The Dalai Lama and the King Demon

Tracking a Triple Murder Mystery Through the Mists of Time

The Dalai Lama
and the King Demon

Tracking a Triple Murder Mystery
Through the Mists of Time

By Raimondo Bultrini
Translated by Maria Simmons

Published by Tibet House US
New York
2013

Published by:

    Tibet House US
    22 West 15th Street
    New York, NY 10011

    http://www.tibethouse.us

Distributed by:

    Hay House, Inc.
    www.hayhouse.com

Printed in the United States of America on acid-free paper.

22 21 20 19 18 17 16 15 14 13   5 4 3 2 1

ISBN 978-0-9670115-23 (paper)

Library of Congress Cataloging-in-Publication Data

Bultrini, Raimondo.
  [Demone e il Dalai Lama. English]
  The Dalai Lama and the King demon : tracking a triple murder mystery through
the mists of time / By Raimondo Bultrini ; Translated by Maria Simmons.
    pages cm
  Includes bibliographical references.
  ISBN 978-0-9670115-2-3 (pbk. : alk. paper) 1. Gautama Buddha. 2. Bstan-
'dzin-rgya-mtsho, Dalai Lama XIV, 1935- I. Title.
  BQ882.B8513 2013
  294.3923

                                2013005212

Contents

Part Four

Part Five

Part Six

Part Seven

Epilogue

Appendixes

Select Bibliography

Without its demons

the world would be imperfect

—Plotinus

Synopsis

A triple homicide committed a few hundred yards away from the residence in exile of the Dalai Lama opens the doors to an unknown universe for Superintendent Rajeev Kumar Singh of the Indian police. With his deputy, Amitabha, he goes over every step of the crime and identifies its perpetrators as members of an exclusive cult dedicated to a demonic spirit with fearsome earthly powers. However, the alleged assassins have escaped to Tibet and the trial judges deem the evidence insufficient to condemn them. The chief suspects include the leading figures of a society devoted to the cult of Gyalpo Shugden, whose headquarters are to be found in the heart of Delhi's Tibetan exile neighborhood. The initial police inquiries over, an investigative journalist decides to open a new trail by reconstructing the mystical aspect of the events. The victims, a respected scholar and two young monks, were translating a commentary on a text of the Buddha known as *The Dependent Origination of All Phenomena*. This ancient treatise seems to indicate the path to follow in retracing the original cause of hatred and incomprehension. But will it also shed light on the identity of the killers?

The investigation takes us back to the beginnings of the cult in the time of the Fifth Dalai Lama, and the death of one of his contemporaries in inexplicable circumstances in the great monastery of Drepung, a stone's throw from Lhasa. The legend surrounding this person's death and subsequent transformation into a demonic entity has come down through the ages, surfacing at critical moments in Tibet's history. The present Dalai Lama discovered as an adult that his tutors and religious instructors were part of a network of power based on the cult of Gyalpo Shugden that had existed since the time of his predecessor, the Thirteenth Dalai Lama. Having himself prayed to the spirit for many years at his teachers' prompting, he gradually distanced himself from its influence, thus creating the grounds for a schism the outcome of which remains impossible to predict. Determined to combat the sectarian outlook fostered in the name of the demon by a group within the clergy of the Gelukpa school of Tibetan Buddhism, the leader of Tibet revealed to the author hitherto secret religious and historical details regarding the impact of the cult. Recent events and developments seem to bear out what was said, since many Shugden followers have found common ground with the Chinese authorities. The links between renegade lamas and the Communist regime are becoming stronger, laying the foundation for an alliance aimed at removing all traces of the Dalai Lama's lineage from Tibet's future. This conflict will involve generations of Tibetans and Chinese together with Westerners interested in the secrets of Asian civilizations.

Foreword

I am extremely pleased to welcome this excellent work of thorough investigation and spiritual exploration by Raimondo Bultrini about the Gyalpo Shugden, or Dolgyal ("king demon from Dol"), cult, both in its modern manifestations and in its historical trajectory. Years ago, His Holiness the Dalai Lama had asked me to research the problem. I wanted to do so, but other commitments prevented me from bringing the work to completion. Mr. Bultrini has gone far beyond what I could have done, so I feel much unburdened from a serious duty as I help in presenting his great work. This is a mysterious and important subject that has not yet received enough attention: I am sure that many students of Tibetan Buddhism and Tibetan history, and the many people who are concerned about the fate of Tibet today amid all the savage assaults on its people and their culture, will benefit greatly from this book's carefully researched information and cogent insights. Finally I am delighted to present this work in the series of publications from Tibet House US, whose founding mission is the preservation, promotion, and defense of the precious, unique, spiritual and scientific culture of Tibet.

The cult of a ferocious "king demon" (Tibetan, *rgyal po*—so classified by all sides in this category of Tibetan demonology), called "Dolgyal" (king demon from Dol) by His Holiness the Dalai Lama and "Shugden" by its proponents, has become a major weapon in the arsenal of those members of the government of the People's Republic of China who think their livelihood depends on making an enemy out of one of China's potentially best friends, namely the Dalai Lama. The original proponents of this cult are members of the majority Tibetan Buddhist order, the Gelukpa, who think they need this fierce spirit in order to dominate members of the other orders as well as hold at bay all persons around the world who hold religious or ideological beliefs other than theirs.

The Dalai Lama, although he also is a devoted member of the Gelukpa order, instead understands its main philosophy as vigorously supporting a true pluralism, not only of different orders within Buddhism, but also of different world religions and world sciences. Therefore, although he was inducted into the cult himself as a youth, after extensive research and personal experience, he abandoned his own participation. He then took it as his solemn duty to recommend that serious practitioners avoid the worship of this "king demon," as it is a hard-to-control worldly spirit-entity with a strong bent toward violence and intolerance. It is inaccurate to say he "banned" the cult, as he has no authority within the Tibetan Buddhist culture to "ban" specific practices. Rather he stated his considered opinion that the cult was harmful to practitioners, and he requested those who chose to continue in its practice not to attend his personal initiations, though of course they are free to follow their religious inclinations on their own as they like.

However, the members of the cult are not content with this situation of having to choose between adopting His Holiness the Dalai Lama as their spiritual mentor or ignoring his judgment and persisting in the Gyalpo Shugden worship. They want to force their supposed mentor to adopt their perspective that the demonic spirit is an enlightened being, almost more important than the Buddha himself, and perhaps also rejoin their worship of it, or at least give them all his initiatory teachings in spite of their defiance of his best advice. So, they feel compelled to attack His Holiness, in order to force him to join their fundamentalist version of a Gelukpa outlook.

Their sustained attack soon attracted the notice and the muscular financial and propaganda support of the strategists of the United Front department of the People's Republic of China government, who imagine that thereby they can weaken the Dalai Lama and ultimately turn the Tibetan people against him. This now makes it an international struggle, a worldwide battle between angels and demons.

This book sheds a tremendous amount of much needed light on the whole story, so I don't have to summarize the tale here. I simply want to welcome it enthusiastically, and then to pose some questions that have arisen while thinking about it, and also to sketch an alternate perspective on the origin of Dolgyal, the king demon from Dol.

First, the question arises: Why has not this "king demon's agitations" been shut down long ago? The Dalai Lama incarnations have been helping the world for a very long time, most powerfully in Tibet since the fifteenth century, and long before that as the incarnations of Avalokiteshvara, the celestial archangelic bodhisattva messiah of universal compassion. The king demon, as powerful as his worshipers think he is, has never yet shut down these compassionate archangelic incarnations: But why can't the opposite have been true by now? Buddhists consider the power of compassion to be overwhelming, the greatest power of the universe, so ultimately evil can never prevail—but why do evil entities keep at it so assiduously? It is a kind of "buddhodicy" problem (Buddhist version of the monotheists' "theodicy" problem about the origin of evil). Perhaps one answer is that the Buddhist movement never tries to destroy evil absolutely, as it would be evil to do so. Instead, it seeks to transform evil into good, turning even demonic entities into "protectors of freedom" (*dharmapala*) or "world protectors" (*lokapala*). To think that evil can be eradicated by destroying an external demon is to miss the "dark side" within oneself, to destroy one's own demonic unconscious potential, and hence actually to be taken over by the demon of one's own egotism. So now and again evil is overcome by heroes in certain contexts, but left to rise again in the future, so other heroes can also overcome it.

This may also fit in with another extremely mysterious even paradoxical teaching in classical nondualist Mahayana Buddhism about the perception of the duality of good and evil. In Buddha's time (whether mythical or historical), his half brother Devadatta was always trying to rival him and destroy him and came to a bad end after causing a lot of trouble. In the Mahayana *Lotus Sutra*, the Buddha mentions that Devadatta in a previous life was his great benefactor, first introducing him to the vision of the *Lotus*! In the *Noble Teaching of Vimalakirti Sutra*, at a certain point, the sage Vimalakirti shocks the enlightened monk Mahakashyapa with the statement that all the devils (*Mara*) of the world that harass and persecute the advanced bodhisattvas are actually themselves bodhisattvas, since it takes a bodhisattva to harm a bodhisattva!

In short, since in Buddhist thought, the ultimate good is so good, it incorporates all sides in the ordinary good and evil dichotomy, so the good bodhisattvas never destroy or give up on the bad demons. They try to hold them in check and then give them interminable teachings!

Second question, to be addressed especially to the worshipers of the cult of Shugden: Why—since the school of Lama Jey Tsong Khapa did so well in Tibet building on the huge contribution of the Kadampa school from the time of Atisha (ca. 982–1054), influencing the basic curriculum of all the other schools—is there need of such a fierce "protector king demon" to terrorize everyone? Is it not rather the case that this "protector" is causing huge trouble to the teaching of Tsong Khapa and indeed Tibetan Buddhism in general? Is not then your alliance with this king demon accomplishing the exact opposite of what you claim you want? Far from enhancing or promoting the cherished teaching of Tsong Khapa, you are perverting that teaching by making its liberative force seem to be a tool of oppression. And your constant attack on the Dalai Lama, doesn't it bother you that it plays right into the hands of the anti-religious forces in communist China that are well on their way to destroying entirely the precious Buddhist culture of Tibet?

This brings me to the one thing I would like to add to the reflections stirred up herein. There seems to be a general consensus from all sides that the Dolgyal/Shugden king demon arose from the death of the reincarnate Tulku Drakpa Gyaltsen in the mid-seventeenth century. Even the Great Fifth Dalai Lama, in a moment of exasperation toward the end of his life, after the death of Drakpa Gyaltsen, exclaimed in writing that he must not have been a genuine reincarnation, but rather a trouble-making impostor. The great Nyingma adept, Terdak Lingpa, was recorded as proclaiming in a dramatic moment that the Dolgyal entity was not at all Tulku Drakpa Gyaltsen, but some other demonic entity posing as the deceased lama, and this opens an avenue of investigation that should be pursued.

Since the presumed motive of the followers of the Gyalpo Shugden entity is to practice and support the teaching of Lama Tsong Khapa, why are they attacking the one person alive today who has done most to make a good name for that teaching, H. H. the Dalai Lama? Why have they rallied around a fundamentalist version of that teaching that so badly alienated followers of other Tibetan Buddhist schools throughout the centuries? If the Gyalpo Shugden entity is so essential to Tsong Khapa's movement, why did that movement spread so widely by doing so much for Tibetan and Mongolian people for over two centuries before the Gyalpo Shugden entity was even thought of? Is it not rather the fact that every time the Gyalpo Shugden movement raised its head since the 1650s, the Lama Tsong Khapa teaching and its practitioners have been harmed rather than helped?

It is recounted in the biographies of Lama Tsong Khapa, that he was seriously ill in the early part of the 1410 decade, and many prayers and rituals were performed to overcome the obstacles to his lifespan. It is further reported that a particularly powerful malevolent entity, who is not named, was not fully overcome, but put onto temporary suspension of negative activities. The close disciples reported to Tsong Khapa that this entity had pledged not to harm Tsong Khapa or his followers for thirteen generations, but in exchange they would have to set up a regular tradition of offerings to it. Tsong Khapa rejected this deal, and told his disciples not to bother, as he was not worried about whatever such a negative being might try to do. If we count from the 1410s for thirteen generations, between fifteen to twenty years per generation, we land right in the middle of the seventeenth century, around the time of the arisal of the Gyalpo Shugden entity. It could be then that it was this longstanding negative spirit that insinuated itself into the drama of the death of the Fifth Dalai Lama's close fellow student, Drakpa Gyaltsen, the politics of the wealthy Gekasa family, and so on, and positioned itself to become one of the most persistent flies in the ointment of the wonderful nation-building work accomplished by the Great Fifth from his accession to the throne of Tibet from 1642 to his death in 1682.

This is all a matter for further research. The main point here is that the followers of the Gyalpo Shugden cult should look into the history more critically and judge the entity by its long-term fruits—clearly negative, and by the uncertainty of its source, and not cling to speculations about its connection with the brilliant Drakpa Gyaltsen, who was after all a lifelong friend and classmate of the Great Fifth, under their revered tutor, the great Panchen Lama, Losang Chokyi Gyaltsen, and would never even have considered causing harm to the marvelous institutions built up all over Tibet and Mongolia based on the teachings of Atisha and Tsong Khapa and the Dalai Lamas and Panchen Lamas, which is exactly what those caught in the grip of the Gyalpo Shugden cult are trying to do today—even collaborating with the Chinese communists who are continuing the utter devastation of Tibetan and Mongolian Buddhism they began sixty years ago.

In conclusion, we owe an enormous debt of gratitude to Raimondo Bultrini for his courageous odyssey of investigative reporting on all levels on the Gyalpo Shugden cult, starting from the thorough investigation of the triple murder in Dharamsala a hundred yards from the residence of the Dalai Lama himself, traveling through history to shed light on the source of the cult, and through the world in tracking how it has metastasized by allying itself with the material and propaganda support offered by the PRC's United Front department and its officials, whose sole aim is to destroy the Dalai Lama and the Tibetan Buddhist teachings and institutions he has done so much to preserve.

Robert A.F. Thurman (Ari Genyen Tenzin Chotrag)

Jey Tsong Khapa Professor of Indo-Tibetan Buddhist Studies,
Columbia University;
President, American Institute of Buddhist Studies;
Director, Tibet House US.
September 17, 2012
Tibetan Royal Year 2139, Year of the Water Dragon

Buddhism and Fundamentalism

Raimondo Bultrini: *Your Holiness, you have suggested more than once that we should try to comprehend the original reasons for hatred in the human soul. What are your deductions regarding the origin of what is known today as "the clash of civilizations"?*

Dalai Lama: I have already said several times, after the terrible and painful events of September 11, that the cause is to be sought many centuries ago, in the twentieth, the nineteenth, and previously. The colonial rule was followed by Western progress, while the Islamic countries stayed behind. But they were not alone. Many Indians and Asians have had problems with the so-called "American cultural invasion." That is another reason why the followers of Islam consider the Western lifestyle a serious threat to their tradition. Then there are the political reasons because America is Israel's strongest ally and so on, but as you know, the list of causes would be multiple. First of all we must take into consideration that this long dispute has created great emotional, poisoned conflicts difficult to resolve with a short-term strategy.

What do you mean by short-term strategy?

The strategy of taking rigid security measures is no doubt necessary but has unforeseen consequences, not always controllable. As a Buddhist, a man of religion, I am more interested in an intensive long-term cure, because it is necessary to reconstruct the immune system of our world. When the system is strong, no small infection can harm us. But when it is weak, we run the risk of illness pervading our body and mind.

And how can we go about reconstructing a weakened system affecting the whole world?

First of all it is necessary to eradicate the root of negative emotions, of afflictions, and to extinguish within ourselves the very source of anger and hatred. Soon we will reestablish respect for our respective dimensions, in the relations between north and south, between rich and poor, between atheists and Christians.

Your Holiness, you must surely be aware that this will need a long time to come about, perhaps too long for us to witness it?

Unfortunately, until now only negative seeds have been planted, with a few people using their intelligence to create as much harm as possible for all of humanity, with no regard for the children, the innocent, their own brothers of the same faith. Therefore these acts are not easy to cancel from human memory. However, what is needed is a countermeasure, so as not to continue damaging the mind with a negative attitude, beginning with the promotion of human values, because we are human beings and we must live together.

What can the West, or an individual Westerner, do concretely in this phase?

Listen to their complaints and reasons. They are unhappy and we must listen to them and share their unhappiness.

Your Holiness, you must admit that this is something difficult to do.

Yes, but if we analyze the problem we see that the limit of the fundamentalists is that they do not even tolerate the idea of a dialogue. The proof is that when they carry out their acts of death they try to make themselves invisible. There exist different interpretations of the Koran between imams, but the final understanding depends on the individual. For this reason there are extremist positions and black sheep, as in every religion.

In Buddhism too?

Yes, of course, in Buddhism too. In 1997, a group of people claiming to belong to the same religious school as I do were strongly suspected of having killed a lama who was very dear to me, the Director of the Tibetan School of Dialectics in Dharamsala, along with two monks who were carrying out the precious task of translating Tibetan texts into Chinese. This same group of people on several occasions has beaten and threatened other Tibetans in the name of a vision of Buddhism that, in my judgment, is fundamentalist. The fact is that they consider a certain "protector spirit," which I myself used to pray to but which I now no longer trust in, as important as the Buddha himself. To affirm this they have made a point of harming their fellow man instead of respecting and understanding him, as taught by one who disseminated compassion five centuries before Jesus Christ. From this point of view our experience is not different from the Christian or Hindu one.

In your view, do the "kamikaze" assassins belong to a fundamentalist army organized on a global scale?

If terrorist organizations find people ready to follow their directives, this will almost automatically cause the seed of terror to take root. Many dear Muslim friends are preoccupied by the actions of those who claim to follow Islam and yet in reality do not, because in both ancient and modern Islam the tolerant bases of religion have inspired generations of luminaries and wise men. For example, a certain banking system is prohibited because it is considered an exploitation of man by man, a noble motivation. A journalist who lived in Teheran during the years when the Ayatollahs were in power told me that a mullah he knew used to receive large donations, which he would distribute equally among the poor. This is compassion. This is why we must not condemn everybody; this would be utterly mistaken. Neither can we Tibetans totally attribute our current condition of suffering to the Chinese. Perceiving one's own errors is the beginning of the process of universal understanding.

Main Characters

Tenzin Gyatso (1935–), Fourteenth Dalai Lama

Lobsang Gyatso (1617–82), Fifth Dalai Lama

Thubten Gyatso (1876–1933), Thirteenth Dalai Lama

Drakpa Gyaltsen (1619–55), reincarnation, contemporary of the Fifth Dalai Lama

Gyalpo Shugden, spirit endowed with a mysterious nature who appeared at the death of Drakpa Gyaltsen

Padmasambhava (eighth century), founder of the Nyingmapa school

Atisha (980–1052), founder of the Kadampa School

Lama Jey Tsong Khapa (1357–1419), founder of the Gelukpa school

Reting Rinpoche (1912–47), former regent of Tibet

Geshe Lobsang Gyatso (1926–97), Director of the School of Dialectics in Dharamsala

Lodoe and Ngawang, translator monks, full names: Ngawang Lodoe and Lobsang Ngawang

Rajeev Kumar Singh, Superintendent of the Kangra Police

Amitabha (pseudonym), Deputy Superintendent of the Kangra Police

Trijang Rinpoche (1900–81), the Fourteenth Dalai Lama's Tutor

Phabongka Rinpoche (1878–1943), Trijang's master

Zemey Rinpoche (1927–96), Trijang's disciple, author of *The Yellow Book*

Principal Lamas of the Shugden Coalition, now the Western Shugden Society:

>   **Ganchen Tulku**, resident in Italy
>   **Kundeling Lama**, resident in India
>   **Kelsang Gyatso**, leader of the New Kadampa Tradition (NKT), based in England
>   **Chimi Tsering**, leader of the Dorje Shugden Devotees Religious and Charitable Society in Delhi

Kalsang Tsewang, arsonist

Dongchung Ngodup, Head of the Security Office of the Tibetan government-in-exile

Chogyal Namkhai Norbu, Dzogchen master

Introduction

Shortly after the first Italian edition of this book was completed, by force of circumstance I found myself in two critical conflict zones: Sri Lanka and a border region between Cambodia and Thailand.

The government on the island in the Indian Ocean, with its Buddhist Singhalese majority, had no wish to concede territorial autonomy to the Tamil minority, Hindu for the most part. During twenty-six years of civil war, bombings and armed clashes were the order of the day, and hundreds of thousands of citizens lived in a constant state of terror until hostilities were officially ended in 2009.

In the district of Preah Vihear, meanwhile, the soldiers of Thailand and Cambodia, both nations inspired by the religion of the Buddha, had daggers drawn, contesting the site of an ancient temple from the Khmer era set to be transformed into a major tourist attraction.

While aware of their very different historical, political, and economic origins, I could not help wondering at the odd contradictions presented in these two sites of tension. Such intense animosity fed by worldly interests is in theory diametrically opposed to the teachings given over two thousand years ago by the Buddha. And yet, in Sri Lanka, Thailand, Cambodia, Burma with its ferocious generals, and Laos, where the Hmong minority are persecuted, the martial impulse continues to rule hearts and minds and to shape human action.

Why preach and declare oneself a follower of the principles of compassion and altruism and then use weapons and violence to make one's views prevail?

At the pagoda of Preah Vihear, I witnessed a significant scene: Cambodian soldiers and their Thai "enemies," their rifles laid on the ground beside them, prostrated together before statues of the Buddha. Then, once outside the temple, they clutched their weapons again.

As in the case of Sri Lanka, there is now apparently peace between Thailand and Cambodia, but the religious, social, and economic fears that caused both conflicts still lurk below the surface.

The subject of this book is a case in which the conflict between brothers and sisters of the same faith is based on reasons that appear more subtle, and less easily understood beyond the relatively small world of the followers of the different schools of what is known as Tantric Buddhism.

But precisely by returning to the roots of the hatred that is so deeply wounding the Tibetan community, both in the Land of Snows and in exile, we can see the paradox that has driven the heirs of a great esoteric tradition to continue to hasten the weakening, and perhaps the very extinction of one of our most ancient and extraordinary cultures. This cycle of birth, growth, development, decline, and disappearance is the fate of every civilization. But if this paradigm is applied to an individual rather than a culture, the symbolic significance of the vicious circle is more evident still.

On the eve of the publication of this English edition, another dramatic chain of events has occurred in Tibet itself, the setting for much of the story below. Almost forty monks, nuns, laymen and laywomen have set themselves on fire, and most have lost their lives. These acts took place in different parts of the country, but mostly in the east, where the Chinese invasion began and the most heinous atrocities were perpetrated against a population almost everywhere defenseless. The same acts of self-immolation have taken place in the region of Amdo, birthplace of His Holiness Tenzin Gyatso, the Fourteenth Dalai Lama of Tibet. The image of the nun Tashi Choezom setting herself ablaze on November 4, 2011, on a sidewalk in full view of passersby has been seen all over the world. Among Tibetans, reactions have been mixed. The Buddhist religion considers as karmic wrongdoing not only killing others but also taking one's own life. One of the foundations of Tibetan Vajrayana Buddhism is respect for the precious human body, a rarely obtained, indispensable means to obtain enlightenment.

The motives driving Tashi and her fellow monastics cannot be compared with the self-interested campaigns of Southeast Asian governments. The Tibetans consider their sacrifice a noble one that will bring the world's attention to their cause, which is to end the suffering of their entire people.

The Dalai Lama himself, vehemently opposed to suicide for any reason, has tried to explain publicly the roots of these extreme acts as a consequence of the colonization of Tibet. "Some kind of policy, some kind of cultural genocide is taking place," he said in an interview. "In the last ten or fifteen years," he added, "there were some hard-liner Chinese officials. So that's why these sad incidents have happened, due to this desperate sort of situation." The story told in these pages reveals the background factors and certain previously unknown aspects of the "policy" to which the Tibetan leader refers.

It revolves around an element that might seem insignificant within the complex and ancient Himalayan religious tradition: the doubts raised by the Dalai Lama about the nature of a deity/spirit/demon in the Tibetan pantheon known as Gyalpo Shugden. His Holiness's request to his followers to abandon the cult has nonetheless created a deep division between a minority of its diehard followers and a majority in the community at large, set on following the advice of its leader.

No single apparent rational motive can explain either the three murders in 1997 that are recounted in the first part of this work or the religious and political controversy generated. Aware of this, I have tried to review the various phases in the "Shugden Affair," beginning with the apparent facts and historical factors, and at times using the expedient of fictional narrative. I cannot claim to have presented an impartial picture, since the results of my research had a deep impact on me. In particular, I was struck by the incredible coincidences that guided the investigations of the Indian police toward a very small group of Tibetans. These were not only followers of the "spirit" but also effective members of organizations and associations that emerged in its name. Those directly involved maintain there was no judicial proof of wrongdoing, but this has yet to be demonstrated, as can be seen by a detailed consideration of each phase of the inquiry.

The context in which the story evolves should be familiar to readers who follow international events. The present Dalai Lama was forced to leave his country in 1959 after trying in vain for several years to reconcile the religious and ethical principles of his people with the atheistic and materialist nature of the powerful invaders. But the origins of this struggle lay considerably further back in history than the advent of communism in China, and can be traced to a time when the lives of the emperors in Peking themselves were influenced by the Buddha's doctrine.

Until the eighteenth century, few Chinese dared to venture into the impenetrable highlands ruled by peoples considered wild and unpredictable. In ancient times, the population density of the empire was in no way comparable to today, so there was no vital need to conquer new territories. Apart from this, any Chinese aims to expand into Tibet would have foundered on the proud resistance of the Mongol tribes of the northwest.

The Mongols were determined in their defense of Tibet, and in particular the Buddhist doctrine, to which they had been converted in the thirteenth century. The lamas of the various schools attached to the Mongol courts since that time had played a great part in transforming these fierce heirs of Genghis Khan. They had convinced them to abolish certain of the more cruel ancestral customs, such as the burial of servants and animals with dead princes and warriors, and the tradition of hurling captured Chinese villagers from the tops of cliffs and precipices.

The Third Dalai Lama, Sonam Gyatso, was the first representative of the Gelukpa school, the Yellow Hats, to visit Mongolia, in the sixteenth century. Prince Altan Khan used the Mongol word *Dalai* to translate his religious name, Gyatso (literally, ocean). This title was applied retrospectively to his two predecessors and has been passed down to the present Dalai Lama, the Fourteenth, Tenzin Gyatso.

From then on, the Gelukpas enjoyed a privileged rank in the eyes of the most powerful Mongol tribes and, thanks to the activities of the Dalai Lamas, their popularity was extended to all three of the Tibetan provinces, U-Tsang, Kham, and Amdo. In 1642, the "Great Fifth" Dalai Lama was made political as well as spiritual head of the whole of Tibet by the Mongolian ruler, Gushri Khan. It was during his reign that Gyalpo Shugden appeared. Both the Fifth and the present Dalai Lama were to describe him as a "spirit of a mysterious and perfidious nature" that has hovered like a shadow for three and a half centuries, influencing the destiny of the Gelukpas, the most powerful spiritual and political community in the modern history of Tibet.

Already, by the death of the Great Fifth, Shugden had begun to be associated with the Yellow Hats in the role of their "Divine Protector." He was central only to this particular school of Tibetan Buddhism, although he had a minor role in the liturgy of the Sakyapa tradition. At the same time, another so-called "protector"—of a very different nature—was about to enter the Tibetan scene: China.

The Manchu Empire intervened in the eighteenth century to fill the void left by the numerous Mongol tribes who, on account of their divisions, no longer had control of the Tibetan territories. Previously, Peking had established with the early Dalai Lamas, particularly the Fifth, a "priest-patron" relationship. At a certain point, the Chinese created a preferential relationship with the more malleable of the Yellow Hats in order to dominate the most venerated of Tibet's reincarnations, and thus the entire population of the highlands. Unlike Gushri Khan, however, they did not let the Gelukpas exercise the same power: for centuries after 1700, China had a dramatic influence on their sect and its highest religious incarnations.

Was it because of this pressure that no Dalai Lama—from the Eighth to the Twelfth—was able to govern his realm? As we shall see, some died when very young or little more than children, while others fell under the sway of regents, faithful to Peking. It was only at the start of the 1900s that the Thirteenth Dalai Lama officially proclaimed Tibet's independence from China. But at almost exactly this time, the mysterious figure of the demonic spirit reappeared with even greater vigor.

Gyalpo Shugden became the bonding element of a barely concealed pact among the most orthodox Gelukpas, whether monks, nuns, or laypeople determined to hinder the policy of opening up and modernizing Tibet, desired by the Thirteenth Dalai Lama. Two of the last century's most celebrated masters inspired and guided them: Phabongka Rinpoche and his disciple, Trijang Rinpoche, junior tutor to the present Dalai Lama. Trijang introduced the cult of Shugden to the young leader shortly after his enthronement. These were the most dramatic years in the country's history, on the eve of the Chinese invasion that began in 1949 on Tibet's eastern border.

It was during the first exile of the fifteen-year-old Dalai Lama in 1950 that Gyalpo Shugden made an appearance on the political and religious scene in the Land of Snows as "vice" State Oracle. His career as exclusive protector of the Yellow Hats and oracular divinity of the government would only be interrupted thirty years later, when the Dalai Lama learned for himself that the main predecessors in his lineage, the Fifth and the Thirteenth, had already condemned the uncontrollable and inauspicious power of the spirit.

During the years of exile, Tenzin Gyatso saw clearly the dangers of a sectarian viewpoint that linked the leader of all Tibetans almost exclusively to the Gelukpa order. Amid the great difficulties of organizing the life of the refugees in India, there seemed little sense in encouraging nostalgia and pride in the ancient power of the order. But while the Fourteenth Dalai Lama strove to strengthen unity and received teachings from masters of various schools, the orthodox Shugden devotees mounted a blatant sabotage of his ecumenical efforts.

It is difficult to say whether Phabongka and Trijang's disciples had foreseen China's being involved yet again in this internal conflict, now enveloped in a secret and mystic aura. We only know that the links between the followers of the cult and the Communist authorities grew steadily once Beijing realized the important potential benefits of a schism between Tibetan Buddhists: a split that first and foremost weakens China's principal enemy, the Dalai Lama.

In 1995, when the Tibetan leader, as requested, identified the reincarnation of the Panchen Lama, the second most important spiritual figure in Tibet, the Chinese government changed the rules and presented its own candidate. During his investiture, the false Panchen received the homage of the highest Chinese Communist Party leaders and—in a pointed strategic move—the devotees of Shugden represented by a lama residing in Italy, Ganchen Tulku.

Among several interesting aspects of this conflict—apparently of secondary interest when compared to the very grave problems in relations between China and Tibet—one has remained almost unexamined.

On a trip to Beijing at the end of 2007, I met in a small suburban apartment two lamas of the ancient Nyingmapa tradition who had been invited by some Chinese devotees to proffer teachings and blessings. Each day, lines of people, young and not so young, came to their door and prostrated on the floor as a sign of their homage and devotion. Among them were many soldiers and policemen, as well as ordinary people, students and intellectuals.

Of course, Buddhism is not as widespread in China as it was at the time of the Celestial Empires, but such scenes are by no means uncommon. Indeed, the ban imposed by the Party and the government on the charismatic Dalai Lama's return to Tibet thus may be prompted by fears of an uncontrollable religious revival. It is no coincidence that thousands of followers of the Buddhist organization Falun Gong remain in prison while the movement has grown beyond the control of the "establishment."

However, in contrast to Tibet's exiled leader, the young Panchen Lama is unlikely to constitute a threat to the Communist leadership: from the start he has been trained to fill the role imposed on him by the Party. He may never gain full acceptance by the people, but this is not a problem for Beijing since the Dalai Lama's advanced age is in its favor. The Shugden followers have proved extremely useful in this plan, to the extent that their mysterious spirit, opposed by Dharamsala, has been welcomed and accepted by the Chinese Communist authorities as a potential "ally."

How much—if at all—these developments will hasten the decline of Himalayan culture, it is too early to say. Similarly, it is hard to estimate the impact of the violence seen in Buddhist countries on the image of this ancient doctrine. At the moment, the conflict has echoed in the West only through the dozens of public demonstrations against the Dalai Lama that have taken place in Europe, America, and Australia in the name of "religious freedom." But the hundreds of articles written on this subject have only made bland references to the issue, without explaining its complex origin.

The first part of this book is dedicated to the story of the triple homicide that occurred in Dharamsala on February 4, 1997, and to the initial investigations carried out by Superintendent Rajeev Kumar Singh of the Indian police. The various phases of the inquiry are faithfully reconstructed using judicial reports and conversations with witnesses and participants, starting with Rajeev Singh himself. The characters cited are for the most part real, although some names have been changed in the interest of safety.

In the second part of the book, I briefly have outlined the general and esoteric features of the Tantric disciplines that are constantly connected to the crimes. I have preferred to avoid as far as possible reproducing extracts of academic and religious texts, which the reader may consult independently, and have relied on my personal understanding gained through my own experience as a reporter and a passionate student of Tibetan culture. In the other sections, I have reconstructed certain historical events and presented the most salient facts regarding the origin of the cult and the perennial controversies that it has generated down to the present.

The essence of the various interviews that His Holiness so kindly granted me over the last eleven years is condensed into the first and last sections of the book. Analyzing the background of the controversy and its possible implications for the future, the leader of Tibet broadens the discussion of the nature of Shugden, whether divine or demonic, to the political plane, and to the bitter confrontation now taking place between his small nation and the authorities of a country well on the way to becoming one of the world's greatest economic and military powers.

In the eleven years or more since beginning this research, I have accumulated enormous debts of gratitude to many people, starting with my own spiritual master, Chogyal Namkhai Norbu, and His Holiness the Dalai Lama. It is thanks only to them that I have been able to tackle a subject as sensitive and elusive as the cult of Gyalpo Shugden.

My heartfelt thanks also go to my treasured consultants, friends, and collaborators, who have made various contributions to this book. Among many I mention Giorgio Del Vecchio, Ugo Leonzio, Jeremy Russell, the Ven. Lhakdor, Ngari Rinpoche, Rajeev Kumar Singh, Dongchung Ngodup and the staff of the Security Office of the Tibetan government-in-exile, Stephen Batchelor, Elio Guarisco, Beniamino Natale, Giancarlo De Cataldo, Susanna Tavernari Terra, Cecilia Brighi, Lama Karma Lhundup, Geshe Kalsang Damdul, and Sonam Ngawang.

I must give particular thanks to John Oliphant for his unfailing encouragement and advice and for his editorial assistance, and to Maria Simmons, who translated the original work and has contributed significantly to the amendments that have enriched the English edition. I am also deeply indebted to Robert Thurman for his vision and courage in taking this book to a wider audience beyond the frontiers of my country, Italy, where it was originally published in Italian by Alessandro Dalai and Cristina Lupoli at Baldini-Castoldi-Dalai.

Finally, I would like to thank my family, who have helped me in every way possible.

I hope to have contributed some information that may help to ease the tensions that continue to afflict the souls of the heirs to a unique, profound culture that is a vital part of our heritage.

This book is dedicated to the numerous victims of sectarianism and religious extremism, and in particular to the memory of Lama Lobsang Gyatso and the translator monks Lobsang Ngawang and Ngawang Lodoe.

Finally, I pay homage to the masters endowed with compassion and wisdom and to all those sincere Dharma practitioners committed to alleviating the suffering of their fellow beings, whichever school or tradition they may follow.

Raimondo Bultrini
Dharamsala, October 2008

PART ONE

Three Murders in Dharamsala

It was not long after six in the evening. Master Lobsang was sitting in the small room where he studied, meditated, and slept, when an unfamiliar cold sensation came over him; this was strange, since his electric heater was switched on and a soft yak-wool blanket covered his legs.

Out on the road, the mules stamped their hooves heavily, weary under their last load of gravel before darkness brought their day of toil to an end. The monk raised his head from his notebook, his train of thought now interrupted by that sound, which beat out the rhythm of his own work from dawn till dusk. *Probably,* he said to himself, *death will come as liberation to those animals after a lifetime spent carrying heavy packs. But where people are concerned,* Lobsang Gyatso thought, *some of their preoccupations weigh as much as or more than a hundred sacks of sand and stones; yet death is dreaded more by humans than animals.* Maybe this was because, more or less unconsciously, a man or woman fears that existence does not end with the body, and that the spirit will bear the burden of the consequences of one's actions in all future lives, until one discovers how to be free from that cycle forever.

In a few days it would be Losar, the Tibetan New Year, and snow covered the mountains around Dharamsala. Before returning to his writing, Master Lobsang drank the hot tea made for him by the novice, Tenzin. Glancing out of the window, he saw the dim lights of the School of Dialectics[1] and those in the windows of the cells of his monk pupils being turned on and off. With a little imagination, they could be compared to the windows of the shops in Hong Kong, where he had just spent two tiring weeks with his Chinese students, teaching meditation and commenting on one of the sutras[2] of the Buddha. Soon, Ngawang and Lodoe would be arriving, and they would continue together their translation into Chinese of the text of their lessons.

---

[1] An important institution adjacent to Namgyal Monastery, founded by the Dalai Lama to

[2] The ancient scriptures of the Buddhist tradition, teaching the paths of renunciation, compassion, and wisdom, taught by the Buddha in his human form, memorized by his disciples, and finally transcribed after four or five centuries.

3

So silent were the now deserted, dark streets of McLeod Ganj that one could make out the slow, dragging footsteps of a few old women devotees on their way to turn the prayer wheels[3] at the temple of Namgyal, which stood opposite the residence in exile of the Fourteenth Dalai Lama. A steep slope separated Lobsang's room from the house of the leader of all Tibetans, but, as the crow flies, they were only a few dozen yards apart, and every day he would gaze upwards at it with filial devotion. His feelings towards his students were equally intense. They filled the emptiness that he had felt in his heart since he chose to renounce his family and his other attachments by becoming a monk.

Lobsang was barely six years old when he first thought of donning monastic robes and entering a college of the Gelukpa tradition,[4] known as the "Virtuous Order." Most Tibetan families would have been delighted at this early calling, but not his. His mother had given him the name Drang-Te, "Garbage Beggar," to divert the attention of spirits jealous of a privileged only son, for whom a favorable marriage had been arranged at birth. She counted on him to manage the property, the cattle, and their land in that corner of Kham where six mountains give birth to the four rivers that nourish the valleys of eastern Tibet, their waters so rich in sodium bicarbonate as to leave a sharp, bitter taste in the mouth.

The parents of Lobsang's parents were *sa ma drok*, small landowners, neither peasants nor nomads; in the winters they moved to lower pastures where the climate was milder. An ancestor had brought a certain prestige to the family by conducting the complex rituals used to unmask thieves. He also knew how to perform exorcisms, a skill perhaps learned from a shaman of the ancient school of Bon, the pre-Buddhist religion that was widely practiced in Tibet before the eighth century. These were rites of such power that, if the client so wished it, the thief could be made to fall sick and die. Another ancestor had been involved in a double homicide,

---

[3] These are hollow cylindrical objects filled with mantras, which are activated with a circular motion in a clockwise direction. During recitation, often paired with visualization, the mantra enables one, by means of the repetition of sound, to reach a mental state of subtle perception.

[4] The most recent and widespread of the four schools of Tibetan Buddhism, it was founded by Lama Jey Tsong Khapa (1357–1419). The other schools are the Sakyapa, the Kagyupa, and the Nyingmapa.

and had entered the maternal family line on the recommendation of a lama who wanted to protect him. This ancestor married his Lobsang's grand-mother, who had no male siblings to take care of the land, and thanks to his efforts the property flourished. Lobsang was born into a family that was therefore relatively prosperous. An uncle, who was a religious instruc-tor, convinced his mother that the boy innately had a sincere predisposition for the Buddha Dharma, and that it would be inauspicious to let concerns about the family's material interest stand in the way of his vocation.

Lobsang was not calm and meditative by nature. Indeed, he was quite violent and always ready for a fight. Nevertheless, from the moment his guru, Aku Me, accepted him as a novice, the youth's one aim was to enter Drepung, the largest of the Gelukpa monasteries, near Lhasa.

His master told him to observe his dreams closely, as they were the gateway to his unconscious mind. One night, while he was immersed in a vision of a forest where he was gathering fruit fallen from the trees, a naked woman appeared to him, riding bareback on a black horse. She asked him to follow her, but Lobsang, frightened at the thought that his monastic vows might be disrupted, awoke, and ran, dripping with sweat, to tell his guru Aku Me everything. "This is an excellent sign," said his master. "That woman was Palden Lhamo,[5] and she wanted to take you to Drepung, for sure." Then, Lobsang dreamed of a man dressed in white, pointing out the direction he should follow. This also pleased his guru, who revealed that the figure was an emanation of the great Nechung, the State Oracle of Tibet, and there now could be no doubts about his choosing the road to Lhasa.

This would be the sixty-ninth Losar since his birth, and the thoughts of "Garbage Beggar," now the erudite Venerable Lobsang Gyatso, Director of the School of Buddhist Dialectics, turned to the two divine beings from his dreams that had comforted him since his childhood. Like watchful

---

[5] One of the principal Tantric divinities of the Gelukpa school. Tantra or Tantrism (the root of the term means continuity without interruption) indicates a particular attitude in the application of spiritual teachings, so that the state of meditation and presence are never separate from the ordinary activities of existence through body, speech, and mind. The esoteric Tantric traditions formally originated in India from the fifth century onwards, although they had been transmitted from master to disciple since time immemorial. The Indian King Indrabhuti is said to have received the first secret Tantric teachings from Buddha Shakyamuni.

angels, they acted as peaceful and joyous guardians, but through the power of his meditation they could transform themselves into terrifying beings, warriors with a fierce gaze who defended him from his enemies, above all his own inner demons.

Lobsang settled the blanket over his knees as, yet again, and not without some anxiety, he pondered the current situation in all its details. On one hand stood his trusted celestial guardians and the universal master, Gyalwa Rinpoche,[6] the Dalai Lama; on the other, certain ecclesiastical figures with exalted titles, remnants of an elite clerical power class, men who were, even now in the poverty of exile, well-positioned in the hierarchy of the Tibetan community. Who, if not they or their disciples, could have written the threatening letters piled in his drawer? The latest to arrive was the most coarsely worded yet: "Why don't you show some guts and come and confront us in Delhi, like a louse meets a thumbnail?" it said. Although he was by now used to this, Lobsang had to exercise all the patience acquired in his years of meditating not to not explode with anger. His own pen did not always write gently; and he too could hit hard with words and knew it.

Once more, he peered out of the window into the evening darkness. The monk translators, Ngawang and Lodoe, whom he was expecting, were now even later. He returned to the notes he had been making writing as he tried to make sense of the origin of the contradictions found in the tormented religious and political history of his people.

> The Fifth Dalai Lama was a great man who lived on the cusp of two eras that were distinct in their politics and religion. He unified the country and was able to preserve the ancient tradition and promote the new. What real reason might there be to oppose such a sensitive figure, someone who brought together the different schools of thought all rooted in the precious teachings of the Buddha? And how could anyone think that the result of bringing these traditions together would mean their adulteration? The four schools of Tibetan Buddhism have so much in common. I don't know how anyone

[6] The term *Rinpoche* means "Precious" and is attributed to all reincarnations officially recognized by other *tulkus* (reincarnations) and lamas.

could see them as being as incompatible as water and fire. How small-minded can you get?

There! He had let slip more harsh words. But couldn't he stop himself?

He raised his head at the sound of footsteps and greeted his students, who had rushed in without knocking. Numb with cold, Ngawang and Lodoe closed the front door behind them. In the warmth of the room, they took off their cloaks, touching the floor with their foreheads before their master. Ngawang then sat on the room's other bed while Lodoe took a chair.

"Tenzin will be here soon with supper, but meanwhile, please have some tea," said the Geshe, closing his notebook and picking up a rectangular packet wrapped in finely embroidered yellow silk. He touched his head with it in a gesture of deference, and then very slowly removed the silk cover. The Tibetan text, on rough paper yellowed with age, was pressed between two inlaid wooden tablets. He removed the upper one, and on the first page was written, *The Homage of Jey Tsong Khapa to the Buddha for His Teaching on the Dependent Origination of All Phenomena.* Under his breath, he recited a short mantra; and then he said, "You know how important the commentary on this text is. We must finish the translation quickly and do it really well. In a few days Ngawang will accompany His Holiness to Taiwan as his interpreter, and we don't have much time."

"Master, what were you writing?" asked Lodoe, wrapping his hands around the teacup to warm them better.

"Nothing, just a few notes."

"Yesterday another threat arrived, didn't it, Genla?"[7] Asked Ngawang.

The old lama cut him short with a gesture. "We have other things to do right now. I have made a commitment to my Chinese students in Taiwan, Hong Kong, and Singapore, and now is not the time to discuss all that."

Noticing the abashed expressions on the faces of his two disciples, he changed his tone. "I don't have to tell monks what happens when a master transmits a teaching. The *samaya* is like a thin thread—an intimate, deep link, a sacred promise to continue to practice the Dharma[8] together until

---

[7] Teacher, also called Geshe.

[8] Sanskrit term that may be translated as 'truth," 'teaching," "cosmic or natural law," or even "phenomenon." It comes from a verb root /dhr, which means "to hold," so Dharma holds things in freedom or a certain pattern.

mutual realization. It is the cause of liberation from the cycle of birth and death."

The geshe's words seemed to put an end to the discussion. Lodoe thought of the fatigue it had cost him to follow the path of his gurus. From Lhasa he had walked for two months, his feet sinking in the snow of the Himalayan passes, to reach the Dalai Lama in Dharamsala. By the time they finally arrived in India, a number of the initial group who had escaped with him were dead; most were children and the old people, who had died of hunger and pneumonia.

Even now he could feel the pain of that experience and of the separation from his family, but he would never turn back. The Dalai Lama and Geshe Lobsang had become his father and mother and his fellow monks his brothers. With deep affection, but not without concern, he looked at his master who, just at that moment, was peering out the window behind him. "I hear footsteps," said the geshe, "It must be Tenzin with supper. Lodoe and Ngawang too looked at the window, and then at the door. They made out Tenzin's figure through the heavy drapes and heard his familiar voice telling them their food had arrived. He was bearing a tray full of steaming bowls, glasses, a thermos flask, and oranges. The translators got up to help him place everything on a small table piled with books and papers, except for the master's plate, which was served to him by the cook.

They ate in silence, perhaps still thinking of the most recent threatening letter, and of the gloom and darkness of the day just passed. The hours before the New Year (Losar) began were often like this, not only because of the long wait for a warm and luminous sun to rise but also because, since the dawning of their highland civilization, the eve of Losar had less than fortunate connotations for Tibetans, it being a time to exorcize any evil that might linger from the year past. The meat broth and vegetables, the rice and the oranges, were eaten slowly. When they had finished, Tenzin gathered the cups on the tray. After washing and drying his hands, Lama Lobsang broke the silence. "Good, let's get back to work. Please bring tea later, at eight o'clock," he said to the novice, who left the room treading backwards and closed the door.

Many commentaries exist on Tsong Khapa's poetic prayer of thanks to the Buddha for having taught *The Dependent Origination of All Phenomena*. Most were written by scholars of the Gelukpa school, as Tsong Khapa was its founder. Their tradition became famous as the School of the Yellow Hats, and spread in Tibet some 1,500 years after the time of the Buddha's original teachings. It was destined to change the very history of the Land of Snows, by instituting a comprehensive curriculum in the monasteries and revitalizing the rules of monastic discipline.

Geshe Lobsang never ceased telling his young translators that the Mandarin version of their text had to preserve the persuasive force of the Tibetan original and that the words alone could have the power to dispel from pragmatic Chinese minds their ignorance of the laws of karma—the causal process according to which one is reborn in apparently different forms, and which can only end with the discovery and eradication of the cause of suffering. "Let's take this passage," he began, leafing through the pages on his lap. "Nondependence," you said, "is like a flower in the sky." Tsong Khapa addresses the Buddha ecstatically, thanking him for using such a poetic expression to explain how impossible it is to find any phenomenon that is independent of its original cause."

Ngawang was taking notes, but he paused to ask, the lama; "Do you mean that in the world as it appears to us, everything depends on a previous cause?"

"Exactly," answered Lobsang, "We know that the cause of the flower's existence is its own seed, which gives birth to a plant rooted in the earth and certainly not in the sky; just as a plant, given enough water and light, will create a blossom. But the Buddha condensed this into the simile of "a flower in the sky." That's how powerful I would like our commentary to be, reflecting the magnificent simplicity of the meaning of dependent origination."

"Master," said Ngawang once again, "forgive me if I steal more precious time from the translation of this text. But if the law of interdependence is as true for a flower as it is for all other existing phenomena, what about the consequences of criticizing so openly the followers of the spirit? I heard that last month Geshe Thinley, the Abbot of Jangtse College, was badly beaten after he expelled eleven monks who were found to be devotees of the cult."

"Even the granary at Jangtse was burned down," added Lodoe.

Geshe Lobsang put the pages of the text back between the wooden tablets and stared at his disciples with a frown. The numerous wrinkles that furrowed his round, severe face emphasized the annoyance in his expression. But then he quickly relaxed. If his disciples wanted to remind him of the risks that he ran, they certainly did not mean to offend him. They simply needed to understand. "All right," he said. "I know you mean well.

It is true. Yesterday, too, I received more threats...." He showed them the letter for an instant. Then, holding the pages to his chest, he added, "They are just like the people in the past that prevented the opening of our Tibetan world to the rest of the human race. If I have become the target of their criticism, it is because I have felt an intellectual and moral responsibility to talk about it openly, as His Holiness has done. You should know, in terms of dependent origination, that what the cult of this spirit might cause could be far, far, worse, than the polemics and the violence that have occurred in the Tibetan settlements in India. If our leader has put us on guard, there is a serious reason. His Holiness is no ordinary spiritual guide but the incarnation of Avalokiteshvara, the bodhisattva of compassion."

"But, Master, you are taking too big a risk," Ngawang insisted. For some time now he had wanted to discuss this matter, which many other students of the School of Dialectics also took to heart.

Lobsang Gyatso heaved a deep sigh and, after a short pause, continued in his friendly tone, "Earlier you asked me what I was doing. Well, I was writing about the Great Fifth Dalai Lama. It was during his epoch that the conflict over the spirit began, and before we make any judgments on the subject, it might be better to learn some more about it, because there's more to this story than what is written in books."

The Geshe paused to reflect. The sound of the mules had faded away, and in the silence of the small room only muffled, faraway voices echoed through from the streets near the temple. He concentrated, as if he felt the need to revisit that distant moment when much, or at least an important part of this complicated chain of events, had begun.

All of a sudden, he looked up towards the window. The shuffling of footsteps on the balcony was light, but on this silent night it was loud enough to make the monks turn around. They looked at each one another in the grip of a strange agitation. Then they sat down again and Geshe Lobsang resumed, "The Fifth Dalai Lama ordered that a fierce fire rite be performed in the presence of the greatest lama exorcists of the time. That ceremony completely eliminated the evil spirit, even if some still deny it. But who can say if this is the same demon that has survived all these centuries?"

The footsteps began again, louder this time.

"Go see who's there. Maybe they are looking for someone," said the Geshe to Lodoe. The young monk closed his notebook, but as he was rising, the door burst open, and the first intruder entered the room, ripping aside the heavy drapes embroidered with the symbol of infinite love.

The three monks had no time to realize what was happening. Large, silent figures armed with daggers filled the room. Two of the assailants rushed straight towards the master's bed, their daggers pointed at Geshe Lobsang's heart and face. The others set upon the young monks. The attackers' strength seemed unbounded as they struck at the eyes, the head, the neck, and the legs of their victims. Blood poured over the three bodies and the walls and spattered the cushions and the teacups, the books and the gas stove. It stained the carpets, the photos of the masters, and those of the buddhas and the contemplative deities.

One of the killers fell furiously on the body of the dying Geshe, so enraged that he did not notice that his rucksack had been grabbed by the old monk, who clutched it to his chest in his dying spasms. Lobsang was a powerful man and, despite the years spent with his books, his body retained much of the strength it had had when, as a boy, he wrestled the sons of Khampa shepherds.[9] They had already stabbed him seventeen times to be sure he was dead, but the assassin with the rucksack lowered his blade to slit the old monk's throat from ear to ear in a ritual not carried out on the other victims.

Nor were the lives of the two younger monks were spared. The delicate Ngawang had been struck seventeen times and lay sprawled on the floor beside his guru's bed, his skull split open down to the brain. It took thirteen knife slashes to still the sturdy Lodoe, who would be the last to die. His hefty body was now doubled over in the exact center of the room.

All three would bleed to death, though Ngawang and Lodoe were still breathing when Tenzin came back to the room at exactly eight o'clock. He found the door wide open and the drapes torn aside before he noticed the copious streams of blood, a pure brilliant red, gushing all over the floor. Dropping the flask of tea, he flung himself, weeping, on their mutilated bodies, shouting for help with all the force he could muster.

Tenzin's nostrils sensed the smell, and he shuddered at the thought that the demon of death had passed a few moments before him in this very place. He would surely have fainted but for the need to do something for his disfigured companions, from whose throats death rattles sounded and

---

[9] Ethnic group of the eastern Tibetan province of Kham.

clots of plasma spurted. Tenzin sat on the bed, oblivious to the pools of blood that soaked the blankets and the mattress, and delicately placed his master's head in his lap. Only then did he see the enormous wound on his neck. As he tried to staunch it with the hem of his robe, he noticed the rucksack, colored blue and black, its strap wrapped around the geshe's forearm.

When he realized that no one had responded to his shouts, or come to help, Tenzin ran out onto the balcony and found a frightened monk. It took what seemed an eternity before the open space in front of the house filled with monks and nuns, curious onlookers, Indian beggars, and motor rickshaw drivers. Tenzin hurriedly sent one of them to summon a renowned doctor who lived nearby. At that point, the neighbors appeared timidly in their doorways but quickly retreated within.

They thought perhaps it had been a drunken brawl, a playful scuffle gone wrong. Something similar had happened earlier that very evening among several revelers who had had too much to drink, and someone had gone around saying they were monks. Knives were drawn, and only when the men collapsed on the ground, exhausted by their wounds, had passersby stopped to patch them up, medicate them with alcohol and gauze, and send them home.

Few immediately realized the seriousness of what had happened. It was hard for anyone to conceive of such violence on this still, cold eve of Losar, right beside the sacred temple of the Dalai Lama.

One of the more enterprising in the crowd searched for an ambulance to move the wounded to the hospital, along with the Geshe, although he was beyond the help of any doctor. Ngawang and Lodoe were taken together to the Gelek hospital, a small medical center run by Tibetans a few miles kilometers down the mountain. Ngawang was already dead by the time they arrived, but Lodoe was still breathing. The doctors said that they could not save him with the hospital's inadequate equipment, so he was lifted back into the car and rushed off towards Chandigarh, five hours distant. But on the way he too stopped breathing.

Those who assisted him in the ambulance heard very clearly the rasping murmuring of the mantra of compassion of Buddha Avalokiteshvara, through his throat punctured by knife wounds: "Om Mani Padme Hum"— "Om Jewel and Lotus [Holder] Hum." This mantra accompanies every Tibetan from birth, or even previously, in his or her mother's womb.

At the scene of the murders and in the nearby temple of Namgyal, monks who had word heard of the crime swarmed towards the geshe's house, intoning sacred mantras, long, sad, dirges mourning their unfortunate companions. On the ground floor of the apartment building and along the street where a mule still ambled by, a noisy crowd had gathered. Most prominent were the monks from the School of Dialectics and from the Namgyal Monastery, where the personal disciples of the Dalai Lama study. They fingered their mala rosaries[10] frenetically as they paced up and down between the small veranda of the lodging and the road, accompanied by the chants of the faithful, who had hurried to the temple when they learned the news. These were followed later by the traders and shoppers from the bazaar about half a mile away. The maroon and ochre of the monks' robes colored the street where the reciting of the prayers merged with the weeping of those in the first shock of hearing about the horrible massacre. In the School of Dialectics, as in every microcosm where people gather around a common belief and spend long hours of their life together, friendships become as strong as deep-rooted trees. This is especially so for among the young, torn away from their families too soon and unready to master their earthly attachments.

In the first rush of panic, nobody had called the police, or even the Tibetan government-in-exile's own security officers, and for several hours, confusion reigned. The monks from the School of Dialectics and a number of eager citizens ran up and down the streets of McLeod Ganj chasing men and ghosts, as word spread that certain spirits had been involved in the killings before vanishing into the moonless night. Some roamed in groups in the vain hope of finding one of the culprits with a bloodied dagger still in hand. Others got into cars and drove around in circles for hours between Dharamsala, Kangra, Chandigarh, and the further side of the mountain in the forests of Tushita, where Western Buddhists come to experience for a week or two the asceticism of monastic discipline in intensive courses.

Finally, news reached the Head of the Library of Tibetan Works and Archives, known to everyone in Dharamsala simply as the "Library," a little more than a mile away from the scene of the crime. He in turn called the Chief Superintendent of Police of the District of Kangra. When

---

[10] Rosary with 108 beads.

the first police officers arrived with their tracker dogs, it was too late to give chase. The animals smelled the blood, the floor trampled by the killers, every object in Geshe Lobsang's room, the stone paving, and the dust on the dirt stretch in front of the house. But after midnight the torches were switched off and the dogs lost their sense of direction in the dark. By the time a rational investigation began, the killers had a night's start. And a winter's night in India is a long time: time to hide anywhere or to sleep; and then resume one's flight unhurriedly.

The Superintendent Arrives

Rajeev Kumar Singh, the Kangra District's Superintendent of Police, reached the hilltop village of McLeod just after nine o'clock on the evening of February 4, 1997. He had a slight feeling of vertigo since he was used to the lower elevation of the valleys and the smooth plains of the sacred Ganges.

Singh was born in Allahabad in Uttar Pradesh, birthplace of Nehru — the father of modern India — who had welcomed the Dalai Lama and his followers when they fled from the Chinese invasion. There, the Ganges and the Yamuna, each with its own sacred source on the roof of the world, join only once to form the invisible, legendary river, the Saraswati. Singh was aware of the deep mystic significance of his birthplace and had always thought that the water of those rivers was like the breast milk of Mother India, flowing from the full, pristine peaks of the Himalayas.

The village of McLeod rises on one of the first spurs of that great mountain chain, and for Rajeev Singh, this the place had a special meaning. This very group of houses, scattered around what was once an English colonial hill station, had over the years become one of India's centers of prayer and pilgrimage. It was a destination for thousands of the faithful, not only from Tibet, but from all over the world.

Several hours had already gone by since the triple homicide his switchboard operator had told him about so excitedly, and the superintendent knew that every moment was now precious. His wife asked him what the hurry was, especially since she knew that he usually sent his deputy, Amitabha, to the crime scene first, even in the most brutal cases.

With the men from the local police station beside him, Singh entered the small room and found himself surrounded by the stench of blood. He took in the overturned chairs, the photos of lamas and the pictures of the Buddha, strewn sheets of paper, books, religious statues — the blood everywhere of a red turned so dark it seemed black.

It was immediately apparent to him that hundreds of feet had already trampled over the now utterly filthy floor, but he still took care to touch as little as possible as he moved around, practically on tiptoe. There was no more time to waste in looking for a first clue in the search for the killers. "Who said they were dressed as monks?" he asked Amitabha, who was buzzing in and out of the room. "Someone said so. We're getting some

15

leads from neighbors here," replied his deputy, "but I don't understand when and where they were seen...."

Singh noted that many hands had by now touched and moved the objects in the room. He observed a small gas stove, two glasses, and a pair of slippers, ballpoint pens scattered, papers, and oranges that seemed to shine in the indescribable chaos of the floor. The overturned chair where the monk Lodoe had been sitting was probably the only thing left as it was just after the attack took place.

The mess told him that the blows, dealt with such incredible violence, were the work of many hands and that at least five or six people probably were involved. Rajeev Singh half closed his large eyes; deep and magnetic, they resembled those found in certain Hindu statues. His hair, swept back with oil, was well groomed and sleek, and his bald spot gave his round face with its small moustache the enigmatic quality of one who observes the world with no apparent emotional involvement. Now, however, his deputy, Amitabha, saw that Singh's imperturbable expression, which usually so reassured his men, was gone. Shock had transformed it to one of dismay.

Singh had seen numerous crimes, the widest range of atrocities: heads cut off, bodies disemboweled. But the sheer quantity of congealed blood, filling the monk's small room with a sickening odor, horrified him. Tightening his moss-colored military greatcoat around his chest as if to contain the ugly onslaught of unpleasant sensations, he looked around in search of a clue to the meaning of this slaughter, as if the objects and the blood itself could transmit some inkling of what had occurred a few hours before in that very space.

Singh asked his men if any of them had known the slain Geshe, but all of them shook their heads. "The way he faced the killers, he certainly wasn't short of courage," said Amitabha. Singh gave no sign of having heard him and continued to study the objects, the oranges and cups—the last traces of life before the cataclysm. He took a camera out of his shoulder bag and began taking flash photographs from every angle, waving aside the forensic experts huddled over the evidence as they searched for fingerprints.

There were no eyewitnesses, and the superintendent had to make do for the moment with the descriptions given by the cook, Tenzin, who was still in a state of shock. From his men at the hospital he Singh learned more details, of the multiple bruises suggesting that a number of attackers had been responsible. His eyes roamed the room once more in an attempt to reconstruct the sequence of the fearful struggle in this tiny space. Most of the pieces of furniture and objects had ended up on the floor, especially those near the bed, which also served as a sofa, where the bodies of the Geshe and Ngawang were found.

The superintendent considered the theory of his colleague in the forensic unit who suspected the use of chloroform. But given the layout of the room, the killers would have found it too difficult a way to subdue the victims. Singh looked out of the window and was struck by the large party of monks, who seemed identical to the victims. They were staring in, following his every movement. He gave orders to his men to make up an inventory of all the objects, numbering the books and notebooks, and summoned for the following morning the most reticent of the neighbors. His men were told to seek out others.

All of a sudden, he could not stand being in the room another moment. The blood, the tension, and the odors of the place had been oppressive enough, but most suffocating of all was the sense that he was not equal to this task. Long experience in dealing with daily occurrences of like crimes of honor and disputes over cattle ownership and dowries[11] was inadequate preparation for such a challenge.

He glanced around one last time before going out into the fresh air to clear his nostrils of the sickening smells. After issuing a red alert to every police station in his district, he wiped his shoes thoroughly on a grassy patch to rid them of the caked blood and got back into the police car. Amitabha, who had been unusually quiet since they arrived at the crime scene, got in beside him, and their driver set off at high speed for Delek Hospital, navigating the narrow curves where there was barely space to squeeze past another vehicle.

Along the way, Singh looked out of the window as childhood memories came to mind. He remembered hearing about holy men in maroon robes who had appeared like Martians in the mountains that overlooked the valley. McLeod had then been well known among more prosperous Indians, who came to enjoy the cool air when summer scorched the rest of the subcontinent. This small village of Indians and Kashmiris, was a hill

---

[11] The money or treasure paid by the bride's family to the husband, often the cause of disputes and crimes masquerading as domestic violence.

station in the days of the British Raj, but in the 1960s it had been transformed into a miniature copy of a Tibetan city, with its temples of inlaid,
painted wood, houses with decorated windows, chanting pilgrims, and
smells of rancid butter and pungent incense. Frayed cotton prayer flags
fluttered in the wind, while shops sold statues and *thangkas*, those richly
colored religious paintings.

Indians too, thought Singh, *live in the sphere of the sacred, like
figures in a nativity crèche eternally adoring the highest, the absolute, the
unfathomable—a god, both visible and invisible, who for Hindus is present
in every atom of creation.* But the Tibetans in exile offered him and others
they met a very different, indeed almost opposite, idea of faith. Their god,
whether the Buddha or one of their own many divinities, which rivaled
the Vedic[12] pantheon in number and variety, did not create the world, nor
claim to be manifest in human beings, animals, plants, or rocks.

Rajeev Singh had heard their lamas say that everything around us—
mountain, river, or desert—was part of a great illusion. Like a magic box,
the human mind could constantly construct its surrounding world and
populate it with beings whose circumstances were the direct result of
actions performed in this life or others before it. But he could not regard
the blood-drenched room as some sort of macabre conjurer's trick, still
less could he link the geshe's fate to his behavior in a previous life. His
own thoughts stemmed from his Hindu mindset; they came from a vision of
an in response to seeing his ancestral land shrouded by the pitch darkness
of night. Firelight showed an indistinct figure, perhaps a shepherd, huddled
up near grazing horses. It was a scene of absolute peace, removed from the
realm of human folly, which could turn even a paradise into a hell.

They arrived at the hospital to find an atmosphere of frenzy. In the
turmoil Singh found officers from the McLeod station, colleagues from
Kangra, a doctor in white, a group of monks, and one woman who seemed
more desperate than the others. Instinctively, the two policemen headed
straight for her, almost as if a female presence was needed beside them

---

[12] The Vedas consist of the corpus of ancient knowledge and writings or oral traditions at
the base of Hindu religion and culture from the time of the first Aryan invasions from Persia
and Central Asia. The deities of the Vedas represent different aspects of the primordial
power of creation and can assume human, semihuman, or phenomenal forms.

when going in to see the horribly mutilated corpses. She told the super-intendent that her name was Dolma and she was the geshe's neighbor. Knowing him well, she went often to see the luminary from the School of Dialectics for advice on spiritual practice and guidance in daily life, also discussing her fears about life and death. The woman begged Singh not to let the crimes go unpunished. "It's not that I want revenge," she explained, "their karma will take care of that. I just want everybody to know the truth. When the truth about this comes out, everyone will finally understand."

She was an educated woman from an aristocratic family, and Singh bowed slightly to indicate that she should step into the morgue first, aware of the absurdity of such etiquette in the circumstances. Dolma took the shawl from her shoulders and wrapped it around her head, as she walked down the long corridor, stopping before the last door. Superintendent Singh noticed several dark stripes on the floor, surely dried blood mixed with earth from outside that had been left there by the hospital aides bringing in the corpses. In fact, most of the bloodstains trailed off outside the room where the bodies of the monks had been placed, and what he now saw before him was more chilling than the crime scene itself.

Slowly, as he approached the geshe's dead body, Singh saw that one side of the neck wound was much deeper. This showed that the killer had plunged the knife in to finish his victim off as quickly as possible. The thrust that caused the rest of the wound had no effective purpose, and seemed only ritual. Try as he did might, he was unable to retain his profes-sional detachment in conducting his examination and so resorted to taking photographs of the wounds in every detail, just as at the scene of the murder. Later he would study the prints, some enlarged, some reduced, all the while focusing on details, setting them beside one another, side by side and turn-ing them around to view them from every possible angle. Among the wide range of wounds, one that he had overlooked at first now stood out. It was a small, neat puncture, which began at the geshe's right hip and seemed to penetrate his bowels directly.

That night he was restless and slept uneasily. His wife had never seen him so upset, and they discussed the case for hours. "You need some rest," she said to him when dawn was approaching. "If you had a real assistant, rather than that useless Amitabha, you might be able to spend more time in bed."

Singh was a peaceful type and rarely responded to such remarks from his wife. "He's a good policeman," he replied, drawing up his blankets. "A good policeman doesn't get drunk every night or dump his family while he goes chasing anything in a sari," was her immediate response.

Singh went back to sleep, thinking about Amitabha and the rest of his team, and how nervous they all seemed; even Rahu, the driver, and the young orderly, Unni, who seemed the most worked up of all after seeing the crime scene. They had talked about it for the entire journey home, while in the glare of the headlights the trees on the side of the road seemed to flash by like phantoms in the dark night. "Superintendent, we've asked around everywhere—down to every hovel. The local police have, too, but no one has seen or heard anything at all. Doesn't that seem a bit strange to you?" said Unni. Rahu added, "I have heard some Tibetans say there are spirits mixed up in this. I don't believe it myself, but I can't deny that in cases like this…!"

From the back seat, Singh looked directly into Rahu's eyes in the driver's rearview mirror just for a second, so as to avoid an accident. "Rahu," he said pointedly, "'spirits' do not carry knives…."

"But, Superintendent," said Unni, turning around from his seat beside Rahu, "the first eyewitnesses monks said there were no footprints or traces of shoes on the floor of the room. With all that blood everywhere there should have been, especially if there were five assassins, as you say."

Singh shook his head, exhaling heavily as he did so. "Use your brain! A few human bodies losing blood from points with a lot of veins can flood a very large floor if no one staunches the wounds."

His men then kept silent until they arrived at his apartment, where they turned in the front seat and said good night with a slight twist of their heads.

The morning after the crime, Singh found the waiting room at his office full of monks ready to offer evidence, and his desk piled high with papers collected from the geshe's room. Most of the papers were spattered with blood, and all were now in plastic folders. One pile of yellowing sheets, placed precariously on another piece of furniture, attracted his attention. On top were some documents bound together, along with an exercise book of the type students use, with an opaque cover. He picked these up, and, when he saw they were written in Tibetan, he called in one of the monks from the School of Dialectics waiting in the anteroom.

A young student, with a weary expression, and wearing tortoise-shell glasses, came in. Singh took a page at random and asked him to translate it. The monk read a little in Tibetan. It was one of the geshe's old articles, he told the superintendent, adding that these had been collected in a book widely circulated in the Tibetan monasteries in north India. He made a rough translation of a passage, "You, who seek to discredit the Dalai Lama and our government: whatever you do will only harm yourselves and the true disciples of the Gelukpa school...."

Other monks had by now come into the room, despite the guards' efforts to stop them. Singh asked them if they knew who the geshe's enemies were. The student who had begun translating acted as spokesman and told the superintendent it would be best to speak to Kalsang Damdul, who was Lobsang Gyatso's assistant and deputy. At present he was not in McLeod, but the government's security service could inform Singh of his whereabouts.

Only then did Singh notice, standing among the monks, a wily old noncommissioned officer from the Central Bureau of Investigation in New Delhi, sent to offer the benefits of his considerable experience to the case. The man spoke in Hindi and reminded him that there had been reports from several police stations in Tibetan settlements in both in north and south India. Small acts of violence, death threats, incidences of statues displaced or destroyed, had all been recorded, and the Central Police Office had never really understood the motive, although he was in fact aware that differences existed between the cults of certain deities.

Singh was reminded of a phrase that his father, a respected figure and a good teacher, was fond of repeating: "A researcher does not arrive on the scene of his research with results already in hand." A philosophical man, he was also a practical one. From him, Singh had inherited his love of investigation, even if his father would have preferred him to have more scientific or literary interests. Meanwhile, Singh sought to use his acumen to further the cause of justice, although he knew he was working in a system that was, in a number of ways, quite corrupt within.

In the reflection of the windowpane, Rajeev Singh fleetingly noticed a face. Someone was staring at him, but only for a moment. He turned around and saw a female figure walking with slow, harmonious measured steps towards him. She wore a traditional Tibetan dress, and her braided hair fell in waves down her back. It was Dolma, the Geshe's spiritual friend and devoted neighbor. But how changed she was from yesterday!

Singh attributed his feeling when he saw her drained face to the deep suffering Dolma had experienced, which touched everyone around her. Aware of the lengthy investigation that lay ahead, he decided to forego the niceties of gentlemanly conversation and asked her directly to join him and the cook, Tenzin, in an examination of the objects found in the room. Dolma said nothing, but slightly nodded her head in agreement. She stepped firmly into one of the rooms in the local police station, where objects and photographs of the evidence sent for analysis to Simla had been laid out.

The police station was a rather ugly cement building. Every wall, outside and in, was a uniform grey color, except those behind the desks of the inspectors and their assistants, which were a nauseous green. They then went up to the second floor, where the officers on duty offered a military salute with no great enthusiasm. Dolma was taken into another room whose with walls were covered with sheets of paper and green and black box files were piled high. In one corner were bags, backpacks, knives of every type and size, teak sticks, and much else. In another corner, objects taken from the crime scene were arranged in a row, and she and Tenzin, who had joined them, were asked to identify them.

The two witnesses indicated the monks' plastic sandals, the Geshe's shoes, a paperweight, photo frames, a wooden incense burner, and other objects. They both paused as they focused on a blue-black trekking rucksack. "This," said Dolma, "certainly did not belong to the monks or to Genla." Tenzin had the same shuddering sensation he'd experienced beside his master's corpse. It was he who had tugged the bag away from the Geshe, who was clutching it so tightly. He said so to Singh, who signaled to his deputy with his eyes to let Tenzin pick up the object. Amitabha quickly read the reference, "Rucksack—blue and black—Adidas brand with markings in orange on upper part; made in Thailand. Contents: a torch—Apollo Jeevan Sakti brand—with blue plastic around the glass, one pair of black leather gloves, one small pink handkerchief, one whole peeled orange, one publication in Tibetan." Amitabha took the pamphlet and showed it to the two witnesses. By the expression on their faces, the policemen could tell that this was something important.

Singh left the pamphlet with Amitabha for him to get it translated and was on his way back to the station head's office when he heard the Geshe's cook call out to him. "Yesterday, with everything that was going on, I forgot to tell you something, Superintendent. In his last few days

Genla said we should be very careful over Losar because a lot of Tibetans and Westerners traditionally come to the temple and it would be very crowded. He asked me to keep a close check on everyone who wanted to see him and only to allow them in if I could recognize them personally." The novice buried his face in his hands in a theatrical gesture of remorse. "I didn't protect him," he sobbed, while Dolma gently placed an arm around his neck. "No one could have done it," she said in consolation.

On the way to the police office, the superintendent was jostled by some journalists who had been waiting avidly for news. He pointed to a small group sitting around the police station entrance, clearly in a state of shock. "Ask the neighbors," he told them, with a grimace indicating his disapproval of their failure to intervene. "But please let them talk to us first." One of the reporters shouted out that they had already interviewed them, but nobody had seen or heard anything. Singh shrugged his shoulders as he entered the office and replied with a wry smile, "Then you know as much as I do."

The men at the McLeod police station had a hard time letting the witnesses neighbors in one at a time, as they were all so keen to be rid of their disturbing obligation. Nothing had really struck any of them: neither the cries of the victims, nor the killers' heavy tread on the balcony, not their flight into the dark crowded streets; they had not even heard sounds of anything resembling a struggle. One old nun, who lived in the room below, said that she was asleep at the time. The six youths who lived in the apartment next door had not even noticed the bloody footprints on their landing. "We had a bit too much to drink last night," they said by way of explanation.

Luckily for Superintendent Singh, there was that rucksack. The secondary witnesses' testimonies were recorded and they were shown out. He was now alone with Dolma, the cook, and the inspector from Delhi, who was to remain with them as part of a special unit. Tenzin, his eyes still red from his tears, began speaking before he had even been asked a question. "When I went into the room I called out for help. Then I tried to get Genla's body onto the sofa. I was stunned, shocked by what they had done to my brothers. But I couldn't help noticing that rucksack because Genla was clutching it and his arms had gone rigid. I'd never seen it before, but it never occurred to me to wonder what it was or who it belonged to—or why he should be clinging to it like that."

The inspector from Delhi, who had not uttered a word throughout as the witnesses testified, stepped towards the police superintendent's desk and poured out the contents of the bag, which had already been touched by far too many hands. Out came the leather gloves, the handkerchief, the torch, and the peeled orange, now almost dried out. Then he gestured to the pamphlet still being translated and asked the superintendent, "Have we learned anything else?"

Singh nodded to Dolma to reply on his behalf. She explained that, as far as she understood, it was a text written by a group of monks about whom her late, lamented friend the geshe had made barbed criticisms. Tenzin nodded in agreement.

Dolma then asked, "Superintendent, have you ever heard about His Holiness's advice on not practicing the cult of a certain demonic spirit?"

"I have heard vaguely about something that may have been behind some incidents among Tibetan communities in India," he said, glancing at his colleague from Delhi, who had just been telling him about these quarrels in the settlements.

"They may just may be incidents, but they are a source of great worry for His Holiness," said Dolma. "Geshe Lobsang was forever telling Buddhist practitioners they should follow our leader's counsel."

Singh asked the name of this demonic spirit and, for the first time, an enigmatic expression came over Dolma's face. "Gyalpo Shugden. That's his name. His worshippers call him Dorje Shugden... unfortunately, that name has been on people's lips for far too long. I warned my poor Genla, I felt that the less the spirit was talked about, the better it would be for everyone.... That pamphlet, the one you found in the rucksack, came from his followers. Read this. See how it's signed: "Dorje Shugden Devotees Religious and Charitable Society, New Delhi.'"

She lowered her eyes, and Tenzin the cook did the same. The superintendent and the inspector from Delhi exchanged a significant glance: their colleagues in Intelligence and the experts from Security of the Tibetan government-in-exile could have the book pamphlet analyzed.

Singh wanted to find out why the cult had been banned, and much else besides. But he instinctively felt that Dolma was not the right person to ask, nor was this the right moment. Replacing the torch, handkerchief, gloves, and orange in the bag, he started to instruct his team on what to tell the press. "Say that we have sent some interesting samples to be examined in our laboratory at Simla."

"But they'll want to know what lead we're following," interjected a lieutenant.

"You can tell them we're not ruling anything out."

A jumble of thoughts and emotions flooding through his mind, Singh got into his car. He knew how to handle criminal investigations and had never ducked a challenge. But, whereas ordinary cases with determined elements could be classified as crimes of passion, madness, or revenge, this one knew no logical rules. Here, every explanation he constructed foundered on one detail or another, and none of those flashes of intuition that had helped him in his career had come to him yet.

For example, that pamphlet in the killer's bag—what could it mean? And that signature, "Dorje Shugden Devotees Religious and Charitable Society?" Why on earth would the killers go around with such obvious evidence incriminating their group—if the Delhi society really were was responsible? Then he thought about the expression he had seen on the faces of Dolma and the cook when they named the spirit. How would the more superstitious among his own men react when they learned of this Shugden's existence? But this was no time for theories and reflection—it was time for action, and Delhi was his next destination.

The superintendent returned to Kangra that afternoon to call a meeting of his closest collaborators, along with Amitabha and the inspector from Delhi, who had followed him in his own car. He told his deputy to contact their colleagues from the Criminal Investigation Department, the Central Bureau of Investigation, and the Central Police Office in the capital. He needed permission from each of these to transfer his special unit from Kangra to Majnu Ka Tilla, the Tibetan refugees' neighborhood in Delhi, where the "Shugden Society" was based.

A Complex Investigation

The eleven specialist detectives making up his team were convened in his Singh's meeting room, which also served as the lounge of his office. Several of them had arrived the night before from Delhi, Chandigarh, Simla, and Dharamsala, and all were told this was an assignment that might take weeks, if not months. Once assembled, everyone studied Amitabha, the deputy, with a degree of suspicion, perhaps tinged with envy. His weaknesses were well known, and they were not altogether happy to have him around, especially since, as Deputy Inspector, he would be their superior on this case. All knew, though, there would be no leeway for personal likes and dislikes once work began.

Rajeev Singh got straight to the point. "With the Delhi Central Bureau of Investigation's agreement, we have decided to set up this a special unit, which will cover a number of angles on this triple homicide. Besides establishing the origins of this secret society and its membership, we have to examine the economic, political, and religious implications of the crime."

Singh got up from his seat at the table and walked around his colleagues, showing each of them the photocopy of the "Shugden Society" pamphlet found in the rucksack of one of the killers. "These are our main suspects, and today we must concentrate on this group: who they are; what they want; and, what was their intent in committing a triple murder of this kind and then leaving their calling card on the corpses...."

Asha, a female detective from the Dharamsala Division, asked why a killer who later tried to cover his tracks would go around with such incriminating evidence on his person.

The superintendent replied that he had already asked himself that question, but it was too early to form a theory.

"As far as we can make out, the killer probably had no intention of leaving it in the room. The cook arriving with the tea, or his haste to get away may have made him forget its importance. Besides, he did not leave it deliberately; it was wrenched from him. So, for the moment, we have to focus on what we know now—I stress the word *now*—regarding the divisions in the Tibetan exile community that seem to be at the source of this crime and give it a rather complicated context. You all know that the

26

Geshe killed was very close to His Holiness the Dalai Lama, so this case is being followed at the very highest level."

Singh made an appropriate gesture to emphasize the last point: in fact, he meant the political classes in Delhi, government ministers included, and the Foreign Ministry in particular, which had already sent an emissary. Several of those present opened their notebooks.

He returned to his seat and went on to explain that he and his section had not yet fathomed the complexities of this particular religious conflict, nor had his predecessors. Up to now, the clashes between various Buddhist groups had been given little attention and were attributed to more mundane matters such as struggles for power and influence over the exile community.

"This is our first task," he said, "to be well prepared for our questioning of the leaders of this Delhi-based society that opposes the Dalai Lama. Many of them are well known in the exile community and were so even before they set up the "Shugden Society."

The police officer from Chandigarh asked what the word "Shugden" meant. "In your folders," Singh replied, "you all have a copy of a rough translation of the pamphlet found in the rucksack I showed you earlier. The cult's viewpoint will be clear from that. Gyalpo Shugden is the name of a spirit, or demon, or something of that sort, considered to be negative and dangerous by the Dalai Lama. The Dalai Lama has asked his followers to no longer pray to him. This has brought protests and created a lot of spiteful resentment among a large faction of lamas, monks, nuns, and laypeople."

The superintendent had wanted his tone to be relaxed and informal, but he knew that when it came to matters of deities, angels, and spirits, Indians were no different from Tibetans. Indeed, small signs of unease appeared on some of the faces of those there.

"I am aware that even among my own men, the other world has its terrors. I must say that if any of you have has doubts or fears, you should speak up right now and state clearly whether you're ready to work together rationally. If not, it would be better if you stepped aside, because there is absolutely no place for emotion in a case like this."

His words were met with silence, and after what seemed an appropriate pause, Singh resumed. "For now, all we need know is that the results of this split among Tibetans have been right under our noses for a long time, and we have to admit we have underestimated the seriousness of the situation. Now we have to get down to work, and, with this in mind, check out some past episodes."

"What sort of episodes?" asked the detective from Chandigarh.

"Many of you know that around 1994–95, the entire Tibetan community in Dharamsala was about to be transplanted to lands allocated by our government at Gurgaon, near Delhi airport, because of the continual clashes with the local Indian Gaddi people. Barely a day went by without an exile's shop being burned down or damaged because the Gaddi felt put out by the new arrivals' business success. Many of the Tibetans were far better businessman than the Gaddi, and within a few years the Tibetans had gained control of all the local production. At the same time, at the height of the tension, we learned that McLeod was more than usually full of Chinese spies. Our 'neighbors' had even planted a cook in the Dalai Lama's kitchens. The man was discovered by pure chance and confessed that he was being paid by Lhasa through a local contact and was meant to send simple information about the goings-on in the Tibetan leader's residence. Needless to say, when we tried to locate this contact, he had completely disappeared."

"But how is all this you're telling us connected to our three murders?" asked Asha. Singh looked around, him as if to satisfy himself that he could trust everyone present. "That's the background, or at least an angle on this crime, that I wanted to sketch for those of you who haven't much detailed knowledge of local affairs. But forget about China, the spies, and all the rest—that's classified information. Let's get back to the technical points of the case, since they're the most important for us. There's something else, though—just to give you the whole picture. I'll pass you over to my colleague from the RAW, the Research and Analysis Wing."

The special intelligence officer was well known because he carried out his work in secret in Dharamsala for the Research and Analysis Wing (RAW), the state's espionage service. He told them about an incident a few months ago earlier when a Tibetan girl was had been kidnapped, raped, and brutally murdered on the road to McLeod. "We were all very worried, weren't we, Superintendent? What with that happening, along with the burning down of an Indian shop, it seemed that we would be forced to transfer the whole Tibetan community to the land north of Delhi, as the superintendent mentioned. There's no doubt something serious would have come about, probably a vendetta against the Gaddi. They were the first suspects in the rape case, but luckily the dogs found a trail leading to a Tibetan's room. The man worked in the Dalai Lama's office and was called Dhundup Tsering. When he saw the police coming with dogs, he tried to escape. Then he made a full confession. He too admitted receiving money from the Chinese in Lhasa to be their spy in Dharamsala, but refused to reveal whether the murder was connected to his clandestine activity. We, instead, suspected it was part of a plan to discredit the community in exile and the Dalai Lama. But we found nothing concrete in the way of evidence, only confirmation from our own informers. From what I've just told you, it seems clear that given what happened on February 4, we can't exclude the involvement of outsiders or, likewise, even Tibetan dissidents."

This contribution from the RAW agent made everyone present more aware of how delicate this investigation was going to be.

Seizing the moment, Singh asked if there were any questions. A detective from Dharamsala raised his hand. "So, then, can we attribute the burning down of the 'Famous Studio' photography shop to the antagonism between the Tibetans and the Gaddi community, since it was owned by an Indian immigrant?"

"A good question, Inspector. That episode may prove very significant because, just like the kidnapping and the rape, it came about when the tension was actually decreasing between Tibetans and Gaddi. We could suppose that the fire was even part of a strategy to keep the atmosphere hostile."

Singh briefly paced up and down in front of his desk then paused, "Are there any further questions?"

Amitabha, his deputy, asked if all this had been explained to the emissary from the Foreign Ministry, who happened to be in Kangra the day after the crime. "Naturally, he received all our reports," said the RAW agent.

"But when China is involved," Singh intervened, "no mention of spying can be made explicit in any official report, otherwise it has to be officially investigated at government level. That involves the Home and the Foreign Affairs Ministries, and then the diplomatic channels..."

"I think Indo-Chinese relations are troubled enough already without us bringing up this whole affair," said the RAW agent rather pompously.

They all agreed, and now Singh was anxious to move on to another topic.

"Have you made any plans for the raid on the Tibetan quarter in Delhi?" asked one of the detectives sent up from the capital to join the team.

The superintendent nodded towards the Chief of the Coordination Department, also present, to indicate that he should answer this. "It is highly advisable to ask for support from the local police station, but only once we've arrived there. We have to be very careful—Majnu Ka Tilla is a tough zone to keep under control. You've got various Tibetan groups living by their wits, many families involved in gambling, prostitution, illegal bars—and some of our colleagues are not immune to female charms or to making some money on the side," the man added, without looking at Amitabha, but smiling knowingly at his neighbor.

"You're right," said Singh who had no time to spare on for defending his deputy from insinuations, "We'll go in on tiptoe, but we will go in. Read this." Taking from his drawer an envelope containing a book and two letters, he handed them to his nearest colleague. The content of the letters seemed identical. "These are letters from the "Shugden Society," that reached the lama a few days before his death. One was posted in Kangra and the other in Delhi. The code number for the latter, B97, identifies the post office as the one in the Tibetan Colony, Majnu Ka Tilla. We're waiting for the translations, but we know the letters are not an exchange of compliments. We have to find out if this "Dorje Shugden Devotees Charitable and Religious Society" has the means and the manpower to translate words into action."

He looked over his team one by one and added, "My deputy, Amitabha, seems to me the right linkman for this special unit. You are going to work with the secret service on the background of the crimes—under my supervision, of course. Each one of you," he looked pointedly at them again so as to stifle further sarcastic responses regarding his deputy, "must report any findings to this office for the simple reason that all the threads will get tangled otherwise."

"Our section of the Inspectorate will check the financial records of the Institute school and the foundation directed by the murdered geshe. We'll look to see whether there may have been any quarrels over the distribution of the funds, which came largely from abroad. We shall have to work closely with Interpol and its representative here, Agent Abhey. Meanwhile, we're still waiting for the findings on those objects and the fingerprints from Simla."

The guards came in with tea, and when everyone stood up to drink it, Singh announced that they would all meet again soon, after the raid on the Delhi headquarters of the Shugden Society. He showed them the letter from the Central Bureau of Investigation with its red corner indicating top priority and utmost secrecy. "As of now, our mission is active. I'll say it again, whoever has any doubts of, let's say, a mystic nature, had better say so openly right now, so as to avoid problems later."

Amitabha, who had been silent throughout the meeting, already had in mind a strategy of his own that would show his colleagues, ever ready to pass their moral judgments on him, what a real detective was made of. He was going to exploit one of his apparent weaknesses, one of his numerous female friends.

The Special Unit

Phuntsok worked in one of the offices of the Tibetan government-in-exile. She had a daughter from a relationship with a man who had later preferred to go off to America alone, rather than take care of them. Deputy Superintendent Amitabha swore his love constantly and strove to convince Phuntsok that only fear of his wife and her family's reaction deterred him from a deeper commitment. Phuntsok knew these were lies, the usual sort that men told. But deep down she didn't really care that much. Amitabha was very generous, especially when he left her side. Usually this was only when he could stand steady on his feet again after a serious bout of drinking.

That morning she heard the deputy superintendent calling her from behind the thick cotton curtain, embroidered with an auspicious Tibetan symbol, that covered the window in the little room where she lived, on a street near the library. "Phuntsok! Phuntsok! It's me, Ami. Are you there?"

The young woman sat him down on a small sofa squashed between the fridge and her bed. Hers was a small, bare home — a single room containing a kitchen, bed space, and a small closet. The deputy superintendent accepted the tea that she poured from a thermos and told her that he needed her. This time, however, he spoke differently. It was a tone Phuntsok had not heard before. In fact, come to think of it, this was one of the few times she had actually seen him in daylight, and sober. She positioned herself on a small stool so as to take a better look at him. Amitabha's short hair framed a handsome face with prominent cheekbones and an expression that seemed all the more intense because of his way of staring at you when speaking.

She asked him, seriously, "Problems with your wife?"

"Bah! That goes without saying. It's work. Can I trust you?"

"This is about those monks that were murdered, isn't it?" asked the girl, who had the sharpness of mind of most women in the Tibetan community in exile.

"Yes, it is about that. Tell me everything you know on about the Dorje Sudden Society."

"You mean Shugden," she said with a grimace that he found hard to decipher.

"Yes. Exactly. What do you know?"

"They're fanatics. They have it in for the Dalai Lama because he has spoken out against their cult of the spirit, Gyalpo Shugden, and now they want to make all his Tibetan followers pay. You saw what they did to that Geshe..."

"So, you're inclined to help me. If you do well on this case, I will put you in touch with a big shot in the secret services in Delhi who can get you onto the list of informers. You know they've got deep pockets. They don't have to keep a record of their expenses, as they don't appear in the budget. They're almost unlimited, at least compared to the miserable sums they give us at the district...."

She observed him suspiciously. Phuntsok had never liked spying, and, on principle never would have started, even for this good cause, despite having heard that a lot of people, including beggars, were on the RAW payroll. She knew her policeman friend well: generous he could be, but he could also leave you high and dry if things became problematic. The deputy superintendent had to keep up some form of decorum, avoid divorce, and keep his name out of reports whenever he was found in a drinking den or brothel.

Tibetan women appealed to Amitabha because they were strong and straightforward like Indian women, but could also be sweeter and more romantic. Certain clues told him at a glance whether they had recently immigrated or had arrived a long time ago. As they spent more time here in exile, their skin became smoother and their figures more shapely, while their features softened, making them more attractive to him than the girls who lived on the cold, dry highlands beyond the Himalayas.

But right now, Amitabha's only concern was to impress his boss, whom he held very dear. Singh had always defended him, however bad the scrape. Under the superintendent he felt secure, convinced that his boss's authority would be of help in overcoming his problems, even if rules had to be bent. Indeed, all too often things ended in humiliation, and he had to touch the superintendent's feet with his hand in a gesture of devoted submission usually reserved among Hindus for a guru or a respected *sadhu*.[13] Amitabha knew his superior was a little bothered by these prostrations but, having a kind heart, he always could be persuaded to help out one more time.

[13] Hindu mendicant renunciant.

He said goodbye to Phuntsok with a kiss she did not return and went back home, hoping his wife would not be as tense and irritable as usual. This was not to be, and Amitabha spent the night trying to persuade her that it was she alone that he loved, until they fell exhausted into a deep sleep, just a few minutes before it was time to take the children to school.

The Geshe's Enemies

Rumors spread from the School of Dialectics to the bazaar and reverberated around the great courtyard in front of the Dalai Lama's residence, where the old folks, monks, and nuns whirled their prayer wheels and prostrated with particularly fervent devotion before the images of buddhas and bodhisattvas. All the butter lamps were constantly lit, while auspicious white scarves were piling up on the statues around the main altar.

Stories were told and reminiscences exchanged about Master Lobsang's life entirely devoted to religion and teaching: he rose at four, practiced until six, and then circumambulated the temple for an hour. At seven he recited mantras with students from the School of Dialectics and at eight he would breakfast before going to his work at the Institute. From ten to half past eleven he taught, and after lunch he finished his writing of religious commentaries or texts for publication by the government. Sometimes he gave lessons in the afternoon, too, which lasted until suppertime, never continuing beyond half past five. Afterwards, the master would return to work until it was time for the debates to start. The Geshe liked to listen to the monks' exchanges, which were accompanied by sweeping, dramatic gestures, hands raised to the sky as if to call the heavens to support the point of doctrine that was about to be unleashed on an opponent. Watching the debates was one of his few pastimes. At eight he drank tea, and at half past nine he would pray and then go to bed.

All this Singh learned from his men's reports. They had gleaned this information by frequenting every one of the Tibetan community's meeting places. But, from the summary prepared for him by Amitabha, one of those best informed, something resembling a craggy rock lay menacingly in the calm waters of the life of the former peasant turned scholar. The letter pamphlet in the killer's bag seemed to confirm that it had wreaked havoc quite often.

His students knew that rock as "Gyalpo Shugden, Gyalchen or Dolgyal," to whom they referred to as the most treacherous of enemies because of the spirit's effect on their master's mind. It occupied his every free moment for reflection, eroding the calm meditative state gained in his practice. It hurled him back into his boyhood inferno of worldly emotions, when, bearing the name "Garbage Beggar," so naïvely given him by his mother, he landed in many a fight.

Singh learned from Amitabha, whom he complimented on his excellent sources, that Shugden had become the most terrible of all demons in the collective Tibetan imagination, even though the ban on the circulation of his descriptions and pictures meant that few of the young monks and novices would recognize his image. This fear had grown greater since the Dalai Lama's announcement that he had removed Dolgyal from his prayers and considered him a negative force, against those seeking enlightenment, the government, and the people, as well as a danger to his own life.

From the information relayed to him by Phuntsok, now established as his secret source, the deputy superintendent passed on the rumor that Geshe Lobsang Gyatso wrote and dispatched a great number of letters on the subject to all those Tibetan centers where the cult of Shugden was fervently practiced. Amitabha had attached to his report a very old one of these from the 1970s, which Phuntsok had somehow obtained and translated as best she could. Singh read it quickly, running over a series of names that meant nothing to him. "Lobsang Namgyal, you and others who are trying to discredit the Dalai Lama and the government, no matter what action you take, you will only end up hurting yourselves. You may be considered among the most erudite,[14] but if you look back on your lives you will see little but dirty deeds. I never believed in you and I do not now. If you were mules, a good lashing would do your minds no harm. My speaking ill of the followers of Shugden, you among them, does no damage to the true disciples of the Gelukpa School and indeed may be just what is needed to protect its growth."

The lamas mentioned, Amitabha indicated in his note to his superior, were followers of the cult now scattered all over the world. In common, they were all disciples of Trijang Rinpoche, the Dalai Lama's Junior Tutor. Amitabha explained that Trijang was probably the most revered and charismatic of all the lamas who escaped Tibet in 1959, following in the footsteps of their leader. This seemed to confirm to Singh that the Gelukpas dominated the microcosm of the Tibetan community in exile to an equal, if not greater degree than they did the whole country in the centuries when they held spiritual and temporal power in Tibet. It was not easy to fathom to what extent the Director of the School of Dialectics had intended to

---

[14] This letter mentioned the names of Kelsang Gyatso, Ganchen Tulku, Dagom Tulku, Geshe Tendar, Lobsang Ngodup, and Chatreng Yeshe.

create so direct a confrontation with a lama as powerful as Trijang in that small, and gossip-ridden community dominated by eminent clerics.

Singh wondered whether the Dalai Lama was aware of the slowly growing rancor. Amitabha's notes answered this question. "The Tibetan leader," he wrote, "had often advised the old scholar of dialectics to take care when choosing that subject for his writings."

It was still not clear why the assassins—if they really were worshippers of the demon—chose to kill the young monks too, when their only apparent offense was having translated some Tibetan texts into Chinese. Why had they not waited until the old monk was alone? Even the staff of the government-in-exile could not provide a clear answer to that question. They pointed out that the deaths of Ngawang and Lodoe had made the Shugden followers unpopular across the Tibetan community and threw a sinister shadow over the real causes of the conflict. Could their translation have had some connection to a motive for the crime? Singh knew the investigation had barely begun and these knots would be unraveled in time, if only he could get a lucky break. Even when an investigation seemed lost in a pitch-dark tunnel, there was always something to grasp onto—or, as his father used to say, "Above even the darkest clouds, the sun is shining brightly."

The superintendent gathered up his papers. The first two intense days of the investigation were drawing to an end, and he telephoned Amitabha to check that the officers leaving for Delhi had all their instructions clear for the raid on the Tibetan quarter. Then he called his friend Ngodup in the security services of the government-in-exile. From his office Singh got all the information needed about who the followers of the Shugden Society were and where in India they were located. It was quite a long list that also confirmed that various branches existed overseas, although they operated under different names. The superintendent called one of his assistants and pointed to an old computer in the corner of the room. Without explaining too much he started to dictate. "Write...Addressed to: The Ministry of Education. Copies to: The Ministry of Home Affairs. Central Police Office. Interpol. To Whom It May Concern. Re: Request for Information; Urgent."

Dictating the formal "red-cornered" letter, Singh asked for all the reports available on the Indian network of the "Dorje Shugden Devotees Religious and Charitable Society" and listed all the names, monasteries, and addresses revealed by his secret source in the Tibetan government-in-exile. Then he had the fax sent off.

By now he was so exhausted he could hardly keep his eyes open. After his assistant left the office, the Kangra district police superintendent stretched out on a small leather sofa, its surface worn as thin as the scales of a dried-out old snakeskin. He woke up after just a few minutes but had to drink a whole pot of piping hot coffee before feeling ready to start work again. Next, he read the report on Lobsang Gyatso's recent trip to Hong Kong. This dossier, several pages thick, told the whole story of the Geshe's dealings on the island, once a British colony before it was returned to Chinese control.

It all began with one of the Geshe's first disciples, Tenzin Jamchen, a half-Tibetan, half-Chinese monk, who had lived in America since the 1950s and came quite regularly to Dharamsala to attend Lobsang Gyatso's lectures at the Institute School of Dialectics. These he transcribed and published in Chinese, and they became very popular in Taiwan and all over Southeast Asia, where Tenzin Jamchen had opened many centers by the start of the early 1990s. Even the sutra commentary on which Lobsang had been working with Lodoe and Ngawang was mentioned in the file as about to be translated and distributed in Chinese.

He looked swiftly over the rest of the report, which explained that the money raised in the Geshe's Asian centers was used mainly put toward completing a study division in Kangra, to be connected to the Institute School of Dialectics. There was also a reference that Singh could not fully understand, although it seemed to be relevant somehow. The new institute, like the School of Dialectics, "would be dedicated to the study of all traditions of Tibetan Buddhism in accordance with the nonsectarian policies of His Holiness." The report ended by stating that Lobsang Gyatso had always declined to travel to Taiwan for fear of embarrassing the Dalai Lama, since China considered the island as much a part of its territory as it did Tibet. Therefore, many Chinese who wanted to follow the teachings in his presence descended on Dharamsala, often booking entire hotels. It was only in the last few years that the Geshe had decided to go personally to Hong Kong. The last visit was shortly before his death.

Superintendent Singh closed the dossier and thought about the remunerative international engagements of these exiled Tibetan masters and scholars such as Lobsang Gyatso. Together with the donations of generous

Western disciples, they played a large part in ensuring the survival of the refugee communities in India.

On reflection, he had seen too many frauds posing as *sadhus* and *maharishis*[15] in his own society to completely exclude the possibility of there being some illicit dealings in the background to the murders. Besides, the interweaving of finance and religion among the Tibetans already had a name, "Dharma business." The problem now was to identify the type of money interests that could be hidden behind the murder of Lobsang Gyatso.

However, an examination of the Geshe's bank accounts and those of the government-in-exile showed nothing but regular donations, many from abroad, and it was soon clear that nothing useful to the investigation could be gained by looking at bank statements and deposits. As for the other standard motive, sex, even though the victim was a monk, it would be inappropriate to discard this possibility so early on. In any case, it was Dolgyal or Gyalpo Shugden, or whatever he was called, who seemed to cast an indelible occult shadow over these three murders.

There was little to do but wait, at least for those the dark clouds to disappear from his horizon until those events, whose meaning as yet eluded him, appeared in a new light.

---

[15] Literally, "great teacher" or "great sage."

A Conversation Regarding History

The monks of the School of Dialectics were living like recluses behind the gates of their Institute. They felt not only robbed of their spiritual leader and guide, but also surrounded and intimidated, prey to the hostility that their late master's rough outspokenness had attracted.

Kalsang Damdul, the murdered director's assistant, rushed back to Dharamsala the moment he heard the news and immediately took charge of the funeral rites for both Lobsang Gyatso and the two young monks, and the running of the school.

Rajeev Singh knew him only by name. He called his office, as Ngodup suggested, and made an appointment for that evening, after the special squad had been dispatched to probe the Majnu Ka Tilla area of Delhi.

Singh arrived with Amitabha and his driver, who parked the car in the open square near the Dalai Lama's temple. It was almost nightfall, probably the same time when as the killers bore down on their victims.

An icy gust of wind penetrated the folds of his coat, freezing his chest and kicking up whirls of dust that carried the stink emitted by the rubbish bags spilling out from filthy boxes on the side of the road. Below them, the valley resembled a lunar landscape in the blurred light cast by the distant villages, with spirals of smoke and a purple-streaked sky. *Maybe the valleys of Tibet look like this*, he thought to himself. In his mind, images overlapped of processions of pilgrims and monks heading for the monasteries of venerated, powerful masters, incarnations of earlier lamas and of the gods, seated on thrones and surrounded by sacred icons clad in incense smoke.

Rajeev Singh slipped into the maze of corridors and staircases of the Institute school, following the directions he had been given on the telephone. He pulled aside the curtain at the entrance to Kalsang Damdul's office and found him at his Mac, his face lit by the glow of the computer screen. It was a surreal image in the sober, austere, mystic atmosphere of the monastic complex that housed the school, made even more evocative at that twilight hour by the silence of the dusk that enveloped every building.

"Come in, Superintendent. I'll put on the light for you," the monk said hospitably, as he stood up to meet him. "I was replying to an email from one of our benefactors. You see, a lot of foreigners help us financially, and without their money we couldn't hold all our courses or support the monks. But we don't allow personalized sponsorship. It was our poor Geshe Lobsang who decided that. "It is better not to let the boys have money in their hands," he said, "easier for them to avoid temptation." I wouldn't have been so rigid about it, but that was the way he was, and so I am respecting his rule until the new director is appointed."

Geshe Kalsang Damdul's words flowed easily. His expressive eyes set in his round, wrinkled face and his shaved head gave personality to an otherwise ordinary figure. He resumed singing the praises of his predecessor, "...Besides, our late, lamented director did so much to preserve Tibetan culture here in exile. Thanks to the School of Dialectics, generations of monks and scholars have been trained to respect not only our Gelukpa tradition but all the others, too."

Kalsang Damdul saw from the questioning look on the policeman's face that he had touched on a point of great interest. Then he realized he had not yet offered his guest a chair. "Forgive me. Please have a seat. You too..." he said to Amitabha, who had appeared in the doorway followed by another serious-looking monk with a folder under his arm. "May I present my assistant, Tashi," said the Geshe, "...We can speak freely, since he knows as much as I do." The monk sat down behind the other computer in the room, wearing the same impassive expression as when he had entered. Kalsang Damdul continued, "We monks take it for granted that everyone knows all about our Buddhist schools. When I say 'Geluk,' I mean the Yellow Hats, to which His Holiness belongs. For centuries, it was the most important of all the schools and had most political influence, spiritual power, and the most famous masters...."

"As far as I knew until the other day," Singh told him, "I thought that everyone who followed the Buddha's way was of the same religion. But after these crimes, it seems to me that things are a bit more complicated. Isn't that so?" Then he added, "Of course, I'm not interrogating you."

The Geshe's laugh multiplied the wrinkles around his eyes. He rose to speak, making broad gestures with his arms as he did so. "I'll do my best to point you in the right direction, especially as your inquiries are our main hope of obtaining justice."

Singh tried to get straight to the main points. "Had you taken any measures to protect your director after you learned about the threatening letters? Did you take them to be serious or just word games?" he asked.

"Serious, Superintendent, very serious. You must have heard about what happened in the south in the monasteries and in some other areas where exiles live. There were a lot of clashes, often very violent, and fires. But a crime like this? No, I can't believe anyone could have imagined anything of the sort, even if many of our late director's students were very worried for him. But then Genla always said, "If I don't speak out, no one else will respond to the lies written about His Holiness.... I can tell you in confidence that even the Dalai Lama advised him to be careful. He asked him to end his long dispute with a well-known Geshe in that cult, which was already common knowledge."

Here, the monk Tashi interrupted. Placing his folder and his elbows on the table, he said, "His Holiness told both of them to end their harmful correspondence. The insults exchanged were unbecoming for masters of their rank."

"The Dalai Lama was certainly aware of the consequences of his imposing a ban of that type," said Singh, who was now proceeding by instinct and was still far from understanding what was going on.

"Not a ban, Superintendent," answered the Geshe, "the Dalai Lama had simply said it was not appropriate for someone to receive Tantric teachings from him if that person continued to dedicate practice to a spirit like that. Whoever wished to participate in the cult could do so, but they shouldn't attend his teachings or religious initiation ceremonies. There was a clear conflict, but I don't want to bore you with a story which that goes back a long way."

"Well, sooner or later I have to get to the bottom of it."

"In that case I'd advise you to read this text," replied Geshe Kalsang Damdul, as he stood on the tips of his toes to take down a folder from a shelf holding catalogued files. He held out some sheets of paper written in English. "If you have time to have a look at these, they will give you some idea of the reasons why His Holiness decided to take such a delicate decision. Of course it won't be easy to get to the bottom of this affair, but I"m sure it these will help to make some parts of it clear."

Singh read the introduction: "Speech made by His Holiness the Dalai Lama on the worship of Shugden on July 13, 1978, at his residence...." There followed a detailed list of the abbots and monastic officials present. On it was a reference to "two teachers from the School of Dialectics." The superintendent asked if one of them was Lobsang Gyatso.

"Of course. Our director was very close to the Dalai Lama and was certainly among the first to be told of the decision. Both of them inspired our institute to have a nonsectarian approach to the teachings from the very beginning. As I said earlier, here one studies the whole body of the teachings of every tradition, with no discrimination."

The superintendent scratched his chin. "Perhaps," he said, "we had better proceed step by step. The very first report I received on the case also referred to this sectarian aspect."

"To use a fashionable term," answered the Geshe, "we might consider the followers of Shugden to be 'fundamentalists.' Essentially, they will not tolerate what they see as the corruption of the practices and the original point of view of the Gelukpas, whose name, you will remember, means 'the Virtuous Ones.' These practices, they say, must never be confused with elements drawn from other schools of religious thought, particularly from the Nyingmapa tradition—which is actually the oldest."

The emphasis that the Geshe had put on the word "Nyingmapa" made the superintendent curious, and he asked again, "Is it a dispute over the interpretation of the teachings of the Buddha?"

The monk smiled: and replied, "You see, from its very beginning, between the seventh and eighth centuries, the development of our religion in Tibet was not based only on the original teachings attributed to the Buddha. It came to us in a form that was more elaborate, let's say more complex, than what the Enlightened One presented to his first disciples 1200 twelve hundred years before."

"I thought religions didn't change with time...."

The monk grew more serious, and shifted his position in his chair, indicating a careful answer was needed. "Between the era of Buddha Shakyamuni and the introduction of Buddhism into Tibet, many centuries passed. Thanks to other masters, teachings that had evolved as different schools of thought were incorporated. Schisms were overcome and deep differences over the interpretations of words and meanings of the doctrine were resolved. Just to show how complicated it all was, Tibet was a case apart. The pre-Buddhist tradition there was more or less shamanic, but not as wild as some historians would have us believe. In an ancient Tibetan kingdom called Shang Shung, near the sacred mountain known as Mount Kailash, which you Hindus consider the abode of Shiva, ancient treatises on the nature of the mind had been kept from a time many centuries before the Buddha himself lived. Besides, the Bon masters[16] knew techniques to control the elements, the deities and the spirits of those highlands. To replace this religion, something more than knowledge of the teachings of the Buddha gained from the sutra on the dependent origination of all phenomena was needed. At first, attempts were made to use just the scriptures and the commentaries of the great Indian sages, then...."

The two policemen had so far listened in silence. Although Buddhism began in ancient times in India, Singh and Amitabha, like most other Indians, knew very little about it. The superintendent raised his hand as if in a gesture of surrender. "I beg you, Geshe.... Everything you have told us is very interesting, but I'm afraid we have to get back to the present if we are going to achieve something concrete. Do you think this group of Shugden devotees actually had a real motive to eliminate Geshe Lobsang?"

Kalsang Damdul spread his arms wide then drew them into his chest. "A real motive? I wouldn't know.... In general, they want to bring into their cult as many Tibetans and foreigners as possible...." The Geshe stroked his shaved head. "What do you think?" he asked the monk Tashi, who replied, "Maybe they wanted to demonstrate something—something to do with their demon—to show he really existed and that he punishes those who cross him, just as the famous *Yellow Book* says—the one that so shocked His Holiness."

"What book is that?" asked the two policemen almost in unison.

"That's another rather long story, Superintendent, and it's very closely tied up with our sects and their differences.... You see, what I was telling you about earlier was not unlike today's events. As you know, karma can work out over centuries, and not only individuals but whole nations have collective karma."

"You said the killers might have wanted to demonstrate something. What, exactly?"

---

[16] Bon (the term derives from the verb "to recite") is the ancient religion of Tibet, formed thousands of years ago by the great master Shenrab Miwoche. After the advent of Buddhism, Bon integrated and absorbed the new teachings from India, and vice versa, the Vajrayana embraced numerous divinities from the original Bon pantheon. For an in-depth analysis of this topic, see *Drung, Deu and Bon—Narrations, Symbolic Languages &and Bon in Ancient Tibet*, by Chogyal Namkhai Norbu. Dharamsala: Library of Tibetan Works and Archives, Dharamsala 1995.

"Try to understand, Superintendent. We're all still in a state of shock. It's not easy to find answers without explaining a lot of details that aren't part of these...these..."

"Crimes?" suggested Amitabha.

"Not only crimes. Once again, it's a long story. Told briefly, when the ancient Bon priests and the deities of seventh-century Tibet hindered the spread of Buddhism by producing mysterious and disturbing natural phenomena, a great master exorcist called Padmasambhava was invited to Tibet. He was immediately venerated as a new buddha, and demonstrated that he had the powers to subdue even the spirits controlling the elements. Tantric texts of his secret practices circulated in the land. In his teachings, philosophical discussion was kept to a minimum, renunciation of the world became of secondary importance, and a new type of knowledge was spread, which enabled a transformation both of one's inner and outer human existence by means of the development of certain innate powers. Afterwards, there came to the throne a king who was an enemy of religion, and the spread of Buddhism was halted for over a century until after his death, when other masters, both Tibetan and Indian, once more journeyed across the Himalayas. They brought with them new translations of additional sutras, which were suited to intellectual study, closer to the monastic way and to the original interpretations of the works of the Buddha. During this second phase, or wave, of translations, the secret Tantras of Padmasambhava still continued to circulate among his followers, who were called the Nyingmapa, the 'Old School'..."

"Do you mean the school that the Shugden Gelukpas oppose?" asked Amitabha, thus earning an admiring glance from his superior.

"Exactly. This is why I have been burdening you with this long preamble. Many masters from the new schools which that emerged between 1100 and 1400, the Sakyapa, Kagyupa, Kadampa, Jonangpa, and later the Gelukpa, practiced the secret Tantras, but only those Tantras that had been recognized as valid and, above all, connected to the traditional sutras. It was the Kadampas in particular, and later the Gelukpas, who cast doubt on certain Nyingmapa Tantras, even though our founder, Tsong Khapa, received many teachings from masters of the Nyingma school. However, the more orthodox maintained that it was too difficult for people to use such practices without training, and especially without the compassion needed to use them for the benefit of others. Besides, these texts often were discovered by yogis who claimed to have found them amongst rocks, in caves, under stones in rivers, or even in visions or dreams of Padmasambhava himself and his disciples. Many Gelukpas did not believe them. The entire Buddhist canon was revised, and subsequently those teachings were excluded. However, these continued to develop among the Nyingmas, the Kagyus and especially in what was considered the highest Tantric tradition, Dzogchen. I don't want to add to your confusion, but a number of Dalai Lamas used the ancient practices, as His Holiness does today."

The superintendent nodded. "You're right, Geshe, it is all very interesting, but also extremely complicated. We wouldn't want to get too deeply into it."

"But you should bear in mind that the present Dalai Lama regretted not having followed the tradition of his predecessors from the start, limiting himself to the practices of the Yellow Hats as he did. He made this clear when he imposed the restriction on the cult of Shugden. He admitted that he had made a mistake."

"By the way, you mentioned earlier a *Yellow Book* that links all this to the present. Does the color chosen have to do with the school?" asked Singh.

"Yes and no. It was the color of the cover, but it also was intended to be connected with the tradition. It was written in the 1970s by Zemey Rinpoche, who was a disciple of His Holiness's tutor, Trijang Rinpoche. Some say that it was Trijang himself who inspired it. Anyway, it listed a great number of problems experienced and the mysterious deaths of famed masters and ministers, including the former Regent of Tibet, which happened just before or just after the death of the Thirteenth Dalai Lama. And what do you think Zemey thought was the reason for all those deaths?"

"The Geshe is pulling our legs," said Amitabha with a knowing smile. "We're just two poor policemen who've come here to question you, so you shouldn't be asking us riddles."

Kalsang Damdul laughed. "The reason was that Shugden had punished them all for having abandoned the Gelukpa practices, or else of for corrupting them with those of the Nyingma Tantras, just as they claim the present Dalai Lama has done. That's why that book was seen as a direct attack on His Holiness."

There followed a few seconds of silence as the Geshe waited to see if the policemen had understood.

Amitabha was, once again, more prompt than his superior. "But how did this Shugden get to know what kind of Tantras those unfortunate fellows were practicing?"

Kalsang Damdul laughed heartily. It was Tashi, the monk, absolutely serious as always, who decided to answer instead. "One of the practices absolutely forbidden to Gelukpa monks is that of sexual union. However, with the excuse that they were emulating the Nyingmapa yogis, some of the Gelukpas had sexual relations with women. In a small and gossip-ridden community such as Lhasa's in the early 1900s, very little stayed secret. In the eyes of the orthodox, even laypeople should not indulge in certain techniques with their partners; however, according to the Nyingmapa Tantras, physical pleasure should be used as a means to control one's attachment to sensation. But I think such details are not really relevant to your investigation...." For the first time, Tashi's face showed the hint of a smile.

"So then, the *Yellow Book* says Shugden punished the transgressors. But why was such a fuss made about it, and why would they want to upset the Dalai Lama? Surely His Holiness doesn't practice Tantric sex?"

This time Tashi laughed as loudly as Geshe Kalsang. "No, His Holiness is an impeccably behaved monk. Now, as to the sixth reincarnation...." At this, the two monks started laughing again.[17] The Geshe continued, "His Holiness was upset because it was an indirect and barely concealed attack on his nonsectarian approach. Read here..." He rose to point out something in the batch of photocopies he had given the superintendent. He brought the lamp closer, and Rajeev Singh scanned what was written:

> It does not matter which prayers I say in my own room. I represent all Tibetans and I favor no particular group, neither Gelukpa, Nyingmapa, nor Kagyupa.

Singh skipped down a few lines:

> Zemey was perfectly aware of my point of view on sectarianism, then and now.

Kalsang Damdul gathered the pages carefully. "No, no, it's best if I give you a summary so you don't get confused. First of all, you should know that His Holiness had already informed his tutor, Trijang Rinpoche, that he no longer wanted to depend on Dolgyal as principal protector. This was

---

[17] The Sixth Dalai Lama was a practitioner of Tantric sexual methods and was obliged to abdicate at the beginning of the eighteenth century.

because the oracles of Nechung and the divinity Palden Lhamo had already indicated clearly in divination ceremonies that this spirit was a dark force. The Dalai Lama recounted how he had been asked by the State Oracle to dedicate an offering ceremony in the main temple to Guru Rinpoche, another name for Padmasambhava—you remember who he is, don't you? The year of the Wood Hare, 1975, was the first time since the flight into exile that the Gelukpas had paid homage to Padmasambhava in public. Just read what His Holiness says:

> Padmasambhava is the guru of all Tibetans; his compassion and power have a particular influence in these degenerate times when darker forces, both human and otherwise, are gaining power. That is why it is important for Tibetans to turn to him in prayer."

"I'm sorry, but I still don't understand," said Singh, glancing at his deputy, who seemed equally puzzled.

"You see, many monks and nuns did not come to that ceremony, much to His Holiness's surprise. When His Holiness asked why, he learned for the first time of Zemey's book, which spoke explicitly of misfortunes, disasters, and calamities, all provoked by Shugden, that were experienced by the Gelukpas who performed Padmasambhava's Tantric practices. Those absent feared that something similar would happen to them if they attended the prayer ceremony. If you now read what the Dalai Lama said, you will see why that incident was so important. Such was the fear of the demon among his followers that they no longer responded to a decision made by their master."

> After making inquiries, I heard about the *Yellow Book*, entitled *The Oral Transmission by the Intelligent Father*, which Zemey Rinpoche had kept secret from me.... Only when I asked why the nuns refused to practice with us did I learn that the book had been distributed publicly. And when I received a copy two days later, I felt truly downcast.

Rajeev Singh was beginning to have a clearer picture. It had not been easy to follow this long story, but he now realized that the schism was not merely about theories. He asked for confirmation from the Geshe. "So Padmasambhava was a sort of enemy of Gyalpo Shugden, if I have it right."

"That side of things is not quite so easy to explain, Superintendent, because Shugden did not exist in Padmasambhava's time. But, in a certain sense, the answer is 'yes.'"

"Of course, all this is not going to help me find the killers," said the superintendent with a sigh. "And I still wonder how differences over doctrine in your religion could lead to such horrific crimes. But maybe I'm mistaken in thinking that religions at least hold out something good for the world...." Having said this, he made turned towards the door.

"Frankly, Superintendent, it's a difficult issue for us to deal with, too," said the Geshe, rising to see him out. "All our practices and prayers, everything we learn as children, is meant to help us develop compassion for others, even our enemies. As a matter of fact, our enemies are often our best teachers. As His Holiness often says, they teach us the patience we can't practice with those who are kind and obliging toward us."

"Geshe, you look very tired," Amitabha said to him.

"It's true, these days have been wearying and painful," replied Kalsang Damdul. "The funeral ceremonies for our brothers needed long and elaborate rituals, then the strain of dealing with the young monks who have felt devastated, the demands for news, the telephone calls, letters, emails, and visits every day from Americans, Indians, English, and Italians; above all the Italians and the English—which is interesting, isn't it?"

"Why?"

"You may know that there are several lamas among the principal followers of the cult. One of them has about twenty centers in Great Britain and another is quite famous in Italy and also has a lot of friends and influence in China."

"Just as we were speaking about all this," said Rajeev Singh, "I realized that I haven't had time to read the Interpol reports that mentioned this cult's branches overseas. For now, I'll say thank you, and be sure I'll be in touch soon."

Tashi asked the two policemen to wait while he took photos from a drawer. One was an image of Padmasambhava in fine, colored robes wearing a pointed hat. The other was of a strange winged being surrounded by flames, with a fearsome expression. Its lower body was shaped like a dagger. Two figures with large monks' hats were speared on its blade.

"Who is this?" Singh asked.

"Padmasambhava changed himself into this form during his rites to control and subject demons. The blade is called a *phurba* in Tibetan.

Shugden followers claim that Nyingmapa practitioners still use the *phurba* rite[18] against their protector."

The superintendent put the photograph in his pocket, shaking his head, and then gave a military salute. With Amitabha beside him, he set off quickly for the large, rubbish-strewn square. Someone had set fire to the plastic, rags, and wastepaper and the glow lit the wall surrounding the school and the temple, revealing a pair of beggars wrapped in torn clothes, their bodies stiffened by the cold. On a compassionate impulse Singh tossed them five rupees, and they immediately began to argue over who should pocket them.

---

[18] The *phurba* is a dagger or stake with a three-cornered blade used in specific sacred rituals. It is considered a kind of magic weapon used to defeat the most terrible demons. It is also the symbolic instrument for destroying impediments that bind us on the path toward inner liberation.

The Meeting with Ngodup

Their driver, Rahu, was waiting in the open space where usually only taxis parked. Seeing two shadows, one broad and one much thinner, emerge from the weak neon light cast by the school, he guessed that it was the superintendent and his deputy. He quickly thought he should turn off the engine so he couldn't be accused of wasting taxpayers' money, but then he left the key as it was in the ignition. His superiors would find a warm car to climb into from the freezing cold. In fact, when the superintendent got in and made no comment, Rahu could see that he was pleased.

The conversation Rahu had with Rajeev Singh and Amitabha that night made a deep impression on him. They had never before spoken so freely with him and probably never would do so again. The superintendent said this case went beyond the imagination. His skills, acquired in years of experience in fifteen districts of India, from separatist Kashmir to Nagaland by the borders of Burma, with its generals and the heroin Golden Triangle, now seemed completely inadequate. He knew those ethnic groups and their customs, together with the historical and political causes that had reawakened in these settled peoples their ancient warrior instinct for rebellion. But the fate of Tibet seemed the saddest of all. Perhaps this was because, of all the defeated minorities forced to assimilate by their conquerors, the Tibetans had the strongest memory of their own tradition. And what a remarkable tradition it was! Their seraphic buddhas, their awesome wrathful Tantric divinities, their kind natures combined with a martial spirit. Almost everywhere he went, Singh heard Tibetans reciting the same mantra, "Om Mani Padme Hum," dedicated to their spiritual father, Avalokiteshvara, the Buddha of Compassion, who is incarnated in the Dalai Lama. But the boycott of the prayer ceremony dedicated to Padmasambhava by hundreds of monks and nuns seemed to have damaged that relationship. He asked Amitabha if that really were so.

His deputy replied, "Those monks and nuns must have been terrified." Jokingly, he added, "They were so afraid that they no longer trusted their own leader. Maybe we too had better be a bit careful of the powers of this spirit."

But the superintendent glared and reproved him. "Don't say that again."

"Please don't take it so seriously, Superintendent. It was only a joke. Remember what the Geshe said, 'It's to our enemies we should show true compassion.' So show some to your poor old deputy, at least."

"Once," answered Singh, "a Tibetan refugee told me that the Dalai Lama, with his divine nature, would help them return to their homeland one day. Who knows? Maybe compassion sometimes needs to be shown by means of force and violence." He pulled the terrifying image from his pocket. "Look at this. There's a lot we still don't know about these people...."

At first unable to sleep, Singh pondered what he had seen and heard, and somehow he connected his long conversation with the Geshe to Tibet's future rather than its past. There was a political twist in the background of this triple homicide, and maybe not just in the background. Then, his exhaustion overcame him and he fell into a deep slumber.

Accompanied by his driver, Rahu, and his deputy, Amitabha, Singh arrived in good time for his appointment with his friend Ngodup from the Tibetan secret service in Dharamsala. Everywhere in the world, experts from the field of security and their counterparts in criminal investigation get on best over a good meal, and so Singh decided that later, over some steaming dishes of meat *momos*,[19] he would ask Ngodup to explain how it came about that his people's situation had so deteriorated.

With his case folder in hand, Singh dismissed Amitabha, who went back to the car. Just then he noticed on the steps of the library the woman who had been beside him at the morgue during the identification of the dead bodies. He heard the unmistakable voice of Ngodup behind him, saying, "Miss Dolma is so engrossed in her practice and her books that she seems to be living in another age."

The superintendent turned and saluted his friend in the military fashion before lightly touching him on the arm.

"How far have you got with your investigation?" asked the secret service agent.

"I'm getting the feel of it."

"In what sense?"

---

[19] A type of stuffed ravioli dumpling typical of Tibetan cookery.

"You know how I am. I don't like to work on a case without examining every possible motive. This time the religious one seems the strongest—but then, what do I know about religious motives?"

"It would be nothing new; people have always killed in the name of their beliefs."

"That's true. A Hindu does it because he's a Hindu; a Christian does it because he's Christian, the same goes for Muslims, Buddhists, and so on. But what kind of religion is this that unleashes a massacre of monks, butchered because of some invisible spirit? I had a long talk to with the teacher at the School of Dialectics. It has helped me understand your world a lot better. There's a more disturbing side to it than the Shangri-la tales of those enchanted valleys, sacred mountains, and limpid rivers of the Himalayas. The other evening, I realized suddenly that I can't limit my search to the murderers and whoever sent them, if we ever do catch them..."

"Sure, on their way to China..." said Ngodup ironically.

Singh turned more thoughtful, smoothing his moustache. "You Tibetan exiles are like those activists in the '60s who saw the CIA behind everything, down to their favorite sports team losing. For you, instead, everything has the stamp of the Chinese on it—"

"But that's exactly how it is! You think Geshe Damdul is biased. It's true. But he's on the side of our oppressed people who have to live far away from their homeland because a stronger army defeated us and imposed other laws and other ideals—the things that are most important for human society."

Ngodup, whose work obliged him to be discreet at all times, grasped Singh's wrist as he said all this into his ear. "As for the Chinese," he continued, "they can only benefit from a schism like this. They're enjoying it and think the Dalai Lama will be discredited and his image as Nobel Peace Prize winner tarnished. Why wouldn't they favor someone creating that division? It was you yourselves who discovered the cook spying in His Holiness's kitchen, and the other four spies with maps of his residence—not to mention that maniac who killed the girl thrown onto the rubbish dump—all paid for by Chinese money from Lhasa!"

"True, true! Let's not keep going back to the same point. Have you brought the map of Majnu Ka Tilla and the names of your contacts down there?"

"They're in my bag. Do you want them right now?"

"No. I say we go and have some good *momos*."

"Do you like them fried or boiled in soup?"

"Both...we can share."

Ngodup spoke in Tibetan to the monk waiting on their table, who promptly brought a pot of tea. Singh continued, "What's more, fear of this spirit has infected my men too. I've had to draw the line more than once regarding their superstitions."

"For you, they may be superstitions, but to really understand this case, you have to start by recognizing that for us Tibetans there is no question about believing in divinities and spirits. We grew up with them around the same mountains and rivers. We breathe the same air. The fact that they can't be seen doesn't mean they don't exist."

"I agree that it would be presumptuous of us to think we are alone in the universe; I've always believed in the existence of other worlds and other beings, but not here, with us..."

"And why not?"

Pausing with his *momo* dipped into the soy sauce, Rajeev Singh stared at his friend. Ngodup's theory seemed convincing enough, but it was too distant from what was preoccupying him most just then. He asked Ngodup if Shugden might be one of the spirits to which he was alluding.

The Chief of Security shook his head. "This is one of the most difficult knots to undo. His devotees don't consider Shugden to be a demon at all, but the manifestation of a positive deity, as enlightened as a buddha."

"So I can strike him off the list of suspects," replied the superintendent. "If he's so good-natured, what am I supposed to tell the judge? I deal with people—flesh and blood—not angels. It's the knife-wielding killers who will have to go to prison, and maybe those who gave them their orders."

Ngodup nodded. "As you know, we have very clear ideas about that. But I think you have some clues already. They tell me there was a bag with some interesting contents left in the Geshe's room. Is that so?"

"Don't play dumb with me. You know very well what that's about. Your men are working constantly with my team. Let's be serious now. We need all the information we can get to act in Majnu Ka Tilla: a map of the area with its meeting places, addresses. You have all the documentation on the immigrants, old and new?"

"Yes, but you know a lot of them slip through the net. We can't keep tabs on everyone. Luckily, we've had our eye on this bunch for some time now."

"I'm just a bit worried you may be biased against them."

"You know we want to get to the bottom of this as much as you do, although I must say we have very little doubt about who is responsible."

"The problem in my case is that it's more personal, let's say. It's the first time I have ever encountered a crime so...weird, so..."

"What about us? It's like being hit by a thunderbolt—for the government, the administration, and the exile community. You know how we, or most of us, survive in our simple way on financial help from the West and from a few Asian Buddhist countries. I can't deny that I know of some terrible cases of hardship—entire families have no work and not enough food. But they can never return to Tibet because they are on the records for having taken part in a demonstration or because a relative is suspected of being part of the underground resistance." Ngodup paused, as if wondering whether he should speak so openly. Even though he was a friend, the superintendent was nonetheless a civil servant of the nation that offered his people hospitality. Ngodup decided it was worth the risk. "There is a sort of solidarity among us, but you mustn't think Buddhism has saved all Tibetan minds from the worst demons of all—avarice and selfishness. Look at the younger generation that grew up here, the ones who can afford to go around McLeod Ganj all dressed up and showing off their motorbikes. Some of them get by on petty crime. And the prospects for the future seem even worse. The young don't always have a sense of belonging to a culture that is up to them to preserve."

"Is the situation in Tibet all that bad?" asked Singh.

"Forget Tibet. Finished! Enough! If the young Tibetans here and in the West can't do something, if we in India can't—here where we're free to practice our religion and study our language and culture—tradition certainly isn't going to save our people in our own country under Chinese Communist rule. It is true that in Tibet, Beijing has decided to rebuild a few monasteries for the tourists, modernize the cities, and bring electricity to a few more places. But if young Tibetans want to earn money, they have to turn to the Chinese, who have the power to give them jobs on condition that they speak their language. So, right from when they are very young, children speak Mandarin to each other, and often do so even at home. Slowly, the words of their new language are replacing Tibetan words."

Ngodup paused again, unsure if he should continue. "Sorry," he said, "My little outburst is of no use to your inquiries."

Singh meanwhile had emptied his plate. "Allow me to decide what's useful. What you've been telling me makes the murders seem even stranger. Since your people have so many troubles already, I wish the crime hadn't been committed by one of you. Now, there's that book pamphlet in the bag, there are suspects dressed up as monks...monks indeed! Maybe they even were! They may have spent years at prayer, but then one day they pick up knives, go across India, burst into a room, and cut the throat of an old lama who had insulted a deity, or a demon or whatever, that he didn't believe in. Now what sort of a god is behind that?"

"It's not a god," Ngodup interrupted.

"As you see," Singh resumed, "I'm getting carried away here too, but this is what's been going through my mind all morning. I'm pretty thick-skinned about things like religion, but I'm trying to understand why there is so much hatred. I'd like to start by assuming the heretics are right. But if this spirit really is a deity, and moreover a compassionate one, how could it have inspired such butchery, such contempt for life?"

Ngodup looked at his friend, moved. Relations between Tibetans and Indians had always been difficult, but in that moment, over a plate of *momo* dumplings, in a teashop full of silent monks, each absorbed in his thoughts, the superintendent seemed to embody the soul of India. This country had played host to a community of at least a hundred thousand of his people for nearly forty years, offering this mountaintop and other villages so they could settle and recreate a little piece of their Tibetan homeland.

From their table they could see the entrance to the Library, where dozens of Westerners were streaming out of one of the courses on Buddhist philosophy and doctrine taught by the geshes. Others were going in to consult some of the thousands of books carried over the Himalayas in 1959, when the Dalai Lama left Tibet. Ngodup thought about the problems the refugees must have encountered dragging that weight, the sheer number of mules and horses needed to bear the Buddhist canons, Tantric scriptures, and sacred images in that sad procession that left the Land of Snows on what might have been, and indeed did turned out to be, a journey with no return.

As Ngodup watched the Westerners coming and going, he decided that it really had been worth the effort. The books certainly would have been burned and the images destroyed, as had happened in eighty percent of

Tibet's monasteries during the Cultural Revolution, and the world would have lost a precious part of its heritage.

The head of security meanwhile gobbled down the last of the *momos* and drained his cup of tea. Then, as if there had been no intervening silence, Ngodup resumed, "Do you know why I think all this happened? Not even our religion, though vast and deep as the ocean, was able to overcome human limits. Just think how many schools emerged with different versions of the Buddha's words and different ways to apply his teachings." He found it hard to continue. What he wanted to explain was beyond his understanding of doctrine.

"I'll ask you another question," Ngodup said to his policeman friend. "What do you really think of us?"

"Of you Tibetans?" answered Rajeev Singh, a little surprised at this shift in the conversation.

"Yes, at least of we us Tibetans here in exile. By now, you know us well enough to express an opinion."

As he searched for a diplomatic response, Rajeev Singh looked at Ngodup for a good few seconds, taking in his lean frame, his raven hair, and his deep-set eyes through the smoke haze that always surrounded him. Recent events made it difficult to forget his prejudices. But he thought, and said so, that he found Tibetans not much different from his own people, though he had noticed a certain craftiness among Tibetans who had been working a long time in tourism, business, or civil service. This guile was completely absent in those newly arrived from Tibet, whom he met in the Commissariat offices, or when inspecting the refugee camps for new arrivals.

Then Singh thought of his compatriots, even those considered high caste, with their calculated, unfeeling ways, protected by their privileged positions. He recalled one of his most successful cases, resolved a few years earlier. A local politician arranged for his supporters to pay him through his brother, who was well rewarded for his role as intermediary. When this money-laundering brother refused to hand over a certain very large sum, he was found stabbed to death in his bedroom. Singh had ordered an examination of the politician's house, and bloodstained clothes were found in the laundry. Analyses showed that the stains were made by the victim's blood. Even after all these years, it angered Singh to remember how the district judge dismissed the case for lack of evidence, won over by the swagger and rhetoric of a swarm of lawyers brought in from Delhi and Bombay…and no doubt by a handsome gift…

Ngodup left the superintendent time to reflect and then picked up the bill, indicating it was time to go. The superintendent rose too and regained his professional manner, shaking Ngodup's hand and thanking him for the excellent lunch. "Come to my place one day. I have a great cook," he told him, "she'll make you love dal and chapatis[20] as much as you do these *momos*. I guarantee it. Then there's the dessert my wife makes. But you'll have to earn it." Ngodup's handshake went still, and he looked suspiciously at his friend. "What do I have to do?"

"Quite simply, don't feed me too much propaganda. This is a really serious affair for us."

Ngodup nodded and walked with him to his car, reminding Singh that he was just a humble functionary whose job was to reduce the sense of paranoia in the already troubled exile community and the Dharamsala hierarchy.

"You, on the other hand, have a lot of work to do, as these are by no means the first crimes connected to Shugden."

"What do you mean? You're telling me this now?" answered Singh in surprise.

"Don't worry! The crimes I mean were committed decades and centuries ago, way beyond the time limits for legal prosecution. But Tibetans have never forgotten them."

"Well then, go and discuss them with the history faculty at Nehru University," said Singh with a laugh as he went off.

---

[20] Typical Indian dishes: dal is a spicy dish consisting of lentils, tomatoes, onions, and various condiments; a chapati is a type of flat unleavened bread.

Operation Majnu Ka Tilla

Superintendent Singh summoned to his office the men who were to leave for Delhi at ten o'clock on the morning of February 7. The cars were ready, and it only remained to give them their final instructions. "Every single piece of paper that can be traced to the Shugden Society," Singh told the squad leaders, "any correspondence whatsoever found in the offices or homes of their leaders must be seized and catalogued. The language experts with you will check it quickly so you can select what's worth taking. But it's better to bring back too much rather than too little, and regret it later."

"Do we have an address or do we have to comb the whole area?" asked one of the Dharamsala inspectors in a tone that Singh found irritating.

"'B 97 Tibetan Colony Majnu Ka Tilla' is written on one of the instruction sheets given to every patrol leader this morning. A document we are translating was posted from there, and it seems to be one of many warning letters received by the murdered Geshe. It turns out that it's here the activists have their Shugden Society headquarters, and where many of their leaders live. Every step forward the investigation takes will depend on your skill, your efforts, and—why not say it?—a bit of luck. One of the most important things to find out is whether any groups of people left the neighborhood on the evening or night of January 31 for Dharamsala. As you know, there is a regular bus service from Majnu Ka Tilla. Try to get names, and don't forget to check the taxi companies that go back and forth. Any questions?"

"Yes, one. When do you think we will be coming back?" asked a young special agent chosen for his athletic prowess, which could prove useful in chases and fights.

"That depends on the circumstances and our luck. Why do you ask? Have you got a new fiancée?" asked Singh jokingly. The young agent gave a hint of a smile, but seeing the wooden reaction of the rest of the men present, Singh realized the tension in the air. "What's the matter? It seems you are afraid to go on this mission. If the Punjabi terrorists were threatening you, as they once did me, what would you do then?"[21]

---

[21] Punjab is a state in Nnorthwest India. The Sikh separatist movement was defeated after the massacre at the Golden Temple in 1984, ordered by Indira Gandhi. She later paid with her life for having sent troops into the sacred place of Guru Nanak, founder of Sikhism and the first of the ten Sikh Gurus's followers.

"When was that, Sir?" asked the same young agent.

"A long time ago," replied Singh, "but let's not waste any more time. Tell me what the problem is, don't be afraid."

Amitabha, who had been leaning against the wall beside his chief's desk the entire time, said that, in his opinion, the "Tibetan spirit" was the problem. "They're afraid of this Shugden," said Amitabha.

The inspector from Dharamsala in charge of the patrols was clearly peeved. "Why do you say that? I find it disrespectful to all of us."

"Calm down," said Singh's deputy, "I just wanted to lighten things up. Superintendent…"

Rajeev Singh rose to his feet and approached the men about to leave on their mission. Although he was not tall nor yet forty years old, all knew him as a competent policeman and an upright person, and his authority remained unchallenged.

"This isn't the first time we've spoken about this matter. I've already told many of your colleagues that only those who believe in justice and not in spirits can work on a case like this. We must make every effort to see that such a crime, committed in a town under our jurisdiction and visited by people from all over the world, does not go unpunished. We still don't know much about the background of this case, but we do know that the group you're about to investigate is deeply involved."

A veteran officer from his own police district spoke up: "But there's no getting away from the fact that the Tibetans are famous for their magic arts, black and white. This doesn't mean, God forbid, that I'm afraid myself, but I quite understand that some of us here may be…"

Singh returned to his seat. "I don't want to keep going on about this. There is a lot to do in our province, and my department has six hundred officers available. Two hundred are working solely on this case, and those I've chosen can't allow themselves to be conditioned by a fear of spirits. You still have time to switch and join the other four hundred. Nobody will blame you if you do."

No one said another word, and just before midnight, Singh dismissed the meeting. All seventy-five members of the team, officers, agents, and drivers, got into police cars, ready to leave for Delhi. Other cars from Dharamsala and Chandigarh would be joining them along the way.

The superintendent decided to set off in the afternoon. He wanted to stop by to visit friends on the way to swap some ideas. These friends were well informed and relatively high ranking in the RAW. As such, they were able to filter information at various levels from Asia and America. In the meantime, he would go home to his wife, who was always unhappy when he went off on a tough assignment without knowing when he would return. At least they would have lunch together, a simple one of dal, rice, and roti.[22]

Singh's wife was affectionate throughout the meal. She asked him if he would be directly involved in capturing members of the cult. Rajeev He reassured her, "That's not the superintendent's job. I'll be interrogating them, rest assured, but capturing them..."

"The truth is, you're acting as if it's a matter of routine, but this time you all seem to be finding it a bit thorny."

"Not so. It's simply that each one of us has a role, and mine is to direct operations and evaluate my men's reports constantly as the mission evolves."

Singh finished his lunch and washed his hands in the basin. He put on the jacket of his uniform and placed by the door a small case with the items he needed for two or three days. He kissed his wife and two children as if he were leaving for a long time. Actually, he hadn't traveled much recently, and the family was becoming used to him being at home. But, for whatever reason, their farewell reflected the pressure that had been accumulating over the three long days since the murders had been committed.

Singh regretted that he had reproached his team so publicly. *After all,* he thought, *we are all afraid of something, especially when we are not sure enough of ourselves.*

On the journey, Rajeev Singh tried to take a nap. It was a magical night, and he could see all the constellations through the car window. The white Ambassador drove under the silvery sky, with just a few weak neon lights indicating the provincial road. Meanwhile, the convoy of cars from Dharamsala had separated, its progress disrupted by carts, funeral processions, oxen wandering unconcernedly on the road, and other sudden interruptions.

As they traveled south the temperature rose considerably, and the superintendent asked Rahu to turn off the heating so they could enjoy the fresh air of the valley. That recent moonless night on the very eve of the Tibetan New Year was at the center of the superintendent's thoughts.

---

[22] Typical unleavened Indian bread, cooked on the grill.

Forgetting that his companion was a down-to-earth soul, Singh began to talk about his investigator's intuition, which had suggested a strategy to uncover the killers. "The imagination," said Singh to the bewildered Rahu, "must be cultivated like a rare plant. It will not grow unless we nourish it with the water of observation, fertilize it with care, and integrate it with our experience."

Rahu nodded his head, although he had very little idea of what the superintendent was talking about. But he trusted him because he was direct and frank with his superiors, and he liked the way he defended the bumbling Amitabha. He had a father's way of scolding and forgiving him by turns, even when the deputy deserved much more severe reprimands.

To change the subject, and to help himself stay awake through this long night, the driver asked Rajeev Singh if he thought Amitabha would ever have what it took to become a fully ranking superintendent.

Breathing deeply, Rajeev Singh continued to look straight ahead. This was what he invariably did whenever Amitabha approached him with that unmistakable expression of contrition on his face. It always accompanied a request for help that would require his complicity. At those times, Singh knew that he alone could help him, although giving his protection had more than once cost him the goodwill of those above him, his superiors in the police force. But he could not let Amitabha sink. That would have meant suspension, with all its money problems and permanent damage to his status.

However, the superintendent's generosity towards his deputy was not solely altruistic. Of all the minds that he had examined before finding someone to fill the role, Amitabha's was the most brilliant, quick, and intuitive. Other candidates might have been more reliably servile, less of a risk to his image and reputation. But what he needed was someone who knew the detective's craft, who could formulate his own theories on the motivation for a felony or other crime, not just wait for orders from above before acting.

If Amitabha had been that type of subservient assistant, he already would have been killed the day Singh needed someone to appease a crowd of peasants enraged by the rape of a Gaddi girl. They had surrounded the farmhouse where the girl had been taken by force, violated, and held the whole night. The mob had almost broken down the door to pull the man out and lynch him when Amitabha arrived. The driver had tracked him down at his girlfriend Phuntsok's house, where he was settling down with his favorite whisky. Maybe, on this occasion, the alcohol gave him a fortunate recklessness, because Singh's deputy immediately took control of the situation by firing shots into the air and shouting like a lunatic. Then he jumped onto the roof of a car, still firing his gun like a cowboy, and said he would shoot dead anyone who went through that door. As if in the Far Wild West, he took aim at the sign on a telephone pole nearby and blew it off.

The mob stopped bellowing for a moment and let him through with a few weak protests, so that Amitabha was able to slip in the front door alone but armed. The crowd resumed its baying and began throwing stones. But by then the entire force from the barracks at Kangra had arrived, and their sirens dispersed the crowd. No one wanted to feel the blows of the long riot sticks used by the police.

Singh was about to tell his driver the story after the long pause since his question, but suddenly his eyes closed and he finally fell asleep.

When they had almost reached their destination, Singh woke up. "Here we are," said Rahu. The road that branched off the highway was not the one that headed straight for the heart of the city. They turned and took a small lane that went up towards a hill in total darkness. For an hour they followed the dirt road.

Eventually, a pack of barking dogs and a faint light in the distance told the driver and the superintendent that they had arrived.

Jeff, as he liked to be called, having studied in America, welcomed them in an elegant Japanese robe ill-suited to the country scene of mango trees and lentil fields surrounding them. But the force of his personality was unmistakable, and his voice was warm and powerful. Singh had known him since his days at the academy, where he had been one of his favorite instructors. They became better acquainted over the years and ended up friends. Jeff brought the superintendent a whisky and soda—he knew what pleased those he liked—gave him a broad smile, and invited him to take a seat. The veranda was enormous and sealed like a birdcage by a mosquito screen so light it was almost transparent. This allowed a view of the garden, notably a great tree with its trunk wrapped in cloth of different colors. Other plants had been allowed to grow under the care of expert gardeners. These were illuminated by a bright light swaying in the wind. The noise of a nearby brook gave the place a magical, flowing feeling.

Jeff spoke first, congratulating his former pupil on his rise to superinten-dent, "They've given you the most sensitive case of your career." Singh lowered his eyes modestly, as he had done as a child when he showed his father that he knew how to read and write without anyone having taught him. "But you know that I need your expertise," Singh told him.

"I'm the one who needs you!" Jeff replied impulsively, placing both hands on his chest.

Singh was surprised, but he had an idea of what the master spy was talking about. "Without your intuition," Jeff continued, "and especially your knowledge of the facts, I would be of no use whatsoever in the investigation. But they've gone and given me the job of coordinating the intelligence side of the whole operation!"

"I don't see anything so strange about that. You are the greatest expert on Tibet and Tibetans the RAW has, you've lived among them for years…you've even had lovers…"

Laughing, Jeff scoffed. "Don't muddle me up now with that debauched deputy of yours."

"I'd never dream of doing that. I only meant to say you're the right person for this job. As for myself, I'm not so sure…"

"What troubles you, my son?" joked Jeff, tilting his head in the manner of a priest taking confession.

"Nothing too bad really, but I've never felt so like a loser at the start. Let's be frank, we'll never catch those killers!"

Singh could only confide in Jeff like this because he knew that, like chess players, they saw the game's end in their minds: killers running free over the border, their paymasters concealed by a plethora of differing tales from witnesses manipulated by skilled lawyers. His one hope was that the guilty ones would not be able to afford the legal fees, but something told him that was not about to happen.

Jeff agreed with his former pupil that this was an exceptionally problematic case without much glory to be shared at the end. "But still," he told him, "You're barely forty, and the experience will be useful to you later on…. How large is the team under your command?"

"Six hundred," replied the superintendent, aware that this was a good number.

"And how many have you put on this case?" asked the secret agent, taking a puff on a long pipe, the stem of which cooled the thick, acrid fumes.

"Two hundred," replied Singh, waving away the clouds of smoke from Jeff's pipe like bothersome flies.

"I think I've understood what's wrong. You see, my dear Rajeev, you think you are the only one who understands this convoluted affair. And it's probably true that, in theory at least, only you see the entire picture. But how many brushstrokes did Raphael's assistants contribute to the great works of the master while he was teaching them the secrets of mixing and spreading color, so that every centimeter would enhance a part of the grand design born in his imagination?"

"I see what you're getting at, but if you're accusing me of not knowing how to delegate, you should know how much I use my deputy Amitabha."

"Delegating to him is not enough. You have to set it up so Amitabha then delegates to someone else. Is he up to it?"

"In theory, yes, but in practice no one respects him much because of his human weaknesses; that could lead to disobedience or even anarchy among the staff. I prefer to handle things myself as much as possible."

Jeff stretched out in his armchair and inhaled strongly through his nose. "Forgive me, Rajeev," he said, "You're the boss in Kangra and you know what you're doing. The days are gone when you came to me for advice and comfort with that crestfallen look of yours."

Singh smiled as he recalled the time when Jeff was the instructor and he the cadet. "In fact," he said, "You're about to get your invitation to the post-raid dinner. At that point I'll need your advice. But in the meantime, can you assure me your sources in China are active?"

"You know they never sleep. And they know that when the Dalai Lama's involved, they have to be very careful."

"Maybe this time they'll turn off the taps."

"Don't worry. That's my neck of the woods. You take care of your demonic spirits."

Rajeev Singh instead was thinking about his team, which surely must have reached Delhi by now, ready for action. There were fewer than four hours before dawn. He asked if he might lie down, because he wanted to get some rest, and set off early, and reach Delhi by the end of the morning to interrogate some of the leaders of the Shugden Society.

"You'll find one of them rather interesting," said Jeff slyly.

"How is that? What's that about? Tell me..." the superintendent was almost imploring.

"I've had to promise my Chinese friends not to burn him right away, and promises are sacred. Besides, you'll meet him soon enough. Knowing you, I've no doubt you'll recognize Beijing's agent."

The Raid

The ringing telephone awoke the superintendent with a start. He had instructed Amitabha to call him at his friend's number only if problems arose. Looking out of the window, he saw it was still dark. This could only mean that something very serious was afoot. His deputy told him that the head of the North Delhi police department had called a few minutes before. "He told us not to go in today because it's Tibetan New Year and we won't find anyone there."

"But he knew very well it was New Year when the date of the operation was decided!" exclaimed Singh. "What else did he say?"

"That since Majnu Ka Tilla is a very congested area, full of undesirable elements, where many families run brothels and bars, he insisted any independent action by the Himachal Pradesh Police, that means on our part, would be 'most inadvisable.'"

"That was obvious too, from the beginning."

"Yes, but the big shots at North Delhi North want to emphasize it. Maybe they have to keep their officers at Timarpur happy, since they control the Tibetan neighborhood. They told us they knew a lot about the tension among the exiles, and that a couple of months ago reinforcements were sent down there because there had been a stabbing."

"Was it linked to the Shugden Society?"

"It seems so."

"All right, let's try and to turn this unexpected delay to our advantage. Now get a bit of rest, and then send some officers in plain clothes to check out the place—without taking any action, naturally. Best contact that Tibetan from Security in Dharamsala whom we'll be using as an external consultant. Ask him to bring along all the evidence that he has collected on the Shugden Society, starting with the addresses of their leaders. You go in person to the chief of the Timarpur Station and tell him we won't do anything without their agreement and participation. I'll be there before lunch and we'll organize everything. We'll wait till our targets get back— just before midnight, I predict."

Singh's team spent the day walking around, eating snacks and observing life in the neighborhood's alleys—bunched homes, small hotels, shops, and bars all side by side on mud streets. Behind all this, swampy fields brought the danger of malaria epidemics every summer. The large number of monks and Tibetans of every age, most dressed traditionally, gave Majnu Ka Tilla a certain exoticism, especially at those times of day when the sound of mantras, cymbals, and drums came from the small temple in the square, the only open space in the camp area.

The officers Singh had sent down were used to the atmosphere of Tibetan settlements, even though Dharamsala and McLeod were jewels of cleanliness and elegance compared to this dirty, dismal place. Their impressions were affected by the knowledge this might well have been where the three murders were planned. The officers were instructed not to go more than once past B97, on one of the last alleyways at the southern end of the settlement. Amitabha gave his final instructions: "We mustn't raise any sort of alert. If these are our culprits, they may know by now that we've found the rucksack with the pamphlet in it. So behave like casual visitors, split up, and phone me every so often to keep me posted."

The first call came from a phone booth inside a travel agency. Suresh, the young athlete in the squad, said he had already made friends with the young woman working there and she had given him some information.

"What information?" asked Amitabha.

"It's a bit soon to talk about it. I'm just being superstitious…it's to do with a particular taxi."

Amitabha called the superintendent, but Singh had already left. By now he would be on the road. Amitabha was as excited as if on his first case, and felt fresh and full of energy, his desire for drink completely vanished. Leaving the office provided for him at the Timarpur station, he began to walk towards a famous Sikh temple nearby. Among all the religions that existed in the world, he had yet to find one suited to him.

The day passed quickly. When Superintendent Singh reached Timarpur in the early afternoon, there had been many comings and goings in Majnu Ka Tilla between among the homes of the Tibetans, who had given them precious information on the leaders of the Shugden Society and their organization.

Singh read their reports, and the first name to strike him was that of Chimi Tsering, the secretary of the society, described as its real leader. The notes revealed that Chimi had two other names, Drakpa Gyaltsen and Lobsang Sherab. He also possessed two different identity cards, the personal registration documents issued to Tibetan exiles by the Indian government, and he lived between B97 in Majnu Ka Tilla and N230 in Delhi's Greater Kailash area. The religious college he was affiliated to with was listed as Shartse, in the Ganden Monastery at Mundgod, in the state of Karnataka. Singh thought these reports were not much use, although he was struck by the use of the double name Drakpa Gyaltsen, and the fact of the two identities. *"He's going to prove a tough nut to crack,"* his intuition told him.

He gave the others a quick glance: Geshe Konchok Gyaltsen, another monk from Ganden Monastery; Lobsang Nyima, who came from Chatreng in eastern Tibet; Lobsang Tupten, also from Chatreng; Kalsang Tsewang, the president of the society; Chatreng Yeshi; and Chatreng Gyurme... Chatreng, Chatreng, was it just coincidence? The last name on the list also had a record of being involved in militancy in Mustang.[23]

One of the first calls Singh made was to the Head of the North Delhi Department. They had never much liked each other, since the time of a small misunderstanding of the sort that often arises in any field of work. His colleague's curt answer showed that the mutual ill feeling had not subsided. Singh was advised to think twice before putting handcuffs on anybody. The judges in those parts were reluctant to fill the prisons any further, since they already had too many mouths to feed there and were running out of space.

The superintendent knew that in the long run it was best to keep up good relationships with his fellow police in the capital. But when he was told yet again that "the Tibetan quarter is difficult to control," he found it hard to measure keep his answer measured.

"We'll try our best to manage," he replied, explaining that it was vital for everyone to collaborate, as the eyes of the world were on this case. He hadn't wanted to sound boastful, but his colleague from North Delhi took it the wrong way and hit back with heavy irony.

"Oh, yes, the international press, my dear Perry Mason. I hope all those articles they're writing about you won't have gone to your head... actually it's only been four days since the crimes. What can they expect from poor cops like us?"

---

[23] Formerly an independent kingdom, now part of Nepal.

Once more, Singh tried to keep his calm and managed a joke, "This time, though, even the Delhi police will get into the papers...." At the other end of the line, the police chief dropped his mocking tone and said he would report to his superiors. He added that he was on hand for "anything you need."

Singh hung up the phone and thought of all the effort involved in the operation and the risk that the pamphlet in the rucksack might not be sufficient evidence. And what if the judges threw the whole case out right away?

He called his deputy and told him to have the men ready. Within half an hour, North Delhi had sent its approval, and the team of thirty-five handpicked agents went off to meet up with their colleagues already in place. It was eleven thirty.

The superintendent told Amitabha, in charge of the operation, that he was afraid some of the leaders of the society could have left the country, as the killers probably already had done. But he was counting on the fact that sudden flight would imply an admission of guilt.

On the wide street that flanked the Tibetan quarter, Singh and his team found the cars promised by North Delhi and Timarpur waiting. A detective already had paid a discreet visit to the lobby of the guesthouse where many of the leaders of the Shugden Society identified by the Dharamsala police lived. Forty officers were deployed between their headquarters and the apartments in Greater Kailash where several of the five wanted members resided. When the police arrived, a few were asleep, some had just returned, while and others were awake and drinking in the large lobby that served as meeting point, drinking den, restaurant, and TV room. No one offered any resistance. They all said it must be a mistake and that they certainly would be demanding their rights.

Singh arrived at Majnu Ka Tilla in the middle of the night. The street lamps threw a pallid light on the roads of the exile quarter, and not a soul was to be seen. No doubt, news of the raid, however secret it was meant to be, had leaked out, and circulated around the area so the bars normally open late had closed early. The odd stray dog was burrowing in the rubbish heaps, whose smell was made worse by the still-glowing braziers used for burning both plastics and organic waste. Singh got out of his car in the car park. One had to go down the narrow, deserted alleys on foot, and he was accompanied to a three-story building where the sign "Chatreng

House"—that name again—was written overhung above the entrance, beside the name of the society.

There was a lot of noise for that time of the night, and Singh noticed that the Delhi police had taken charge of the operation. It was they who were carrying out hundreds of confiscated documents. He called Amitabha and asked whether they had been evaluating the type of material seized. His deputy explained there was little he could have done. Someone important, perhaps even at the highest level of command, had seemed to want to limit their movements in the building, and he had even been obliged to do without the interpreter, who had gone to the residences in Greater Kailash. "Anyhow, we're finished here," said his deputy, "and the other translators should get to the barracks today."

"But are they reliable?" asked Singh, distrustful.

"The detectives say they have tried them out, and they vouch for them."

"Are they all faithful to the Dalai Lama?"

"You can swear to that, Superintendent."

While his officers carried on with the identifications and taking statements, the superintendent headed up to the floor above, from where he had heard cries of protest. A deep, somber sound also attracted his attention. Moving towards its source, he went down long, dark, corridors guarded by local police officers, watched by men and women in dressing gowns who appeared riled and frightened. Some of them held small, sleepy children in their arms. The sound came from a room at the end of one of the hallways. He opened the door and saw an old man sitting cross-legged with a mala in hand, reciting mantras, his eyes turned towards a large glass altar on which he Singh could make out a statue completely covered with white silk scarves and screened by a curtain, also white.

Curiosity overcoming his respect for religious observances, the superintendent moved the curtain aside and found a statue of a figure whose face had three terrifying eyes and what seemed to be a bloodstain issuing from its mouth, astride a beast that might have been a lion. In its right hand it brandished a sword. All the while, the old man had not stopped reciting his prayers addressed to that monstrous image. Singh pointed towards the statue in a gesture of inquiry, and the old man, interrupted his prayers for a moment and said: "Dorje Shugden." Then he resumed his chant, whose gloomy, cavernous sound seemed to come from the center of his chest.

A detective came up to tell Singh that a number of people had already been transported to the station for questioning.

Singh left the area under the hostile stares of the residents, with a strong sense of the sinister nature of the place. But he did not want to be influenced by that. Up to now he had only one suspicion, but it was a strong one.

Amitabha told him that he would join him soon at the barracks: he had to check out a report sent by the young athlete of the unit. The travel agency clerk he befriended had checked all the taxi hire companies, and only one car had left for Dharamsala on the night of January 31. It had, with six Tibetan passengers. Amitabha went to see for himself, and Singh went back to the police station to look over the confiscated material and complete the interrogations.

When Singh arrived, he was shown some letters seized at the house of the President of the Shugden Society, Chatreng Yeshe. The postal stamps revealed they had been sent from Suja, Mandi, and Dharamsala, and Singh asked for them to be translated immediately. "As soon as you've taken down the names and addresses," he said to one of his assistants, "send a telex to the Kangra District Police Station. We need to search the apartments at these addresses. Specify that it's 'red corner.'"

Singh went to sit down in the room set aside for interrogations and asked for the witnesses and suspects to be brought in to him, one at a time. But he soon realized that many more officers were needed to deal with the constant flow of people protesting their rights and declaring their innocence, and all demanding to do so at the same time. Singh soon adapted to the chaotic working conditions and, after extensive sessions with the other detainees, managed to talk face-to-face with the organization's leader, Chimi Tsering.

He made the suspect sit opposite him on the other side of an old desk, and then stood up and began to walk slowly around him.

"I have heard you mentioned as the leader of this society, or association."

"I am just its secretary-general."

"A very important post!" exclaimed Singh, "Often more important than the presidency itself..." The detective soon realized that he must first study the personality of his interlocutor. "Could you explain to me what your role in the society consists of?"

In turn, Chimi Tsering scrutinized the superintendent before replying. "I am asked to counter the arguments against the cult of Shugden and to defend our practitioner brothers who are isolated and persecuted within the Tibetan community."

"Was it you who wrote these letters to the deceased Lama Lobsang Gyatso?" asked Singh, passing some photocopies towards the monk.

"Whom did gave you get these from?" asked Chimi.

"That is not your concern. Please tell me whether you wrote them."

The monk remained silent for a few seconds. His name was on most of those letters, and it would not be difficult to establish if the signature were his too. "Yes, some of them are mine. But if you think my quarrels with the Geshe in McLeod are proof that I am a murderer, you are making a huge mistake."

"In this letter found in the room where the murder took place, you write directly to this man of religion, calling him the embarrassment of the School of Dialectics."

"That's what he was..."

"I beg you to show a little more respect, if only for the fact that he is dead. Here you say you went to Dharamsala three times and were unable to find him. Then you ask, 'Where were you hiding, in the nunnery?' You go on to accuse him of being ignorant, and finally you write, 'Instead of busying yourself with useless arguments, come to Delhi and find out if you can see what's between a louse and a fingernail...' Is that the correct translation? What does it mean?"

"Louse and fingernail is an expression. In Tibetan it means come and distinguish between facts and falsehoods."

"Then you write: 'If you don't want to come because of your dirty conscience, we can come to Dharamsala to see who's telling the truth. Just let us know when.'" These seem like threats to me. At least they show your feelings are very hostile. And it is a fact that one of the men who came into the room to kill the Geshe and the monks had with him a rucksack with one of your propaganda pamphlets in it."

"And who told you that bag belonged to the killer?"

"Witnesses."

"I can imagine your sort of witnesses!" answered the monk defiantly.

Singh paused for a moment to take a deep breath and to let a wave of antipathy pass. "I advise you to modify your attitude. Simply answer my questions," the superintendent rebuked him. "Now tell me how your society is financed."

"Donations. A lot fewer than Lobsang Gyatso receives.... Why don't you see how much money the Geshe has received from Hong Kong? Or how many payments from Taiwan are in the Dalai Lama's coffers? That way you'd find a lot of the answers to your questions about the crimes." The contempt and sarcasm in his tone were evident.

The superintendent tried to remain polite. "Let's get back to your letters to the murdered lama and the tone of your publications. They show enough hatred to justify those crimes. Where does such powerful hatred come from? Doesn't the Dalai Lama have the right to tell his followers which spiritual practices are right and which are mistaken?"

The Geshe shot the superintendent a burning look. "This is not a controversy about Dorje Shugden, but about a fabrication spread by the Dalai Lama's office. If you were better informed you would see that things are not as black and white as Dharamsala would have you believe."

Singh did not feel like going on with the interrogation without all the facts in hand. There would be other opportunities. He decided to turn Chimi Tsering over to his men for them to record all the details of his movements and his statement on the nature of his disputes with the slain Geshe.

He left the room under the challenging glare of the monk, who had not moved once from his position. The moment he left, a group of people swarmed into the room, evidently to ask Chimi Tsering about his interrogation and to offer him their support.

In the police chief's office, one of the men who had participated in the raid on the houses in Greater Kailash handed to the superintendent a leaflet. The interpreter said it was identical to that received by Geshe Lobsang two days before he died.

Singh was beginning to think that Majnu Ka Tilla might be an inexhaustible mine of clues, and he should gather as many as he could as quickly as possible. He told his officers to have a few hours' rest, as there were dozens of witnesses to interview in the morning and clear heads were needed. "Our ideal objective," he instructed his deputy to tell the team, "is to have the name of everyone who entered or left this camp in the last week."

It was an arduous task, and in the end, the information from the athletic Suresh was the most interesting. Those six youths who rented a taxi with the license plate number DHA 4283 on the night of January 31 became Singh's focal point for the next twelve hours.

The taxi driver had been traced to his home and answered all the questions put to him. "Did you take six young Tibetans to Dharamsala recently, on the night of January 31?" Suresh asked him.

"I take a lot..." answered the taxi driver, "but yes, a few days ago I took a small group. They wanted to follow a car."

"A car? What car?" asked the young policeman, now curious.

"It was a monk's car. I don't know more, someone who had just got to the airport or who had taken their baggage by mistake. That's what they said, but I didn't really believe them. Anyway, it didn't matter much to me, as they were paying."

Suresh was a smart young cop, and he made sure every word of the taxi driver's testimony was recorded. "The witness Mangat Ram made the following statement. "The night of January 31, 1997, I agreed with six sturdy young Tibetan men on a price to take them to Dharamsala. We left at dark—around eight in the evening—from Majnu Ka Tilla. The clients wanted to follow an Armada Jeep along the road to Dharamsala. It had left the airport with a suitcase that it was very important for them to recover. They told me they wanted to get to McLeod, but at Ambala the car broke down and needed a repair and my clients were very annoyed. I tried to fix it so we could go on, but the six men said they were in a hurry and would find another car. Two of them went to a phone box to call someone. The others walked to a taxi rank and hired another taxi.[24] At that point I left them to themselves and went to sleep in my car while I waited for a mechanic's shop to open."

An hour later, when Rajeev Singh read the report, he couldn't help exclaiming, "They telephoned! Now we're getting there." He blessed the law that obliged every public telephone facility to register all data electronically. Singh immediately made had Amitabha send a telex to the Ambala Police Command with a request for a complete listing of all the long-distance telephone calls made after ten o'clock on the night in question. That done, he looked out of the window and saw that a pale white sun had risen over the city. It must have been past midday. Feeling a little hungry, he realized he had only drunk coffee since the evening before. That last witness's statement had restored his good humor. If, as it seemed,

---

[24] In Indian cities at night it is not uncommon to find taxi drivers asleep in their cars, waiting for clients.

the six were had been following the Geshe, it was not improbable that they were the killers. Next, Singh ordered a check on Lobsang Gyatso's vehicle to see if it were was an Armada Jeep. If so, there would be no doubt.

Meanwhile, back at the Timarpur station, the legal representatives for Chimi Tsering and the others had arrived. Things were in a hubbub, and one of his colleagues from the capital told Singh that the suspects had hired some of New Delhi's best-paid courtroom lawyers. The superintendent could see that his presence in town was no longer needed, and he was about to arrange his journey back to Kangra when Amitabha introduced him to one of the interpreters. "Chief, Mr. Nyima says that he must speak to you in person about one of the publications seized in the house of the Shugden Society's president."

Singh showed him in, and the man pulled a leaflet out of his bag. "When I found this, Superintendent," he said, "I remembered having seen it during the inspection of Geshe Lobsang Gyatso's room in McLeod. It looked to me like a simple list of names of leading Tibetan figures: the Dalai Lama; the president of our government-in-exile, Samdhong Rinpoche; ministers; civil servants; and Lobsang Gyatso himself. Today I read it more closely and found all of them are cited because of their role in opposing the cult. There are even the addresses of their homes with directions on how to get to them. The copy received by the victim, though, wasn't sent from Delhi but instead was mailed from Kangra just two days before the crime."

Singh reflected for a moment without saying anything. He remembered the discovery of the map in the Chinese spies' apartment in McLeod. With a touch of sarcasm, Singh asked Amitabha if there had been any response from the Delhi magistrates.

"Not yet, but actually I wanted to ask you how we should handle the leaders of the society. Tonight the deadline for keeping them in protective custody runs out."

Singh replied that, as far as he understood, the lawyers and judges had already decided to release them and it was just a matter of waiting for their order to do so.

"But there's so much evidence against them!" exclaimed his deputy.

"I might be mistaken, but I think we'll have to make do with summoning them to Dharamsala in a few days with an order from the Kangra magistrates. We'll question them there along with our colleagues from RAW and the Central Bureau of Investigation Office."

The Arsonist

Amitabha was about to leave the office with the interpreter—a little disappointed at his boss's cool response to the revelation of the blacklist—when Singh spotted the name of Kalsang Tsewang as he looked down the list again. He had been included among the leading activists, although he was officially unemployed and had dropped out of the school for exiled children and youths in McLeod. Singh read the report of the interrogation, in which he had not participated, and saw that it was a very bare testimony. Kalsang revealed almost nothing about himself, but there was one detail that stood out. He had done odd jobs for members of the Shugden Society, and specifically for Chimi Tsering. The superintendent began to sense see a small glimmer of hope, finding this chink in the wall that the secretary of the association had built around himself.

He called Amitabha back and told him to bring in Kalsang Tsewang.

The young man arrived half an hour later with his head hung low. He was the only suspect taken in the night before who had not adopted an arrogant manner. Singh kindly asked him if he wanted something to drink, so as to put him at his ease. Then he slowly shifted strategy, to frighten the suspect into revealing something more, even though he was unsure how much Kalsang actually knew about the others' activities.

"We're investigating three cases of murder, a crime punishable by life imprisonment," he told him. "Do you want to risk going to trial just like the leaders of the society? Basically," he continued with a friendly pat on the shoulder, "you are just a former student who has ended up in this mess in exchange for food and lodgings. You could be doing a lot of other jobs. Weigh it all up and see if it's worth denying what you've done..."

"What have I done? I've done nothing!" replied Kalsang.

"Now come on, if you admit it yourself, you'll be well treated at the trial. I'll say you collaborated fully and you won't spend a single day in prison."

"But what have I done? I didn't do anything," the youth went on repeating, nervously wringing his hands and rubbing his knees.

Singh recognized that reaction, especially in the young, as an indication that the person had something to hide, even if it might be something very small. He continued to stare at the suspect, his expression ever more serious.

From the room next door came the sound of mantras chanted in deep, lugubrious voices by the monks who had been arrested. Kalsang's anxiety seemed to grow by the minute. He held the hem of his shirt and twisted it, swallowing mouthfuls of saliva and rubbing his face so hard it was almost painful to watch.

Singh felt the right moment had come. He called a guard and told him to take Kalsang to an isolation cell. The young man leaped to his feet, shouting "No!" with all his might. Singh felt sorry for him, but he knew this was the only way to loosen his tongue. He gestured to the guard to take him out of the room. The superintendent didn't know whether Kalsang had played a part or not, but something told him that even his admitting a small episode would be useful and could break the code of silence shared by the youth in the world of Chimi Tsering.

It had only taken one meeting for Singh to see that this ice-cold monk was a key figure. He could not judge whether he was guilty or innocent, but his dedication to his cause, be it a deity or a demon or whatever, gave him a haughty demeanor and his face an abrasive harshness, at least in the eyes of someone like Superintendent Singh, who did not share his beliefs.

The youth seemed to have stopped tormenting himself and looked pleadingly at Singh. Amitabha was about to enter the room, but Singh shook his head to indicate that he should wait. "Do you feel comfortable talking with my assistant here? He's my right-hand man."

Kalsang, his head kept low, did not reply. Amitabha came in and sat quietly on one side of the room. The superintendent was pacing up and down, as he always did when questioning a suspect. At times, it seemed as if he were in a boxing ring dealing out metaphorical punches to the jaw and chest, sometimes even hitting below the belt, as when he told the youth the police knew what he had done when it wasn't true.

But now, Kalsang had something of which he wanted to unburden himself. This, ultimately, was what the superintendent had been waiting for.

"One day last month someone asked me to burn down the 'Famous Studio' in Dharamsala."

Amitabha shifted in his chair, but Singh did not break his rhythm.

"That we knew," said the superintendent, keeping up his bluff. He actually had no knowledge whatsoever about what Kalsang had done, but sensed that he was about to tell him and open up the floodgates.

"I didn't know why it had to be burned down, so I asked if the owner had done anything wrong. They replied he was a dishonest Indian who had come back from Pakistan and disliked the followers of Shugden. I did it for the brothers and because it was a job for which they paid me well."

"We know you got a lot of money—but how much and who from?" asked Amitabha.

"A lot of money? No, not that much."

"Let's look at it this way," Singh cut in. "If you tell us who gave it to you, we'll turn a blind eye to that bundle of rupees you still have hidden somewhere. Otherwise, we'll have to seize it and we'll get the name of who paid you in a few days anyway."

Kalsang began to tug at his shirt again. Then he said, "Geshe Chimi gave it to me."

"Chimi Tsering?"

"Yes. But don't say anything to him, for heaven's sake, Superintendent. It mustn't get out. You forced me to talk, and now what's going to become of me? I didn't tell you! I didn't tell you! You won't really get me into trouble, will you, Superintendent? I beg of you! I beg of you!" he pleaded in tears.

Amitabha was moved to pity: The deputy superintendent thought about how difficult it was when times were hard to keep from bending to the will of others, and he felt very sorry for Kalsang. He waited for him to recover from his outburst, and then led him to an adjacent office where an old computer hummed like a swarm of bees. The room was small but comfortable, and Kalsang listened to his own testimony, read back to him from a transcript, with great anxiety. The former student had confirmed a payment from Chimi Tsering and even specified the amount as 10,000 rupees. This was an important piece of incriminating information, but Singh and Amitabha both knew that under Indian law a confession without hard proof was not sufficient: for if the young man denied it, he would be exonerated.

"Read and signed."

"Put your signature here. Can you read English?"

"Not very well."

"All right, I'll translate it into Hindi for you."

When Amitabha had finished reading the report, Kalsang burst into tears again and did not want to sign. But it wasn't too difficult to convince him. That boy was pretty easy to bend.

The Return Home

Rarely had clues been so directly connected, so unequivocal. The team from Ambala found out that only two calls had been made from their district after midnight on the night of January 31. One of these was to a number in Delhi belonging to the Shugden Society.

The RAW agents learned from their sources within the Society that the phone number in question was Secretary-General Chimi Tsering's. Superintendent Singh, well pleased to find some of the many strands of the investigation coming together, decided to return to Dharamsala to discuss recent developments with his colleagues in the special unit. But first, Chimi Tsering had to be grilled again about the latest twists to emerge.

This time he was surrounded by a host of lawyers and his fellow society members, both senior figures and foot soldiers. As on the previous occasion, they came in and out of the room in chaotic fashion. Singh had the door locked so that only the monk and his lawyers remained. As always, Amitabha was at Singh's side, and now the men from the Office of Central Bureau of Investigation also were present. One of them began the questioning.

"Mr. Tsering, you received a telephone call from Ambala on the night between January 31 and February 1. Do you remember the nature of the call?"

Chimi replied, "I didn't receive any calls from Ambala."

"You can't deny it. It was recorded on the STD public telephone, and the number dialed was yours. Here it is," said Inspector Singh, showing him the receipt sent by fax from Ambala with the number, 011 293 2536.

"You've seen this building and how many people live in it. I don't even know how many numbers there are here, but that one's not mine. Anyway, what are you accusing me of? What crime is there in getting nighttime phone calls from Ambala?" asked Chimi.

Singh had, in that very moment, a clear flash of how this could all turn out in court. *Certainly*, he said to himself, *that group left Majnu Ka Tilla the night the Geshe arrived from Hong Kong*. That, however, could have been coincidence, and the same applied to the telephone call made that night to Chimi Tsering, or to whomever it was, on the road to Dharamsala. But the crime had been committed four days later, and his detective's hunches could crumble if firm evidence showed this to be nothing but a simple chain of circumstances. But how could anyone deny that these details could also become significant pieces of incriminating evidence against a man and an organization that had sent threatening letters to the Geshe?

His colleagues in the department remained silent, embarrassed. Then Singh held out to the monk the sheets with the statement taken from his hireling, Kalsang. It contained the accusation against Chimi—that he had paid the youth to burn down the "Famous Studio."

As he read it through, Chimi Tsering's face seemed to transform into a series of masks, each one more ferocious than the last, until the icy, absent expression worn in his previous interrogation returned.

Singh noted these shifts, which confirmed his sense that it would be hard to resolve this case simply by hoping for this suspect to make a mistake.

The monk turned to his lawyers, who huddled closely around him and hung on his every word, and then said, in an apparently casual tone, "Get a copy of this letter—we must denounce those responsible for the interrogation—for 'abuse of authority.'"

"Geshe Tsering," said one of the lawyers, "if this description was obtained under duress, there are grounds for..." The monk silenced him with a wave of his hand. He stared hard at the superintendent and said nothing.

Singh smoothed his moustache and responded with a slight sideways shaking of his head, as if to say, "Very well, then." The battle had commenced with the start of the Tibetan New Year, and both men knew with certainty that it would be a long one. None of the other police officers present shared that feeling, except Amitabha, who knew his chief's thoughts. But he, too, seemed more pessimistic now that Chimi Tsering had been interrogated and had denied every charge made by Kalsang.

They had just left the station and were on their way to have a bowl of dal when Amitabha told Singh how he felt. But Singh's reply gave him pause for reflection. "When you and I, and the others from headquarters, began this investigation, many of us believed we were searching for spirits. Instead, we've learned that someone left this place with the intention of committing a murder—not riding winged horses or lions—but in an old taxi that even broke down on the way. I think that, for the moment, everyone is convinced there's very little to be superstitious about. Chimi Tsering knows that, for us, a coincidence is a fact and two coincidences make a near certainty."

Amitabha nodded.

After lunch, Singh packed his bag for Dharamsala. He would decide on the way whether or not to stop and see his friend from the world of espionage.

The return journey was tedious, but he preferred to go straight home without stopping at Jeff's villa. When he reached Ambala, where the taxi had broken down and the six men got out to telephone, he told his driver to stop. Rahu looked at him quizzically.

Singh got out of the car in the middle of a deserted road lit by a weak reddish glow from a chai seller's stall. The fragrant aroma from the milky tea spiced with ginger, cloves, and cinnamon whetted his appetite. Rubbing his hands together to warm them, he invited Rahu over for a hot drink. Rahu pointed to the sleeping Amitabha stretched out on the back seat. "Let him sleep," said Singh.

But just then Amitabha woke up and asked if there were was any beer to be had. He had been dry for three days, not touching a drop, worried as he was about wasting time and losing his focus during the raid and the interrogations. But now he seemed like a parched wanderer in the desert.

"Come over and have some tea. It will do you a lot more good," said the superintendent, while Rahu nodded seriously.

Amitabha got up reluctantly. The three were silent for a good while before his deputy asked Singh what he thought about that night chase between Delhi and McLeod. Couldn't they have just waited for him at his destination without sticking close in a taxi and leaving another obvious trail?

"I think they wanted to kill him before reaching McLeod," Singh replied. "Committing a crime like that near the Dalai Lama's residence was no easy feat. There were a lot of people coming and going, especially on the night before the Tibetan New Year. If a bolder neighbor or passerby had heard the shouting or if there had been a longer struggle, let's say outside the room, the whole plan would have been ruined. Had the killers been arrested, there would have been far greater repercussions. Then, the Society's members, and that Chimi Tsering, really would have needed some divine protection, not just their lawyers." By the way, how are the inspections going at Suja, Mandi, and the Shugden members' houses? Have you called the office?"

Amitabha gestured with his arms wide. "I haven't been able to reach anyone yet. I hope Kangra and Dharamsala haven't been idle these past few days."

They got back into the car, and both Singh and Amitabha slept for the remainder of the drive.

Waking up, Singh realized that he had completely forgotten to tell Jeff he wasn't coming. He looked at Rahu and asked him if he was tired. "No, Superintendent, it's fine. But you seemed restless in your dreams. Don't worry. Now that we've discovered that we're dealing with men, we'll get them all, sooner or later. And if not, Shiva the implacable will take care of it...."[25]

Singh looked at him in surprise, but said nothing. There had been a lot to do with magic and spells recently; by now, enough mysticism for one night. Dharamsala was getting close. He stretched his limbs and thought about the vanilla dessert his wife made whenever he came back from a trip.

---

[25] In the Hindu religion, Shiva is considered to represent one of the aspects of God. He is known as the Destroyer, which is the third entity in the Trimurti, also known as the "Hindu Trinity," composed of Brahma, Vishnu, and Shiva.

Incontrovertible Proof

Exceptional security measures were adopted to ensure that the leadership of the Shugden Society would not be harmed or killed by Tibetans loyal to the Dalai Lama. Singh wanted the inspectors to maintain a low profile and to keep the suspects isolated for a few days, so they were sheltered in a secluded guesthouse, with all expenses covered by the government.

Their legal representatives immediately questioned the procedures used in what they defined as a kidnapping, and they produced medical certificates denouncing the physical and psychological stress to which it was alleged their five clients were being subjected.

In fact, Chimi Tsering had kept his nerve and held up the morale of the others so they would not give in an inch. To do so would have meant admitting they would use any means, however unorthodox, to see the power of Gyalpo Shugden prevail.

The morning that the society members reached Dharamsala, the superintendent ordered Amitabha to go over to Kalsang Tsewang's cell. The Dalai Lama's security office had told him there was a similarity between the description of one of the killers and someone who had tried to murder a Tibetan jeweler from McLeod and that of the "Famous Studio" arsonist.

When Amitabha entered the small cell, he found the Shugden Society's young factotum huddled up in a corner like a child fearing a beating. Actually, he was desperately reciting mantras, to his god, who may not have been listening. He gave a start when he saw the deputy superintendent and did not return his smile. Amitabha crouched down and asked him if he needed anything, and if they were treating him well.

"I want to get out of here, I'm going mad," said Kalsang. "Please, Officer, I have confessed. What more do you want of me?"

"To be validated, the confession must be full and unconditional. Full means that you tell us all you know and everything you've done. Unconditional means you don't expect anything in return. This time there's no way out, we have proof it was you."

"Who did what?"

"Tried to kill the Tibetan jeweler in McLeod."

Kalsang's head dropped and he hid his face in his hands. "You know that, too…. I've already told you, we were sent by Chimi Tsering. I wasn't alone. He wanted to stir up, divide, and threaten the Tibetan community of McLeod and Dharamsala. He said that his life's aim was to restore Dorje Shugden's lost dignity."

When Amitabha reported Kalsang Tsewang's words, Superintendent Singh grew ever more certain that the monk heading the Shugden Society would not confess, even under torture, a method he never approved of — although his men sometimes did get heavy handed.

Singh decided that even if not much was to be expected from the meeting, some fertile lead could emerge. He reached the guesthouse that was serving as a holding cell for the society's elite. There he found colleagues from the Criminal Investigation Department and two members of the special unit awaiting him. As soon as they heard about Kalsang's recent story, they were eager to interrogate Chimi Tsering. They were growing ever more prejudiced against the suspect.

The monk had been transferred, along with his three lawyers, to a room in the hotel set aside for the interrogations. When the police entered, he was the first to speak out: "Why are you keeping us shut up in here? How can you expect to have a normal conversation in such conditions?"

The superintendent spread his arms and asked whether he knew of a better way of getting information from prime suspects.

"I've already told you to look elsewhere. Look for the money received from Taiwan and Hong Kong by the Geshe and His Holiness's private office—"

"Okay," the investigator from the Central department cut him short, "let's drop all of that."

The policeman was by now familiar with the religious aspect of the conflict and told the suspect that there are different ways to prove one's point, be it in religion or politics. Killing and intimidating, he said, were undoubtedly the most deplorable.

Chimi Tsering retained his composure. "You'll certainly know that in Tibet religion and politics have always been inseparable, but I don't believe this is true only of Tibetans. Here in India, Hinduism is supreme among religions, in Rome there's the Pope and his cardinals…the list goes on." He paused to observe his interrogators' faces, then continued: "You know, or you should, that the Tibetan Buddhist Gelukpa school was the most widespread one for centuries and had the most appeal. This caused jealousy and rivalry. That should be your starting point if you to want to understand something."

"Yes," interrupted the investigator, "but the Gelukpa order, political conflicts, Tibet itself, these are all things of the past. Nowadays, you and your acolytes are mere refugees, and instead of respecting the country that hosts you and behaving like decent citizens, you go around causing a lot of trouble. You tell your religious and political leader what he should and shouldn't do, and perhaps you even kill those who disagree with you."

Chimi Tsering turned to his lawyers. "This is not an interrogation, it's a series of serious insults." The lawyers all came forward together at once, their voices rising above one another, but when Singh had the guards called, the lawyers meekly returned to their places. Chimi Tsering saw very clearly that ultimately he would have to fend for himself.

"Some of you have been living here for a while," he said in an almost menacing tone, "and you know how superstitious Tibetans are, whatever class they belong to. If one has a certain dream, trips on the stairs, or falls ill, it's all Dorje Shugden's fault. Yes, now he's the demon, the evil spirit…but until recently he was the fierce protector of the Gelukpas that the Dalai Lama prayed to and sought advice from. How do you explain that change?"

The inspector from the Central department answered, "Nobody has the right to judge someone who bears the responsibility for the whole exile community living under Indian law."

He went on: "As far as I know, today His Holiness does not consider the Gelukpa sect to be better or worse than the others, but sees it as just one important element of the Tibetan heritage, and he thinks perhaps there is no longer much sense in having a private guardian angel."

"I see that you are more familiar with this subject than Superintendent Singh. What you do not know is that the Gelukpa school was founded precisely to challenge the many false masters who had invented an equal number of fake divinities, sham cults, and adulterated practices instead of adopting the way of renunciation and study."

Singh butted into this erudite conversation, asking the suspect and his colleagues to get back to the main point of the interrogation: the involvement, which he now regarded as blatant, of the Shugden Society in the three homicides.

"Unless," he said, addressing Chimi Tsering, "you are hoping to justify what happened with historical reasons, I'll remind you that we aren't looking at a crime committed centuries ago but at a triple homicide committed on February 4, 1997, for which, in addition to previous acts of intimidation and violence, you and others are responsible. In Delhi, you told us that two coincidences can't be considered proof. We've got more evidence now, and with it all put all together the picture is clearer. It's a complex story that we've reconstructed from your followers' movements. Coming from the capital and from other settlements, they reached this area, met up with other members of the society then disappeared like ghosts. You, as secretary-general of your organization, certainly knew the movements of your men. One of them you treated as a faithful servant whom you sent to eliminate enemies and to burn down stores."

Tsering addressed his lawyers, "Please make it clear to the superintendent that I don't know what he's talking about. Who disappeared? Who would I have wanted to eliminate?"

"You have no proof and cannot accuse our client of anything," said a lawyer.

"There is evidence, and there will be plenty more. You'll have the right to appeal, and perhaps you'll win the case. My duty is to hand you over to the authorities on the basis of my convictions. Then, others will decide, not me."

Chimi Tsering kept quiet, but swirled his sandalwood mala in his hand for a long time. The superintendent figured that his silence and those gestures had a specific meaning. This was no longer the man who had been answering questions up to now, but the performer of a rite. He was taking refuge in the spirit that was supposed to protect and guide him.

The superintendent had some chairs brought for the lawyers and apologized for not having thought of it before. Meanwhile, Chimi Tsering kept on fingering his mala, not saying a word, while his lawyers busied themselves formulating sentences denying all accusations.

When Singh returned to his office after the interrogation, the police officer sent from the Dera station had been waiting for him for over an hour. He produced a sealed envelope, the contents of which reinforced Singh's conviction regarding the six youths in the cab from Majnu Ka Tilla.

Six was the number of passengers picked up by the cab driver, Mangat Ram, and six Tibetans checked in on the afternoon of February 1 at the Grand Hotel, close to the old bus depot in Kangra.

The statement was taken from the hotel owner, Kumar Surinder, who clearly remembered those youths. Being a fussy type, he recorded their entrance at exactly 17:03. The six had told him they were there on a sightseeing trip to the mountains above Dharamsala. They signed the register with one name, Chaba Jalsingh, which turned out to be false, before carrying their own luggage to their rooms. It was their "strange behavior, unlike 'regular tourists,'" that caused Kumar Surinder and his staff to observe the group with some curiosity. When the policemen showed them the picture of the blue and black rucksack with its orange hemming, there was no longer any doubt. That bag had attracted their attention, and they had seen a flashlight taken out of it one evening. But they couldn't confirm if that it was the same one as in the snapshot taken by the superintendent at the crime scene.

As Singh finished reading the statement, the phone rang. It was Amitabha, telling him about the raids in Dharamsala, Suja, and Mandi on the activists' houses, where they found letters written under the letterhead of the "Dorje Shugden Devotees Charitable and Religious Society" in Delhi. The deputy had spent another sleepless night, as Singh could tell from his slurred speech, but he was incredibly excited. "Boss, what'll we do with all this material? There are letters, pictures, the society's documents..."

"What pictures?" inquired Singh.

"Many. They're of parties, day trips, ceremonies, friends at dinner. These people really love to be photographed."

Singh told him to bring everything to his office as quickly as possible. Soon, detectives from the special unit would be there, and they would examine them together.

The superintendent broke the news to the other members of the unit and told them his subordinate would arrive soon with the evidence, but Amitabha was late. Singh began to wonder if he hadn't made a slight mistake. He could have begun the meeting by discussing the other developments in the investigation, but now everyone's attention was on what had been seized from the Delhi society's headquarters, and thus on the expected arrival of his deputy. Singh felt that the awkward silence enveloping the room was connected to the commonly held prejudice against Amitabha. Unfortunately, his colleagues might not be altogether wrong, and he feared this lateness was due to his habitual problem.

He apologized, left the room, and went in person to ask the driver to go and look for his deputy in the usual spot, behind the liquor seller's. But just as Rahu was leaving the police station, he bumped into Amitabha, who appeared sober but had that shine in his eyes that typically followed an outing to a drinking den. Singh noticed immediately and was able to intercept him, sending him to throw water on his face and put on dark glasses before he went into the meeting room. Amitabha entered a few minutes later, apologizing for his lateness, and said he had an eye allergy.

He took a stack of documents and a lot of pictures out of his folder. These were the fruit of the raids on several apartments. He flourished the bundle of pictures, put them on the table, and then raised them one at a time. "Now that we've got two important witnesses, we can find out whether the six youths who reached Kangra in a cab on the first day of February are in these pictures. The principal witness is the cab driver, who claims to remember his clients' faces perfectly. The second witness is the owner of the Grand Hotel in Kangra. At this very moment, our officers are showing him and his staff the originals of these pictures, and soon we'll know how they responded. We scanned and emailed the images to Timarpur station to show Ram the cab driver. Now we have to decide which of us will go to the various monasteries in the south that we've had reports on."

The whisky bottle, Amitabha's companion that morning, had given him a certain confidence, which impressed his colleagues from the special unit.

When the telephone rang in the middle of the meeting, everyone present looked at it simultaneously. As he spoke on the phone, Singh's expression was triumphant.

After hanging up, he said, "At the hotel in Kangra they recognized two of the youths in the picture." Singh called his friend Ngodup and asked him to join him as soon as he could to start investigations across the exile community.

One of the members of the unit asked the superintendent whether they shouldn't keep the Tibetan authorities up to date with these latest developments.

"There truly is a danger for the whole community," he answered, "Nobody can be sure that other crimes aren't being planned, especially now that we've found a list with the names and addresses of the leaders of the government, including His Holiness the Dalai Lama. The murderers may have already fled the country, probably across the Nepali border. You all know about our constant problems with our Nepali counterparts, the total lack of cooperation that allows dangerous criminals to come and go as they please across our borders. We recognize the legitimacy of the Tibetan government-in-exile, since we host it in our country. We probably wouldn't have got anywhere without their collaboration."

They all agreed to assign detectives to the various monasteries and settlements across India. They also realized that raking through the exile community, spread all over the subcontinent, would be an arduous, if not impossible task. They therefore decided to wait for the results of the other inquiries and the grilling of the Tibetans whose pictures had been confiscated. Their link to the Shugden Society in Delhi was obvious, given their frequent correspondence.

The policemen who had shown around the photos at the hotel reached Singh's office and pointed out to the members of the unit two people circled on the pictures. "They were unsure about the others," they said, "but the witnesses had no doubt when identifying these two as their guests."

Singh had the police station photographer come over and asked him to blow up the details of those two faces. The pictures portraying both of them were quite clear. One person had a bull neck, a large nose, and bushy eyebrows, and wore a baseball cap. In the picture he seemed chubby, but it might have been the angle or the lighting, since those in the hotel seemed to remember him as lean yet muscular. The owner thought the rucksack belonged to this man.

The other image was of a man with a long, sharp face and a remarkably large nose for a Tibetan. Like the man in the first picture, he was well built. Singh thought of sending Amitabha and some men with the pictures to interrogate the Shugden Society members searched in Suja a second time.

It was they, in fact, who had taken, or at least had in their possession, the pictures of the two suspected passengers in the taxi, whom Singh regarded as the probable murderers. The deputy superintendent pointed out that it would not be easy to get the witnesses in Suja to name the men in the photos. He advised his boss to get the RAW agents to activate their local informants and, with discretion, grease a few palms to find out who those two men in the picture were.

RAW replied that they needed a couple of days to organize things without arousing any suspicion and asked for a fax authorizing the request, without which they would be unable to proceed.

What was really needed was a justification for the release of a sizeable amount from the special fund, considering how sensitive the case was.

The men at RAW were complaining that the members of the Shugden Society were proving just as expensive for the secret services as Chinese undercover agents. This answer caused some murmurings among the members of the special unit.

The superintendent called RAW headquarters, "Isn't two days a bit excessive? I'd like to point out that these are probably the monks' killers, and a month has already gone by since the murders." They answered that they would do their best. That very evening, Singh and the members of the unit obtained two names, but they were too common to give a solid lead.

The two youths in the picture were called Tenzin and Lobsang, just like thousands of other Tibetans. But the RAW also knew where they came from—Karnataka. Singh phoned Ngodup immediately and was told that the largest number of followers of the cult came were from that region. The main seat was Bylakuppe, near the monastery of Sera; the other, Mundgod, was home to the Gelukpa monastic college of Ganden.

The superintendent carefully studied the photographs that had been seized from Kalsura in the Mandi District. They were pictures of a group on an outing, but the subjects seemed to share something more than the bond of comradeship between camaraderie of young fellow exiles.

Amongst the various Tibetans in Western clothing there was one monk. Singh wondered how he had not recognized him immediately. It was the Secretary of Delhi's Shugden Devotees Religious and Charitable Society, Geshe Chimi Tsering.

Singh studied his long face, his small, round ears sticking out from his shaven head, his low forehead, and his prominent cheekbones. That picture offered yet another small strand of evidence to increase his suspicions of Chimi Tsering, but could it be useful as proof? Both he and the other ringleaders had already been released, as Singh feared from the start, despite the discovery of the alleged killers in the cab, the phone call to the society's office, and now these pictures found by the police in the north.

In an attempt to cheer up the superintendent, the man from the Intelligence Bureau in the special unit told him that down in Karnataka there were two excellent Tibetan agents at their service, Nyima and Gyurme, and he would get in touch to let them know that detectives were on their way to identify the suspected assassins.

The first team, four men led by a chief inspector, left Kangra on the morning of March 3. After a stop in Delhi to look up some information in the immigration files, they reached Bylakuppe in Mysore District and found lodgings in Kaushalnagar, about eleven kilometers from the Gelukpa settlement near Sera Monastery.

Nyima joined the team on the morning of March 8 on their drive to Camp Number 2, where several hundred refugees were living in conditions similar to those of the Tibetans in Dharamsala. After looking carefully at the photographs, a policeman at the local station said that one of those the two faces was well known around there. He recounted a check he had carried out a few weeks earlier for the RAW, when a German woman suspected of being a Chinese spy travelled with the suspect on his motorbike around the Bylakuppe area for a few days.

The policeman took the team to meet the Tibetan official in charge of the camp. From him they learned that Tenzin was a resident monk in Sera Monastery. There also were others named in the list of suspects, all guests of Pomra House, where monks from eastern Tibet, and in particular from Chatreng and Lithang, were accommodated.

The detectives from Himachal Pradesh asked if they could organize a raid on Sera the next day, but the local representative of the Tibetan government-in-exile strongly advised them against it: "Tomorrow a big puja, that is a ceremony when food, alcohol, and incense are offered to the deities, will be held by the monks and lamas in the main temple all day long. The offices of the monastery will be closed." Then he added something that left the policemen perplexed: "You should keep in mind that seventy percent of the monks and laypeople living in that wing of the monastery perform the practices of the Shugden cult." The team leader communicated this news over the phone to Singh, who was about to return to Delhi.

The superintendent reflected at length on the phenomenon of this cult, which many people, including Ngodup, tended to describe as marginal. "Certainly Sera is exceptional," said Amitabha. "My informers tell me this monastery is renowned for the practices tied to this spirit."

"Sure," said the superintendent distractedly, "but there is starting to be too much of the exceptional in this story. We know too little about what happened, what's happening, and what's going to happen."

Amitabha looked at him with a worried air. "Do you think something else is in store for us?"

"Isn't that what we're here for?" Singh responded, slapping him affectionately on the shoulder. "Keep focused. You'll stay here in the police station to oversee the operation while I'm in Delhi. There's no need for me to tell you this, but in this situation one of your screw-ups could be very costly, and I won't always be able to defend you."

Amitabha gave him an official salute and watched him get into the car, which then disappeared around the curve in the road. He was tempted to go straight off and have a drink, but chose to resist the urge. He asked the superintendent's assistant to bring him some tea and received his first telephone call as coordinator of the investigation. It was the inspector from the team in Bylakuppe, confirming that the raid on Sera had to be postponed because of the ceremony. However, they had begun to search in the archives for foreigners' identity certificates and had narrowed down the suspects to a group of youths with the same name: Tenzin. Some had already been questioned and were immediately removed from the list of suspects. The team was counting on the information that they would be able to retrieve from the raid on Sera.

Amitabha thanked him and wished him good luck, urging him to call if any problems arose, even at his home number. At the other end of the line, the inspector was about to ask for the number of the liquor shop, too, but he kept the joke to himself.

The Southern Monasteries

On the morning of March 12, the Himachal Pradesh unit, the local police, and the officer from the Intelligence Bureau, backed up by a squad of guards and two colleagues acting as interpreters, reached Sera Monastery.

There they learned that a man named Tenzin had stayed a long time in Room 20 of the Dokham Khamtsen Hostel attached to the Pomra Khamtsen College. According to one of the police informants, who did not pray to Shugden, the youth had been expelled from the monastery some time earlier for "unbecoming conduct." The informant recalled that his behavior had been slightly suspicious from the moment he first arrived at Sera. Subsequently, he had been noted several times as one of the most active members of the groups of monks and laypeople who went around intimidating Gelukpas and other Tibetans opposed to the cult of Shugden.

Tsering Lhakpa, in charge of the monastery, was himself a worshipper of Shugden and was Tenzin's protector, the informant explained. And this was not all. The head of the Sera Mey College, Thupten Paljor, did everything he could to hinder the inquiries of Singh's men and had even tried to conceal the official registers. But in the end, the team from Himachal Pradesh got what it was looking for and found the names of the three Tenzins on the guest lists of Sera Mey. One had the surname Rabyang. He was 35 years old, and had arrived in India in 1985, and his certificate number was 400. Another Tenzin, with no surname given, had certificate number 3069, was resident at the address of an exile from Chatreng, and came to India in 1991. Finally, the third and last Tenzin, Tenzin Choezom from Chatreng, was registered as number 308 and had immigrated in 1985.

When the photographs were shown around at Sera Mey and Camp Number 2, it was only the Shugden practitioners who pretended not to recognize him, even though some of them told the police in secret they knew who it was—the third man on the list, Choezom, was quite a well-known figure in the Tibetan community. The data matched the early information on the guest in Room 20 in Sera Mey's Pomra Khamtsen College. Further inquiries helped establish that one of the reasons why he had been told to leave the monastery was his connection with the pro-Chinese groups in the exile community.

But, as the team found out, Tenzin continued to live at the college despite his formal banishment. He simply changed rooms around periodically, although he usually lodged in Room 53. The young suspect had also worked in a Tibetan restaurant, The Lachi, but this seemed to be more of a cover than a real job. It turned out that Tenzin spoke reasonably good English, Hindi, Tibetan, and Chinese, just like Chimi Tsering. Furthermore, from the second half of 1996, he began to receive quite a lot of money. His companions at the college didn't know much about its source, but everyone was sure that it wasn't his earnings at the restaurant. Tenzin had left Sera Mey in January 1997. This also fitted in with everything else.

Amitabha recorded all the information from Sera and was overcome by an irresistible urge to go out and relax over a beer. He had been in his office all day, submerged in paperwork and telephone calls, and felt he deserved one. He called his wife and told her he would be back late. Aware of the mountain of work this case had brought him, this time she made no objections.

At his favorite drinking spot near the Grand Hotel, Amitabha ordered a bottle of whisky, some soda, and a glass of gin. Settled in the corner of the room, where the windows looked out on the steepest side of McLeod Hill, he first poured himself the gin with a bit of soda, squeezed in the lemon, and devoured a packet of peanuts. Then he moved on systematically to the whisky, at first mixed liberally with soda, and as this ran out, with some ice cubes.

Normally, there were very few customers in the bar at that time, and no one had ever bothered him or asked him who he was or where he came from. But that evening, a young man with rather an artistic air about him, his long hair tied back in a ponytail, stared at him for several minutes. Then, finally, he spoke to him from across the room, "I know you," he said, "I've seen you before with Phuntsok."

Hearing the name of his Tibetan girlfriend, Amitabha raised his head from his glass and asked him the young man over to sit with him. "You know Phuntsok? It's been a while since I heard from her. Is she well?"

"Now she's okay, but she went through a bad time."

"What happened to her?" asked Amitabha, alarmed. He was by now feeling the effects of the gin.

"Someone stopped her one night and beat her up. She couldn't tell if it was a drunk or a monk, or who knows what. He was gripping her so hard he almost broke her neck, but luckily a motor rickshaw was just passing by in the alley near her house and the man ran off. Now she can hardly move her head, and the neighbors have to take care of her daughter."

Amitabha thought the incident could have something to do with her gathering rumors to pass on to him. Or else, it might have been some personal mission of her own with the idea of selling information to the Indian secret services—something he himself had advised her to do. "How about coming with me to see her? I'll bring some beer along. Are you up for it?"

The young man introduced himself as Changchub. They drained their glasses and got up together. When they reached the small room where Phuntsok lived, a few hundred yards away, they found her in bed, unable to move.

She was surprised to see them together and, with her eyes, she signaled that the policeman shouldn't reveal his identity to her friend Changchub. "You've no idea how much it still hurts. That man bent my neck wanting to break it, I'm certain. I'd never seen him before, but it was like he was waiting for me. Luckily that taxi…"

Amitabha told her he would have given anything to have been there. "Do you remember what he looked like? Do you feel up to looking at some photos?"

Changchub turned sharply towards Amitabha. "You're a policeman? And I thought…"

"No, no, take it easy," Phuntsok interrupted him. "My friend Amitabha works at the foreigners' registration office and wants to help me. But I don't think I'd be able to recognize the man, and I don't really care. I know what to do if I ever find myself face to face with him again," and saying this, she smiled as she showed them a knife kept in a silver sheath studded with turquoise and ruby-colored stones.

"It's an ugly business," said Changchub, after they all had been silent for a while. Amitabha offered him a beer, and they spent the evening drinking together, until the deputy superintendent fell asleep in his chair like a log.

Phuntsok asked her friend to call a taxi and take Amitabha home. He probably would not wake up until he got to his front door. "His wife will deal with him," she said.

The detectives sent to Ganden, the other great Gelukpa monastery in Karnataka, had traveled through Mundgod to reach Hubli. There, the special unit from Himachal Pradesh had contacted Mr. Naick from Intelligence and learned that Lobsang, the second man in the photo, was actually a former resident of Mundgod and had last been seen there a few months earlier.

The team was joined by Superintendent Karta from Research and Analysis, and the Tibetan local security officials. They told the agents from the north that Lobsang had a record of repeated acts of violence against opponents of the Shugden cult. However, when they got to the monastery to check the list of residents, no Lobsang matching the description was registered.

They had more luck with witnesses, though. The secretary of Ganden, Mr. Changchub admitted almost immediately that the young man in the photo had lived at Ganden and had left around June or July in 1996 for Dharamsala. He said he had to move to take care of an uncle.

With this information in hand, the detectives began to question monks and laypeople in Ganden and Mundgod and learned a number of things about the young murder suspect. The youth had arrived from Tibet well trained in the martial arts, and his guru was Geshe Jamyang, a teacher at Dhokhang College, known by the nickname Ami. The Geshe recognized the man in the photo and admitted that he had lived at Ganden for several years before leaving at the end of 1996 to be with a relative in Dharamsala. The details matched the information from the secretary of the college. The Geshe also gave his personal details as registered by the college administration. "Name: Lobsang Chodak, born in Chatreng in 1972. Certificate of registration number 534. Entered India in November 1991. Arrived at the hostel in December of the same year."

Strangely, his code number was not in the general register, but to clear up any doubts, it would be sufficient to question the other Shugden Society members in Mundgod and Ganden. A list was also compiled of the leaders of the devotional society in Karnataka. There were eight of these, and the president was Geshe Lobsang Gonpo. Amitabha collected the data from the Mundgod team, along with that sent by telex from Sera Mey and Bylakuppe. The information confirmed that Pomra House was the heart of the cult's activities. A profile of twelve leaders emerged: nine of them were from eastern Tibet, notably from Chatreng and Lithang. Among these was a certain Yongya Tulku, alias Kusho Thupten, at present residing in the United States and considered one of the links between the Shugden devotees and the Chinese authorities. He was the teacher of at least one of the other Tibetans in the photograph; all were suspected of playing a part in the Dharamsala slaughter.

The detectives collected a good deal of classified information that converged on one point: both Tenzin from Sera Mey and Lobsang from Ganden had left India to hide out in Kathmandu, in Nepal. The RAW men also sent their addresses: the Nyalam Phelgyeling Guest House in Swayambhu and Dagom Rinpoche's center in a monastery at Boudanath. They added, however, that attempting a formal verification at these two places would reveal nothing.

When Superintendent Singh had compiled all his information on the two main suspects, he asked Amitabha to begin checks on the other four men, whose identification was less certain. It took several more days to get replies: For him there was no doubt that those were the missing members of the band of six who had left Delhi to kill the Geshe. He looked at the record sheets and photos obtained from the Tibetan government's security department; all of them had been photographed without their monk's robes. Try as he would to remember their names and match their faces, they all still looked alike: Ngodup Chodhen, 39 years old, from Lithang, ex-monk from Pomra House, disciple of Yongya Tulku: Lobsang Phuntsok, 28 years old, from Dappa in eastern Tibet, also from Pomra House: Chodak Kelsang, 28 years old, from Chatreng, a monk at Ganden's Shartse College: and, finally, Lobsang Tsultrim Daplha, 28 years old, born in Yangting, a monk at Ganden.

He tried to match the small photos on their identity cards with the snapshots of the group found at Suja and Mandi, but it wasn't easy to recognize them, even with the help of the Tibetan informers. It was, anyway, only a formality. He was by now more than certain that these were the other four killers of Lobsang Gyatso. When Amitabha came back with the results of the inquiries, the final traces of doubt vanished: all of them had left the country.

The RAW reconstructed their last movements across the border into Nepal until their trail was lost in Chinese-controlled Tibet. It had not been too difficult to get that information, vague as it was, from the well-paid informers in Lhasa. Rajeev Superintendent Singh took the photos, the telexes, and the notes and put everything in a folder. This he placed in the cupboard for investigations partially completed and, formally, still open.

He sat down again with a feeling of unease. The Shugden case, he knew, would be one of the last, if not the very last, in his career as a criminal investigator. He had already heard things, unofficial whispers, from Delhi. He did not know where he might be going, nor did he know when, but he felt he would soon be leaving this post.

But Singh did not want to think about the new life awaiting him just yet, nor to make plans when he had yet to solve a case to which he was so committed. He went back to turning over in his mind all those coincidences, the places the suspects came had come from and their frequent visits to Nepal, before they vanished into thin air. He knew they would never set foot in India again.

The investigator superintendent was particularly struck by the detailed list of their tutors, the masters in the monasteries where they were had been educated. This was something that it had only occurred to the Tibetan authorities thought to compile, and their reason was very clear; their teachers were in a sense considered responsible for the actions of their disciples. Judging by the large number of these tutors, many other monks in their charge could be candidates for a commando squad of killers. He had collected dozens of pages of reports, in sequence, of hate crimes involving the cult members. To be sure, even the Dalai Lama's followers did not always turn the other cheek, but they had certainly never murdered anyone.

He sent for Amitabha, and, after a few minutes, his deputy appeared before him with a slight bow. He stood waiting for an order, but when he saw the superintendent leaning back with his hands joined behind his neck, and looking out of the window, he knew it was clearly something personal his superior wished to say. He hoped this wasn't going to be a scolding.

"Ami," Singh said in a confidential tone, "if we find we are no longer working together, I want you to know I am very grateful for everything you've done in this investigation."

"Please don't say that, Superintendent. I've done nothing special. Indeed, if I've caused any problems or done something embarrassing, please don't hold it against me."

"We've given it everything we've got, but I think we are going to have to trust in the justice of karma as far as these killers are concerned," said the superintendent with a smile.

"I hope it punishes them severely," replied his deputy seriously.

"It would be interesting to know what their conscience is telling them," Singh commented, "Maybe they think they've fulfilled a mission for their god...hah! Say, how about going out for a beer?"

A broad smile spread across Amitabha's face. The two men took one of the station cars and invited Rahu, the driver, to come out for a drink. They decided to go into McLeod, and drove by the bazaar and its shops. There, they saw the swarms of monks talking and joking along the streets and sitting in the tiny Tibetan restaurants. They were like young soldiers on leave from their barracks. Singh could not tell which order they belonged to, and he thought once more about how the Dalai Lama in exile had to represent all the religious views of his people. Those monks seemed to be the proof of a harmonious integration, and their mantras couldn't really have been so very different from one another's. Or was this not true? He was beginning to realize that he had become deeply involved in this "case"—perhaps too deeply. He had not just been working on it as one of the duties of his job—that was for sure.

As he walked in silence beside Amitabha and Rahu, he thought destiny had given him a chance to encounter a different, truly mysterious culture. Many centuries ago, Tibet had taken from India the seeds for a new spiritual era, and as an Indian, he could have felt proud of this. But recent events had made his country feel the weight of Tibet's woes rather than appreciate its positive aspects. It was almost as if India were saying: "There you are. You taught us to use the powers of the mind for enlightenment. But those powers are also terrifying, devastating, and uncontrollable. Exactly like Shugden."

The three policemen drank, but in moderation, and offered toasts without any great joy, aware that they had done their duty to the utmost. Soon their paths would separate forever.

PART TWO

A Journalist's Sources

Of all professions, that of the journalist is perhaps one of the most stressful. One becomes involved in the life lives of others about whom we knew virtually nothing before events thrust them into the limelight. The reader must be provided with superficial information thrown together in a few hours from press agency bulletins, police reports, depositions, and sometimes even rumors that later prove baseless.

I had worked as an investigative reporter for many years, and all too often I found I had played a part in damaging the reputation of those under scrutiny, especially in the preliminary inquiry carried out by investigators who were sometimes less than scrupulous.

When the news of the crimes in Dharamsala reached my office, only a few hours remained before the press deadline. What was to be done? From abroad, it was impossible to contact Superintendent Rajeev Singh, in charge at the start of the investigation. The Indian press already had given the story wide coverage because it was the first time blood had been shed on this scale in this small, usually peaceful town where the Dalai Lama had his residence and the Tibetan exile community was based. But I knew that the coverage had been limited. Reporters all over the world have to hand in their articles after a mere day or two of research, except on rare occasions when time allows for more detailed reporting.

Then news of Superintendent Singh's investigation began to circulate, with more details and theories regarding the motives for the crime. I decided immediately to get to the bottom of the story once and for all, even if it were to take me years. There was one particular reason why I chose to get involved with this and not some other story: all the protagonists in the triple homicide in Dharamsala belonged in a certain sense to that world of ancient teachings that had become, over the years, an antidote to the contagious cynicism that undoubtedly had been fuelled by members of my profession.

Besides, it was a "family" crime, if not exactly between close cousins, at least between distant relatives. The complexity of the plot also offered enough clues to satisfy my curiosity, both as an investigative reporter and as a beginner in the study of Tibetan Buddhism.

Like the victims, the alleged assassins were religious figures belonging to the Gelukpa or Yellow Hat school, though they had refused to accept

the Fourteenth Dalai Lama's request to relinquish the cult of Dolgyal[26]—
this spirit with a demon's appearance they considered the main "guardian"
of the pure tradition of their order.

I was quite surprised to discover that a large number of articles, comments, and internet Web sites had been dedicated, both in Europe and in
North America, had been dedicated to this enigmatic spirit who is said to
have arisen over three centuries ago from the dark shadows of the Kingdom
of Böd,[27] at a time when the Land of Snows was just emerging from a long
fratricidal war. The Fifth Dalai Lama, with support from the Mongols, had
by then assumed full power over all of Tibet, from the Himalayas to the
Chinese border.

I also read the considerable number of speeches on Shugden given by
that powerful Dharma monk-king's successor, His Holiness the Fourteenth
Dalai Lama, Tenzin Gyatso, the Nobel Peace Prize recipient who has been
obliged to live in exile in northern India since 1959. Initially, in his first
speech in 1978, the Tibetan leader used a certain amount of caution when
speaking of the spirit in public. One sentence caught my attention:

> If you ask what definite conclusions I have come to, I
> cannot say what the ultimate identity of Gyalchen may be.
> If, amongst human beings who we can see directly with
> our own eyes, we cannot gauge the nature of another, how
> then can we know the nature of a deity?[28]

I immediately noticed that though he had advised against the worship
of this entity, the Dalai Lama, in his first speech in 1978 then still defined

---

[26] The "king demon from Dol," the way the Dalai Lama prefers to name the entity called
"Shugden" by its followers.

[27] Böd is the Tibetans' own name for their country, made up of the provinces of U in the
center, Tsang in the south, Ngari in the west, and Kham and Amdo in the east. Lhasa (pro-
nounced Hla-sa), the capital of U, was governed in the fourteenth century by the Phagmo
Drupa family, which was faithful to the Kadam and Geluk schools. In the fifteenth and
sixteenth centuries, the Rinpungpa and Tsangpa dynasties, devoted to the Kagyu school,
gained the upper hand, and severely pressed the popular Geluk school. In the mid-
seventeenth century, the Mongolian warrior king Gushri Khan unified the country and
made the Fifth Dalai Lama the political ruler.

[28] From the the Dalai Lama's speech given on June 25, 1980, to the monks from the
monasteries of Drepung, Ganden, Sakya, and Nyingma of Mundgod.

Shugden as a deity, whereas in successive years he would choose a decisively negative term, describing him as a being of an ambiguous and dangerous nature.

The Indian press reports on the inquiry into the triple homicide soon started to refer to an international search by Interpol, and there were Shugden devotees under investigation not only in India, but also in England and in Italy. The English center belonged to the New Kadampa tradition, whose head was an erudite lama and author of many widely read books. A few months before the crime, this lama's disciples had staged a demonstration in London accusing the Dalai Lama of religious intolerance precisely because he had requested Buddhists to stop praying to Shugden. Indeed, the Tibetan leader, eighteen years after he first discussed the subject with his closest advisers, the Tibetan leader no longer described Shugden as a deity but as a dangerous demon. I attributed this use of different terms to altered circumstances following his decision to end his own daily practice, rather than a reversed judgment on his part. The Dalai Lama's opinions on Shugden were made known by lamas such as Kelsang Gyatso in England and the United States or and Ganchen Tulku in Italy to many people who did not always know of the historical and religious background of the affair.

In the mid-1990s, therefore, the Dalai Lama wished to make clear to all concerned his opposition to this cult that was creating such divisions among Tibetans and foreigners too. To do so he employed terms more appropriate for those ignorant of both the scope and the nature of the controversy.

It is difficult to explain simply that the demons and deities of Tibet are part of an intricate cosmic mandala, a symbolic pattern in which there is no real separation between them. In other Tantric practices such as the Chod, in which, using visualization, the practitioner offers one's own body to all beings, and even demons are invited to feast on one's flesh; this signifies the overcoming of attachment to one's most precious worldly possession.

His Holiness explained to me that, as these were high practices, many ended up experiencing only a conceptual transformation into the state of a divinity, thus creating more harm than benefit to their spiritual progress. Others, in contrast—a limited number of master yogis—were authorized to continue the practice of such "king demons" as Gyalpo Shugden. Evidently, they were considered capable of using the demon's worldly power to develop their own meditation and not become his slaves, as was the fate of many others.

"Some Tantric practices are difficult, even for the Dalai Lama," he said with great humility, but with an indirect reproof aimed at those who attempt them lightly.

The Italian group cited in the police reports was run by Ganchen Tulku, a well-known lama residing in Milan, recognized by the United Nations as a "messenger of peace." Unlike those of Kelsang Gyatso, none of his disciples had ever protested publicly. But Ganchen Tulku was the first link in the chain of events and characters that widened the international scope of the mystery to include China. This lama maintained frequent and intensive contacts with the authorities in Beijing, especially after the Chinese government imposed the selection of its candidate as the reincarnation of the Panchen Lama, the second most important religious figure in Tibetan Buddhism. A six-year-old child named Gyaincain Norbu, he was totally unaware of the fate that the strategies of the Communist politicians had in store for him. It was too early to say whether Gyaincain's fate was somehow connected to the cult of Shugden. The only certainty was the sudden, but hardly mysterious disappearance of a boy of the same age called Gendun Chokyi Nyima, initially designated by the Dalai Lama as the "authentic Panchen." As soon as that was declared in 1995, the little Gendun vanished from sight, along with his parents, and Gyaincain took his place. Since then, nobody has seen nor heard of Gendun and his parents.

Ganchen's original monastic residence was very near the monastery of Tashi Lhunpo in western Tibet, the residence of the previous Panchen Lama. This previous Panchen Lama, who, after being imprisoned for over a decade, emerged in the 1980's as a member of the Central Committee of the Chinese Communist Party (CCP), until he died in 1989 in circumstances that have remained unclear. On November 22, 1996, the little Gyaincain had his formal investiture as successor in a ceremony broadcast by all the state television channels. In the first row of lamas offering the traditional white *kata* scarf to the new Panchen Lama was Ganchen Tulku.

However, there was no concrete link between the Italian and English Buddhist centers and the international investigation of the murders, nor was it evident to what extent the Western and Tibetan disciples were aware of the esoteric and political aspects of the cult of Shugden.

Meanwhile, numerous pieces of the puzzle were beginning to take shape at different latitudes and at other points of the compass.

The Law of Cause and Effect

The story of the three murders is but one of the horrendous events in the news during those years. I read of human sacrifices offered in the manner of the Aztecs; witch hunts in India, in Indonesia, and Papua New Guinea; and in Africa, massacres attributed to satanic cult followers inspired by a warped Christianity. Then there were the "modern" versions of human wickedness: the destruction of the environment; the squalid speculations of so-called globalization at the expense of the poorest nations; and the numberless brutal crimes in the prosperous, educated societies of the industrialized world.

It is difficult to pass judgment on the senseless behavior patterns genetically transmitted in our species. But the particular forms of Buddhism that developed in India and Tibet in the centuries following the birth of this religion were based precisely on the conviction that reality could be modified by discovering the origin of the process by which our mind encounters phenomena and produces emotions, both positive and negative.

The Buddha called it the theory of the "law of cause and effect," known as "karma," or the "dependent origination of all phenomena." Doubtless, it was only by chance that Lobsang Gyatso was working on a text on this subject when he was killed and two fellow monks were killed as they translated his commentary into Chinese. "Dependent origination" had been studied for many centuries and interpreted by countless Buddhist scholars and practitioners. Thus, the Geshe's work was only one of the many details of secondary legal importance that emerged from the files of the investigation.

Nevertheless, this fact attracted me with a magnetic force. It was an intuition that I could not lay aside, as the Indian investigators following the tracks of the killers had been forced to do earlier. I was not similarly obliged. What interested me was precisely the original cause of those crimes that had been given a religious significance. For this reason, I began with the very subject of the text that the deceased Director of the School of Dialectics had intended to translate into Chinese.

The theory of dependent origination is quite simple to understand, at least in its elementary principles. All phenomena essentially arise from others that came before; and all are interdependent, with no exceptions whatsoever. Fruit is born from its seed, which becomes a tree and bears its own fruit which contains another seed; ice comes from water, which, when heated, melts; a child is born of her or his parents and in turn may become a mother or a father; and matter is born from the action of water and wind in space, the intervention of human beings, the joining and separation of atoms and molecules.

But the law of cause and effect, with its interdependent links tied to diverse causes and circumstances, contains numerous unknown factors. Following its logic, a good deed should generate a positive consequence and a bad deed the opposite. But how many variations may ensue? As one example, we give money to a beggar, and as soon as he has turned the corner he buys himself some heroin and dies of an overdose. Our intention was good, but the effect was disastrous.

The case of the slain Geshe demonstrates that the heart of the enigma lies precisely in the difficulty of understanding the meaning of two kinds of truth, one relative, one absolute. Certainly Lobsang Gyatso was motivated by good intentions when he began to challenge the followers of Gyalpo Shugden, using the arguments of his guru the Dalai Lama. The ruler of Tibet himself long had pondered the appropriate moment to raise the issue publicly. His decision to do so may have been a contributing factor to the murder of his three disciples.

There was an apparent contrast between the Dalai Lama's earlier declaration that he was not aware of the nature of Shugden and the fact that later he called it "a harmful spirit" or a "spirit born of dark forces" and advised against practicing the cult's prescriptions. What had the Dalai Lama discovered in the interim that was so serious that he decided to impose restrictions on the cult, despite the danger this could cause to himself and his followers? A first response could only refer to fragments of relative truth: his own dreams; the oracles' divinations; and political and doctrinal reasons. He had to put the facts together and find more significant details to fill the empty spaces between them.

It was not important to establish whether what may have been a misinterpretation on his part could have justified the violent reactions of the Shugden worshippers. Nothing could make sense of the barbarity of the massacre of the three poor monks. But such ferocity was born of a hatred that neither began nor ended with their sacrifice, as events over the last few turbulent centuries in Tibet show.

At the time when the Dalai Lama first publicly declared the dangers of venerating the Dolgyal Shugden, some Western scholars of Himalayan religions were surprised and disconcerted, considering that the Tibetan leader had prayed to and invoked the *gyalpo*[29] for at least three decades, beginning from the time of his childhood. Stephen Batchelor, an essayist and a former monk in both the Tibetan and Zen traditions, explained to me that one of the reasons for surprise was that the Dalai Lama's initial devotion to the spirit came from the tight "lineage" bond that he had with his tutor, Trijang Rinpoche. Trijang was one of the most famous lamas of the Gelukpa School and was himself the disciple of another eminent personage who lived at the time of the Thirteenth Dalai Lama, Phabongka Rinpoche.

Every lama in Tibet has been in turn the disciple of other past masters, so that complex lines of transmission, or lineages, have been formed over centuries. Some lineages evolved into schools, orders, or monastic institutions. Others became extinct, and still others were differentiated into more specific traditions that integrated various techniques of meditation focused on the cults of deities and celestial guardians. Some struggled for supremacy over one another.

Both Phabongka and Trijang could be considered heads of a new lineage that raised Shugden to the rank of a principal protector of the widespread Gelukpa tradition, even though this spirit had not even existed when the school was founded in 1400. According to his devotees, he appeared in the time of the Fifth Dalai Lama, in the mid-seventeenth century. Phabongka's mother had worshipped Shugden in her family tradition, and Phabongka himself and had been initiated by Dakpo Rinpoche. Therefore, Phabongka and Trijang Rinpoches were not the first to promote the cult, but thanks to their fame, they were able to disseminate it in the first half of the twentieth century, both among Tibet's religious and political aristocracy, the monks, and the Tibetan population generally.

When the Dalai Lama stated publicly that the nature of Shugden was not, in his opinion, that of a buddha, it was as if he had officially called his tutor, and thus indirectly Phabongka, liars. This he did knowing full well that many of the Gelukpas who had moved to the West and many of those who remained in Tibet were their disciples. In no small number they were assailed by painful doubts and torn between their devotion to

---

[29] According to the Tibetans, this term, literally "king," refers to one of the eight classes of demonic beings who can create obstacles such as diseases or accidents.

Trijang and Phabongka and their love for their leader, himself the holder of a lineage going back several hundred years.

It is hard to find a more fitting parallel for the emotional reaction of some Tibetans than that of a child perturbed by its parents' quarrels. Furthermore, the transmission of teachings from master to disciple is considered more important by Tibetan Buddhists than physical nourishment because whereas the body dies, the mind continues forever. As Sogyal Rinpoche writes in *The Tibetan Book of Living and Dying*:

> Who is this outer teacher? None other than the embodiment and voice of our inner teacher. The master whose human shape and human voice and wisdom we come to love with a love deeper than any other in our lives is none other than the external manifestation of the mystery of our own inner truth.

It is said that one day the celebrated Naropa,[30] having given symbolic initiation and spiritual instructions to his disciple Marpa, wanted to test him. He created the form of the Tantric divinity Hevajra[31] in the sky, with another eight celestial figures around him. Marpa immediately prostrated himself before the divine figure, which Naropa quickly caused to disappear, dissolving into himself. He then said to Marpa, "Where there is no guru, you cannot even hear the name of the Buddha. For thousands of eons the buddhas have depended on a master to enable them to appear because they are his manifestations."

The sacred nature of the transmission methods of Tibetan Tantra through the guru is one of the many variations of this religion from the original teachings. Gautama Buddha, in fact, invited his followers first to evaluate his words to see if they were helpful in understanding how to liberate themselves from the mental suffering of fear and attachment to the material world. The Buddha attributed more importance to the teaching and the method used than to the guru—not emphasizing study and memorizing theories, but, instead, application in daily life. Only this way, he said, can we discover if the teacher's experience is valid for the

---

[30] He inspired another of the four principal schools of Vajrayana Buddhism, the Kagyu.

[31] Hevajra is a contemplative divine buddha with many arms imported to Tibet in the eleventh century by Drogmi, *(Brog mi)* 993–1077 CE, who founded the Sakya order.

student. Only through experience does true knowledge arise. Certainly his teachings were not simple, especially if only intellectually analyzed, as two of the most hermetic affirmations of his doctrine demonstrate: "Life is like an illusion," and "Illusion is born from the void." For a great number of his disciples who did not possess his capacity to understand, developed over years and years of strict asceticism, it was like listening to a description of a sweet taste without ever having tasted sugar.

Buddha advised his disciples to reach this understanding gradually, without immediately asking themselves unanswerable questions such as whether or not a God or creator exists. He gave this example:

> Attachment to worldly life is like being struck by an arrow with a tip that slowly releases poison. The moment you learn that within a certain lapse of time the poison will provoke suffering and death, there is no point in keeping the arrow in your body, looking at it and wondering where it was shot from, north or south, if it is made of wood or metal, long or short. It is more important to extract the arrow.

This was definitely not an invitation to commit suicide, but advice to liberate the mind from the conditioning of this poison, which is the attachment to a self, or an individual "I," which generates fear. This is not just the fear of physical and mental suffering on leaving this life, but it also refers to the terror created by the uncertainty of the fate of the self, or "I," after death. Once free of attachment and tension, the mind also could eventually discover the existence of a higher reality beyond suffering, called "nirvana."

The logic underlying the theory of dependent origination seemed in any case to deny the possibility of an eternal and immutable creator. As the Buddha stated, there exists an infinite number of variations of the possible combinations that give origin to life. There are so many in the continual evolution of phenomena, by their very nature interdependent on one another, that no fixed point exists, only a series of causes and conditions that in turn are the effects of other causes and conditions.

This is why the Buddha substituted the notion of "emptiness" for the idea of "God." He discovered voidness or emptiness as the nature of ultimate reality, in contrast to any presumed immutability of a creator. This emptiness is all phenomena's lack of any intrinsic, fixed reality whatsoever, which allows all those phenomena to manifest—according to different circumstances. But emptiness is not some sort of thing-in-itself either. Form is indistinguishable from emptiness and emptiness is indistinguishable from form. Like a reflection in a mirror, form is the shining surface of emptiness. All things are free to manifest according to changing circumstances, as a lightning bolt appears only after a sudden gathering of clouds. Just as suddenly, as if by enchantment, the clouds change and disappear, leaving a transparent, clear sky.

The particular form of Buddhism that developed in India toward the end of the first millennium CE, intensified the asceticism of the Theravada and the world-transforming compassion of the Mahayana's Universal Vehicle by creating the Vajrayana, the "Thunderbolt" or "Diamond" Vehicle, beliefs and practices enabling the capable practitioner to reach enlightenment in a few lifetimes, or even in a single lifetime. This "triple vehicle" form of Buddhism is the one that was imported to Tibet beginning in the eighth century. The most popular sacred iconographic depiction of Padmasambhava, the first Tantric master to arrive in the Land of Snows, shows him holding a *vajra* (*dorjey* in Tibetan), which symbolizes the power of lightning and the indestructibility of a diamond, the king of stones. The *vajra*'s five prongs symbolize the transmutation of the five poisons of delusion, hatred, lust, pride, and envy, into the five wisdom — mirrorlike, primordial perfection, individuating, equalizing, and all-accomplishing wisdoms.

According to the Vajrayana, the primordial mind of every individual is not restricted to the physicality of the body and has the same creative potential as the freedom of emptiness, the same ineffable essence of space that allows the lightning bolt to manifest, like the reflective surface of the mirror. But when the mind becomes attracted to and distracted by the reflections, by what it sees and perceives, then it loses its true nature beyond discrimination and attachment to form. Instead, it falls into ordinary vision and follows thought, which arises like the reflection of the moon in water. Through this distraction, one remains imprisoned within the relative dimension of existence and becomes a victim of the ignorance of causes and conditions that have been accumulated previously through this very distraction.

It is impossible to establish when this process started, that is, when "mind" entered into "habitual vision," which Buddhism calls "dualistic," in which a subject thinks about and judges an observed external object that is desired or rejected.

The supreme Indian sage Nagarjuna lived in the second century after Christ and wrote the seminal treatises on emptiness. He is also considered to be the "noble father" of Vajrayana Buddhism, and taught the essence of the Buddha's revelation on dependent origination:[32]

> From unawareness, karmic[33] impulses come forth;
> From them, consciousness; from that, name and form;
> From them, the cognitive senses are developed;
> And from them, contact, as the Able Sage declared.
>
> From contact come sensations;
> From sensations arises craving;
> From craving, grasping is developed;
> Grasping leads to the impulse for further existence;
> And the impulse for further existence brings rebirth.
>
> From rebirth comes a great mass of suffering,
> Such as sorrow, sickness, aging, loss of the desired,
> Fear of death, and death itself;
> So, by ceasing unawareness and rebirth,
> All of these [sufferings] will be stopped.[34]

The Buddha started to explain what he had discovered, beginning with the perceptions of ordinary man. He spoke of 'the Four Noble Truths." The first is the suffering that we all experience in various forms; the second is the cause of suffering, the source of all the other possible relative causes: desire and especially delusive ignorance; the third is nirvana, the freedom from suffering achieved by destroying ignorance; the fourth truth is the path to that freedom, the various methods of liberating oneself, depending upon one's capacities, through ethics, meditation, and wisdom. Every one of the Buddha's followers can engage in the practice that he or she finds most effective, and definitions of greater or lesser vehicles matter little, since their common aim is to transcend the *samsara* (literally,

---

[32] Pratītyasamutpāda.

[33] Evolutionary actions.

[34] From *Letter to a Friend* (*bShes-pa"i springs-yig*, Skt. *Suhṛllekha*), written by Nagarjuna as advice to a South Indian king. The letter has since become very popular. It comprises 123 verses, and it covers the whole Mahayana path.

"ocean of suffering") of earthly suffering existence and to extend compassion to those still suffering in that realm.

In the early sutras, the Buddha advised Indian peasants some 2,500 years ago on the usage of a slow but sure system, the Individual Vehicle, the Path of Renunciation, which is based on a gradual path of purification of past obscurations by means of abstaining from negative actions of the body, speech, and mind, and practicing meditation and the wisdom of selflessness. Ideally, it is the path of the monk or the layman who makes a pact between the Buddha and himself. The pact includes the solemn vows of renunciation, not one but often hundreds, such as promises to not kill, steal, and lie. The accumulation of the merit obtained for having respected the vows and thus having avoided creating any negativity for others is the condition for obtaining a better rebirth and, after a long learning process, liberation from the cycle of death and rebirth.

This method[35] requires many lifetimes and generally works for only one "individual passenger" at a time: one must think above all of one's own personal salvation, and if it proves impossible to help others onto one's unsteady raft, at least one tries not to hinder the rafts of others. By purifying oneself, one also purifies the surrounding environment.

The Buddha, though, was aware that a world filled with only hermits and monks would be a paradox. He started with the assumption that before liberating the world completely from suffering, an incalculable amount of time would have to pass, and human beings have an important role to play in this long process. He explained to his contemporaries that the possibility of obtaining rebirth in a human form rather than that of an animal is rare and precious. How could he then deny that sex, one of the main vows of renunciation taken by his monastics, had a positive valence in the grand design of the liberation of beings from suffering?

So Buddha taught the Mahayana, the Universal Vehicle, for laypeople who needed or wanted to retain the option of family life, emphasizing compassion and altruistic ethics. And for a special few—those who had mastered to a sufficient degree the renunciation of blind bondage to the passions, the conception of the altruistic spirit of enlightenment, the vow to become a perfect buddha for the sake of all beings, and the wisdom of selflessness, the freedom from fixed identity while recognizing the relativity

[35] Used by the Theravada Buddhists of Southeast Asia.

of the continuum of the ever-changing self—he gave the esoteric teaching of Tantra.

The Buddha admitted that, unlike lesser beings, all human men and women can progress in their own way and realize their divine nature without renouncing the world. But there is one condition, everyone must overcome involuntary attachment to passions. This means not simply repressing the passions themselves, which are part of human nature, but both recognizing them as a principal cause of attachment and simultaneously using their potential. Pride and envy, for example, are emotional poisons but can also be medicines. They become poisons when they separate us from others through anger and violence, but they can be turned into medicines when directed by wisdom. Pride can stimulate self-respect and envy can be turned into respect toward others, as we progress together on the path of knowledge. For this reason, after the "Path of Renunciation" of the Theravada, Buddha laid the foundations of the "Path of Transformation" by teaching the Universal Vehicle for the bodhisattvas, based on the transcendent wisdom of emptiness. Within that Universal Vehicle, he taught the Vajrayana of the Tantras, which were practiced in secrecy for many centuries, and only a thousand years later developed into mainstream depth practices in India and became a central focus in Tibet.

Like nuclear power, with its great beneficial capacities but potentially devastating risks, the Tantras could not and cannot be understood and used by just anyone, but only by individuals aware of and able to use their power for the collective good. There is a precise reason: attachment and desire increase proportionately with pride and the mental and physical pleasure that develops by means of certain Tantric techniques of body and mind. Therefore, these practices can become counterproductive instead of facilitating the development of the liberating power that comes from controlling desire and pleasure. The ultimate aim of every method is the control of ordinary mind, which, once obtained, enables one to discover the relaxed state that is the abode of the superior and altruistic mind, devoid of expectations of personal benefit.

The Buddha transmitted special practices to disciples of superior capacity who were not content to leave *samsara* behind aboard their own little boat, but instead were disposed to return continually to shore to bring back the last remaining shipwrecked being. These special students are referred to by the Sanskrit term *bodhisattva*, literally "enlightenment hero" or "heroine."

Like the captain who is always the last to abandon ship, the bodhisattvas are the last to reach nirvana. To develop this resolve, they can draw on the philosopher's stone of Tantra, the alchemical secret that frees human beings from attachment to the material and is capable of transforming impure vision into pure vision. The Sanskrit version of this Holy Grail is called "*bodhichitta*," which can be translated as the "seed of enlightenment," "spirit of enlightenment," or "spirit of awakening." Only those who possess true *bodhichitta* are authorized to act beyond conventions, that is, at another level of the relative truth of cause and effect.

Regarding the path of supreme asceticism explained in *The Sutra of the Great Promise*, it is written:

> When one is secure in the Buddha's vehicle,
> Then, even enjoying the five passions and five sense
>   objects,[36]
> One's morality remains intact,
> Like a lotus [(that grows)] in mud.

The idea that there exists a teaching beyond the law of cause and effect, based on a different interpretation of dependent origination, is considered dangerous by all the traditional Buddhist schools. This apparent contradiction is one of the great enigmas, impossible to understand without knowing the principles of the Tantras.

I have often asked myself if certain methods were really within the grasp of the limited mind of an ordinary man (such as myself). I was comforted by the words of Nagarjuna in his previously mentioned *Letter to a Friend*:

> Whoever has realized the Dharma [in themselves]—
> They are not, in fact, beings fallen from the sky;
> They are not [beings] who have sprung up,
> Like crops, from the womb of the earth;
> They were once merely [ordinary] people,
> Who were dependent on their disturbing emotions.

According to the Vajrayana path, to develop one's *bodhichitta* correctly, one must follow a true master of knowledge and do so with ex-

---

[36] Form, sound, smell, taste, and texture.

treme caution. That master is chosen for certain essential qualities, such as loving compassion toward every form of creation, and not for the simple capacity of knowing how to explain in words the meaning of dependent origination or of the Four Noble Truths. The master or the lama in the initiation ceremony is imagined to assume the role of the Tantric deity so as to channel to the student the power of knowledge and its relative blessings.[37]

The subtlety of this path is evident compared to the first teachings of the Buddha on the importance of method over that of the guru. In Tantra, only a master able to abide in the state of natural mind and in contact with the dimension of the deities is capable of helping the disciple develop the true *bodhichitta* of compassion, which goes beyond the techniques of meditation. Only in this way can one reach liberation and not some inferior, or worse yet, diabolical realm, where one is driven by the pride of possessing mundane magical powers developed by means of Tantric practices. All Tibetans, from an early age, whether they become monastics or not, request from lamas the initiation of the Path of the Bodhisattva and of relative *bodhichitta*. But someone who does not possess the *siddhi*[38] of clairvoyance cannot justify an action contrary to conventional ethical principles, even if theoretically it was committed to achieve a good end. From this stems the secrecy of Tantra, validated by the ritual of initiation, and by the link of dependency on a true master. From this there also emerges one of the main problems raised by the Dalai Lama on the nature of Shugden and the behavior of the lamas who transmitted his practices, including his own tutor, Trijang.

---

[37] *Chinlab* in Tibetan.

[38] Nonordinary powers such as mind-reading, telepathic communicating, remote seeing and hearing, conscious out-of-body travel, invisibility cloaking, flying though the sky, and so forth.

The Great Master of the Lightning Bolt

With some trepidation, I waited for the first appropriate opportunity to talk to the leader of all Tibetans, whom I had encountered in the past. Finally, word came that he would shortly be arriving in Italy to receive an honorary degree from the University of Bolzano.

I began to read more closely the numerous and incredible accounts from past and present that impinged on the affair of the Dharamsala murders. Some I felt skeptical about, and I thought of the great majority of people, who ignored the existence of such an esoteric universe. In my view, their sense of incredulity and their dismay were justified. But it was not a question of accepting or rejecting a thesis. Precise facts and circumstances involving human beings of flesh and blood and the identity of the assassins were merging into the complex shadow of the plot.

From the very beginning of my research, I had an intuition that this "war" between spirits and lamas would put the survival of Tibetan culture and traditions at stake. A desperate effort would be necessary for the Tibetans to avoid the fate of the Sumerians or Etruscans, with all their wisdom and secrets, gradually reduced over the centuries to artifacts in museum exhibits and subjects of academic studies.

For some time now there has been an attempt to expunge from the history of Tibet a figure not so well known in the West,[39] outside the circle of scholars and practitioners of Tantric Buddhism. The Tibetans call him Guru Rinpoche, Padmasambhava or the Lotus-Born Guru. He appeared at the time of King Trisong Detsen, around the middle of the eighth century, when this ruler dominated a vast empire stretching from the westernmost Himalayas to the borders of the Chinese empire. Trisong had conquered and absorbed into his own the pre-Buddhist kingdom of Shang Shung around Mount Kailash. He intended, for political and religious reasons, to supplant the ancient beliefs of Bon, which were taught by priests adept at controlling the elements and the guardian spirits of mountains, and particularly expert in using exorcisms and black magic.

Buddhism in India had little to do with shamanic ritual, and systematically discouraged focus on miraculous manifestations. It would have been

---

[39] See the account of the destruction of the statues in the final chapters.

impossible to convince a people of nomads, farmers, and warriors, savages in the eyes of their neighbors, to accept a new doctrine based on theories and writings with no practical purpose.

This influenced Trisong Detsen in his strategy. At first he invited to Tibet, Shantarakshita, the foremost scholar from the Buddhist university of Nalanda,[40] in Bihar. But the learned pandit[41] did not even manage to set foot outside the castle where he taught the literature of the Theravada and Mahayana sutras, and the basic Tantras to the royal court. Terrible storms, repeated cyclones, and famines devastated Tibet, and the Bon priests sought to convince the sovereign that all this was caused by the native gods, angered by his decision to supplant Bon with Buddhism. With this accusation, came also the logical consequence—according to the mentality of ancient Tibet—that the Buddhist faith was not able to overcome these obstacles. For this reason Shantarakshita advised the king to invite Padmasambhava, a great adept, celebrated not only for his knowledge of literature, but also for the his ability to realize the true powers of the Tantras. He was a great yogi, whose primordial mind was capable of controlling the five elements of which the physical universe is made up. He was also able to connect to the powerful cosmic entities that protect the universal order.

No novel or science fiction film could match what happened when Padmasambhava arrived in Tibet; fire was transformed into water; exorcisms were accomplished; rivers and lakes sprang forth as if by enchantment; resurrections—all miracles that history can only justify by the end achieved. The result was the complete conversion of Tibet to the new creed within a few decades. For Tibetans, it is beyond dispute that this was achieved by Padmasambhava's conquest of the ferocious spirits. No human being without the special powers derived from a mastery of the inner sciences of the Tantras could have accomplished such a task.

In the following centuries, some sought to diminish the importance of Padmasambhava by transforming him into a legend. But with the exception in recent centuries of those extremist Gelukpas devoted to Gyalpo

---

[40] The great Indian monastic university that was completely destroyed by Muslims in 1193.

[41] A learned scholar of the Indian Buddhist universities, expert in ethical, psychological, and philosophical texts.

Shugden, all the Tibetan schools, with a Vajrayana focus, considered him a historical person, and even a "second buddha." He was a man of action equipped to fulfill not only the task assigned to him in the eighth century, but also the present task. He is prayed to and invoked daily to resolve the present challenge of restoring to the Tibetan people the sovereignty and justice lost in the 1950s. According to some, Padmasambhava continues to live in an earthly paradise and, like the return of the Messiah, his return to Tibet is awaited perhaps in other forms, to defeat the new enemies of the country and spread the teachings of the Buddha. This the Dalai Lama himself made clear in his first speech to the abbots and monastics, when he revealed his decision to break with the practice of Gyalpo Shugden.[42]

Twelve hundred years ago Padmasambhava's teachings were at the origin of the Nyingma, or the "Ancient school," the first Tantric order established around the famed monastery of Samye. The principal deity of Samye was Pehar, considered the most powerful of a class of beings whose name will appear again in these pages. Padmasambhava converted Pehar to Buddhism, along with the other gods, spirits, and demons of the highlands. In subsequent centuries, Pehar's emanation, Dorje Drakden of Nechung Monastery, became the State Oracle of Tibet and Protector of the government led by the Dalai Lama. Even today, Nechung regularly takes possession of the official medium,[43] charged with transmitting, while in a trance state, the advice and instructions of Pehar to the Tibetan leader and his ministers in exile.

Another of the important phases of Tibetan history connected to the story of Gyalpo Shugden is known as the second diffusion of Buddhism. Between the time of Padmasambhava's disappearance and the new wave of translations of Sanskrit texts from India after the year 1000, there was an interval during which Langdarma, a king opposed to the new religion, persecuted the ancient Nyingmapas and all the followers of the exorcist guru, destroying a great number of their sacred texts. However, both Padmasambhava and his twenty-five leading disciples had hidden numerous Tantras in various secret locations, having clearly foreseen this epoch

[42] See the discussion between Rajeev Singh and Geshe Kalsang Damdul of the School of Dialectics and the interview with the Dalai Lama.

[43] Currently the Venerable Thupten Ngodup of Drepung Nechung Deyang Monastery of Dharamsala.

during which "dark forces" would prevail. These secret places were not only physical, such as rocks, holes dug in the ground, or hollow tree trunks. Many teachings were entrusted to divine female beings known as *dakinis*, while others were placed in the minds of disciples capable of reincarnating and remembering the sacred formulae sealed in their memories.

In the meantime, other masters had journeyed to India to translate the Mahayana texts at Nalanda, a prominent center of learning, and to invite various scholars from there to come and spread the knowledge of these teachings in Tibet. Thus, the new orders of the Kadampa, the Sakyapa, and the Kagyupa were established. The Kadampa tradition in particular, founded by the Indian sage Atisha,[44] did not look favorably on the diffusion of some of the old Tantras, thought to originate from uncertain sources, and falsely attributed to Padmasambhava. These Tantras the Kadampas considered tainted by the shamanic techniques of deviant forms of Indian Shaivism and ancient Tibetan Bon.

Atisha and his disciples in the eleventh century, and later in the fifteenth century, his spiritual heir, Jey Tsong Khapa, constructed great monasteries where the teaching of Mahayana thought and practice according to a precise scholastic curriculum, the *Lam Rim*, the Stages of the Path, was set in motion. Their tradition was also focused on the marvelous path of the Tantras for those advanced practitioners who could use them safely, but their systems aimed to cultivate the larger numbers of Tibetans step by step, through the gradual path of the Vinaya (monastic discipline) and the Mahayana sutra philosophies, to prepare them for the swifter paths of the Tantras. The curriculum of the monastic universities, like that of the great monasteries of India, was based on study and the systematic application of the simpler Buddhist theories and practices, such as the accumulation of merit by means of virtuous actions, the renunciation of the passions through monastic celibacy, the cultivation of empathetic compassion, and the deepening of the wisdom of emptiness.

Their advice was not to venture into experiments in experiences they considered dangerous without adequate preparation and certainty about their practices' origins and effects. But no master versed in these new

---

[44] From Bengal originally, he was invited to Tibet in 1042 CE. For more citations, see the biography of Atisha edited by H. Elmer, *Nam thar Gyas pa, Materialen zu einer Biographie des Atisha.*

schools could deny the power of some of the Nyingma methods, which had enabled many yogis to attain enlightenment in one lifetime, sometimes realizing the "Body of Rainbow Light."[45]

Both Atisha and Tsong Khapa, in fact, had knowledge of Tantras of every type. No one was more erudite than Atisha in the traditions of the so-called secret mantras. Yet, when he arrived in Tibet and visited Samye, founded by Padmasambhava and King Trisong Detsen, he discovered some manuscripts in Sanskrit collected as *The Treasure of Pehar Ling*, of which he had never heard. He praised the ancient kings of Tibet highly and said, "It seems the teachings are propagated more in Tibet than in India."

Atisha actually recognized a Nyingmapa master as the reincarnation of his Indian guru, Krishnacarya. Three centuries later, Tsong Khapa applied at length the teachings of Padmasambhava, receiving them from a famous Kadam-Nyingmapa master, Lhodrak Namkha Gyaltsen. However, Tsong Khapa, like Atisha earlier, feared that the secret sciences, in the hands of those who were not prepared and lacked compassion in applying them, could be a source of trouble rather than liberation.

Today, the followers of Gyalpo Shugden maintain that their protector has been charged with the responsibility of punishing those who transgress and break their commitment to follow the gradual path indicated by Atisha and Tsong Khapa. This path may be slower, they say, but its effectiveness is proven. There is a prayer of invocation to Shugden revealed in the *Yellow Book*, written by Trijang's disciple Zemey Rinpoche. This is the controversial text that prompted the Dalai Lama to denounce the cult. It states:

> Praise to you, protector of the Yellow Hat tradition,
> You destroy like dust,
> Great adepts, high officials, and ordinary people,
> Who defile and corrupt the Gelukpa order.[46]

---

[45] Highly developed Tantric yogis are considered able to absorb the physical dimension into the original condition of the elements, leaving behind after death only the impurities of hair and nails.

[46] Excerpt from The Yellow Book by Zemey Rinpoche. Full title: *The Ambrosia That Flowed from the Mouth of the Heroic Lama Father: Account of the Protective Deity Dorje Shugden, Chief Guardian of the Geluk Order, and of the Punishments Meted Out to Religious and Lay Leaders Who Incurred His Wrath*.

Because of this sectarian attitude—which may sometimes have been expressed in violence that went beyond words—the cult of Shugden, from the time of its arising in the seventeenth century, was the cause of division and conflict; both within the Gelukpa and Sakyapa[47] orders where it developed, and in their relations with other traditions, such as the Nyingmapa and the pre-Buddhist Bon religion.

In fact, Gyalpo Shugden is one of the most recent figures of worship to be added to the Tibetan pantheon connected to the Tantric practices. At the beginning of my research he was to me but one of the myriad gods and demons that crowd the renowned *thangkas*, those sacred scroll paintings used by devotees as the basis of their meditation. Each school follows a precise order in the placement of the figures: the Buddha, their founding master, or their principal divine figure at the center; the various masters in their tradition and the bodhisattvas around them; and, the peaceful or fierce deities above, below, or at the sides. These figures are reproduced in the visualizations in the state of meditation, and their purpose is to help the mind to imagine and then realize the dimension of the divine, the buddha-deities in their sacred mandalas.

In Tibet, it is said that the terrifying guardian protectors, ranged around the masters, peaceful deities, and angelic bodhisattvas and surrounded in turn by flames, blood, and corpses, defend those who evoke them. When necessary they manifest fiercely against any danger on the spiritual path, including other beings, visible or invisible, real or created out of fear and the imagination. Faith in such wrathful beings has been a part of Buddhism from its inception in India, and in Tibet fits well with a propensity for spirit worship common to tribal societies the world over. Focus on such worship is discouraged in the vast body of scholastic doctrines of the Indian and Tibetan Mahayana movement, which is based on an immense number of texts, scrupulously translated into Tibetan from Pali and Sanskrit.

The Tibetan respect for the spirits of land and sky became apparent to me during a long journey, made in 1988 and lasting almost a year, into many of the regions of the borderless highlands on the Tibetan Plateau. I was accompanying the renowned Tibetan master, Chogyal Namkhai

---

[47] Founded by Drogmi, a scholar from the University of Vikramashila in India and principal figure in the second diffusion of Buddhism.

Norbu,[48] a lay lama distanced from the traditional monastic schools and considered a reincarnation of one of the great sages of Dzogchen, or path of the "Great Perfection." He is also an eminent scholar of ancient history and was for thirty years a professor at the Oriental Institute in Naples.

On our journey together, every morning, wherever I found myself, whether in a peasant dwelling, in a monastery room, or under a nomad tent, the first act of the day was the lighting of a brazier or a fire. Sweet-scented branches would be thrown onto it, herbs symbolizing purification, and a smoke offering made to the invisible local gods, spirits, and protectors. This ritual, known as *sang*, was announced in monasteries by the deep sounds of long horns and enormous drums, before the mantric prayers of the day began. The rarified air carried the smoke across great distances while the sky began to lighten with the first glimmers of dawn, beyond the mountains delineating the vast valleys between earth and sky. Immersed in spaces that often had no visible horizon, I had the clear feeling several times that certain beings surrounded us, masters of places still isolated from the rest of the world below, lords of rivers, peaks, and planets.

On my return to the West, my perception of these presences almost disappeared among the buildings obscuring the sky, the highways, and the pollution of our frenetic, congested, modern metropolises. Yet I was still certain that in reality, somewhere, high above the skyscrapers and the smokestacks, some "presences" continue to move around us, participating secretly in human affairs while we, perennially distracted, go about our pressing worldly business.

There is a close link between the distraction of our minds, and the illusion containing the enigma of the exotic force of karma—evolutionary cause and effect, often confused with fate or destiny. Both in the original

---

[48] Chogyal Namkhai Norbu born in Derghe, Kham in 1938, was recognized at the age of two as the reincarnation of Adzom Drugpa (1842–1924), a great master of Dzogchen, and then by the Sixteenth Gyalwa Karmapa (1924–1981) as the mind-emanation of Shabdrung Ngawang Namgyel (1594–1621) the first Dharmaraja of Bhutan. Namkhai Norbu, the name given to him by his parents, means "Jewel of Sky." Educated in the monastic colleges of Derge Gonchen and Derge Bontod, he left Tibet in 1960 for Sikkim. He was subsequently invited to Italy by Professor Tucci, and taught at the Oriental Institute in Naples from 1964 until 1992. From the mid-1970s he has given Dzogchen teachings all over the world, and published numerous works on Tibetan history and culture. He is also the founder of the International Shang Shung Institute for Tibetan Studies and ASIA (Asociation for International Solidarity in Asia).

form of Buddhism and in Tibetan Tantra, it is explained that there is nothing in reality that is immutably written in the stars. Each of us can modify our situation continuously and consciously, by being more present in our daily life, concentrating on shaping it like a sculptor molding a clay statue. In rural Tibet, where the physical world is dominated by the sky and the rhythm of life is marked only by the tempo of the passing of day and night, the mind, familiar with the urban dimension, slowly empties itself of earlier constraints relating to space and time. Thus, using a little more awareness, I had a chance to discover that the figure to be modeled— my mind—had been subjected to a long, uncontrolled process made up of instilling prejudices and deep-rooted convictions, which had rendered it extremely rigid and barely malleable.

When I asked Norbu how I could free myself from the weight of the often negative and even self-destructive inclinations of the emotions, he introduced me to the esoteric meaning of the mirror. Exactly like the essential nature of the mind, he said, the mirror shows an image without judging whether the reflection is beautiful or ugly. To understand this, he advised me, I should observe the course of my thoughts as I encountered objects and situations in life without following the first emotional impulse of attraction or revulsion that arises. This was one of numerous methods to avoid unconsciously accumulating more karmic sediment. When I was able to do so, I noted the effect immediately. My mind, overloaded with the traces of the past, was less encumbered, and my thoughts were far less dominant. Previously, I would have considered this a form of torpor; but I changed my opinion when I saw the effectiveness of letting thoughts disappear into the "no place" from which they had come, like birds in the sky, leaving no trace. They were not eliminated, nor canceled out, but they simply did not become disturbing emotions—they didn't change my mood to exaltation when the reflections were gratifying or exciting, or to depression when they were negative.

There was no need even to sit with legs crossed and eyes closed. I could practice this as I read a book or when riding and admiring the mountain landscapes. Namkhai Norbu, besides, is an extremely practical man, engaged in numerous activities simultaneously, who is able to enjoy relaxing moments or to work through the night if necessary. He told me the story of a famous Dzogchen master in eastern Tibet who was interviewed by a Buddhist scholar. To the question, "Is it true that you Dzogchen masters are always in meditation?" he replied, "What am I supposed to meditate on?" His interlocutor said, "So it isn't true that you meditate?" The master answered, "When am I ever distracted from my meditation?"

Certainly, without training and maintaining a conscious presence in the challenging circumstances in which I found myself, I wouldn't have been able to bear the heavy burden of superstition and fear surrounding the three murders in Dharamsala. Among the opponents of the cult, and also among those who left it at the request of the Dalai Lama, I often found reluctance even to pronounce the name "Shugden." It would be a lengthy and useless exercise to recount the myriad anecdotes collected about the misfortunes, real or presumed, attributed to this spirit by those on both sides. I, too, had some moments of apprehension, and I set aside my work for several years with a disturbing sense of its futility, and even uselessness and danger. Any sectarian cult contains a potential threat, and the Dalai Lama himself had warned me during one of our meetings: "Don't be frightened of spirits, but be wary of men with knives."

Among the various tales of fear and superstition, I will only quote the story of a former monk, P., who had received the initiation of Shugden along with two other monks (only three people at a time are allowed to partake in this ceremony). P. taught Buddhism in the West, and though he remained devoted to the lineage of Gelukpa lamas who had introduced him to the cult, he had followed the Dalai Lama's advice.

> In 1981, I asked His Holiness for advice because I didn't feel ready to forsake that protector. But he told me in a firm and irrevocable tone, "You have to choose whether to rely on me or on him." So I went to consult my teacher Lama Zopa, a great lama who used to practice Shugden. He said, "It is not necessary to turn to Shugden to reach enlightenment." Actually, I mainly relied upon the six-armed Mahakala[49] for protection, and considered Shugden as something extra. Shugden seemed a very familiar figure—I'd even call him approachable—though the text of his ritual was many pages long.

---

[49] Maha (great) Kala (black one) is a fierce manifestation of the celestial bodhisattva Avalokiteshvara, the incarnation of the universal compassion of all buddhas.

First of all, it starts off with a summary of the *Stages of the Path* teaching. Then the prayer begins: "Please, Great Guardian, eliminate all obstacles, do not send negativities...." I had very strong, concrete experiences. He was a truly powerful, present entity. However, some time later, after receiving a few Nyingma initiations, I had a motorbike accident. There was a strong gust of wind, and I found myself with my face flattened against the tarmac and my lower limbs tangled up in the wheels. The [resulting] infection lasted a year, and one day the doctors said I would lose the use of my leg. For sure, I thought right away of my Nyingma initiations and of Shugden's vendetta. Then I invoked the protector and I said to him, "I'm here, do what you want with me!"

In 1991, I returned to see His Holiness and I said to him, "I have stopped my prayers, but Shugden helped me greatly in many practical ways and in business." The Dalai Lama answered me, "You can trust in Palden Lhamo. She is more than a sister. She is part of the family of our masters and helps all beings, without making distinctions."

Just as the story of P. describes the personal travails of one former follower of the cult, the repercussions of the Shugden affair have had many other consequences for entire communities of Buddhist devotees, and not only for practitioners of Tibetan Tantra. Besides the three crimes in Dharamsala, the tense climate among exile groups in India, and the public demonstrations against the Dalai Lama in England, there have been quite serious effects on the Italian and the European Buddhist Unions. The differences arose during a delicate phase of negotiations aimed at having Buddhism recognized officially as a religion by the Italian state. Traditionally, the Rome government has been influenced by the Vatican, the reference point for most of the political classes, reared on Catholic principles. The agreement discussed would have facilitated the arrival from abroad of recognized masters of different Buddhist traditions, Theravada, Mahayana, and Vajrayana, with an easing of visa regulations, tax concessions for Dharma centers, recognition of a calendar of festivals, and so forth.

The statements of the Dalai Lama, according to which the practice of Shugden turned the teaching of the Buddha into a spirit cult, made a strong impact on the various Gelukpa centers belonging to the Buddhist Union, apart from that of Ganchen Tulku, who was among the European Buddhist Union's founders. At Pomaia, the main monastery inspired directly by the Dalai Lama, several lamas had been practicing the cult, and not all of them officially declared that they were willing to follow their leader's instructions. Since the Tibetan Buddhist centers were among the most numerous and influential in Italy and they could not agree, even members of the Zen groups (who emphasize meditation on the nature of cosmic emptiness) and the Theravada (who follow the path described in the Pali sutras of the Buddha) had to resign themselves to the impasse, and the negotiations came to nothing.

Chogyal Namkhai Norbu's spiritual center was in fact the only one to position itself squarely behind the Dalai Lama's request. The very name of the teaching, Dzogchen or Great Perfection, of which Namkhai Norbu is an exponent, indicates its nonsectarian, noninstitutional nature. In Dzogchen, both mantra and meditation, visualizations and the external forms of religious practice, are only of relative importance compared to the main objective—to be liberated, or rather, to liberate oneself from ties and conditioning, from mental cages and prejudices, and from the very attachment created by the sense of belonging to a group, a community, or an ideology.

For me, once a Catholic and formerly editor of the Italian Communist Party's newspaper, weary of labeling and taking positions, it was an ideal route, and one that did not require me to renounce living in society, to close myself away in a monastery seeking refuge from the ills of the world.

When I asked Namkhai Norbu for suggestions on the case on which I was still working, he replied that my book could help to clear up a question that was much more sensitive and important than was at first apparent.

One day, while we were traveling from one village to another in the eastern highlands, the master asked me what I thought of the Dalai Lama. Shortly before, the Dalai Lama had been awarded the Nobel Peace Prize, and I answered that I knew of his role as a political leader but not enough of his standing as a spiritual master. Norbu Rinpoche then said something that struck me, "In the past I had some reservations, but now I cannot wait for a chance to receive teachings from His Holiness." I don't know why, but I didn't pursue this point and ask him why he had said this, since my reporter's curiosity normally would have compelled me to. But when the story broke I intuitively connected his words to Gyalpo Shugden.

Namkhai Norbu confirmed to me that not only he, but also many masters from other Tibetan traditions earlier had feared the influence of that cult on the young Dalai Lama, since it had already created deep divisions within the Buddhist community. "Many Gelukpas in the past," he told me, "have been convinced that the success of their school stemmed from the power of their guardian deity. But this is not true, because there was no Shugden at the beginning, and it was the Fifth Dalai Lama who unified the whole of Tibet. He appreciated the value of, and practiced teachings from, all the traditions. The Dalai Lamas had a personal power that went beyond the schools. It was they who gave prestige to the Gelukpas and transformed their great monasteries into state institutions that minted the money. None of the other traditions had ever enjoyed that privilege. The sectarian clergy have continued to believe since that time, however, that all this was owed to the spirit Shugden, and today, in exile, they try to control as far as possible the money that is received from abroad. Even the actors and extras for the film *Seven Years in Tibet* were chosen from their ranks."

As regards the more esoteric aspects of the mystery that unfolded after the killings in Dharamsala, Norbu alluded to the growing power of the class of beings called *gyalpo* ("king demon"), to which, in his opinion, Shugden himself belonged.

I asked him what he was referring to in particular, and Norbu Rinpoche mentioned the great human tragedies provoked not only by the *gyalpo*, but also by other powerful demonic beings. He spoke of disturbances of different kinds, seemingly incomprehensible but nevertheless all linked to precise causes fed by human selfishness, and especially by damage to the environment. "When we build a house, we cut down trees, we dig holes, and we lay cement, and we don't think for a moment that animals live there. But in those places we consider 'our home,' not only animals or other beings that we can see are found. It would be presumptuous to think that we can 'see' everything around us, and that we are the most powerful and intelligent inhabitants of the planet. Among these beings, invisible to us, there are good and bad, just as among ourselves."

Not only were there the conflicts among the schools; there were also the political implications of the links between the cult members and China. Here was yet another slippery slope. I reread several transcriptions and texts of the lectures of Namkhai Norbu on the eight principal classes of beings in the universe, according to the concepts of the original Bon religion of Tibet, which had been accepted, for the most part, by Tibetan Buddhists. Each class could include hundreds, if not thousands of beings, and they lived in rivers, valleys, mountains, countries, continents, and galaxies. Texts on the deities of this and other worlds, spirits, ghosts, and other beings besides, are part of Buddhist and non-Buddhist encyclopedic literature.

I reflected for a long time on these dwellers sharing our planet who have been "victims" of our collective repression. Centuries of enlightenment and rational thought have associated certain ancient beliefs all over the world with "superstitions," classifying every phenomenon anomalous to ordinary perception into the scientific fields of anthropology, philosophy, psychology, and medicine. Freud connected fantasies of demons to psychic disturbances; that is, wicked desires, resisted or repressed instinctive stimuli. And even parapsychology, closest to the spiritual sciences in defining the unknown, speaks simply of "internal" forces in human beings. Apart from the studies of Carl Gustav Jung, the figure of St. George battling the dragon—Evil—with his sword, and the convictions of the odd passionate student of the occult, I had had little success in finding comprehensible analogies to offer Western newspaper readers.

Meanwhile, I personally used to share that tendency to place more value on the visible. I did not want to be estranged, as someone indulging in mystic folly, from the lay intellectual circles in which I moved. But with the millions of planets and galaxies unknown to us, in the infinity of worlds, visible and invisible, such as microbes that exist in the physical dimension of the cosmos itself, it seemed more irrational than logical to deny the possible existence of beings hidden from our ordinary perceptions, yet real and endowed with a nature of their own.

Chogyal Namkhai Norbu started from a simple observation that is difficult to refute. Unaware of the existence or the behavior of these beings, who do not necessarily intend to do us harm for no reason, we can with our actions can disturb them to the point where they are forced to react, causing sickness and calamity. None of us intentionally kills an ant unless it disturbs us, and no ant ever recognizes the being that crushed it.

Rinpoche explained that today we are paying a high price for the harm caused to these unknown inhabitants of the planet, not only by our actions but also through our technologies. He gave the example of the class of beings called *tsan* by the Tibetans, who, when provoked, act upon movement and cause paralysis. The *tsan* also can act upon cells, creating tumors, while the *naga*—water spirits—act on the lymphatic glands, skin, and so forth.

Are these all superstitions? Before Pasteur and the microscope, it was widely believed that mysterious malevolent spirits were responsible for certain inexplicable maladies. Then we discovered previously invisible small beings with complex structures, microbes, bacteria, and viruses, which we sometimes fight with effective medicines, but just as often succumb to without ever discovering the origin—or the nature—of their essence and their antidotes. But even when we find effective medicines such as antibiotics, some organisms have learned to react and strengthen themselves, multiplying their lethal powers.

Science has learned that there also exist benign bacteria, but the lessons of experience have not sufficed to widen the field of research beyond the rational and "physical" factors, and even less so beyond the microcosm of material classified by our ever more sophisticated instruments into infinitesimal particles, split into atoms comprised of protons and neutrons.

If we apply these discoveries to minuscule beings on a larger scale, in the complex macrocosm of the universe, we cannot exclude further surprises. The Tantras work with an instrument considerably more powerful than telescopes and spaceships, the marvelous instrument of the mind, obscured in our relative dimension by the confused and egoistic use we make of it. Like a cloud, this egoism obscures the ultimate truth.

During the terrible period of the Balkan Wars in Europe, Namkhai Norbu cited these conflicts as an example of the human and environmental conditions that formed the perfect humus for the development of the power of the *gyalpo* king demons, capable of unleashing folly and hatred. He said something that even rationalists can find easy to accept; that is, ethnic, political, and religious conflicts, the basic cause of that and all the other wars that bring bloodshed to the world, would not be irremediable if human beings knew how to protect themselves without resorting to the physical destruction of the adversary, by instead controlling their own greedy and opportunistic nature. This means controlling the mind.

Schopenhauer studied Asian doctrines in depth and spoke of *maya*, the illusion at the origin of the world. He wrote that it is not important to establish "what" it is we want, because the "wanting" (a fundamental mistake) can never be satisfied. That is why we never cease to want and life is continual misery.

In Buddhism, ignorance and the distraction of the mind do nothing but sharpen the tension deriving from this wanting, which we call "attachment." The failure to satisfy desire—indestructible as a weed whose root has never been extracted—is not only the origin of conflict and of human and animal rebirth. Even powerful beings—deities or spirits to us invisible but endowed with a worldly mind—have not crossed the threshold of the realms dominated by desire. Some, like the best of human beings, try to engage in beneficial actions, following the principles of universal compassion. Others feed on our very conflicts, entrapped in the dualism of attraction and refusal, and are invigorated by confrontation like a virus in an organism without antibodies. Thanks to human ignorance, they extend their power, and increase their own and others' misfortunes.

The Indian master Shantideva of the Mahayana school once said:

> Maleficent beings are numberless as space,
> And it is impossible to subdue all of them;
> But if you can dominate your own anger,
> That is just like defeating all your enemies.

There are other factors, beyond the physical, that are connected to humankind's innate conflict. Just like a tumor, either genetic or caused by radiation or the quality of one's food, the circumstances created by our ignorance affect our material world at the level of our cells, maddening and destroying them.

Both Chogyal Namkhai Norbu and the Dalai Lama have interpreted another pivotal, historical event, the Chinese "Cultural Revolution," in this vein, regarding it as a much more striking example. During that fanatical political mass movement (1966–1976), millions accused of being "counter-revolutionaries" were killed or imprisoned in the name of Communism. In many ways, its effects were more devastating than the invasion of Tibet in the 1950s, because the Cultural Revolution created millions of victims among the Chinese population. Mao Zedong, who had an enormous influence on the movement's leaders, realized at a certain point that things had taken a mistaken and irreversible direction. However, the people were by then highly charged in an atmosphere of uncontrollable tension and hysteria and continued for years their intensive war on the "old guard," which had begun on the theoretically reasonable principle of overthrowing the feudal system. But for a long time, no one was able to put an end to the delirium of massacre and destruction.

Many we met, especially in eastern Tibet, told the lamas of having seen numerous manifestations of *gyalpo* king demons in those years. One of the visible signs caused by their presence, as Norbu Rinpoche explained, is the appearance of a white light resembling the reflection of rays of the sun on water or a clear surface. But similar signs were described by Zemey Rinpoche, a Shugden devotee, in his *Yellow Book*; the book that prompted the Dalai Lama to speak out publicly against the cult. Discussing the problems that arose near the residence of the Eighth Panchen Lama, Lobsang Palden Choekyi Drakpa (1855–1882), suspected of having "contaminated" the purity of his Gelukpa practice, Zemey describes flashes of bright light appearing like burning flames. Zemey goes on to discuss the unfortunate fate of this lama and that of his successors, in the following passage:

> All-knowing Panchen Losang Palden Chokyi Drakpa was the lord of the Doctrine and from a very young age proved himself as an eminent scholar. He thus had great potential to serve the Dharma and sentient beings. But he did not make the flawless and well-established teachings of the Dharmaraja Lama Tsong Khapa his principal practice. Instead, he studied many treasure texts of the Nyingma order and did meditations on those teachings. They were mentioned in his autobiography. Dorje Shugden repeatedly asked him not to do that. He became annoyed with the deity and performed a wrathful and despicable ritual to burn it. Along with other items, he put a *thangka* of the deity in the fire. But the fire could not consume the *thangka*. Then he took out the *thangka* and put it under the steps of his door in Tashi Lhunpo [the monastery of the Panchen Lamas in Shigatse]. He fell into disgrace, became ill, and passed away at the age of thirty in 1882. It is said that a terrifying bearded monk appeared at his deathbed.
>
> Panchen Lobsang Ngodup Chokyi Nyima Gelek Namgyal (1883–1937), also, faced a great number of problems [as

a consequence]. Although he had no interest in the Nying-ma teachings, because of a misunderstanding between his monastery and the Tibetan government, he had to escape to Mongolia. Later, he wished to come back to U-Tsang, but there were insurmountable hurdles and he could not succeed. At the age of fifty-five he passed away. In 1936 Panchen Lobsang met Phabongka Rinpoche and asked him to go to Tashi Lhunpo to give teachings. He also asked him to take out the *thangka* of the Shugden deity that was buried by the previous Panchen Lama. Phabongka went to Tashi Lhunpo in 1940, and gave many religious sermons. He also took out the *thangka* of the Shugden deity and put it in a shrine in Tashi Lhunpo and worshipped it, and composed a text that was an agreement and understanding between the monastery and the deity.

The tenth incarnation, Lobsang Thrinley Lhundrup Choekyi Gyaltsen, was born in 1938 in Zhago Dzong, in Kokonor, into a family of local government officials. Certain impediments delayed his enthronement. Soon after his arrival in Tashi Lhunpo, he composed a prayer to Dorje Shugden. He entitled this invocation to the five aspects of Shugden "The Spontaneous Melody of Four Activities." There was a statue of Shugden in a shrine in the palace. But when his spiritual tutor, Kachen Ngawang Nyima, saw it, he told one of the attendants to remove the devil's statue from there. When this was told to the Panchen Rinpoche, he told the attendant to keep it where the tutor could not see it. The tutor disliked Shugden and banned the usual practice of propitiating Gyalchen Shugden at Tashi Lhunpo, and the oracle too was banned from invoking the deity. Afterward, many bad omens occurred one after the other. An unprecedented flooding of the Shao River washed away the main residential complex of the Panchen Lamas. People noticed from afar flashes of light like burning flames.

Namkhai Norbu related to me how he had recognized manifestations of the *gyalpo* demon on his journeys in Mongolia, Buryatia, and Russia. A number of dreams made him recall personal experiences from his childhood. At that time, in order to be cured of a serious illness attributed to disturbances he had unwittingly provoked in a temple dedicated by locals to the *gyalpo* king demon, Namkhai Norbu was invited to make ritual offerings to placate it and so recover his lost health. However, his father and several masters advised him against doing so to avoid even worse consequences, since he would have to continue ingratiating himself with the spirit for the rest of his life. Once a *gyalpo* king demon is invoked and worshipped, they said, a relationship is formed, a dangerous bridge that creates dependence, making the worshippers like animals in a cage from which even physical death may not easily free them. The empowerments and temporary benefits that could come from propitiating rites are in the long run transformed into negativities that far outweigh their advantages.

The young Norbu followed the advice of his father and the lamas, but the disturbances continued until he was taught practices that could strengthen his mental and physical defenses and make him immune to the dangers of provocation by those beings. These practices are based on the mental powers of transformation transmitted by Padmasambhava, when he defeated the wrathful deities opposed to the spreading of Tantra in Tibet, thereby controlling their powers. One of the figures capable of taming the *gyalpo* king demon is Guru Dragpur, the lower part of whose body is transformed into a huge sharpened triangular blade.

A Private Meeting with the Dalai Lama on the Subject of Gyalchen Shugden

A long time had passed since the Dharamsala crimes when the Dalai Lama finally came to Italy, to receive an honorary degree from the University of Bolzano. My newspaper sent me to attend the press conference scheduled after the ceremony. To prepare myself for the meeting, I read over some of the first speeches made by the Tibetan leader during the 1980s and 1990s, noting the most significant passages:[50]

> Some of the former civil servants noted that previous administrations had been dependent on deities. It seems that those functionaries were right. Decisions were not taken simply by officials after appropriate deliberations, but a deity was consulted and rituals carried out. If the administration was attached to a particular deity, it would seem strange to leave it unsatisfied.[51] Otherwise, men might be forced to come to decisions alone.... Ordinary people who are greatly interested in food and clothes in this life might be inclined to see the worldly deities as more useful and practical than Buddha Shakyamuni. Because there are no rites to the Buddha that are propitious for obtaining long life, riches, and success in business, when it comes to obtaining these worldly goods, most people will trust those deities with all their hearts.[52] But acting in this way, the practice of taking refuge is thrown to the winds and the person ceases to be a Buddhist.
>
> The Tibetan cause is connected to the preservation of Buddhism, which consists of the entire sphere of the Small Vehicle and the Great Vehicle, which includes the

---

[50] This speech was given by His Holiness on July 18, 1980, to the former abbots and the elderly monks of Sera Monastery, the regional committee of Bylakuppe, and the Tibetan Youth Congress.

[51] That is to say, without devotional acts of worship and ritual offerings.

[52] His Holiness continues to define Shugden as a deity.

Mantrayana (or Vajrayana). Both deities and humans must cooperate for the common good.... I lead the government-in-exile known as the Ganden Podrang established by the Fifth Dalai Lama. Thus, when I refer to the deities I mean the guardian deities, and in particular the black Palden Lhamo, and the red Nechung, responsible for the affairs of state.

You, people of Lhasa, from central Tibet, from Kham or Amdo, you should know that during the struggle for our freedom, under the guidance of the Dalai Lama, we must be sincere with each other, and this goes for the deities too. Our private affairs are another matter, and the deity we trust in is an individual choice. But trusting in Gyalchen Shugden damages our common cause, particularly in the monasteries.[53]

During the press conference, with no small feeling of embarrassment about the sensitivity of the issue, I asked a question about the three murders and the mysterious religious conflict behind that horrendous crime, upon which newspapers all over the world had by then already commented upon. The Dalai Lama responded briefly, as he had done on other occasions, that he considered the practice of Shugden a "spirit cult" that was very negative for Tibetan Buddhism, for himself, and for his country's cause. I thought that I would have to content myself with those few words. But soon afterwards his attendants let me know that His Holiness had agreed to grant me a private interview.

I was shown into a room where there were other journalists and, after some general questions on the political situation in Tibet and relations with China, the Dalai Lama said with his usual straightforwardness: "Earlier you asked me a question on the matter of Gyalchen Shugden. It is difficult to explain in a few words what it is all about, especially in front of your colleagues who may be less interested in this subject."

The others all rose automatically and we remained alone. Then he continued, "If you really want to carry out this research seriously, I advise

---

[53] Spring 1991, from a speech on guardian deities and politics given by His Holiness to Tibetans newly arrived from Lhasa.

you to study the entire history. Begin to do so with no preconceptions. You will understand better why I spoke of a dangerous spirit cult. Not only is it contrary to the principles of Buddhism, it also deviates totally from the very tradition of the founders of my school, Atisha and Jey Tsong Khapa, to whose teachings I adhere scrupulously. Since the followers of Shugden claim to be the last and only custodians of the lineage of these masters, I invite you to make an inquiry that is truly free from schemes and prejudices. It will take you to the roots not only of the conflict over Shugden, but of Tibetan culture in general."

For years, whenever anyone asked me why I was attracted to Tibet, I replied that in the teachings of its people there is no dogma of the forbidden fruit of knowledge. A person can face and challenge directly his or her limits of understanding, above all of creation, God and the devil, death and the possibility of reincarnation. These were basically the themes that seemed to be outlined in this strange story unfolding between Tibet, India, and the Western world.

I asked His Holiness if, indeed, when he used the expression "harmful spirit," he meant a demon, and what was his definition of a devil.

"An obstructive force," he replied decisively.

And how can one defend oneself and overcome the obstacle?

"By meditating on love and compassion with an awareness of the interdependence of phenomena and all beings, and developing inner strength."

Do you believe that Shugden may also have an influence on Tibet's problems?

"If the Tibetan people should turn *en masse* to the practice of Shugden, it is hard to foresee a positive effect on the cause of freedom. It would aggravate an already worrying situation. In any case, an ever-greater number of Tibetans are abandoning it."

How would you reply to those who maintain that your doubts about Shugden are a betrayal of your master and tutor, Trijang Rinpoche, the man who introduced you to the cult?

"You see, the Buddha, after declaring himself as an enlightened one, gave us the chance of investigating his words. "Don't follow with blind faith or without analyzing," he said. So even this humble Dalai Lama says, "Don't take my words in blind faith, evaluate them; this is the Buddhist tradition." My master Trijang Rinpoche was a very important lama for me. From him I received immeasurable kindness from when I was a child, and my veneration for him never lessened. Over Shugden I may have developed very different opinions from him, but that does not mean I lost faith in Trijang, nor did I lose faith in my first tutors and instructors, even though they, like all men, committed serious mistakes."

Could you give me an example?

"Take Reting Rinpoche, the Regent who identified my reincarnation, and to whom I therefore owe my position as Dalai Lama. In a letter written in his hand, Reting Rinpoche approved a plot to take the life of his successor, Kyabje Tagdrak, who led the government when I was a child. As an adult, I saw that letter with my own eyes. But even though it was unimaginable for a Buddhist to justify such an action, all the same I did not lose faith in him, although this was hard to understand. In the same way, my faith in Trijang Rinpoche did not weaken..."

Which is...?

A disciple accepts the physical impurities of the master while the master accepts the mental ones of his student, and they find themselves united on the path to knowledge. But, there are more serious considerations. I come from the same teaching lineage as Phabongka and my tutors. But at the same time, since I am seated on the throne of the Dalai Lama, I carry on my shoulders the responsibilities of an institution. From that viewpoint I must evaluate everything, even the errors of my predecessors. For example, I have already said that the Seventh Dalai Lama was not, in my opinion, fully qualified for the throne. But let's not move too far away from your subject."

Speaking of the past, according to Shugden followers, it was precisely the nonsectarian tendency of the Fifth Dalai Lama that was at the origin of the conflict with this so-called guardian. You, in turn, also practice non-Gelukpa teachings, such as the Nyingma and Dzogchen teachings: is this why the controversy has returned after many centuries to divide you and this spirit?

"What we know for certain is that Shugden was controversial from the beginning. As you can see, even his devotees attribute his origin to the conflict with the Fifth Dalai Lama, with whom I feel particularly close. In his autobiography, he calls him a *gyalpo* or *gyalchen*, the "Great *Gyalpo*." He describes him as a very powerful and perfidious spirit, born in his view from twisted prayers harmful to the Buddha's teachings and to sentient beings. I do not know the origin of this spirit, but in the biography of the Second Dalai Lama there is also a description of the influence exerted on the lineage of the Dalai Lamas by a deity, originally from Tsang, from the *gyalpo* class of beings."

So, when you began the practice, you did not know the previous history?

"No, indeed not. It would take too long to explain it all now—how I decided to advise against the cult, the reasons why I experienced for myself the problems that can arise when one trusts these beings, and my many experiences in dreams and divinations. Anyway, history records many cases of negative associations with the practice of Shugden, like the unfortunate failures of the reincarnations of Phabongka Rinpoche."[54]

Nechung, the State Oracle of Tibet, who is consulted on important occasions, is also an emanation of a gyalpo, *Pehar. What is the difference?*

"Just as with humans, not all *gyalpos* are harmful, even though it is not a good idea to create a relationship in which one depends on any of these beings. Gyalpo Pehar, who was subdued by the new religion through the power of Padmasambhava, has always proved reliable both for me and for Tibet's interests. But here we are speaking of worldly deities nonetheless; and very few possess the powers of masters like Padmasambhava, capable of avoiding the possible consequences of a relationship with the *gyalpos*.

"Many guardian deities and oracles, even the state ones, are wrathful mundane beings appearing in various forms but who have not attained

---

[54] See the final section of the chapter on Phabongka.

the state of buddhahood. If you take as your true refuge[55] an oracle or a nontranscendent deity who is not beyond the limits of attachment, your link with the Three Jewels—the Buddha, his teachings, and his religious community—will be lost. Divination, too, should be carried out imagining the benefit of the Three Jewels, and this gives the answer meaning. The state oracles that we consult leave the final decision to me; by now they know me. They consider me their "boss." Nechung explained this to me when I was only five or six years old, and I treat these oracles as if they were friends or servants, unlike some Shugden followers, who regard him as the highest of the gods, ideally entrusting him with their very lives. The Thirteenth Dalai Lama told Phabongka very clearly that if he trusted one hundred percent in Shugden, his Buddhist vows of refuge in the Three Jewels would be lost."

Many believe that one of the main reasons was, let us say, political. When you and the other exiles arrived in India, the Geluk school no longer had the same power or wealth as in the past. Furthermore, the Tibetans needed a guide who would unite all the traditions, not just one. It is said that the heads of the other schools asked you specifically to abandon the cult of the exclusive protector. Is this true?

"No. No one asked me anything of the sort. The previous Dudjom Rinpoche (1904–1987), one of the great Nyingmapa masters, once told me that Shugden was negative for the Tibetan government. He knew that I venerated him at that time, but we were friends, and the fate of our people and the Tibetan government was dear to his heart. Therefore, in certain situations, he gave me guidance and explained dreams that he had had. When I was still in Lhasa, my practice already included some rituals to Vajrakilaya, which belonged to the Nyingma tradition, and I increased these after I moved to India. In this way, I gradually came to appreciate more the nonsectarian practices. Around this time, some texts on Shugden appeared, like Zemey Rinpoche's *Yellow Book*, of which you may have heard, and then, after long and serious reflection I discovered that there was something wrong."

---

[55] The practice of the taking refuge is linked to the principle of spiritual union with the guru who transmits the teachings.

So then, do you see a direct relationship between your decision to embrace teachings from other schools and the way in which Shugden and his followers distanced themselves from you?

"Yes, I had a first indication when I was erecting statues in the main temple of Dharamsala. When some pieces of the Avalokiteshvara statue from the temple in Lhasa arrived in India, I recalled an incident in 1956 or 1957. At that time, Khyentse Rinpoche[56] suggested we put up a statue of Padmasambhava in the central temple in Lhasa. But the appearance of the statue was wrong.[57] And so, still feeling regret, I decided to construct the statue in its correct form in the temple at Dharamsala. Then I received a letter, unsigned but easily recognizable as being from some Gelukpas, that said, "You have placed Padmasambhava's image in the temple but not Tsong Khapa's." This was the first hint I had of the resentment felt by some small-minded Gelukpas."

The Dalai Lama's secretary approached him to explain that the program of ceremonies was not finished yet, and the city authorities were awaiting him for lunch. I was just asking him when he had come into contact for the first time with Shugden for the first time. He let me finish the question and said, "It happened during my first exile in Yatung, on the Indian border. I was fifteen years old when I met his oracle for the first time. But that's a long story, and perhaps we'll have a chance to talk about this again."

As the Dalai Lama stood up to speak to his secretary, one of the assistants who had been present at the interview called me over and asked me to wait. He took some sheets of paper from his bag, looked them over, them and gave me a text no longer than a few pages. "Since His Holiness spoke to you about his exile in Yatung, read this. Anyway, it might give you some ideas."

---

[56] Khyentse Chokyi Lodro, one of the great twentieth-century masters of Dzogchen.

[57] The statue had a peaceful appearance and did not correspond to the Tantric aspect of the celebrated master, who holds a vajra and with his right hand makes the gesture of dominating the demons that, according to Khyentse's advice, can keep at bay any enemy, including the Chinese.

Before leaving the room, the Dalai Lama came back over to say good-bye to me and invited me to visit Dharamsala, if I intended to continue the research. I felt elated, but not without a sense of disquiet. I thought about the small karmic sculpture that I was modeling for myself. What would emerge at the end of this research? I felt as if I were at the entrance to a tunnel with no idea of where I was going and only a single lit torch: my damned curiosity.

As I turned through the pages, I found plenty to satisfy it.

The Devil?

The evening after the interview, I met some colleagues and university researchers for dinner, among whom was a profoundly Catholic intellectual. Inevitably, we spoke of my meeting with the Dalai Lama and about Gyalpo Shugden. But soon the conversation turned to Satan. The professor maintained that a God who had created all things had no doubt a valid reason for introducing at the end of his work the perfect antagonist for "good," be it Satan or Lucifer.

"Maybe God is himself 'good' and 'evil,' if we start with the premise of one creator," I replied to her.

She reacted somewhat dismissively, "Satan exists because humankind has broken the laws of God, and he has continued this villainous revolt."

"And so?" I replied, "Where does this deviance come from, if not from genesis itself? Wasn't it in the very nature of things from the very act of creation? Why weren't human beings created with an immune system equipped with an antidote to evil?"

"Evil is God's way of testing his creatures," she answered.

"But I still don't see the sense of giving life to beings who are destined to unhappiness from the start, when, with all his powers, he could have done the opposite."

My dinner companion seemed to be gathering her thoughts. But then she said in one breath, "It seems that for you, God and the devil is the same person, creator and destroyer...."

"No, actually creation and destruction are inherent in the very nature of the phenomena perceived by the mind." Then I asked her if she knew about the triad of Hindu gods.

"I know that the Hindus believe in a creator-god and in an infinite number of other gods," she said.

"Brahma creates the world, Vishnu protects it, and Shiva destroys it. Of those three, who is the devil?" I asked her.

"I don't know, but if I had to guess I would say Shiva," she laughed as she briskly cut a piece of watermelon.

"But destruction in Hinduism does not correspond to evil; in fact, it is part of a process of regeneration. Shiva is also the god of cemeteries, he does not fear death."

"Do you mean to say that Buddhist demons have that function, too?" she asked me somewhat sarcastically.

"This is the most mysterious but perhaps also the most interesting aspect of this affair that I have been researching. If you don't mind my saying so, you should read some essays by other Asian masters, not only Buddhist ones. Paramahamsa Yogananda was one of the greatest orthodox Hindus of all time. He explained that the goddess Kali, for example, symbolizes the coexistence of the beneficent and the terrible aspects of nature; and that intelligent minds always have reflected on good and evil because they are life's enigmas. Like the Great Sphinx of Egypt, this mystery is a challenge to human intelligence. Those of us who don't try to solve it pay the price of our own lives."

"That's a rather extreme argument," she commented.

"It may seem so. But Buddhism and Hinduism don't set good against bad—I mean in philosophical or absolute terms—in the same way that Catholicism considers the devil to be God's enemy and thus the enemy of good. For Hindus, each one of the innumerable figures in their pantheon represents a different manifestation of God. For Buddhists, existence reveals itself, as each can experience, in peaceful or terrifying form. Nobody can deny this. Without a problem there can be no solution; without attachment, desire, and misfortunes, there is no human life. But even if they didn't exist as external phenomena, it is postulated that each person is born with an inner enemy. Padmasambhava, the master who first expounded Buddhism in Tibet, clearly explained this principle: "When we come into this world, two things are born with us: the *lha* (the divine, the vital essence) and the *dre*, the inner demon. Our inner *lha* is our *rigpa*, the state of primordial knowledge, and the *dre* is *marigpa,* ignorance, which is its opposite." A famous Indian pandit of modern times, Osho Rajneesh, maintained that "as soon as you create God, you also create the devil," and that the word "devil" originates from the Sanskrit root "*deva*," the same term as "divine." So the devil too, is divine, and the divine must carry within something of the devil."

"It seems to be a kind of original sin in a Buddhist version," she said.

"It is more like the birth of a baby with two heads," I answered. "That is why Tibetan deities have perennially opposite appearances, some peaceful like a buddha in meditation and some terrifying."

"But underlying all this philosophizing, isn't there a vacuum of human values, of love for life, for the beautiful things that God gave us? I have read that Buddhists consider all of creation as purely illusion."

"It's true." I took a metal ashtray off the table and showed it to her. "If you have this object melted down, you can give it a new shape as either a statue of an animal, of the Buddha, or of Jesus Christ. Isn't that so?"

The woman laughed wholeheartedly. When we said good-bye at the end of the evening, she went off shaking her head: "An illusion," she repeated, "If only..."

During the return journey from Bolzano, I opened the folder containing the documents that had been handed over to me and I read them from beginning to end, unable to put them down. The texts recounted not only the history of Tibet before the Chinese invasion, but also the true beginning of the relationship between the young Dalai Lama and the demonic spirit.

PART THREE

The Shadow of the New Spirit

Events thrust the fifteen-year-old Dalai Lama toward the new "Protector."

Enthronement

The danger of a Chinese attack on Lhasa was not just a rumor. On January 1, 1950, Radio Peking[58] announced as one of China's resolutions for the New Year its intention "to liberate" Tibet, Hainan, and Formosa from "British and American imperialism." Ten months later, on October 5, the troops of the People's Liberation Army (PLA) already had crossed the Yangtse and, in barely two weeks, they had overrun the meager, poorly organized Tibetan defenses in Kham.

The new governor, Ngabo, was arrested along with numerous dignitaries. Peking, now sure its army would have an easy march to the Tibetan capital, stopped its soldiers in their tracks, giving the government in Lhasa the opportunity to accept formally the "peaceful liberation" of the country.

The Fourteenth Dalai Lama recently had celebrated his fifteenth birthday. Despite his youth, he already was aware that events were driving him to ascend to the throne of Tibet, replacing the old Regent, Tagdrak. His attendants were urging him to take this step as they recounted the rumors abounding in Lhasa. His tutors also mentioned it, and he noticed the increased deference and devotion shown him, even by the high lamas. Up to now they had treated him with all the respect due to his rank, but still as the young boy that he was. The only things missing were divine omens, which soon appeared.

On October 21, after the news of the defeat on Tibet's eastern front, the National Assembly and the Kashag[59] decided, without consulting the State Oracle, to accept one of the principal demands of the enemy for the first time: the declaration that Tibet was part of China. This was communicated to the Tibetan delegation in India led by Shakabpa, along with the order to undertake a mission to Peking to start negotiations.

This decision created high tension and heated arguments between among the potentates in Lhasa, even though the diplomatic note reiterated

---

[58] Also known as Radio Beijing, now China Radio International.

[59] The Dalai Lama's (or his Regent's) cabinet.

that the power of the Dalai Lama and the government had to be guaranteed, together with Tibet's rights regarding foreign trade and defense.

Tagdrak's position vacillated by the hour, both because he had lacked the foresight to create an army worthy of the name, as the Thirteenth Dalai Lama had intended, and also because many highly placed monks in the monastic hierarchy were displeased with his treatment of the ex-Regent, Reting Rinpoche. Furthermore, there were charges of corruption against his ministers. Though the Dalai Lama had not yet finished his studies, everyone was suggesting that he should assume the leadership of the country.

In those days, the young Kundun[60] resided in the summer palace of the Norbulingka, out of touch with these events. However, he listened with great disappointment to the news of the government's decision to submit to Beijing's wishes. "If we accept that we are part of China, then it will be difficult in the future to do what we want," he said in a tone so imperious it surprised ministers and officials. Then he added, "I think that letter was a very bad idea, and I suggest consulting the guardian deities." If he had been an ordinary person, one could have said the Dalai Lama was going through a phase of adolescent affirmation of his personality, and that he was convincing himself of the strength of his spiritual authority and his ability to settle controversies and resolve disputes.

Perhaps he felt that his intuition was not developed sufficiently for him to take on sole responsibility for decisions regarding the welfare of his whole people, but ever since he was a child, those around him had convinced him that he would always have on his side the divine guardians, bound by oath to serve Tibet, its religion, and its leader.

No one opposed him as at certain other times in the past, and in the shrine of the guardian, Gonpo Chagdruk[61] in the Norbulingka, the cabinet invited the mediums with the ability to host the spirits of the oracles. This time it was not Nechung, but Gonpo himself and Palden Lhamo, both protective deities with historical, indissoluble bonds to all the previous incarnations of the Dalai Lama, who were invoked. Their answer confirmed the thoughts of the young Fourteenth Dalai Lama, and a new, peremptory message reached the delegation in India. Shakabpa was astonished

---

[60] Literally, "The Presence," honorific title of His Holiness the Dalai Lama.

[61] A form of Mahakala.

that the counter order had come directly from "His Holiness the Dalai Lama," who was not yet invested as leader of the land.

Less than a month passed before the mediums of the State Oracles, Nechung, and Gadong, also were called upon, this time to decide once and for all if the Dalai Lama definitely should assume temporal power.

There exist different versions of what happened in that session. But many years later, in his autobiography, *Freedom in Exile*, the Dalai Lama accredited a reconstruction that left no doubt as to how the chain of events unfolded that day. As regards Dorje Drakden (the "minister" of Pehar who communicates through the Nechung Oracle), he wrote:

> It was a very tense occasion, at the end of which the *Kuten* medium, tottering under the weight of his huge, ceremonial head dress, came over to where I sat and laid a kata on my lap with the words: *"Thu la bap"* ("His time has come").

It was the beginning of November 1950, and the astrologers studied the constellations to establish the exact date for the enthronement. This was fixed for the 17th, with two odd recommendations, namely that the Dalai Lama was to wear a green sash and to eat an apple.

In his autobiography, Tenzin Gyatso added a detail more important than the colors and the food to an understanding of the atmosphere in the echelons of power in Lhasa at the time.

> Looking back I understood that I shouldn't have been surprised [that my nomination had been brought forward]. For years, the [Nechung] Oracle had shown obvious disdain for the government while he treated me with great courtesy.

At that time, the Dalai Lama's elder brother, Taktser Rinpoche,[62] arrived from Amdo, where he was the Abbot of Kumbum Monastery. Greatly agitated, he recounted how the Chinese had threatened to kill him if he refused to comply with their demand to submit to the new Communist regime. On that occasion, Taktser, after long reflection, decided to renounce his vows and to attempt to convince the United States to

---

[62] Deceased in September 2008.

finance an armed revolt against Beijing. The newly installed leader of Tibet was deeply perturbed and frightened. This influenced his decision to listen to the advice of the lamas and the oracles and to leave Lhasa.

Nobody could predict how it would end, nor that a new element was about to disrupt the future delicate harmony of the relationship between the Tibetans and their gods. A new protector was about to enter the life of the Fourteenth Dalai Lama and the politics of Tibet.

Toward Yatung

The new head of the government decided to follow tradition and to nominate two prime ministers, one lay and one religious. Letters requesting urgent help were sent to the American, English, and Nepalese governments, and a direct appeal was made to the United Nations.

It took several weeks to prepare for the departure to the town of Yatung, on the southern border with India. From there, the Dalai Lama would be able to escape easily over the frontier by walking for a few hours. Several tons of gold ingots and gold dust from the treasury of the Potala, the Dalai Lama's residence and the seat of government in Lhasa, were sent ahead on mules and horses, and detailed itineraries and strategies were studied to make sure that the first stage of the Fourteenth Dalai Lama's escape would pass unnoticed by the people. More than forty years earlier, his previous incarnation also had left Lhasa in fear of the Chinese, then later returning triumphantly to declare Tibetan independence.

On the night chosen by the oracles, the young Kundun, with a certain excitement, put on the layman's clothes that would enable him to move inconspicuously among his people for the first time in his life.

He looked out the window with a sense of freedom he had never experienced before. This was almost stronger than his fear that he no longer would be able to turn back. He stared for a long time at the clear, starry sky of his beautiful Lhasa, lit by a few dim lights, wondering if he ever would return to the vast palace built by the fifth of his line on the sacred hill of Marpori, the residence of Tibet's first king. Not even his guardian deities could give him an answer, nor would he be able to consult them on where he was going, the monastery at Dromo, over three hundred kilometers away in the direction of the border with Sikkim.

The tragic unfolding of events in eastern Tibet seemed to prove right those who dared to doubt the prophecies of faithful spirits trusted for centuries, such as Nechung himself. What other divine arbiter could have guided the choices of the young god-king along the ever more impervious roads of an unfavorable destiny that stood on the horizons of his land? By himself, he was certain that it would be hard to tell the false from the true, torn as he was by the differing advice offered him on every occasion by his counselors, themselves tormented by doubts, envy, and personal rivalries. Undoubtedly the news from the east brought dilemmas that were too heavy a burden for a boy of his age, surrounded by men who placed a blind and indomitable faith in him. Before leaving, he had asked one of his attendants, who was translating a page from an American magazine, whether during their journey they would see skyscrapers such as those in the photos. "Everything is possible through the prayers of His Holiness," was the reply.

The caravan was made up of dignitaries, officials, and heads of monastic institutions. Among them was Trijang Rinpoche, his junior tutor. Trijang tried to ease his pupil's distress at the absence of the mediums that could communicate with his celestial guardians by telling the Dalai Lama that in Dromo, at the Dungkar Monastery, there was a tradition of evoking the peaceful and wrathful aspects of Gyalchen Shugden, a spirit that regularly took possession of an old monk there. Shugden, Trijang told him, protects the Gelukpa school and would know how to guide them through these dark times.

Trijang was the direct disciple of the legendary Phabongka, who lived at the time of the Thirteenth Dalai Lama and died while the Fourteenth was still a child. The junior tutor had become the direct spiritual descendant of that master, who had made the school of the Yellow Hats so illustrious, despite his direct disagreements with the Thirteenth Dalai Lama over the cult of Shugden.

It was an exhausting journey, like every trip across the high plateau, moving on horseback or on foot when the roads become impassable and the animals risked sliding on the crumbling stones made slippery by the snow and ice. At first the young Dalai Lama switched between riding a white horse and a mule to avoid being recognized. Soon, however, he developed a painful bladder complaint and had to be carried in a palanquin by groups of soldiers who took turns along the way. Before revealing his status by riding in that unmistakably privileged means of transport, he had been able to stop and talk anonymously to peasants and nomads, as his predecessor had sometimes done in the inns around Lhasa. There he encountered many monks drinking *chang*, liquor distilled from barley. The fifteen-year-old Kundun wanted to know if his subjects were satisfied with their government and its taxes, with the working conditions in the state-owned fields, and with the conduct of the religious leaders and aristocrats who held so much of that land. He discovered that the people were not, and he promised himself once more to change the terms governing the lives of peasants and the semi-feudal system itself, which favored the arrogant monastic hierarchies and a few rich families while condemning most of the Tibetan people to material misery.

The Dalai Lama often wondered what his life would have been like if, on that winter's morning in 1937, the emissaries of Reting Rinpoche, nominated Regent of Tibet following the death of the Great Thirteenth, had not appeared to recognize him as the incarnation of Avalokiteshvara, the Buddha of Compassion. He was two years old at the time and was playing carefree in his small village in Amdo, in a house with a turquoise-edged roof, exactly as Reting had predicted in his vision that appeared on the surface of the waters of Lake Lhamo Latso.[63]

The name of the Regent who discovered the Dalai Lama came to his mind because, before his flight, in the glow of the dim lights of Lhasa's deserted streets, he had seen the posters put up by the people denouncing Tagdrak Rinpoche, the man who had replaced Reting and guided Tibet until the time of his own enthronement. Their message was unforgiving, accusing Tagdrak of corruption, incompetence, and failing to handle the crisis with China. No one could forget Tagdrak and his aristocratic supporters' bloody treatment of Reting, even though at that time they were all practitioners of not only the same Buddhist teachings but also those of the new protector, Shugden.

One reason, held secret, seemed to explain the course of events that had been set in motion at the highest levels of the ecclesiastical institutions, and thus the government.

Nine years had passed since the oracles had advised Reting that if he wanted to remain in his physical body for long, he should withdraw to a life of prayer and leave his prestigious worldly office. But those well-

---

[63] As a manifestation of the power of the deity Palden Lhamo, visions were seen in that lake that showed the birthplace of the new Dalai Lama.

informed claimed that the true reason for his renouncing the highest seat in the land was that it was impossible for a Gelukpa monk who had broken his Vinaya vows of celibacy to initiate the Dalai Lama as a novice and teach him the thirty-six vows prescribed by doctrinal rules, which included that of abstinence from sex. This was a duty that fell to the Regent, who also served in the role of senior tutor to the young Dalai Lama. However, rumors of Reting's liaisons circulated continuously, both in the corridors of power and also more widely. The fact that someone in his position pursued the secret aims of Tantric practices in union with a consort had long been criticized by the geshes of the great monasteries, who were faithful, at least in word, to their monastic rules.

Such conduct was typical of the *ngagpas* of the Nyingmapa lineage. These mantric practitioners were unconstrained by any such prescriptions that *a priori* excluded alcohol, sex, or any type of worldly pleasure. But the Regent's transgressions caused concern and anger, especially among the growing ranks of Shugden devotees,[64] who were well-known for the severe punishments they inflicted on any transgressor of the scholastic rules of the "Yellow Hats," or "Virtuous" ones.

No one was ever to learn the exact terms of the agreement between Reting and Tagdrak, who was to assume the role of Regent when the Dalai Lama was barely six years old. It was thought that before he became inebriated by absolute power, Tagdrak had promised to restore the Regent's scepter to Reting, once the latter had purified his negative karma in a strict spiritual retreat to restore his vows and remove the obstacles to his health.

But when Reting sought to return to his position in 1947, Tagdrak did not want to oblige and instead had Reting incarcerated. He was accused of leading a plot to kill Tagdrak, in collusion with a faction connected to Chiang Kai-shek, who was still head of the Chinese Nationalist government.

The young Dalai Lama reflected on how he had been kept almost completely in the dark regarding the circumstances that led to Reting's arrest and, shortly afterwards, to his suspicious death in a prison cell. He was stunned, and the posters he now saw in Lhasa reviling Tagdrak reminded him of how dear Reting had been to him.

---

[64] A full description may be found in *The Yellow Book* by Zemey, which currently is being translated by the Library of Tibetan Works and Archives in Dharamsala.

Did he hate Tagdrak for causing Reting's death? He might well have done so had he still been little Tenzin, the herdsman's son from Amdo. His own mother did not particularly like the Regent either, but now he was the leader of Tibet, the Dalai Lama, the bodhisattva who rises above ordinary human judgment and trusts in the implacable higher law of cause and effect. Besides, who could say with absolute certainty that it was Tagdrak's men who had killed Reting and not, as someone had insinuated at the Potala court, the new ferocious guardian deity?

The adolescent Dalai Lama could not yet know how all these goings-on were in fact connected, even if only in the wishes and the words of others. He thought back over the last few days, before he lay down on the camp bed that his attendants had made up for him in the yak-wool tent pitched at the gates of Gyantse. It was well into December, and snow already covered the highest peaks, while the mountain gorges, like the one that His Holiness's caravan had passed through in its flight towards Yatung, gathered misty clouds as thick as cotton wool. It was the ideal route in case an advanced guard of Chinese dared to climb all the way up there in the pursuit of the fugitives.

It was also known in Beijing that from November 17, the Dalai Lama had accepted the urgent requests of the Assembly to bring forward his investiture. But the Chinese had another card to play, apart from their military dominion. This was the Panchen Lama, the second-highest figure in Tibetan Buddhism.

Now that the responsibilities of adulthood bore down on him, at an age when his peers were still playing games and enjoying their first romances, the young Kundun was beginning to realize that enemies were all around, wearing the same religious robes, invoking the same deities, and sharing the same food as he did.

One of his most perplexing problems was the figure of his closest spiritual brother, the Panchen Lama. Since the time of the Great Fifth Dalai Lama, the incarnations of the Dalai and the Panchen Lamas had been born with significant age differences so that they would be master and disciple to one each another and be able to confirm the mutual recognition of their respective rebirths.

Spiritually, the figure associated with the Dalai Lama is Avalokiteshvara, while the Panchen Lama is connected to Amitabha, one of the five transcendent buddhas, the Lord of Infinite Light, before whom Avalokiteshvara undertook his commitment to act as bodhisattva until the ocean of samsaric suffering runs dry. Whatever their celestial status may have been, both were constantly engaged with all the problems of pride and jealousy that the human form entails.

The Tenth Panchen was almost the same age as the recently elected Dalai Lama, being barely three years younger. Since his birth, he had been steered towards the Chinese enemy's sphere of influence, like his previous incarnation. The Ninth Panchen, in fact, had long disagreed with the Lhasa government and never wanted to come to the capital to pay the taxes asked of him. Such was his fear for his life that he announced he would only travel to Lhasa with an escort of five hundred soldiers in the service of the Kuomintang government. This was not allowed, and he died in exile at Jyekundo. After his assistants recognized a young tulku reincarnation named Losang Tseten (later renamed Choekyi Gyaltsen), they refused once again to bring him to Lhasa, when the Tibetan government requested them to do so in order to confirm that he was the rightful incarnation of Buddha Amitabha. These assistants preferred to place him in the hands of the Kuomintang, the Chinese Nationalist government, and when the latter was defeated by the PLA, the eleven-year-old was handed over to the new Communist rulers of China.

The young Panchen immediately sent a letter of congratulations to Mao and Chu Te, the leader of the army of liberation.

> With superior wisdom and courage Your Excellencies have accomplished the grand salvation of the country and the people.... The success of your army has brought joy to the whole country. From now on, the realization of the democratic happiness of the people and revival of the country are only questions of time and it will not be long before Tibet is liberated. I sincerely present to Your Excellencies on behalf of all people in Tibet our highest respect and offer our heartfelt support.

The Dalai Lama knew well that a master, a bodhisattva who had delayed his departure for nirvana to suffer in the midst of humanity, should not have interpreted those words as a personal betrayal. But his present body shook with indignation, even though the Panchen was obviously dominated "by his Chinese advisers," as he was to write many years later.[65] With hindsight, the Panchen Lama added, "If he and his monks had overcome the differences created by our predecessors, Tibet's disaster might not have been so complete."

The problem was that in eastern Tibet, the flank most exposed to the enemy, the Panchen and his monks were not the only ones to believe in the Chinese "liberation." In the regions inhabited by the fierce Khampa warriors, with their long hair plaited with colored strings, a number of monks and laypeople were aligned with the "People's Liberation Army,"[66] and many had sympathized with the Chinese Communists ever since the Long March in the 1930s.

At the time of his journey to Yatung, the young Dalai Lama was not yet aware of the influence of his master's teacher, Phabongka Rinpoche, over many Gelukpa lamas in eastern Tibet. After the death of the Thirteenth Dalai Lama, Phabongka had resumed his campaign of "purification" against the "shamanic" Bon practices and "false" Nyingmapa lamas and *tertons*.[67] In the 1940s, a large number of monasteries in the most orthodox Geluk tradition sprang up in the regions where many masters of the Rimey movement, nonsectarian and opposed to the exclusive approach of the Lhasa government, had been teaching.

Only many years later did the young Dalai Lama learn that many Tibetans in the east saw the Geluk School as the long arm of Lhasa, imposing taxes and pressing them with physical coercion to convert to the "pure" doctrine of Tsong Khapa and also to the "divine" force of the protector Shugden.

Phabongka's followers had, without the Dalai Lama's knowledge, destroyed numerous statues of Padmasambhava and other deities worshipped in different schools. They spread the idea that reciting the mantras of Padmasambhava was worthless, and burned or flung into the river many copies of the biography of Padmasambhava, the *Padma Kathang*. They challenged the practice of spinning prayer wheels (*mani khorlo*) and disputed the value of weekly ceremonies for the dead. Many monks from

---

[65] My Land, and My People, 1962.

[66] The best known was Geshe Sherab Gyatso, former Abbot of the College of Sera Jey.

[67] *Tertons* are said to be discoverers of secret teachings hidden in the time of Padmasambhava.

the smaller monasteries of the south, in the name of Shugden, went around destroying images of the Buddha, scriptures, and stupas.[68]

At Yatung

On its flight from Lhasa, the caravan reached Yatung on January 2, 1951, after two weeks of journeying. A thick, heavy snow had whitened the monastery and the houses in the villages, barely twenty kilometers from the border of the Indian state of Sikkim. As if by a spell, the excitement over the arrival of the Dalai Lama and his court had transformed the Dromo valley, a place that usually seemed suspended in time, with a pure nature between earth and sky, perfect, impeccable, primordial.

The monks had been waiting since dawn for the caravan, and the novices, little more than children, ran up and down the roofs of the monastery and the houses in a state of euphoria. The elders were fingering the beads of their *mala* rosaries incessantly, trying to calm their excitement about meeting on such close terms the Gyalwa Rinpoche, the boy incarnation of their savior, whom very few had even glimpsed on their pilgrimages to Lhasa.

Here he was, arriving in a palanquin surrounded by monks and his escort. When he came close to the first houses, set like a crown around the valley of Chimbu, white scarves were thrown in the air and men and women prostrated on the road, obliging the guards to remove them by force, while the smoke of the juniper branches from the *sang* rite and the sound of a hundred trumpets, drums, cymbals, and gongs filled the air and the sky itself.

For a month the Dalai Lama established his quarters in the District Governor's residence, renamed for the occasion the Heavenly Palace of Universal Light and Peace, before he moved into the monastery.

In the temple, warmed by butter lamps and made fragrant by incense, the monastic community recited the invocations to the deities as a good omen for the Dalai Lama's sojourn in Yatung, and for his government-in-exile. All were aware that this was no pleasure trip, but a long-deliberated and grave choice. Indeed, the travelers had rested but a few hours when

---

[68] Mentioned in the biography of Jigme Dhamchoe Gyatso, written by Tsetan Zhabdrung, 1910–1985.

messengers from Lhasa arrived with the latest news from India, where the delegation had been ordered to negotiate with the Chinese, with the agreement of the British and American governments. A place to welcome His Holiness had also been prepared there, should he be obliged to cross the Himalayan border to escape the troops from Beijing.

Yatung was an enchanting spot, and his room was simple and hospitable, but the risk of losing his country and his people dominated His Holiness's mind, as yet unprepared for the bitter emotional experiences of samsara. He was especially troubled at what he had learned from his brother Taktser. But what could have been done to prevent things going Beijing's way? Very little. The threat remained, looming, terrible, and the waiting was slow agony.

It was even clearer the following day, when the terms of the latest political agreement provided for the arrival of a Chinese official in Lhasa to negotiate a "peaceful" agreement of the sort India was urging, which indeed common sense appeared to dictate.

The long ritual offerings to the ferocious warrior deities, invoked to protect faithful Tibetan Buddhists from every adversary, had accomplished nothing. Until then, all the efforts of great lamas and yogis, scholars, monks and abbots, and the people themselves, had had no effect: the guardian deities had seemed deaf and mute, blind, indifferent—or else simply powerless.

Certainly, Nechung and Gadong had continued to offer their oracular prophecies, although their interpretations were uncertain and often laconic. But in general, they seemed distant and absent, and the Dalai Lama could not understand what had rendered these extraordinary powers so weak.

It was not the first time since Padmasambhava imposed the Buddha's law on Tibet that the religious and political harmony of this kingdom at the roof of the world risked being shattered. But the young Dalai Lama could not comprehend what had happened in eastern Tibet to so harm the doctrine of the Great Exorcist.

Now that he had assumed the role of leader of his people, he thought that the injustices, the harsh nomadic lifestyle, and the social differences created by rank between monks and lamas, people and aristocracy, could be the true cause of this bad karma and the problems it had brought. The Chinese Communists, for him, symbolized the hostile force created by wrongful action; the enemy allowed to enter the Land of Snows by a ruling elite that had taken advantage of the people's devotion to accumulate riches in their dominion over a powerless multitude.

But his subjects did not deserve this. The people were not to blame, and the young Kundun could not tolerate the Chinese boasts of being the saviors of the voiceless oppressed. He thought of the great spiritual masters such as Milarepa, who lived on nettles, and of Machig Labdron,[69] one of the powerful female adepts who have shaped the history of the Vajrayana, and of the many simple unknown meditators, in the caves of central, western, and eastern Tibet who had served the dharma of compassion and obtained the "body of light."

What would the Chinese do to all those yogis and yoginis secluded in their hermitages preparing for enlightenment? Would they hunt them down and persecute them in the heart of the mountains? Would they empty out the monasteries?

Never before had he studied so intently the figures of the guardian deities in the *thangkas* hung in every corner of his room. Something had happened that His Holiness did not yet understand, something that had destroyed the harmony and interrupted the communication between human beings and their guiding spirits.

Even those he imagined as "good" in the West, such as the United Nations, had refused to help. This led him to consider the legacy of the actions of the clergy, the heads of the great Gelukpa monasteries in particular, who had hindered every attempt made by his predecessor to open his country to the world. English schools had been closed and gifts from Americans and Europeans refused and returned.

As for himself, he still hoped to have a chance to make changes. He had brought along the watch given to him by Franklin Delano Roosevelt, the President of the United States. Its mechanism, which he had so patiently dismantled and reassembled many times, had become for him a symbol of the material world. This world could have its advantages. It was easy to fall victim to its illusions, but it was a dimension in which science had been able to save millions of human lives.

---

[69] Machig Labdronma (eleventh century); the great yogini who first developed and taught the Tantric practice of the "Chod," the aim of which is to sever attachment to the ego and to the material body.

He thought about the great worldly power of technology and was no longer so sure that it was enough to invoke the guiding spirits and guardians to protect millions of Tibetans and their monasteries and stupas; especially if their wishes and suggestions had been disregarded. With all this in mind, an alternative course of action offered by the new and ferocious protector seemed increasingly worth considering. No one had yet explained to him that Shugden was essentially the same spirit that had been worshipped for three centuries by the extremist Gelukpas, the antagonists of his predecessors, the Fifth and Thirteenth Dalai Lamas.

To console him, Trijang Rinpoche said, "The wisdom guardians manifest in worldly form according to the type of being they are in contact with, their inclinations and interests. Sometimes, therefore, they may appear blemished. To those whose minds are not purified and are immersed in dualism, the guardians appear as violent spirits, reflecting their own negative emotions. But for those who dwell in a pure state of mind, they will appear as guardians of primordial wisdom. This means that no guardian, worldly or otherwise, exists autonomously or in intrinsic reality."

As the young Dalai Lama listened to him in silence, Trijang continued, "Depending on the purity of one's mind, Shugden may appear as worldly or otherwise."

With complete faith in his tutor, Kundun sent for the abbot of the monastery. He was a rather old geshe, although his face was unwrinkled and his eyes twinkled like a child's when offered sweets to eat. He prostrated three times and asked what he could do for His Holiness.

"My master Trijang Rinpoche explained to me that there is a tradition in this monastery of invoking Gyalchen Shugden. Can we rely on the medium of this protector?"

"Your Holiness, when he speaks, you would never imagine that the oracle is a poor ignorant monk. You know how many harsh trials a *kuten* medium must undergo, and our medium is even capable of welcoming the spirit of the guardian Sertrap[70] within him when he is in trance."

The young Dalai Lama had the man summoned. Left alone, he thought about the story of the monk who became the State Oracle Nechung. His name was Lobsang Jigme, and he was a child novice. At the age of ten,

---

[70] The spirit that is said to have saved Drakpa Gyaltsen during a fire offering at the time of the Fifth Dalai Lama.

he was struck by a form of madness that made him hallucinate and suffer extreme mental disturbances. He was moved to Ganden Monastery, where the expert lamas immediately understood that the young monk was experiencing true states of trance. It was not, however, the guardians of the teachings that were manifesting, but lesser deities, that created particular psychic conditions and were using the subtle energy channels of the medium. So Lobsang underwent a process of purification that enabled him to receive the principal deity, none other than Dorje Drakden, or Nechung, the State Oracle of Tibet.

In him, certainly, the Dalai Lama had an absolute faith. He recalled, from his childhood, the accounts of the tests the medium underwent. In his trance, he was able to know exactly what was in three sealed folders. For the so-called internal test, he was presented with the prophecies Nechung had given to the Tibetan government in centuries past. They were prophecies known only to a few and kept under waxed seals in the secret rooms of the Potala. The Nechung Oracle repeated their words exactly, and this was but one of many such trials. At the end of the trance came the final exam, when an unmistakable odor came from the mouth of every medium, a sign of the passage of the spirit. Lobsang Jigme, too, had passed this test, although he was now not with them at Yatung.

What would the oracle of Shugden be like? The Dalai Lama did not have to wait long for the answer. But the ever-worsening news from Kham made him edgy, and the slightest divine signal would have been welcome. Unaware of the complications of the past, he had no doubts when he recalled the veneration shown to Shugden by the other great lamas of his own tradition: Dakpo Rinpoche and Jey Phabongka. Among the living, besides his master Trijang and Geshe Zemey with him at Yatung, the former Regents Tagdrak and Reting Rinpoche, Song Rinpoche, and Geshe Rabten were also worshippers.

The Medium of the Spirit

The Dalai Lama immediately recognized the old monk presented to him as the medium of the protector Shugden. On the day of his arrival, he had seen him in his simple monk's robes, but now he was sumptuously adorned in yellow silk and wearing a pandit's hat, which gave him a dignified air. He seemed immensely tall when he entered, surrounded by six monks who stood ready to restrain him in case he should be possessed with particular violence.

Damaru drums, metal cymbals, trumpets, and bells accompanied the slow, almost imperceptible head movements of the head of this increasingly impressive figure. He sat on a throne opposite the Dalai Lama, whispering softly while the deep voices of the monks intoned the invocation to the Hundred Deities of the Joyous Land. The Dalai Lama recognized in those chants the style of Sangphu Monastery, unmistakable to ears trained to attend religious ceremonies during which the resonance of a mantra is calibrated like the pitch of a perfectly tuned musical instrument.

All of a sudden, the medium rose from his throne and started to whirl, as if lifted by the armpits towards some undefined point on the ceiling. From the altar, where several ritual weapons had been laid out, he grasped a sword with remarkable speed. The moment it was in his hands, it seemed to light up like a flame. The monks were impressed and drew back, while the six monks there to hold him back surrounded the oracle in case he came too close to those present, the Dalai Lama in particular. The medium brandished the weapon as if surrounded by a thousand enemies, and just as the abbot feared the worst, his assistants dragged him towards the throne.

The monk then sat down, let them take the sword, and appeared to be frozen in a state of total absence, almost as if his spirit had abandoned his body definitively. But all could sense a presence within that man whose features appeared diaphanous in the shafts of light that seemed to pierce the walls, projecting onto his face. It was a vigilant, attentive, deliberately controlled presence.

The old monk from Dungkar Gonpa approached the oracle at that precise moment, bending forward to touch the ground with his head.

"Mighty Protector, we invoke your transcendent wisdom for the benefit of the teachings and the infinite beings in samsara. I pay homage to you, the deity who defeats all enemies of the teachings of the Yellow Hats. Your manifestation and your actions are an infinite, transcendent, inconceivable magic dance, a jewel that fulfills the wishes of the vase of fortune. I bow before you, who satisfy the needs of the beings of the six worlds."

The medium remained so still he might have been a wax statue, but his eyes began to light up like hot coals stirred by intermittent breaths of wind.

Thereupon the monk read the letter of supplication, written on parchment by His Holiness and the Tibetan government-in-exile, requesting the advice of the oracle. They wanted to know whether it would be useful to bring to Yatung the Tibetan delegation just then at Kalimpong in India, where it was authorized to negotiate with Pandit Nehru's government, and specifically with the Chinese ambassador in Delhi.

Barely a few seconds had passed before the medium rose and, moving with dance steps and sudden jerks, stood directly in front of the Dalai Lama, in whose presence he folded over like a felled tree. In clear sentences understood by all, spoken through the mouth of the medium, the spirit advised that all the Tibetan emissaries then in India be summoned to Yatung. They had to come together to discuss what was happening in Kalimpong and to take new instructions.

Those days in Yatung waiting for the delegation were spent in trepidation. Led by Shakabpa, the Tibetan representatives in India arrived before dark. In the morning, they were called before the assembly of monastic officials, ministers, and other high-ranking dignitaries of the administration. After giving an initial report, they were allowed time to rest.

For almost twenty years, Shakabpa had been Finance Secretary. The special relationship that his family maintained with the former Regent, Tagdrak, was born of friendship with Phabongka Rinpoche. Shakabpa was not tall, but with his bearing and fierce expression, eyes concealed by small, modern eyeglasses, and a steady gaze, he commanded the respect and awe of those with whom he dealt. However, that day it was he who felt a certain embarrassment, as an icy draught draft swept the room where he had been summoned before the highest ranks of Tibetan religious and civil society. He felt as if arraigned as if by a tribunal, almost as if it were he were responsible for the recent international humiliations suffered by Tibet. The Chinese invasion of Chamdo had been met by the world with silence, and the United Nations refused to discuss the issue before the General Assembly. Only cordial but dismissive letters had arrived from the British and the Americans, while India was afraid to confront its powerful and menacing neighbor.

No one thought at the time that the West's cold response might have been the consequence of the path of isolation chosen by Tibet's ecclesiastical hierarchy since the time of the Thirteenth Dalai Lama, out of their fear that the religious tradition of the Land of the Snows might be contaminated by the materialistic West.

Shakabpa did not allow himself to be overwhelmed by the atmosphere in that assembly of officials, even though it had an unfavorable effect on him. After all, he had been brought up in an elite family, and his relationship with the Dalai Lamas had begun long before His Holiness the Fourteenth had been recognized as a *tulku* in his Amdo village.

The young Dalai Lama stared at him with a worried air, and before the hostile gathering Shakabpa gave him an encouraging and cheerful look. He thought back over all the orders and counter-orders he had received from Lhasa before this move to Yatung. He knew they had been the result of some controversial divinations, but he still remembered the embarrassment of having to announce and then immediately deny to the Indians and Chinese, with no strategic or political justification, that he had received the go-ahead for negotiations. He had never been bold enough to tell his counterparts that these changes were attributable to the predictions of an oracle.

The assembly listened in silence as Shakabpa gave a detailed account of his unsuccessful attempts to find international support for the Tibetan cause. The British, who had just ceded their colonial power to a newly independent India, had refused him a visa to go to Hong Kong to contact the Chinese directly. As for the Indian leader, Nehru, Shakabpa said he had expressed solidarity but in practical terms did not feel obliged to do anything, suggesting negotiations as the only plausible option. Both the British and the Americans were aware that China had attacked the eastern region of Tibet with the intention of proceeding sooner or later to Lhasa. However, their diplomatic letters, examined individually, revealed those nations' embarrassment. Great Britain, especially, knew full well how things stood legally,[71] and yet allowed Tibetan sovereignty to be placed in doubt. Her Majesty's representatives let it be known that they thought the bordering nation, India, should protest to Beijing directly.

Objections actually had been made a few days before; two brusque and threatening letters were sent by Delhi to the regime of the new People's Republic of China. But when Mao Zedong replied that this was an

---

[71] The Simla Convention was a treaty signed by Britain, Tibet, and Nationalist China in 1914 that defined boundaries and recognized at least "Outer Tibet" (present "Tibet Autonomous Region") as retaining its own national sovereignty, with China only exercising a kind of "suzerainty" or protector role over the nation. The Chinese plenipotentiary's signature was repudiated back in Beijing afterwards, but that circumstance was provided for in the treaty, and so the provisions of the treaty were considered still binding on Britain and Tibet.

"internal Chinese affair" and he had no wish to harm India's commercial interests, the subsequent steps taken by the Nehru cabinet were decidedly less aggressive.

Shabkabpa summarized the terms of the appeal to the United Nations, which he had written as best he knew how, but only the small nation of El Salvador took the trouble to respond. Every other country, hid behind impeccably measured speeches in the UN General Assembly of November 24, 1959, regarding the chances of a peacefully negotiated settlement. Further discussion was postponed to a date to be determined; but that parley was never to be held.

Was there any reasonable hope now of preventing the Chinese troops from entering Lhasa? The diplomat's bitter assessment was that it did not depend upon him, nor upon the two prime ministers left at the Potala, nor on the consensus of the Tibetan dignitaries, lay and religious, now gathered at Yatung. Neither, it pained him to say, did it depend on His Holiness.

Given the previous complex, sudden changes of strategy and the atmosphere that confronted him at Yatung, Shakabpa was not surprised when the Kashag decided to replace him and instead sent to Delhi a delegation formed by other dignitaries, Dzasa Surkhang Surpa and the Secretary-General Chompel Thubten, briefed to mend relations with the Chinese and to meet their ambassador in Delhi. Shakabpa decided to return immediately to Kalimpong, since the small town of Yatung seemed so filled with hostile energy. But, hostility toward whom? He decided to wait a few hours before leaving, in order to gather his strength and to see some old acquaintances.

The Seventeen Points

After the delegation to meet the Chinese ambassador had left, the monks exchanged opinions in the city streets and in the cells of their monasteries about the latest prophecy of the Shugden Oracle. They took pride in having offered to His Holiness the services of Dromo Dungkar Monastery's preferred protector, their principal guardian.

Even this idea of sending a mission to patch up relations with China seemed the fruit of Shugden's clairvoyance, and when the two emissaries returned to Yatung from India, the general mood of satisfaction seemed justified. The Secretary-General, Chompel, had in fact announced the Chinese ambassador in Delhi's request to send a Tibetan delegation to

Beijing, for talks with no preconditions. He then showed the newly assembled dignitaries a small bust of Mao Zedong, given him by the diplomat. Everyone was impressed when Chompel noisily slammed the statuette of the Great Helmsman on the table declaring, "I have cut off Mao's head and brought it here."

Who is to say whether it was the effect of that ingenious gesture or the Shugden Oracle that influenced the Kashag and the Dalai Lama? The fact remains that the Chinese ambassador's request for a delegation to be sent directly to Beijing was accepted without a single objection. The dignitaries who had left from Lhasa and Yatung met up again in Chamdo with the new Governor of Kham, Ngabo, who had been held hostage by the Chinese since the day of the invasion. Together, they set off for the Chinese capital, Peking.

In this climate of optimism, the young Dalai Lama thought that he should reward the Shugden Oracle, and he proposed his elevation to the rank of Assistant State Oracle.

But this apparent progress proved as ephemeral as the clouds blowing over the valley of Chumbi. Some mistakenly might have considered the ambassador's gesture of giving the present of Mao's head to the naïve Tibetan functionary as symbolically positive. But no one could doubt a trap was prepared for the new delegation sent from Yatung to Beijing. Once there, they had no choice but to succumb to the enemy's pressure. With the rifles of the PLA metaphorically held to their heads, the Tibetan delegates signed practically all of the seventeen articles of the so-called Treaty on the Forms of Peaceful Liberation of Tibet. Foremost among these, naturally, was the recognition of Chinese sovereignty over Tibet.

At the time, however, very few regarded the political forecasts of the Shugden Oracle as mistaken. This may have been because every decision had to take into account the prevailing enemy forces; or, perhaps it was because His Holiness's court by then was already formed largely of followers of the new guardian.

One further detail, though, casts the shadow of the new spirit over this chapter in Tibet's history. Before negotiating each of the seventeen points, the Party leaders asked insistently what the Tibetan government had decided to do about the recognition of the Tenth Panchen Lama. Did they consider him the *tulku* of his predecessor or not? Official documents record that His Holiness, in particular, requested another divination, and that it was affirmative. No one has yet clarified whether the answer came from a simple *mo*[72] divination or from the Shugden Oracle. What is certain is that the guardian had enjoyed a long relationship with some of the Panchen Lamas, including this Tenth, the present one, in whom the Chinese took such an interest.[73]

After the signing of the Seventeen Point Agreement, the Dalai Lama asked a final question of Shugden: regarding whether to return to Lhasa or to leave the country. The answer was that he should return to Lhasa. After his first brief exile and before his definitive escape to India, another eight years filled with difficult decisions awaited him.

---

[72]An ancient form of simple divination performed either with the use of a mala, three dice, stones, colored knotted cords, or sticks, and accompanied by the recitation of a specific mantra.

[73] The Tenth Panchen Lama was a worshipper of Shugden.

War Among the Lamas

Reviewing the events of one of the most critical chapters of Tibetan history, a period the importance of which perhaps has been underestimated, leaves no doubt of the significance attached by Tibetans to the mysterious mediation between human beings and deities. My encounter with the Dalai Lama strengthened my conviction that even today, almost sixty years after he made his difficult start as leader of his people, that secret relationship established with unknown primordial and non-material beings continues to influence his decisions.

In the new equilibrium created over half a century of living in exile in India and cultivating contacts with the rational Western world, that relationship could have proved embarrassing and counterproductive for the Buddhist spiritual leader's cause, especially right after a triple homicide on his doorstep.

Returning to Rome from Bolzano, I told my newspaper's editor-in-chief about my talk with the Dalai Lama, explaining the implications of the police inquiries and the religious and spiritual background of the Shugden case. He asked me to write an article entitled, "The War of the Lamas."

Attracting readers is a vital need for the media, and when there is a crime on this scale, and an esoteric one at that, it is difficult for editors to resist the theatrical phrase. "The War of the Lamas" was certainly more compelling than a simple "Mystery at Dharamsala." Besides, it was not altogether inaccurate; events had unfolded among prominent religious figures, some in the inner entourage of Tibet's spiritual leader. And this was not all. Among the papers found in the investigations was a list of fourteen high dignitaries in the Tibetan government-in-exile. According to the police, these may have been the next targets of those who had sent out the murderers on February 4. That list was headed by His Holiness Tenzin Gyatso, the Fourteenth Dalai Lama.

The suggestion was disturbing, to say the least. To me, it seemed improbable and verged on the outrageous, even if the way in which the director of the School of Dialectics and his two translators were killed boded ill. Certainly, the affair went deeper than a simple crime story. The meticulous planning of the massacre in that small room by near the main temple of Dharamsala, the suspicions surrounding the Delhi group that had formed an organization in the name of this demonic force, the constant

170

tension in the Tibetan settlements, and the repercussions in the various Buddhist centers in Italy and elsewhere in the West all had to be considered. I thought back to the Dalai Lama saying that everything is connected to the roots of Tibetan culture, to the dangerous nature of certain beings. I then recalled a later, stimulating conversation on the topic of the *gyalpo* with Chogyal Namkai Norbu. To be sure, the intriguing question of whether the conflicts were of a human or nonhuman nature was not merely of secondary importance.

A Western scholar, Philippe Cornu,[74] defines the *gyalpos* as "Spirit-Kings" (*gyalpo* also means "king"), or more precisely, "spirits of demon kings or of high lamas whose religious vows have been corrupted." This description seemed to accord with that of the lamas. In his work, *Oracles and Demons of Tibet*, considered a reliable source regarding the so-called local gods and guardians of the teachings, the Lokapalas ("world-protectors") and Dharmapalas ("Dharma-protectors") of Tibetan Buddhism, René de Nebesky-Wojkowitz[75] defines Pehar as "the chief of all the *gyalpo* demons." He also devotes an entire chapter to Dorje Shugden, "Powerful Lightning Bolt," as the name translates, who dwells surrounded by meteorites, flames, black turbulent winds, and the waves of a stormy sea of blood. Nebesky-Wojkowitz describes many details in the official iconography: trees that flower out of season; booming thunderclaps and blinding flashes of light; crows, owls, and flocks of demonic birds; decomposing bodies around a pagoda with a three-tiered roof in the Chinese style made of skeletons, human heads, and hearts; and the carcasses of tigers and lions. Gold effigies and precious stones such as red agates, diamonds, corals, and pearl-studded doors are also depicted.

Inside this fearsome place abides the so-called Lord of Religion, Gyalchen Shugden, "he who possesses total concentration of the mind, the King of the mind, the terrifying being who destroys all those who behave like demons, the enemies of the [Geluk] doctrine."

---

[74] Philippe Cornu is a teacher of Tibetan astrology at INALCO, the National Institute of Oriental Civilizations and Languages in Paris.

[75] The Austrian René de Nebesky-Wojkowitz (1923–1959) was an ethnologist and Tibetologist. He traveled for many years in the Himalayan regions and wrote a number of works on popular religion and the cults of Tibetan deities. He was a consultant to the Museum für Völkerkunde in Vienna.

I had to admit that, leaving superstition and these blunt iconographical descriptions aside, the prospect of a voyage into this world of demons and spirits was not in itself enticing. But in my line of work, I already had been forced to deal with terrorist plots, espionage, the Mafia, and political intrigue. Now, it seemed, had come the moment for me to take on the supernatural inhabitants of the other world.

After the publication of the article, I received numerous phone calls. A woman residing in northern Italy who introduced herself as a former devotee told me she had cut all her ties with Ganchen Tulku's Buddhist center. "They tried to say I was crazy," she added. "But I'm not crazy."

Another reader, an Englishwoman named Yvonne, living in Sicily, was of the opposite opinion. For years, she said, she had been a disciple of a Tibetan lama known as Kundeling who was dedicated to the cult and whom she called "His Holiness." I knew that this honorific was reserved for the Dalai Lama and the heads of the other most important orders, but I had never heard of a "Kundeling." Yvonne continued very politely, saying that she wished to furnish me with information to clarify all the errors in the article. She also told me that "His Holiness" would soon be passing through Milan and was planning to go to Ganchen's center.

My journey seemed about to take a new direction. Was I ready for this? Maybe, as Carlos Castaneda wrote in the accounts of his meetings with the Mexican master Don Juan, I needed an "ally," a figure actually not so distant from the concept of "protector" in Tibetan Buddhism. To be certain, just as Shugden was considered the guardian of one of the schools, the other Tibetan traditions also had their own guardians. There were deities faithful to the old Nyingma, to the Kagyu, and to the Sakya lineages, to the Dalai Lamas; and to Tibet in general.

Just then, Chogyal Namkhai Norbu had returned from one of his lecturing tours, and I went to visit him at home at the foot of Monte Amiata in Tuscany to ask him if the "guardians" of the Dzogchen teachings could be invoked easily. "In Dzogchen the best protection is the practice of awareness," he said. As always, his words left a mark. I had a dream that made a strong impression on my mind. A man wearing a large hat was sitting on a low wall along a busy road that I often used on my scooter. I usually came from another direction, so I didn't recognize that crossroads, but I remembered the man well because of his wide-brimmed hat. I came back to him repeatedly to ask the way until, out of embarrassment, I woke up. This I interpreted as a sign of my fears of wandering, not just aimlessly, but with no reference point whatsoever. Evidently, the dream was a projection of repressed ancestral fears. These were linked to the various scattered activities in which I wasted most of my time, without focusing on a true or meaningful personal goal. In short, I lacked that presence Namkhai Norbu had told me was our main protection in daily life.

When I awoke, I had little doubt that the man in the dream was none other than Norbu Rinpoche. It was he who had made the distant culture of Tibetan Buddhism familiar to me and connected it to my own ways of observing and reflecting. I came to know of him through his work as an academic. His publications on history and religion have been translated into many languages since his arrival in Italy in the 1960s as the main consultant to Professor Giuseppe Tucci, one of the most celebrated Tibetological scholars and archaeologists of all time.

Rinpoche's own principal master ("root lama") was named Rigdzin Changchub Dorje, and Chogyal Namkhai Norbu often said he had learned more from this very old lama, who lived for over 120 years and died in the 1960s, than from his long years of study in the monastic colleges of eastern Tibet. At the end of the nineteenth century, in the village of Khamdogar, Changchub Dorje had founded a community of students who led a simple life, cultivating the land and applying the principles of the Dzogchen Path of Great Perfection. According to the disciples' predispositions, the master explained both the methods of renunciation of the Hinayana tradition and the Vajrayana way of Tantric transformation. But essentially, he did not insist on any particular religious practice, only the "awareness" that Norbu Rinpoche had spoken of to me. Indeed, the significance of his teaching was condensed in this principle of "presence." In Dzogchen, external vows have a function secondary to self-discipline, which is based on the understanding that we alone are responsible for our actions and for our progress in the practices to control the mind. But, in this case, too, the capacity to maintain one's presence in the state of calm does not require any intellectual effort; indeed, the opposite is true.

I remembered that some years earlier, when I traveled in Tibet with Namkhai Norbu, we had reached Khamdogar from Derge, his birthplace, after riding many hours on horseback, crossing the Yangtse River and journeying deep into eastern Tibet. The valley, over 3,000 meters above sea level, was surrounded by mountains, none particularly high, and dotted with many caves where hermits and yogis spent their lives in meditation.

These caves formed a crown over the small village, below which a clear river flowed. In one of the houses, the old master Changchub Dorje's body had been preserved secretly in salt for 30 years. Inspired by the special energy of that isolated haven in the heart of the Himalayas, under skies as blue and limpid as alpine lakes, I asked Norbu an infinite number of questions on the meaning of Tantra, translated in Tibetan as *gyud*, literally "continuity."

"The meaning of this continuity," he told me, "is the natural condition of the mind from the beginning, in which the state of calm and the movements of thought constantly alternate." He explained that the calm state manifests the pure, primordial essence of emptiness, which both precedes and at the same time constitutes the base, or source of all phenomena. The movement of thought is also part of the nature of clarity. It is a nature "without interruption" because the flow of thoughts that arise is incessant; thus, we cannot separate their origin from that "non-place" that is the source of all phenomena. This is an emptiness quite different from the concept of "nothingness," since unlike nothingness, emptiness has an intrinsic creative power. What we perceive through the senses we cannot call "nothing."

"But our true condition," he explained to me, "is like this sky above us, which has no obstacles or knots; there is nothing to loosen and free, nothing to renounce or to transform. In this state of transparency and clarity, it is easier to identify a thought when it arises. You recognize it just as you would a cloud that suddenly crosses pure, uncontaminated space and then vanishes." I reflected on how no cloud—clouds being by nature as ephemeral as our moods and ever shifting like the positive and negative circumstances of our lives—can change or affect the nature of empty space. In the same way, no thought, no concept, no method, ritual, prayer, or curse can modify the essential nature of the mind. Remaining "present," then, means abiding in this original state in which one can perceive and reflect without being influenced by perceptions and reflections. In Dzogchen, this is called "the state of contemplation," and it requires no particular techniques. No vows of renunciation are needed because, from the beginning, the emotions disturbing us are identified as manifestations of the primordial state of which they are part; and so the effort of eliminating and transforming them becomes meaningless. Rather, they become integrated and are "self-liberated."

The refusal of the extremist Gelukpas to consider valid the self-liberation principles of the Dzogchen and Nyingma teachings has been openly contested by the Dalai Lama. In his book, *Kindness, Clarity, and Insight*, the erudite Tibetan leader makes a very clear comparison of the two main approaches; the new Vajrayana translations, particularly the Geluk ones, and the ancient translations, which have by now become part of his own daily practice:

> In the New Translation Schools actualization of the fundamental mind simultaneous with the manifestation of the six operative consciousnesses[76] is impossible. It is necessary first to dissolve all coarser consciousnesses to render them as though incapacitated; only then will the fundamental mind nakedly appear. It is impossible for coarse and subtle consciousnesses, functioning to comprehend objects, to occur simultaneously. However, in the Old Translation School of the Great Perfection, it is possible to be introduced to the clear light, without the cessation of the six operative consciousnesses. Even when an afflictive emotion is generated in an encounter with an object upon which we falsely superimpose a goodness or badness beyond its actual nature, the afflictive emotion itself has the nature of being an entity of pure luminosity and knowing.... Leaving the coarser consciousnesses as they are, the yogi identifies the clear light.[77] When this has been done, it is not necessary purposely to eliminate the conceptions of goodness and badness. Instead, whatever type of conception may arise; it has no power of deception over the practitioner, who is able to remain focused one-pointedly on the factor of mere luminosity and knowing. Thereby, the conditions for generating the improper mental application of making false superimpositions upon phenomena diminish in strength, and conceptuality cannot really get started, gradually lessening in

---

[76] Eye, ear, nose, tongue, body, and mental consciousness.

[77] The natural mind.

strength. In this way the doctrine of the Great Perfection comes to have a unique way of presenting the view, meditation and behavior for someone who has been introduced to the basic mind and has identified it well.... According to the New Schools, at a certain high point in the practice of Secret Mantra the māntrika engages in special practices, such as making use of a sexual partner... as a means of bringing desire to the path and inducing subtler consciousnesses which realize emptiness.

In this passage, His Holiness the Dalai Lama has touched on one the most delicate points of the entire controversy. Can one enjoy the objects of the senses without developing dependence on them, and instead transform pleasure into a vehicle for liberation? In Zemey's *Yellow Book,* which lists the misfortunes provoked by Shugden for those who "polluted" the purity of the Gelukpa practices, the victims were often precisely those who used Tantric sexual methods. It cited as an example the troubles of a great Gelukpa master named Lelung Shepe Dorje, who had, Zemey wrote:

encouraged many pure monks and masters to begin to practice with young consorts and to enjoy inebriating substances with them. On his advice, many lamas, monks and geshes from Sera and Drepung started to practice the Tantras literally, performing sexual union with women. Purchok Ngawang Jampa and Sho Donyod Kedrup[78] had a master-disciple relationship with Lelung Shepe Dorje. On one occasion, when they met in Lhasa, Purchok and Kedrup begged Lelung not to teach in that way. He replied, however, that he had received predictions from the *dakinis* and did not listen to them.

In his displeasure, the Guardian [Shugden] displayed himself to Lelung in his dreams. So Lelung performed the fire offering ritual and other exorcisms to be rid of the disturbances. Despite this, he did not live for long, dying after a protracted illness.

---

[78] A Gelukpa lama of the period.

In contrast, the Dalai Lama, in *Kindness, Clarity, and Insight*, explains how the various techniques applied by expert practitioners in the ancient schools of the Vajrayana, including those using the power of sexual ecstasy, could manifest the clear light of the fundamental mind. He specifies:

> In the Great Perfection teachings one cannot become enlightened through a fabricated mind; rather, the basic mind is to be identified, whereupon all phenomena are to be understood as the sport of that mind.... With such practice it is not necessary to repeat mantras, recite texts and so forth because one has something greater. The other practices are fabricated; they require exertion whereas one identifies the basic mind and sustains practice within that; it is a spontaneous practice, without exertion. Practices requiring exertion are done by the mind, but spontaneous practices without exertion are done by the basic mind. To do this, it is not sufficient merely to read books; one needs the full preparatory practice of the Nyingma system and, in addition, needs the special teaching of a qualified Nyingma master as well as his blessings. Still the student must have accumulated great merit.

He concludes his commentary with two pieces of advice: "Some people, however, mistake the doctrine about the non-necessity of repeating mantras, meditating on a deity, and so forth and think that the Great Perfection is very easy. This is really foolish. It is not easy at all." Finally, having shown the essential unity of all the different Buddhist paths regarding the importance of the mind of clear light, he writes, "Transcending sectarianism, we can find much to evoke deep realization by seeing how these schools come down to the same basic thought."

The Bodhisattva's Secret

All Buddhist doctrines recognize the importance of the human form and the mind as the center and the motor of the process that regulates the harmony of the internal and external worlds. The lama, the master, and the bodhisattva are human beings before they are deities. It is their qualities that make them symbols of the aspirations of every Tibetan seeking to transcend the limits of the material world. From the ordinary person's perspective, whether the lama belongs to one school or another it is not as important as it is for the monastic, so long as they regard him as a wise person. When a lama participates in a religious ceremony, people come from all directions to receive blessings. During my visit to eastern Tibet, I witnessed enormous gatherings whenever Chogyal Namkhai Norbu gave initiations and teachings, and certainly not all of those present were Dzogchen practitioners. Even in exile, great crowds assemble when the Dalai Lama is present, and likewise for His Holiness the Karmapa, the head of the Karma Kagyu sub-school, and His Holiness Sakya Trizin, the spiritual leader of the Sakyas.[79] The previous incarnations of Dudjom Rinpoche and Dilgo Khyentse, principal exponents of the Nyingma tradition, were similarly venerated wherever they went.

In general, it is thought that every authentic *tulku* is capable of recognizing and applying a number of methods to bring the mind to the state described as natural light, the primordial state. This is the only dimension in which contact is possible with the minds of the enlightened beings and the deities; free of the egoistic conditioning of ordinary thought, the bodhisattva can obtain their powerful support in helping the greatest number of beings. The first to benefit are those who have acquired karmic merit, after which come those with karmic connections at different levels.

In Tantra, there exist six realms of existence that include both gods and hell beings. As with everything else, these dimensions are not only external but coexist present within every sentient being. In the human body, they correspond to six places; at the center of the forehead resides the seed of pride characteristic of the realm of the *devas* or gods; at the

---

[79] I have had the opportunity to hear each one of these figures being extremely critical of the cult of Shugden.

178

throat is the *asura* or titan realm and jealousy; at the center of the chest, the human dimension characterized by all the passions; at the navel, the animal realm and ignorance; at the genitals, the realm of the *pretas* or hungry ghosts, who are impossible to satisfy since their throats are so narrow, to which corresponds avarice or greed; and on the soles of the feet, the beings of the infernal dimension dominated by hatred and anger.

A master able to perceive the suffering that stems from each of these uncontrolled passions also can understand which of one of the six mainly afflicts the disciple so that measures can be taken to purify it. Any circumstance—an unpleasant emotional sensation, praise or criticism, or difficulty in grasping a concept—is a pretext for making an effort to understand which of the six dimensions needs purifying. The main instruments are equanimity and clear wisdom, "like the nature of the mirror," an essential part of *bodhichitta*.

For centuries, there has been an unbroken chain of great masters who have transmitted the relevant techniques to develop these capacities, even to disciples who were far from being bodhisattvas. The fruit of their efforts, despite the grave problems that now grip Tibet, cannot be diminished. The immense political and demographic pressure applied by China has not in the least weakened the great devotion of the people towards their religion and those who represent it. This faith has remained steady even though Tibet's leading religious figures no longer live in their own country.

The risks of degeneration, however, never can be discounted. Of the dozens of lamas, geshes, mediums, scholars, and simple practitioners whom I asked for information and their opinions on Gyalpo Shugden, all, without exception, begged me to recount the facts impartially so that the reader could reach his or her own conclusions. Foremost in their thoughts was the fear that these rifts among scholars might hasten the disappearance of their deep and singular culture.

The Tibetan Vajrayana was born, at least in principle, with the noble aim of emptying the ocean of suffering of the infinity of beings dwelling in it. No one, not even the followers of other religions, would wish that such an important element of human spirituality should disappear through human error and the opportunism of a few fanatics intent on creating strife.

In Tibetan Tantric Buddhism, devotion to the tulkus stems from the awareness that it could take millennia to achieve the ambitious objective of interrupting the cycle of earthly suffering. A tulku must learn how to stabilize his or her mental presence beyond the end of each cycle on earth, so as to fulfill the solemn promise to serve other beings even after death. Abiding in the empty, luminous nature of the mind, knowing that this does not end with the burial of one's corpse, the tulku passes undistracted through the phase of the *bardo*, which is the period between the ending of one cycle and another, as described in the *Tibetan Book of the Dead*.

The *bardo* is said to be like a dream in which one is aware of being in a dimension without a material body; a dream from which one will reawaken. It is not by chance that dreams are so important in the development of Tantric practice. Without physical limitations, one can train every night to maintain presence and awareness in order to be ready to face the most difficult task awaiting us all: the moment in the *bardo* when the five elements that constitute us (earth, water, fire, wind, and space) and the mind become prey to the fear of emptiness, to which we are no longer accustomed after a life spent in the cage of the body.

Thus many Tantric masters develop by means of their dreams the capacity and psychic powers that are often impossible to obtain in waking meditation. But, conceptually, the actions of our daily lives can be compared to a long dream. We learn not to give too much importance to the concrete appearance of the world, which will vanish one day along with everything we possess.

The history of Tibet is full of examples of premonitions and teachings received in dreams; they are found especially in the Tantric tradition ascribed to Padmasambhava and his disciples. Although Shugden's disciples considered this type of oneiric transmission a complete falsehood, Tsong Khapa, the very founder of the Gelukpa order, transcribed many teachings that he said he had received directly from Manjushri, the Buddha of Wisdom.

To give an idea of the extent of the system of reincarnations in Tibet, a census carried out before the Cultural Revolution calculated approximately ten thousand recognized tulkus in the various regions. In a recent article in the Chinese press, the number of officially registered "living buddhas," as they are called in Chinese, was just over a thousand. But it is certain that in every area of the highlands, the people recognize many more than have been officially approved. Indeed, the Chinese-nominated tulkus often have no importance for the faithful. Despite this, the government maintains that its control over them is the key to imposing the authority of the state upon spiritual life. This will become much clearer from what follows.

The tulku reincarnations are the bodhisattvas of the Tibetan tradition. They are considered capable of taking on a new form, choosing a new environment and a new embryo. Life after life, they evolve as they pass through the ten different stages of realization, culminating in enlightened buddhahood. The Tibetans venerate these figures as intensely as a child does its parents.

Foremost among them, the Dalai Lama is the prince of bodhisattvas in human form, and his perennial task is to act with pure and compassionate intentions. His helpers and allies on earth are the tutors and masters who instruct him throughout his entire life, beginning with the most delicate phase of infancy, when they must reawaken the capacities of his mind in his new human form. It is presumed that his teachers too are bodhisattvas, as are the non-human protectors and guardians faithful to the teachings. One of these, Palden Lhamo, is the female manifestation of a deity considered to be beyond the worldly dimension. The other, Nechung, is instead the male form of a worldly deity, and as such is extremely powerful, being able to offer advice and divinations through human mediums. But a worldly deity is still conditioned, as the Dalai Lama is, by the limitations of the sphere in which it operates, such as the degree of approval and support of the people to whose benefit the deity is devoted.

Both the Dalai Lama and the other tulkus, once recognized, must undergo particular tests, such as the identification of objects that had belonged to them in past lives. In the imperfect human world, there is obviously the risk that a mistaken choice may result in a false reincarnation, and this has occurred previously. But for Tibetans, it is a risk worth taking. Even if "erroneously recognized," certain lamas, well-trained from infancy in study and practice, may nonetheless become able to recognize the state of their natural mind and, subsequently, instruct other disciples.

A *tulku* need not be a monk, although for the Gelukpas especially, this is often an indispensable condition for transmitting the formal initiations of the school. The Dalai Lama may have supernatural, mystical experiences thanks to the mental powers acquired during different lifetimes, with the progressive development of *bodhichitta*, but he cannot and should not demonstrate physical powers. If he did perform a miracle, it would only be by the intercession of the divine bodhisattvas with whom he shares the altruistic aim of bringing all beings to final liberation from samsara. The deity of whom he is considered to be the emanation in human form is, as we have seen, Avalokiteshvara, called Chenrezi in Tibetan.

Being an enlightened bodhisattva like the Buddha, Avalokiteshvara can take any form. In the world of Tantric deities, he manifests as Mahakala, who belongs to a very potent class of beings that only can be tamed or controlled by a bodhisattva of their own level, preventing them from unleashing all their devastating power.

The bodhisattvas in human form, instead, work in situations with historical determinants that cannot be completely overturned by miraculous intervention. The earthly dimension is influenced by conditions created by humans in the context of their actions and power struggles. Some may argue that what befell Tibet in its political "liberation" by Chinese forces paradoxically could be considered but one stage in the long process of the "liberation" of an entire people. It is an undeniable fact that neither the Dalai Lama nor a host of *tulkus* thousands strong, nor even the Chinese leadership can alter the fact that a country inhabited by six million Tibetans stands against more than a billion Chinese. Tibet before the occupation was no earthly paradise or Shangri-la, and the Dalai Lama himself often has said that his country is paying for the negative karma accumulated over centuries.

It must be borne in mind that it was Chinese religious persecution that spread beyond the Tibetan plateau a religion confined for centuries to the few million inhabitants of the Land of Snows and the plains of the Mongolians to the north. It could be that, without China, neither the Dalai Lamas nor the myriad *tulkus* and masters who fled to the West could have spread the Dharma to the same extent over the past fifty years. The Dalai Lama, in particular, has become the symbol of an ancient knowledge that preaches compassion and nonviolence. For this, in 1989, he received the Nobel Peace Prize, the highest recognition awarded by Western institutions. This has great symbolic worth, as it reflected the international community's condemnation of China's treatment of Tibet. It also had a more utilitarian value; from 1989 to the present, thousands of new Buddhist religious centers have sprung up all over the world, and tens of thousands of teachings have been translated, published, and distributed in bookshops in every country.

This striking trend, unprecedented even when the West's interest in Indian gurus was at its height, is not due to the merit of Tibet's leader alone. Other masters before him had spread the teachings in the West, but the Dalai Lama certainly has given a decisive impetus to the cause of Buddhism and thus to that of his people, who otherwise would have remained totally isolated under Beijing's dictatorship. If the world's interest had not been engaged by his constant journeys to every continent and his welcomes by heads of state and cultural leaders, perhaps the Tibetans would have remained as neglected as other minorities, like the Mongols and the Manchus, once leaders of their own empires themselves, and now absorbed and assimilated entirely in the new empire of the Han.

One fact that is not accepted by many of the Dalai Lama's new critics, particularly the Shugden practitioners and the independence movements that challenge his "Middle Way," is his request for full autonomy rather than total political separation from China.

In his time, the Thirteenth Dalai Lama also faced incomprehension from and obstacles created by his own collaborators. Perhaps it was no coincidence that one of his many troubling concerns during his reign was the spreading of the cult of Shugden by one of the most authoritative lamas of the time, Phabongka. Nor was it coincidental that at the age of fifty-eight, when he realized that his government and the heads of the great monasteries were not following his advice, the Thirteenth departed the world ahead of his natural time, leaving a terrible prophecy[80] that warned of the future consequences of the errors committed. He even went so far as to forbid any dignitary, lay or religious, to visit him in the last hours of his life.

---

[80] See the interview with Togden Chawang.

A Coalition of Lamas

Yvonne sounded enthusiastic when she called me a few weeks later, "His Holiness Kundeling has just arrived from the United States, where he took part in the demonstrations against the Dalai Lama in New York. Have you heard about them?"

I knew nothing at all, but I asked her if I could meet Kundeling Lama. "We are going to Milan together to a meeting planned with Ganchen Lama. His Holiness must tell him how the demonstrations went in America."

It seemed that Ganchen not only had been to China to meet the young Panchen Lama nominated by the Chinese, but he also was involved in the protests against the Dalai Lama in the United States. No doubt this would be an interesting chance to see how things were developing.

Ganchen Tulku's headquarters was in a narrow street near the city center, with a large courtyard from which one enters a *gonpa* temple in the Tibetan style, quite spacious and decorated in the traditional fashion.

We all met in the courtyard; Ganchen, Kundeling, and the woman I had spoken to on the telephone. They invited me in to see the temple, and I looked around everywhere for some image of Shugden, but there were only buddhas and painted *thangkas*, all resembling Ganchen with his portly physique, bald head, and a beard that exactly followed the line of his round, chinless jaw.

Lama Ganchen invited us to sit down in his office, promising he would be with us shortly. We went up the stairs of the anonymous small, nondescript 1960s building and found ourselves in a simply furnished apartment with a large veranda where some girls were sitting, engaged in discussion.

Kundeling was a youthful man with a long face and the appearance of an intellectual rather than a lama. He gave me a press release, in a folder with the logo of an international organization named "Dorje Shugden International Coalition." It contained clippings from newspapers, press statements, and a book with a flaming sword on the cover.

Among the names of the representatives of this coalition were those of Dromo Geshe Rinpoche, resident in the United States,[81] Dragom in

---

[81] The reincarnation of the master of Lama Govinda, the German author of a famous work of literature on Tibet, *The Way of the White Clouds*.

Nepal, Tritul in Taiwan, Panglung in Germany, Guru Deva in Mongolia, Kelsang Gyatso in England, Ganchen in Italy, Lobsang Yeshe in India, and Kuten Tenzin Choepel in the United States. There then followed a list of monks and laypeople from North America, Europe, Australia, and Brazil. In its pages was a small "errata" slip: Dromo Geshe Rinpoche begged not to be included in the list.

Lama Kundeling had waited patiently for me to finish leafing through the pages, where I saw various articles from American newspapers with his photograph and those of the other participants in the demonstrations that had taken place during the Dalai Lama's visit.

"Are you, Ganchen, Kelsang Gyatso, and everyone else listed in this pamphlet connected in an organization?" I asked.

"We are connected for the same reason, but it is not individuals who organize demonstrations, but rather the Dorje Shugden International Coalition of Dorje Shugden. We have also held many press conferences."

"I would like to learn a little of your history. How is it that you, a Tibetan, have come to be the leader of an anti-Dalai Lama organization? Were you encouraged to do the practice by your family?"

"No, my father was a monk before he met my mother, but in my case, I did not receive the practice from my parents. The Dalai Lama is not the only person in the world who can make observations and draw conclusions. I had no connection with Shugden until a few years ago, and I came to my beliefs through my own observations."

"That didn't happen out of the blue. You had 'signs' from Shugden, I imagine."

"I read a lot of material and historical accounts of Shugden, and from my understanding of these, I feel that this is really a profound practice. I have never had a dream or paranormal experience."

"So your approach was intellectual?"

"Over the years of my studies in the monastery, the Tibetan masters whom I met had unique spiritual qualities and knowledge, and they convinced me that this was an effective practice. I'll tell you something. The day I received the initiation of Shugden from a famous lama, the late Kyabje Song Rinpoche, it was late autumn and it was constantly raining in south India. Right after the initiation, the rain ceased and the sun shone brightly, and this was considered an auspicious experience."

"At that time, no one publicly challenged the practice. But when the Dalai Lama said that it was better not to engage in it, what did you think? Did you think he was mistaken, that he had gone crazy?"

"The first time the ban was made official was March 7, 1996. At that time, I was a fan of the Dalai Lama. I had no connection with him, but, like every ordinary, practicing Tibetan, I believed that whatever he said or did was absolutely correct, and a hundred percent good and marvelous. At first, I did not see it as a ban. At the time, I was even was helping the Tibetan cause, the Youth Congress, the Women's Association. Whenever I went to the United States, I said the same things as everyone else who supported the Dalai Lama, 'China is terrible, the Tibetans are suffering in Shangri-la.' I believed this."

"I hear some irony and bitterness in your words. Is it not true that the Chinese oppress religion and force the Tibetans to obey them in their own country?"

"From a Buddhist point of view, there is no enemy other than your own illusion, your own attachment. Every religion teaches that you must not hate your enemy; you must not stress nationalism, or the superiority of one ethnic group. The Tibetans generally believe themselves to be a special race. But Hitler also thought his to be a special race, and we all know what he went on to do."

I felt a bit annoyed by that comparison. But the lama went on, "You see, the Tibetans feel that their nationalism is connected to the identity of the religion they practice. But this is utterly confused. In every culture, one comes across unique people who believe themselves to be special and boast of it. Melvin Goldstein has written a book that has been read even by members of Congress: it takes no side but analyzes the China-Tibet situation. He says that the Dalai Lama had many chances to establish a normal relationship with the Chinese, who intended to reconstruct the Tibetan cultural identity within the mother country."

"Frankly, I believe that the Dalai Lama and others had little to trust in, as the armed invasion and the treaty imposed by military threat showed."

"But actually, his leaving the country created only division. And ever since the Tibetan people began to feel the need for unity of some sort, the Dalai Lama has created the cult of himself, as a sort of idol. This is something started in the last few years. To be equally frank, there never had been this idealization of the cult of the Dalai Lama in the past, and this is something most people don't know. The Dalai Lama's area of influence was limited to central Tibet, which consists only of U, the central-northern region. Meanwhile, the central-southern province of Tsang, was under the Panchen Lama and his administration. There, the people regarded the Panchen Lama as their ruler."

"Forgive me, but I don't see what the cult of the Dalai Lama has to do with the Chinese invasion."

"There were several regions in Kham and Amdo that already were under the command of the Kuomintang (KMT). And in the KMT, there were many Chinese who were village chiefs, or ministers, as in Qinghai and Gansu. Before the KMT came, these Tibetans were governed by regional leaders and were completely independent and autonomous, and not controlled by Lhasa, since the capital had no telephones, telecommunications, air transport, or other infrastructure. Subsequently, when the KMT was defeated and its leaders fled to Taiwan, the Communists took possession of these territories. Think about this; just eighteen years ago there were old monks from Amdo and Kham who told me they never even knew the Dalai Lama was the leader of Tibet. Titles such as "Gyalwa Rinpoche" ["Precious Victor"] or "Kundun" ["The Presence"] also were used for lamas in those areas. In Kham and Amdo, there were many mighty figures with powers and roles similar to the Dalai Lama's. In fact, they controlled far larger areas than he did. What I wanted to say, in short, is that the Dalai Lama's present claim to have political authority over a Tibet that includes Amdo and Kham is not realistic."

"Having visited several of the areas mentioned and studied a bit of the history," I said, "I know that the central Tibetan government in Lhasa actually was criticized for the excessive authority shown in the eastern regions, but I did observe great devotion to the Dalai Lama."

"Are you sure? I have never heard anything of the sort. Well, perhaps the young...or maybe in Amdo for nationalistic reasons, because the Dalai Lama is from there. That's why the Dalai Lama, ever since he got to India, has focused on the need to save Tibet's cultural identity and has included Kham and Amdo in 'his' Tibet. The people of those regions, under censorship or not, come to learn what the Dalai Lama says by various channels. The monks who escape from Kham and Amdo are brainwashed when they arrive in India so as to purge their Communist ideology, which says, 'religion is bad.' They end up trapped in another ideology that includes religion, but where they are under the illusion they also will find freedom, organization, and work. That is why Chinese brainwashing does no good, because it then offers those same brainwashed minds to someone who says, 'You see, this is the real Tibet that wants to stand only with the Dalai Lama.'"

"Listening to you, it almost seems as if you want to advise the Chinese to exploit religion rather than suppress it."

"Allow me to repeat that the idealization of the Dalai Lama has become a popular cult in Tibet, India, and the West because it serves as a myth; a superman against the fearsome Chinese. But what the Dalai Lama says—that, earlier, everyone lived together happily in Tibet, no one harmed anybody, everyone led a religious life—is not true. Initially, the development of this myth was needed to attract help and support. There are many documents and studies, and also books on the old Tibet, including research by Westerners themselves. When you read these, Tibet becomes less romantic. The truth is very different and it is emerging."

At this point, Ganchen Lama entered the interview room. He invited us to follow him as he disappeared again behind a door, trailed by two of the girls.

I wanted to dispute the point with "His Holiness" Kundeling that the Dalai Lama had idealized the old Tibet. He instead had wanted profound change. But this was not a debate, and I simply asked him if, in his opinion, the controversy over Shugden was religious, political, or both.

"Shugden is not a political controversy. The Dalai Lama's government has made it a political fact. A controversy is what the Christians have in their ranks between Protestant and Catholic priests over being gay, marriage, and having relationships. Instead, at Dharamsala, their mental approach is like in their feudal society when, from 1600 to 1959, there was no separation between church and state. Not even today, in exile, can one challenge the Dalai Lama; it is blasphemy. If you do not love him, it is heresy—you have sold your soul to the devil. What is really important is to see what has happened within Tibetan society."

"Catholics and Protestants, despite their arguments, don't dispute the main aim, reaching paradise and so on. In your case, the Dalai Lama and others maintain that, instead of the way of the Buddha, you follow the way of a spirit, and so you don't practice Buddhism but instead follow some other religion."

"The fact is that Shugden is not a spirit and ours is not another religion. It is a long story, whose original sources are well-documented, and it is emerging slowly. This is the Dalai Lama's biggest lie. It is not a cult of spirits, because if it were, he, too, would be a worshipper of spirits, and not one but five: Palden Lhamo; Nechung; Tsering Chenga; Gadong; and Tsampa Karpo."

"But the Dalai Lama says that he considers them to be celestial servants, angels, let's say, to whom one makes offerings to obtain collaboration and protection. They are not realized buddhas, as you regard Shugden to be."

"Shugden too is part of our practice, but we don't say that he is the central figure. We say the same things they do. The Dalai Lama uses certain words to brand us as a sect, a demonic cult. For example, when he says we regard Shugden as a buddha and worship him as a buddha, and that this is against Buddhism, we can say the same thing about him, because instead of following his own spiritual guide and master, Trijang Rinpoche, he turned against his teachings. In the Mahayana, it is essential to regard one's master as a buddha and to grant him even more respect. When he states that Shugden is a worldly deity, he is not considering what his tutor taught him. Trijang never told him that doing the practices of Shugden is less important than practicing those of the Buddha. All the declarations against Shugden never were suggested by his tutor, who was a Gelukpa master. Why did he not speak out when his spiritual guide was alive?"

"Actually, the Dalai Lama stopped the practice when Trijang was alive. He spoke to him in 1978."

"But he didn't tell him everything."

"Anyway, he wanted to make it clear that the idea of Shugden being the exclusive protector of the Gelukpas was mistaken, and that for him, all schools were equal."

"But this is not an exclusive practice, as if we were talking about 'owning' a woman. The Sakyas also have their exclusive idols. The Geluk lineage of Tsong Khapa has its own."

"You always come back to the lineage of Tsong Khapa, but the Dalai Lama, whose power you want to diminish, is one of the most important figures in that very lineage."

"The lineage of every master—Padmasambhava, Marpa, Sakya Pandit—serves to preserve the transmission of knowledge. It is not the disciple idolizing a teacher; instead, it is knowledge being transmitted to the disciple. The Dalai Lama is an important person in the Gelukpa tradition, but he isn't the boss of the Gelukpas; the Ganden Tripa is. So he has no right to tell us what we should and shouldn't practice."

"The 'boss' of the Gelukpas, as you call him, also has spoken out against this exclusive cult. What's more, the Dalai Lama actually only said that whoever wished to continue the practice should do so privately, and whoever wanted to take teachings from him had to make a choice: follow his way or that of Shugden. He didn't forbid the practice. Perhaps some monks were expelled from the monasteries..."

"No perhaps about it! Many monks were thrown out."

"That's true. But if they had no feeling for the Dalai Lama, why didn't they leave by themselves?"

"The Dalai Lama is still the Tibetan leader, and in any case the monks only have refugee status, and to go away they need the yellow passport that is issued by the government-in-exile. Try doing anything without the Dalai Lama's okay. Either you have Indian citizenship, and that's not easy, or you go to another country. Once you leave the monastery, you leave the entire Tibetan community. This is because the Indian authorities regard them as refugees. Such people have no money, no food."

"Is Shugden a being of the *gyalpo* class?"

"We maintain that the practice of Shugden is not a cult. It is not imposed by an authority such as the Office of the Dalai Lama. The idealization of the Dalai Lama is a cult. Shugden is a realized being that has manifested. Buddha can present himself in a thousand forms—even as a criminal or a prostitute. And so he even may manifest as a *gyalpo*, but he is not a *gyalpo*. If the Buddha manifests as a criminal in order to teach criminals, this does not mean he is a criminal. Thus, Shugden is only an apparent criminal. As for the spirits whose practices the Dalai Lama performs, those are all *gyalpos*."

"You organized a demonstration in America in the name of a coalition that includes an organization that, in Dharamsala, is suspected of three murders."

"The Supreme Court in Delhi and the district court in Dharamsala found the three murder suspects innocent. The Dalai Lama's government is distorting the facts. There is a letter sent by the Secretary-General of the Dorje Shugden Society to Lobsang Gyatso a month before his death. He wrote, "You have written a lot of rubbish against Shugden that you know nothing about. Why did you do that? If you want to, come here and check the facts with us.""

"To tell the truth, I read in the newspapers that other words were used, more like: 'Come and meet us like a louse under a fingernail.'"

"No, that's a Tibetan idiom that means crush or kill, but it's obviously a manner of speech."

Ganchen Lama reappeared in the doorway with his assistants. The atmosphere around us seemed to be getting edgy, and more of the Milan-based lama's disciples started to materialize—all of them women.

I asked the lama to sit down and talk a little, but Ganchen was defensive. After the almost perfect English spoken by Kundeling, Ganchen's words were hard to grasp. He did not speak Italian either, and I gathered that the lama preferred to change the subject of the conversation to peace and the work of the Lama Ganchen Peace Foundation.

When I asked if he were prepared to talk about Shugden, Ganchen Tulku placed one hand on his heart and raised the other: "The Dalai Lama," he said, "is my guru." It became clear to me why Ganchen was so well loved in the world of entertainment. His theatrical face, his gestures, his mime, his intuitive way of adapting to the situation, the glint in his cunning eyes, all suggested he had a way of playing with others like a cat with a mouse.

For a while, without my asking another question, he talked about cultural identities, saying that in this world there was no special place for national and ethnic roots. "Here in Milan, you also see many Chinese," he explained. "For everyone, whatever their ethnic background or religion, reality is made up of money and having a good time."

I tried to steer us back to the subject of the Dalai Lama and Shugden.

"The Dalai Lama is pure. It is his advisers who create all these problems," he said.

"But is it likely that a Nobel Peace Prize recipient considered to be the Tibetan spiritual leader, author of dozens of books, and respected all over the world, would let himself be manipulated by a bunch of wicked counselors?"

"It certainly is possible that these bad counselors can manage to influence the Dalai Lama in a difficult moment, because he is pure, but this is not a pure world."

The lama continued at length on the theme of the purity of the Dalai Lama contrasted with the perfidy of his advisers. As far as I knew, he had received many teachings and initiations from the Tibetan leader and was trying to avoid breaking the link between disciple and master.

I asked him then if he engaged in the practices of Shugden and transmitted initiations in his center. I did not understand the entire answer, but was able to grasp some of it.

"The discrimination against Shugden was unnecessary. For many years I did not give initiations, until I realized that the problem was not spiritual but political. The Dalai Lama had long said that it was a very high practice that must be kept secret. So I held to that view. Later, however, he declared that Shugden was a truly evil spirit. It then occurred to me that he was not expressing his own opinion but that of others, his political advisers. I am not involved in politics. But after the ban, the unity of the whole community was destroyed."

He then went on to talk about the Gelukpa tradition and Tsong Khapa, but there too I could only understand bits of what he said.

"Now I am in Italy," he said, "Now I am Marco Polo Lama." He continued, "Ninety percent of Tibetans have had to sign a pledge not to worship Shugden. But that doesn't mean that it is really so. A signature means nothing.... The Buddhists say that everything is karma. Good or bad is karma. If the people are as they are, that is karma. Because Shugden is karma. If he is such an insignificant spirit, what is there to be so afraid of? Why create the fear that he goes against the freedom of Tibet? If Shugden is a diabolical spirit, since there are millions of guardians, why don't they kill him? We are all connected like father and mother. If the Dalai Lama is the bodhisattva Chenrezi, he cannot abandon any of his children. How could he turn away hundreds of thousands of Tibetans?"

Then he spoke in the third person: "Ganchen has never been involved in politics. He loves his culture and the Dalai Lama. He works hard to promote that culture, while others engage in politics."

I asked him how it had come about that he journeyed to Beijing to pay homage to the little Panchen Lama chosen by the Communists. "All the Chinese television broadcasts showed you offering a *kata* and bowing before this child. If you believe the Dalai Lama is the leader of Tibetans and a pure person, why did you not follow his reasoning when he chose another child; one who later was made to disappear, literally? How could you be sure that the child chosen by the Chinese was the right one, and not the Dalai Lama's choice?"

"It is easy to know," replied Ganchen, his cunning eyes smiling, "because the moment that Jiang Zemin, head of one of the most powerful countries on earth, kneels down and offers a *kata* to someone he considers the reincarnation of the Panchen Lama, it becomes clear that this child has such spiritual power that he could only be the manifestation of a realized being; also because Jiang Zemin, by kneeling down before him, was kneeling before the Tibetan people."

The significance of his answer was clear enough and would become even more so as time passed. At this point, Ganchen summoned to the room a girl with a pale face and an innocent air. "Tell the journalist what happened in Dharamsala." Then he turned to me, saying, "This English girl went to take money to the poor Tibetan families in the settlements, as we do every year. Listen, so you can hear with your own ears what happened."

She looked at her master, moved, and then blushed as she began to tell me how a year ago she and others from the Ganchen Peace Foundation had gone to some refugee families. "They were very poor families," she said, "We went into their houses and realized how difficult their conditions were. Yet when we got out some money and tried to offer it to them, they drew back and looked at us, almost with fear. They said, 'We cannot accept it; it's Chinese money, money given to the enemies of the Dalai Lama.' I was stunned.... I knew how greatly those people needed help...." Her eyes filled with tears at the memory. She began to sob, and another woman from the group hugged her and took her out of the room.

I realized the suffering that had been brought by the schism over the cult, and I left the apartment with a certain sadness mixed with admiration for those families that were so devout as to refuse financial help from the enemies of their leader. When I went back to the organization's official headquarters, I saw on display Lama Ganchen's videocassette on self-healing. I took a copy, and after saying good-bye to the two lamas, Yvonne accompanied me to the door and asked me for my impressions of her master. "His judgments on the Dalai Lama seem pretty final," I told her, "He reasons like a true politician. He seemed to me a bit too pro-Chinese."

The English lady smiled, staring straight ahead of her. "You got that impression?"

I asked her, "Are you really convinced that praying to Shugden is essential? Couldn't they all do without it and avoid all these problems?"

Yvonne answered, "If you do practices dedicated to a deity for a long time—and I was initiated three years ago—at a certain point you know whether they are damaging or not. If you see that your mind is calmer, stronger, then you understand that this is the right practice. All Shugden practitioners, simple ones like me or greater ones, have experienced how effective it is. Even Chimi Tsering, the Secretary of the Delhi Shugden Society, had great doubts at the beginning."

"Wasn't he a disciple of Trijang and Zemey?"

"That's precisely why. He was reluctant at first, and his master said to him, "Try. Investigate. Don't do it in blind faith." The Buddha said the same thing. He investigated and then he decided. I myself have heard him say, "I would give my life for this cause.""

"The cause of Shugden?"

"Yes, the cause of Shugden."

"Did you meet him in India with Kundeling?"

"Yes, that's so, we were together."

"So then, this International Coalition is pretty strong now."

"Oh, yes. It's very strong. There's even a new center in Kathmandu, in Nepal. The lama who lives in Nepal, Dragom Rinpoche, is very important. And Lama Ganchen has a large center there, too."

"But doesn't it seem dangerous to spread internationally a conflict that has divided so many Tibetans?"

"The problem is that the Dalai Lama is so insistent on this ban. At the beginning of this year, after the Monlam, he was supposed to give initiations to thousands of monks, but once again he said that Shugden practitioners could not attend. So Dragom Rinpoche came down from Nepal to Bodhgaya and gave the initiations himself."

I asked her if she knew what had happened to the young reincarnations of Trijang Rinpoche and Song Rinpoche.

"They are two extraordinary young men and they are following in the footsteps of their predecessors," she answered.

"Even in the practices of Shugden?"

"Certainly, but it remains to be seen when they are older how they'll respond to everything that's going on."

"Do you think Trijang could be a leader in your coalition?"

"Oh, yes," she answered decisively, "surely. As for Song Rinpoche, his personality is more eclectic. It seems he is determined to continue the practices of Shugden, but he goes regularly to His Holiness's teachings. Do you see? We and our masters have nothing against the Dalai Lama. But he, instead, does practices and ritual to exterminate us all...."

Yvonne laughed then said seriously, "How can a master like him be so fearful? We Buddhists who have a spiritual refuge know that nothing and no one can touch us. Has the Dalai Lama no such refuge?"

When I got home, I put Ganchen's cassette in the video player. The film opened with an image of the lama surrounded by rainbow lights, first alone, then with the previous Panchen Lama.

The title, "Tantric Self-Healing for the Body and the Mind: A Method to Find the Inner and Universal Peace That Connects This World to Shambhala," was followed by images of *thangkas* of various buddhas and one of Ganchen wearing a wig of long hair tied up in the style of Tantric yogis. The self-healing exercises on the video consisted of various sequences in which the lama made a series of symbolic hand movements— probably mudras—over different parts of the body, to communicate with the deities. I had witnessed dozens of ceremonies in India and Tibet, but those arm movements, the raising and lowering, often like a bird in flight, were something completely new and almost surreal. There was Lama Ganchen, suspended over snow mountains, before the great stupa of Boudhanath in Kathmandu with its two giant painted eyes, or gliding over soft clouds, continually moving his arms and hands, now in traditional sacred gestures, now snapping his fingers to the right and left, backwards and forwards.

While the lama sang mantras, accompanied by a chorus, a girl read out the benefits of self-healing using Lama Ganchen's video: the curing of impotence and frigidity, infections, headaches—the list went on. According to the parts to be cured, Ganchen snapped his fingers or appeared to tie and untie a knot. To symbolize ultimate peace, instead, he placed his hand on his heart while the film's special effects carried him heavenward in his golden robe.

To Dharamsala

Finally, an opportunity arose to go to India and research the crimes thoroughly. I learned that Commissioner Rajeev Kumar Singh no longer was the Superintendent for the district of Kangra and that the investigation practically had been suspended once the certainty was established of the killers' escape, first to Nepal and then to Chinese Tibet. I was counting on meeting him anyway so that he could tell me the background of his long inquiry. Before I left, I asked my Indian colleagues where I could contact him, and I also sent a series of emails and letters to some of the most authoritative lamas of the different schools of Buddhism to learn their views.

I reached Delhi at dawn. Since I had to wait for the bus to Dharamsala, I decided to spend the day in the Tibetan quarter of the capital. Overcoming some embarrassment, and unconsciously a bit fearful, I looked for the guesthouse that had been indicated as one of the meeting places frequented by members of the "Dorje Shugden Devotees Charitable and Religious Society," which was at the center of the judicial inquiry into the murders. It was in a narrow, feebly lit street and had the same dreary atmosphere as the large building that housed the headquarters of the group.

I was received by a deputy of the secretary, Chimi Tsering, who was suspected of ordering the crime on February 4. A geshe seated at a desk asked me to wait in the a spacious room, where there were several photographs on the walls, including a black- and-white one of the Dalai Lama as a young man. I was surprised at this, and the monk explained that members of the cult still hoped for "a change of mind on the part of His Holiness." He added that the Dalai Lama, too, had been the disciple of their venerated master, Trijang Rinpoche, and was therefore their brother, and also a master from whom many of them had received Tantric teachings and initiations.

The conversation went on for some time, with the geshe speaking of the numerous instances of discrimination and marginalization to which, in his view, the Tibetan exiles belonging to the society were subjected. "The government-in-exile," he said, "has stepped up its aggression and the use of force to purge Tibetan society of any trace of the cult. Those who have had the courage to bring the matter to the public's attention have been forced into hiding." He showed me a film made by Swiss television in which exiles from the settlements in the south gave evidence of being threatened and attacked for not obeying the Dalai Lama. Very old monks who had escaped across the Himalayas with the Tibetan leader recounted with tears in their eyes how they had suffered from being forced to choose between their devotion to their leader and to the guardian Shugden. They swore that it was thanks to their oracle on March 17, 1959, that the Dalai Lama had been able to depart from Lhasa on a safe route and to reach India with thousands of monks and laypeople in his wake.

I made an appointment to talk to Chimi Tsering on my return from Dharamsala and left the office of the Shugden Society under the taciturn scrutiny of all those I passed on the stairs and in the corridors of the building.

Only a few minutes remained till the departure of the old "deluxe" bus that left Majnu Ka Tilla every evening, crossing northern India to unload the Tibetan commuters, mostly monks, nuns, and traders, in the square of McLeod Ganj, just above Dharamsala. I could barely sleep because of all the bumping caused by the innumerable holes along the hundreds of kilometers of disconnected roads, and I was dazed when I arrived in the village just before dawn.

I already knew Dharamsala. It had been the final stage of my Tibetan journey, and it was there that I, along with other Westerners, had met the Dalai Lama. I remember that we talked for a long time about the ancient Bon religion and my pilgrimage to Mount Kailash, the supreme sacred mountain. The Tibetan leader listened attentively to every detail, trying, through our stories, to return in his mind to those places he had left forty years earlier. I had the impression of an extremely sincere man, and the meeting dissolved my earlier judgments regarding his role at the apex of a rigid and hierarchical institution.

As I got off the bus and looked around, breathing in the fresh mountain air and the fragrance of the spiced tea from the stalls opened for the travelers who had just arrived. I loved that little miniature version of Tibet in exile, where I rediscovered the colors and scents of the Land of the Snows. Small hotels, restaurants, and Internet cafes had sprung up like mushrooms in the ten years since my last visit, not to mention the now far denser, foul-smelling traffic of motor rickshaws, old Ambassador cars, and buses. The guesthouse was newly painted and its windows opened onto the valley of Kangra. Right below stood the residence of the Dalai Lama. Situated in Himachal Pradesh, on the first foothills of the Himalayas, Dharamsala had from the 1960s welcomed most of the exiles who escaped

with the Dalai Lama after the Chinese invasion. Since then, different generations have been born in India. The young have changed in their fashions,
their way of thinking, and even in their physiognomy, but not in their religion. Many residents are members of the government-in-exile and in
most cases belong to the Gelukpa tradition. Others are owners of small
businesses connected mostly to the growing religious tourism. The larger
communities of monks from the three main monasteries, reconstructed
with their original names, Drepung, Sera, and Ganden, live in Karnataka,
while the followers of other traditions are more dispersed and have settled
mainly in Sikkim.

At the Department of Information and International Relations of the
Tibetan government-in-exile, the starting point for my research, I encountered a certain reticence, justified by the embarrassment the entire community felt at finding itself judged in the eyes of world over for the involvement
of a demonic cult in a triple homicide on the Dalai Lama's doorstep. But
thanks to the solicitation of His Holiness's private office, which had been
informed of my visit, I was treated with extreme politeness and allowed
to rummage through their small archive of materials relating to Shugden,
which had been meticulously assembled.

The material information related was mostly from 1996, the eve of
the crimes, and vividly depicted the atmosphere among the exiles, a community scarcely known to the rest of the world.

April 5: Taking advantage of the Abbess's absence, the statue of Shugden
in the nunnery of Ganden Choeling in Dharamsala is destroyed
and thrown into the rubbish. It had been consecrated by some of
the highest lamas in exile, Ratoe, Song Rinpoche, and the Dalai
Lama's two tutors, Lama Trijang and Ling Rinpoche. (I noted that
this seemed strange since Ling Rinpoche, the senior tutor, was
not officially a devotee of Shugden, unlike Trijang and the others.)

April 9: The "Tibetan Freedom Movement," linked to the Dalai Lama,
forbids the cult among its membership.

April 13: An anonymous letter is distributed around Dharamsala: "The
Dalai Lama and his asinine Tibetan functionaries must resolve
the problem (Shugden) honestly or else our last desperate resort
will be a bloodbath."

April 18: A circular bearing the letterhead of the Department of Health requests government employees and their families to stop worshipping the spirit. They are asked to sign a formal declaration of abjuration.

April 25–30: Representatives of the Dalai Lama's office visit monasteries and Tibetan settlements in India to explain His Holiness's position on the controversy. The cult's followers denounce the imposition of the requirement that the monks sign a statement declaring their renunciation of the practice, the wounding of one of its adepts, and the performance of rites of exorcism [against Shugden]. In Ganden and Drepung monasteries, tension is rising between among the monks, with clashes and injuries. One monk belonging to the cult, from Jangtse College in Ganden Monastery, is taken to the hospital.

The night of April 30: Tenpa Soepa, a representative of the Dalai Lama, reaches Mundgod with another functionary. That night a group of Shugden practitioners, some dressed as monks, surrounds their small building. The assailants capture one of the bodyguards but find the place is protected by other volunteers. So they leave a knife and a message for the officials that states, "We could not meet you this time. We hope to the next."

May 9: Shugden worshippers from different parts of India meet in Delhi and decide to organize. Dozens of letters denouncing their "persecution" are sent out to the Tibetan exiles and the Indian authorities, including the police chiefs and the prime minister.

May 10: The Dalai Lama speaks to six hundred people in the main temple. He cites a passage from the biography of the celebrated Gelukpa lama, Phabongka Rinpoche, that relates that a Shugden medium had announced "in exultant tones, the approaching death of the Thirteenth Dalai Lama."

May 14: The government-in-exile declares officially that no employee has been persecuted or dismissed on account of religious belief.

May 15: The first demonstration against the Dalai Lama is held in Ganden and Sera monasteries in south India. The supporters of Shugden denounce an attempt to arrest their organizer.

May 23: The "Dorje Shugden Devotees Charitable and Religious Society" is registered formally [in Delhi] to defend and disseminate information regarding the cult.

May 27: In Mundgod, unidentified assailants attempt to kill the former abbot of Jangtse College at Ganden, setting fire to his house with gasoline. Khensur Wangga had been asleep and was seriously injured in his escape from the fire. Lobsang Choedak, one of the alleged killers of the three monks in Dharamsala, is among the arson suspects.

June: Shugden followers denounce serious injuries sustained by Kundeling, a former minister of the Dharamsala cabinet, after he expressed his dissent from the Dalai Lama's position on the Middle Way (autonomy rather than independence for Tibet). A few weeks later, the former minister denies the account and denounces Shugden practitioners for entering his house illicitly. For the first time, this episode connects the struggle over Shugden to the Dalai Lama's policy regarding autonomy.

July 13: A new demonstration against the Dalai Lama is organized by a group of monks at Ganden Monastery. Ten days later, at Jangtse College, the site of earlier incidents, the general assembly of the monks threatens a hunger strike if members of the college who took part in the demonstration are not expelled. Eleven monks are obliged to leave the college and protest in newspapers.

July 25: A letter sent out to the various monasteries indicates that, as a course requirement, participants at "Dharamsala's Institute of Dialectics (directed by the geshe later murdered) must not be Shugden practitioners."

August: A nebulous "Secret Society for the Extermination of Tibet's External and Internal Enemies" makes death threats to the two young reincarnations of Trijang Rinpoche and Song Rinpoche, ages thirteen and eleven, respectively, who had in their past lives been were among the main proponents of the cult. The government-in-exile suspects this is a move to take the young *tulkus* away from their course of studies under the patronage of the Dalai Lama. The two child lamas are moved to Eurc̗ᵖᵉ. Trijang subsequently resides for many years in Switzerland.

August 8: A new song is taught to schoolchildren: "All Tibetans follow the Dalai Lama and trust in the pure guardians."

Posters plastered outside the Thekchen Choeling temple in Dharamsala suggest that Gyalchen Shugden worshippers should not participate in the Dalai Lama's rite for the deity Guhyasamaja, a Tantric divinity from the Geluk and Sakya traditions.

Six oracles take part in a religious ceremony with the Dalai Lama. Two of the mediums are women. During her trance, one of them gets up and shouts, "Here in this ceremony there are people who perform the rites of Shugden." The other points towards a monk saying, "This lama is not good, he does the *gyalpo* practice, take him away, take him away!" She then begins to tug at him and scratch his face. A fight breaks out among the monks attending the lama and those from Nechung Monastery. The man is taken away and he threatens to sue. The Dalai Lama persuades him not to.

Reading the notes, I was struck by the words shouted out by the medium, "He does the *gyalpo* practice." Once more there was a reference to this class of beings—a sign that the mystery of conflicting supernatural entities continues to surround the crimes.

August 22: The Sera Jey Monastery in Bylakuppe expels Geshe Kelsang Gyatso, founder of the New Kadampa tradition in England and organizer of the anti-Dalai-Lama demonstration in London. In the expulsion order, he is described as being "possessed by a terrible demon," and all Tibetans and Buddhists are urged "to have no relationship with him."

November 22: In the file there is a photo of Ganchen Tulku participating in the investiture ceremony for the young Panchen Lama nominated by the Chinese.

November 30: Chinese authorities in eastern Tibet arrest Venerable Lobsang Choejor in Lithang. He is accused of circulating among his monks the Dalai Lama's warning not to do the practices of Shugden and then closing the room where the cult was practiced.

After the arrest, the room was reopened on the orders of the Chinese administration.

January 1997: Geshe Thinley of Jangtse College (evidently the turbulent center of the dispute) is beaten up in the Tibetan quarter of Delhi and suffers serious injuries.

January 9: The granary of Jangtse College is destroyed completely by fire.

The papers, piled in chronological order, contained myriad accounts of such episodes, until, fatally, they came to the day of the three murders, February 4. A few lines described what happened in that room, which I intended to visit very soon. On the basis of the police investigation, the alleged killers were identified as members of the fraternity devoted to the spirit, and even if a judicial error had been made, there was little alternative to that theory developed in the exile community—unless, of course, one believed the suggestions of a plot organized by the Chinese secret services. But the latter possibility was discounted by the Tibetan security service itself, although spies from Beijing had been arrested earlier on suspicion of trying to use the Shugden affair to divide the exile community and to create a climate of rebellion against the Dalai Lama. This striking sequence of events showed unequivocally how the conflict began.

In the room where the murders took place, nothing had been stolen. Indeed, there was probably very little to steal in that small space, a few square meters where Geshe Lobsang Gyatso lived extremely simply. The rucksack that "marked" the crime, seized from one of the killers by the geshe as he died, left little doubt. There also was the series of matching clues in the files of Superintendent Singh's investigations. The faces of the youths who had tried to follow the geshe's car had been recognized by both the taxi driver and the owner of the small hotel where they stayed. Their names and surnames had emerged in the investigation into the exile community, and the dossier even contained their photos and the dates of their entry into India, with their official registration numbers. Almost all of them came from Chatreng in eastern Tibet, an area under the influence of the previous incarnation of Trijang Rinpoche, the leading proponent of the cult in recent decades.

While the judicial case was destined to be dismissed, the underlying problem was deeply rooted and certain to resurface again. But as with every conflict born of religious and ideological sentiments, in this case,

two distinct stages were evident; the emergence of an emotional component shared by several thousand people; and the birth of a "party" to
consolidate this base and later to engage in open warfare. Reading through
the files in the Tibetan archive, I had no doubt that this latter stage had
been reached and that new developments were on the horizon.

In the silence of the deserted, brightly lit room, I went over the principal events, down the centuries to the latest phase of the conflict.

A Conflict Centuries in the Making

The Seventeenth Century

The Gelukpa monastery of Drepung, on the outskirts of Lhasa, held seven thousand monks in 1630, but only two *tulkus* consciously connected to their previous lives. One, Lobsang Gyatso, son of a family linked to the ancient Nyingma and other non-Geluk schools, was recognized as the Fifth Dalai Lama, the reincarnation of an important disciple of Tsong Khapa, Gendun Drubpa, later known as the First Dalai Lama. He lived in a monastery complex called the Lower Residence, also known as the Ganden Palace. From his enthronement in 1642 by the Mongol ruler, Gushri Khan, until his death forty years later, he was the leader of all Tibet, from the Himalayas to the Chinese borders of Kham and Amdo (today Sichuan and Qinghai). Around 1650, he moved to the newly built Potala palace that dominated Lhasa from the hill of Marpori, the seat of the first Tibetan king in the eighth century.

The other *tulku*, Drakpa Gyaltsen, was considered the reincarnation of a number of great scholars, starting with another disciple of Tsong Khapa, Dulzin Drakpa Gyaltsen. He inherited the so-called Upper Residence, which led to suggestions that his rank may have been higher than that of the Dalai Lama. His mother and certain other religious figures were convinced that he was the true Fifth Dalai Lama. This was a potential source of jealousy and conflict between the two *tulkus*. At the age of thirty-eight Drakpa Gyaltsen died in mysterious circumstances, perhaps from an infectious disease, perhaps suffocated by a scarf. His disciples believed the latter theory of murder and accused the Dalai Lama's ministers of having killed him. One hypothesis is that Drakpa Gyaltsen was the head of an extremist religious group opposed to the Fifth Dalai Lama's decision to practice and promote the Tantras of schools other than the Geluk, particularly the Nyingma.

In his autobiography, the Fifth Dalai Lama writes that Drakpa Gyaltsen's death resulted from an attack by a demon, and "because of his distorted prayers," he was himself transformed into an evil spirit. A number of disturbing signs arose, including noises coming from his mortal remains, sudden misfortunes to the region, and the deaths of monks. The Dalai Lama ordered a Tantric fire offering ritual to be performed in order to eliminate the disturbances, but the spirit reappeared, first at Tashi

Lhunpo, where he was chased away by the local deities, and then at the monastery of a master of the Sakya school, who gave him a small altar and the rank of a minor "guardian." Over the following centuries, other masters of the Geluk school also offered propitiatory rites and concluded he was a divine ally with a buddha-nature. Among the various names given him was "Dorje Shugden."

From the Seventeenth to the Twentieth Century

A series of unfortunate events, the sudden and sometimes mysterious deaths of all the Dalai Lamas from the Sixth to the Twelfth, left Tibet frequently under the influence of regents, ministers, and foreign armies; Mongolian, Manchurian, and Chinese. Even the Thirteenth Dalai Lama experienced an assassination attempt that made use of occult forces, but he survived and consolidated Tibet's independence from China. In his time, Phabongka Rinpoche emerged as an eminent teacher from the ranks of the Gelukpa clergy. From his master, Dakpo, and his mother's family he inherited a connection with the cult of the spirit Shugden, which urged him to break with every practice not linked to Tsong Khapa's main lineage. After a long illness attributed to a lack of respect for his commitment to Shugden's admonition to practice only the pure doctrine, Phabongka spread the cult of the spirit among the aristocracy and also in the great monasteries of central and eastern Tibet. Thanks to his propaganda, abbots and other dignitaries, fearing the contamination of the country's religion and the weakening of their school's power, blocked every attempt at modernization or opening to the rest of the world. Their efforts clashed with those of the Thirteenth Dalai Lama, who deliberately sought to oppose the cult. In 1933, the Shugden Oracle announced to Phabongka the precise date when the Tibetan leader would die. The Thirteenth forbade any Gelukpa dignitaries from to coming to his deathbed and left a terrible prophecy in which he predicted religious persecution and the Chinese invasion of Tibet.

The Era of the Fourteenth Dalai Lama

After the death of the Thirteenth Dalai Lama, those disciples of Phabongka devoted to Shugden, including the Regent, Reting Rinpoche, had full control of most key positions. Although he had discovered the reincarnation of the Thirteenth, Reting however was suspected of breaking his vows as a Gelukpa monk and was forced to resign. Another Shugden practitioner, Tagdrak Rinpoche, replaced him, while Trijang Rinpoche, a favorite disciple of Phabongka and himself a proponent of Shugden, became the tutor of the young Fourteenth Dalai Lama. After Reting was denied his return to the Regency, he was convicted of an attempt on the life of Tagdrak. He was imprisoned and died in a prison cell, probably poisoned or suffocated. Over the next three years, negative events escalated in Tibet. China invaded the eastern frontier, and the Dalai Lama assumed power at the age of fifteen. During his first exile to the Tibetan border in the Chumbi valley, His Holiness trusted in the political and spiritual advice of the Shugden Oracle, and this led to a deep involvement with Shugden that was encouraged by his tutor, Trijang. The young Dalai Lama returned to Lhasa in 1951 and spent the next eight years trying to establish a satisfactory relationship with the Chinese military leaders and Communist officials, which efforts proved ultimately unsuccessful.

The Escape to India

In the early years after the flight to India in 1959, the Dalai Lama continued to perform the practices of Shugden, together with those of the other traditional deities, Nechung and Palden Lhamo. While Trijang Rinpoche transmitted the practices to other lamas and practitioners, including foreigners, the Dalai Lama began to receive transmissions from various traditions, particularly the Nyingma, and in exile he established a deeper and more direct relationship with the masters of all the other schools. These dialogues, together with his personal dreams and the State Oracle Nechung's divinations, convinced His Holiness that doing the practices of the exclusive protector of the Gelukpas could damage the harmony among the different traditions and could undermine his own authority as the undisputed leader of all Tibetans

At the beginning of the 1970s, this new nonsectarian tendency was made more evident in public, with a great ritual offering ceremony conducted for Padmasambhava, the master of the ancient Nyingmapa school. When many Gelukpa monks and nuns did not participate in the ceremony, the Dalai Lama learned of the publication of *The Yellow Book*, written by Zemey Rinpoche, a disciple of Trijang. It lists all the deaths and misfortunes attributed to Shugden's interventions when important religious and lay figures "corrupted" their Gelukpa practices. Given the nonsectarian tendencies of the Fourteenth Dalai Lama, the book contained a clear threat to his person.[82]

The Dalai Lama decided to criticize the author of the book publicly. Citing his own dreams and the divinations by the State Oracle, the Dalai Lama warned of the dangers that can result from worshipping Shugden. Far from experiencing the wrath of that supposedly fearsome deity, the Dalai Lama instead became deeply respected around the world and received the Nobel Peace Prize in 1989. In contrast, Zemey Rinpoche had a severe stroke and was unable to speak from the time of his book's publication until his death a decade later.

In the second half of the 1990s, the conflict was discussed more openly and became public knowledge, while the Shugden affair acquired disturbing political dimensions culminating in the triple murder on February 4, 1997.

China's leaders meanwhile discovered that certain lamas and practitioners of the cult were potential allies against their foremost international enemy, the Dalai Lama, and decided to support these individuals in the media and also by means of financial assistance, both within Tibet itself and abroad.

---

[82] See Superintendent Singh's interview with the assistant at the School of Dialectics.

An Ancient Monastery

The Dalai Lama was abroad, but his invitation had opened for me the doors of numerous offices and public archives of the government-in-exile. I spent many days in the Library of Tibetan Works and Archives, studying ancient and modern texts with the help of one of the leading Western translators from Tibetan, Elio Guarisco, an Italian who had been a Gelukpa monk before he began following the Dzogchen teachings of Chogyal Namkhai Norbu. Together, we met officials, lamas, geshes, scholars, students, and teachers at the School of Dialectics, in addition to people from all walks of life. We encountered both active and former devotees of Shugden, and, obviously, many followers of the Dalai Lama.

To study the abundant material collected, I looked for a quiet room, away from the bustle of tourists and pilgrims in McLeod's bazaar. I found one on the ground floor of the Tara Guest House, less than a hundred meters from the place where the three monks were murdered. The only constant background noise was the passing of the mules carrying building materials. Pouring rain from time to time transformed the slope opposite my room into a waterfall that drowned out every other sound. Elio returned every day from the library with his latest translations of biographies, historical texts, and articles. I read them avidly, transcribing the most important passages late into the night. They primarily discussed the origin of the spirit.

Amongst the accounts by lamas and monks, one was more compelling than the rest. This was the autobiography of a contemporary of the Fifth Dalai Lama, Drakpa Gyaltsen, whom many believe was the last human incarnation of Gyalpo Shugden. I found myself immersed, captivated by his description of Drepung, its atmosphere and its paved stone pathways in the seventeenth century. I had visited this once majestic monastic city on my journey to Tibet, and it was not difficult to imagine it as it was all those centuries ago. Neither I nor anyone else can guarantee that events unfolded exactly as he described them. But the texts from the period, and those reconstructed recently from various sources, have many points in common. I have remained faithful to these, and along with my vivid perceptions, they form the basis of my story.

208

PART FOUR

1656—The Life and Death of Drakpa Gyaltsen

> For something undertaken all of a sudden
> Or something I did not examine well,
> Even if I have given a promise about it,
> It is proper to examine, "Do it or give it up?"
>
> —Shantideva

For some time, Drakpa Gyaltsen had not left his room in Zim Khang Gong, the Upper Residence of Drepung Monastery. Locked away in this castle dominating the largest monastic complex in Tibet, probably in the world, the erudite monk was spending the twilight of his brief worldly existence in strict isolation.

A scholar and a practitioner of those secret arts leading to knowledge of the supreme laws of cause and effect, he was aware of his own responsibility for the events that now were taking their final shape. Despite the reassuring predictions received in divinations and dreams, the signs of his unexpected and imminent demise were present. He slowly took a few steps and sat down by the window to read once again the sheet of parchment that he long had thought contained the secret of this mood. "Oh, Great Conductor of the caravan of beings and of gods! It is important to keep your promise!" Then he focused on the images of the protectors of the doctrine with all the intensity he could muster and tried to transcend his thoughts, his outer perceptions, and his own presence.

The warmth of the summer sun took a long time to disperse the clouds until, with dazzling clarity, it uncovered the crown of mountains overlooking the foggy Kyichu River valley, crossed by the steady, elegant flight of eagles.

Observed from the highest viewpoint, the buildings of Drepung resembled grains of rice flung against the mountain, scattered here and there. But inside the monastic city, each path, each temple, and each building interlocked like the cells of a beehive in which worker bees, dressed in maroon and ochre, came and went. The over seven thousand monks were divided among five colleges (*dratsang*); within each one, they resided in various monk hostels (*kamtsen*), assigned according to their home regions. This city had seen a vast increase in its ascending alleyways, temples,

211

libraries, and prayer halls, and in the number of the novices' dormitories and chambers for the masters of the doctrine.

In a calm state, free of mental constructions, the lama clearly observed his mind as it became crowded by thoughts that accompanied the rising of emotions. To avoid being overwhelmed, for days on end he had rarely looked out of the window of his apartments, the splendor of which was unrivaled either in Drepung or in any other Gelukpa monastic city in Tibet. On that morning he tried to watch life going by under his window with as much detachment as possible. But, as usual, it was difficult for him to do so, since the walls of that monastery had witnessed the playing out of the cycle of his recent lives.

Drakpa Gyaltsen was born in 1619. Many years had gone by since his mother, Lady Agyal, an influential noblewoman from the Tolung aristocracy, had arrived in Drepung from the town of Gekhasa, north of Lhasa. She was determined to meet the most eminent dignitaries there: "The night my son was conceived, I dreamt of the Fourth Dalai Lama," she told them after being shown into the great audience hall. "The omniscient Yonten Gyatso spoke to me, saying, 'Give me a home.'" She pointed to her stomach abdomen, swathed in a traditional apron with horizontal stripes, and everyone present noticed that she was pregnant.

Two years later, Lady Agyal invited the wise Panchen Lama, Lobsang Chokyi Gyaltsen,[83] to her beautiful home surrounded by vast cultivated fields and scores of yak herds. This high lama had been tutor to the unlucky Fourth Dalai Lama, the only Mongolian in that reincarnation line, who died at the age of twenty-seven, struck down either by illness or by assassins. For some time the Panchen Lama and the Abbot of Drepung, Desi Sonam Choepel, the government's appointed regent, had been searching for the Dalai Lama's reincarnation. But these two venerable figures already had received prophecies concerning a special child, and the divine omens did not indicate Gekhasa as his place of rebirth.

However, the influence of the family within the aristocracy, the insistence of the mother, and the need to examine more than one candidate all suggested that the Panchen Lama go to Gekhasa as requested. Lady Agyal and her husband proudly showed him their little Dondrup, whose name means "he who will realize his aim." By their account, the infant had

---

[83] 1570–1662.

smiled and spoken as soon as he emerged from his mother's womb. The Panchen Lama bestowed a long life initiation upon him and recognized that he was not an ordinary being. Giving advice to the parents on how to care for the child, he announced that they would soon be hearing news. But when they did, the message was not what Lady Agyal had been hoping for.

The Panchen and the Abbot of Drepung had already decided that another child was the predestined heir of the Fourth Dalai Lama. The oracles and their own long meditations at the altars dedicated to their patron deities had directed them to Chingwa Taktse of Chongye, in the valley of the ancient kings of the Yarlung Dynasty.

When, after a long journey, Abbot Choepel arrived at the house of the chosen candidate, the child ran to him and jumped onto his knees, asking, "Why have you waited so long to come looking for me?" Thus began the religious career of Lobsang Gyatso, who was to go down in history as the "Great Fifth" Dalai Lama. Word of his recognition was kept secret because at the time the King of Tsang, devoted to the Kagyupa sect, was threatening to wage a war against the Yellow Hats to gain control of the Lhasa region.

Nor was life serene for the little Dondrup. After his mother's disappointment at his failure to be recognized as the *tulku* of the Fourth Dalai Lama, a gang of Mongol marauders attacked the Gekhasa estate and kidnapped the child. Negotiations for his release were begun immediately and, with luck, the envoys of the Panchen Lama and the governor of the area were able to bring him back safe and sound. However, Dondrup Gyaltsen was to suffer from a painful, indelible memory of the bandits. They were coarse, ignorant men who would threaten him with their swords as they forced him to eat the meat of sheep whose throats they had just slit before his very eyes. When the little Dondrup Gyaltsen child was freed, he found that this experience had left him with a tiny boil on his tongue that kept him from tasting any food and affected his recitation of mantras.

Meanwhile, the new Dalai Lama was passing the test of recognizing the objects that had belonged to his predecessor. However, quite a few Gelukpas had raised objections and insisted that the child from Gekhasa also be put to the test, as requested by his mother, Agyal. They pointed out that the *tulku* discovered in Yarlung was descended from ancient sovereigns, and their lineage included many practitioners of the Nyingma, Jonang,[84] and even the Kagyu schools, the latter presently the sworn enemies of the Geluk order. How could he be the heir to a central lineage of the Yellow Hats?

The Abbot of Drepung, Sonam Choepel, argued that the child's special signs had been noticed by representatives of those traditions and that all had demanded the right to examine him, each convinced that this was the reincarnation of one of their own gurus. So the fact that the Gelukpas had appropriated the young prodigy had enhanced their own sect's prestige and glory.

As a result, the candidate for the throne of the Dalai Lama made a triumphant entry into Drepung and was lodged in the apartments of his predecessor in the Ganden Palace, also known as the Lower Residence.

By the time everything was ready for the ritual of the cutting of his hair and the novitiate ceremony, the little Dondrup, his junior by two years, had also been recognized as an important reincarnation and had arrived at the great monastery. He was assigned to the Upper Residence, where his past reincarnations, great scholars such as Sonam Drakpa, a former Abbot of Drepung, disciple of the Second Dalai Lama, and master of the Third, had lived. Dondrup immediately had recognized a statue and some objects that had belonged to the previous abbot, and he had been authorized to start his studies after taking lay vows and the name of Drakpa Gyaltsen. At the age of eight, Drakpa became a novice monk and received teachings and initiations from the same master as the Dalai Lama, the Panchen himself, who had been a family guest in Gekhasa.

In his autobiography, which was to raise questions for posterity on the subtle mortal struggle that took place in Drepung, the Great Fifth did not deny a certain unease in finding himself constantly placed alongside the tulku of the Upper Residence in ceremonies and festivities such as the Monlam, the most sacred prayer ceremony of the year. On these occasions, two thrones of the same height, one for him and one for Drakpa Gyaltsen, were placed next to each other in the center of the great hall of the Jokhang. The challenge intensified as continuous doubts were raised over the meaning of the definitions Upper Residence and Lower Residence,

---

[84] A religious order rooted in the teachings of Yumo Mikyo Dorje, Choku Odzer, and Thukie Tsondru, which developed between the years 1000 to 1600 and survived to our day through the successors of the master Taranatha.

which nominally seemed to situate the Dalai Lama beneath the *tulku* from Gekhasa.

Eight years old and by now established in his rank, Gyaltsen had learned to read and write perfectly the ancient characters of the Lanza Sanskrit script, on which Tibetan printed script was based. One day his instructor gave him a text[85] from the Nyingma tradition, from the time of the first diffusion of Buddhism in Tibet. The little *tulku*, who had been educated with the writings from the New Tradition, especially the Geluk and Kadampa ones, knew nothing of the mantras of this school. But in his mind he associated the teachings of the Ancients with those of the Bon shamans. He had heard of a certain practitioner who would drink unconcernedly the consecrated beer of the ritual offerings from human skulls.

That afternoon, playing with two other boys, he was distracted and forgot to study the text. Then his instructor called for a stick with which to frighten him and asked, "Have you finished memorizing?" Drakpa answered, "The author is not a Gelukpa lama, and furthermore, I have met some obstacles caused by the language and by the people surrounding me." The instructor then said, "There is no teaching that has not been proffered by the Buddha and there is no difference between them. If you behave like this you will create negative karma. All your predecessors, from Sonam Drakpa to Gelek Pelsang, were erudite lamas. You are considered their reincarnation. It is truly pathetic that you are unable to memorize this text."

Saying this, he picked up the cut bamboo brought to him and, after scolding the boy, beat him ferociously. He told him to learn the text for the next day and sent him to bed. Drakpa's wounds bled copiously, and though he felt very sad, he understood that the strictness of the members of his retinue was meant to develop his qualities for his own good, and he bore no grudges. During the first part of the night he was unable to sleep, having one of his recurring dreams; a man dressed entirely in black tried to carry him away on a horse, and he was afraid that he would not be able to find his way back. A voice invited him to take a path from which a strong gust of red wind had suddenly risen. In its midst appeared a dark figure riding a horse as black as the knight who then gripped him by the waist and dragged him off. Drakpa anxiously thought that he never would

---

[85] *Manjushri Nagaraksha*, a liturgy of a rare form of Manjushri.

return when an old man with shiny white hair and beard appeared between the trees. This figure struck down the black knight with a spear, and
Drakpa Gyaltsen saw his kidnapper vanish in the windy vortex. At that
point he partially awoke, thinking this dream was a sign of demonic interference hindering his path toward the Pure Land. But then the dream resumed, and he went to a lake that seemed to be in Shambhala, the legendary
northern land of practitioners of the *Kalachakra Tantra*. Two albino monks
appeared and told him, "The sun has come up and breakfast is ready."

Opening his eyes, Drakpa did not remember that his tutor had beaten
him but realized that somehow he had memorized the entire text. This he
recounted to his two fellow students, but they did not believe him, saying
his teacher would strike him again. However, after recounting his dream,
Drakpa recited the text in its entirety without a single mistake, to the great
pleasure of his instructor.

This and other memories were jumbled in Drakpa Gyaltsen's mind and
like dry wood fed the flames of his anxiety. Meanwhile, a fever slowly
rose from the soles of his feet to the top of his head, leaving him trembling
and weak. The doctor said that it was an infectious disease,[86] an invisible
enemy that lurks treacherously in the body and conditions one's energy
and mind.

By now he had learned he should no longer give much weight to the
pain of existence, and without even being aware that he had just come
out of a state of fevered unconsciousness that alarmed the adepts of the
Upper Residence, he called his assistants, Jangmo and Lingto Choegye, in
a hoarse, faint voice. But Jangmo and Lingto could not hear him, as they
had gone to implore the Dalai Lama in the Lower Residence to come up
and visit their master. Drakpa Gyaltsen, not knowing their absence resulted
from a good intention, felt his sense of solitude grow. Meanwhile, the weak-
ness that moved his bowels was mixed with waves of heat and nausea.

The words of the great Shantideva came to mind:[87]

> Mind, immaterial, cannot be destroyed by anyone any-
> where.

---

[86] According to some sources, he was infected by the plague.

[87] Indian master of the Mahayana who lived in the eighth century and authored the
Bodhicharyavatara, (*Entering the Path to Enlightenment*).

It is hurt by suffering only because attached to the body;
Humiliation, rudeness, disgrace, do not hurt the body.
Then why, O mind, are you angered by them?

The door was opened timidly by the custodian, and the *tulku* asked this monk for some warm water. He drank and closed his eyes, secretly invoking the help of the divine protectors. But just as in reality his trusty assistants had not come running, in his meditations his guardian angels kept their distance. Meanwhile, the light in the room was slowly fading.

The *tulku* of the Upper Residence could not seem to see the facts in their rightful perspective. He yearned for the day when the meaning of the promise that he had transcribed on the parchment would be revealed. He was privately certain that the resurgence of this memory would put an end to his painful worldly existence. Yet there was nothing he desired more than the chance to dedicate himself to the practice of the sutras and Tantras studied since childhood.

Despite his youth, his master, Panchen, also had made him Abbot of Kyormo Lung, a small monastery not far from Drepung. Tsong Khapa had studied ethics there, and it was therefore sacred to all Gelukpas. But even this role had ceased to hold any particular meaning for the *tulku* of the Upper Residence, though he had proudly invited the Dalai Lama more than once to his rooms there to restore a touch of its former prestige to the old monastery.

Owing to the disappearance or destruction of many of the tulku's writings, it has not been possible to trace even the slightest hint of what happened after the tumultuous events that preceded and followed 1642, the year of the Water Horse. This was a time of glory and jubilation for his classmate, the Dalai Lama, who had become the King of U and Tsang provinces, and also the spiritual and political leader of the entire people of the Land of Snows, from Tachienlu to the borders of Ladakh.

The powerful Mongol Emperor Gushri Khan, devoted to the Geluk lineage, as were most of his people, had won the war against the King of Tsang and donated vast new territories to the Dalai Lama, and to his government at the Ganden Palace of Drepung. The use of a foreign king's soldiers to kill fellow Tibetan monks was distressing to all the lamas, but was justified by the need to save the sect and presented as a victory of the forces of good against the supposedly evil coalition brought together by the King of Tsang.

The construction of the Potala in Lhasa was advancing at great speed. In consequence, the designation "Upper," which had always distinguished Drakpa Gyaltsen and his predecessors' seat, had lost all meaning.

The *tulku* from Gekhasa knew with certainty that there would be no place for him at the new Potala palace. It would be residence only to the Dalai Lama, the man who, according to his mother, had usurped his own destined position from birth. As the high walls of the imposing white and red building, visible from anywhere in the Lhasa valley, took shape on the summit of Marpori, the hill sacred to the first divine king of Tibet, Drakpa felt a heightened awareness of his solitary mission on earth. It was a sensation that resembled defeat, if submission to such a learned and powerful Dalai Lama, his spiritual brother and master who had given him initiations and teachings, could be considered a defeat.

This scholarly monk would have been hard pressed to explain precisely why and when the seed of this virulent conflict had sprouted. A feeling of melancholy and impotent rancor at the outcome invaded his pure soul and entangled him, transforming his very physical appearance. Drakpa Gyaltsen's face was broad and oval, and his narrow, long eyes gave him a haughty, impassive air that was accentuated by thin, level lips and small ears without lobes. His curved shoulders protected his chest and shielded the secret resentment in his heart.

Omens of his imminent end had been communicated by the divination of the Oracle of Lhamotang, who told him to prepare to serve the Dharma in the Mongol regions of the north and in China to the east. But the sentence had been cruel and beyond appeal. "At the age of thirty-seven you will meet obstacles, so you will have to intensify your practice," the deity had said. "At forty-nine or fifty, you will depart for the next world. Do not fear, look upon all beings with compassion, and protect the teachings of the Gelukpa school."

Subsequently, the fierce protector Mahakala appeared to tell him that malevolent people were conspiring against his life and nothing could be done to avoid it.

An ordinary person facing a death sentence, even delivered as abstractly as in a dream or the reading of an oracle, reacts with fear and desperation. But, with growing expectation, Drakpa Gyaltsen continued to contemplate his visions, so lucid and intense. And there was that voice—an inner voice? or was it external? or divine?—repeatedly reminding him of his promise. It certainly suggested a greater design, like a missing wedge in a mosaic, without which his destiny could not be completed.

Once the war fought to defend the Gelukpa lamas and banish once and for all the Tsangpa threat was over and its dead buried, the teaching of the Yellow Hats spread like lightning to every corner of the highlands. Something happened that showed the *tulku* from Gekhasa the missing fragments of the celestial scheme. By now, the Dalai Lama was ensconced firmly in his seat, displaying an inner confidence as he practiced the Tantras learned from masters of different schools and from his own family. Meanwhile, the displeasure of the orthodox Gelukpas, suspicious of Lobsang Gyatso from the beginning, continued to fester. The court jester, who was allowed to ridicule any sacrament, would carry around unashamedly in his belt a large *phurba*, the three-faced ritual dagger that, in the Nyingma school, skewers the *gyalpo* demons and severs instantly all worldly attachments. This was interpreted as a warning that unorthodox symbols were becoming commonplace, and the idea that swift enlightenment could be gained by practicing the ancient Tantras was becoming more popular. Therefore, the gradual, sutric path of renunciation, the slow and methodical preparation for the superior stages of the Tantras, the progressive maturation by means of reading and reflection, were increasingly seen as becoming less important.

Many of the abbots, lamas, and monks from the three great monasteries thought the Great Fifth at least should have kept secret his heresies, as other masters had done. Quite a few Gelukpas had received the secret instructions of the direct path that can liberate one from samsara in a single lifetime. But they did not flaunt them openly, and, above all, how many were truly capable of understanding and applying them correctly? If they followed the Dalai Lama's example, the people might conclude that the teachings of the Gelukpas were only useful for achieving scholastic excellence in philosophical debate, but were impractical for other purposes.

What had become intolerable in the eyes of the traditionalists was the Dalai Lama's open dependence on his visions, which were transcribed and made available everywhere, suggesting to masses of uneducated peasants and nomads that their state of mind, since it was pure from the beginning, could self-liberate and dissolve into the clear light arisen from the void.

The Nechung Oracle, the manifestation of the divine Gyalpo Pehar, was elevated to the rank of protector of the Tibetan government with the consent of the Dalai Lama's Nyingmapa patrons. To build him an abode worthy of his new status, the Great Fifth started the construction work near Drepung monastery for Nechung Dorje Drayang Ling, the "Diamond Garden of Melodious Sound."

As the Dalai Lama's prestige grew, a conviction that the Nyingmapa practices also developed an invincible worldly power was gaining ground in many devotees' minds. The fact that, formally, the Gelukpas dominated Tibet and even minted the currency was insufficient. For the high ecclesiastics seated on the thrones of Ganden, it was no longer the Yellow Hat doctrine but solely the Dalai Lama's star that now shone at the heart of the constellation of Vajrayana Buddhism. All the rest risked being reduced to a mere simulacrum.

The suspicion of a dangerous alteration in the equilibrium of the Lhasa clergy increased when the erudite monk Drakpa Gyaltsen, of all reincarnations in Drepung the most faithful to the traditional precepts, was demoted to the category of third-rank *tulku* in the year of the Water Horse. This rank did not correspond in any way to his lineage or to his fame, which had spread across Tibet to Mongolia. Was Drakpa Gyaltsen not the reincarnation of the great Sonam Drakpa, the head of the Gelukpas in a former generation, whose treatises dominated the curriculum in many courses of Tantric study? Had he not renounced all worldly goods to place fidelity to his vows and the doctrine above his filial duties?

No personal comment or note by his biographers records the reaction of Drakpa Gyaltsen when the regent, Choepel, and the governor, Nomsu Norbu, decreed his relegation. Was the Dalai Lama aware of this? Or had it been kept from him? Like a white yak taking leave without lament from a herd of black yaks on the high pastures, so Drakpa Gyaltsen retreated in solitude to prepare silently for his final choice.

> As a child cries in distress when his sand castle is destroyed, so does my own mind appear to me at the loss of praise and fame.
>
> —Shantideva

These events may well have persuaded Drakpa Gyaltsen that the omniscient Dalai Lama, his master and spiritual brother, had fallen prey to the demon of pride in worldly power, the very demon overcome by Tsong Khapa two centuries earlier when he declined the Chinese Emperor's invitation to visit him in Beijing. Drakpa Gyaltsen's conviction was reinforced by the might of the Great Fifth's escort when he set off for the Celestial Empire, with three thousand dignitaries and assistants in tow. The tulku of the Upper Residence briefly accompanied the procession too. But while the new King of Tibet proceeded to be covered in glory, Drakpa Gyaltsen returned to lock himself away in his hermitage to meditate. Had he not been demoted in rank, he might also have gone to Beijing to visit the earthly kingdom of the man whom all described as the incarnation of the Buddha of Wisdom, Manjushri, the champion of the Manchu dynasty, who had come to power shortly before.

One consolation was that if the oracle's prophecy proved true, Drakpa Gyaltsen himself also one day would go east, if not to demonstrate his worldly power, certainly to serve the Dharma. But, in what form? As a great lama? A king or a minister? An enlightened buddha? A divine spirit?

His train of thought may have stemmed from a great illusion: created by the oracles; his visions of divinities; the statues speaking to him in his dreams; even the glorious lineage of which he was recognized as holder by his devotees in Drepung, but which that had been systematically denied him.

When he had taken the novitiate vows, a master of chants from the College of Loseling, Tashi Oesel, had composed a series of praises in his and all his predecessors' honor. The Master of Chants named some of the greatest sages in the history of India and Tibet, all considered emanations of the same Manjushri, the Kashmiri masters Shakya Shri, Sakya Pandit, and Buton Rinpoche. However, the verses of praise were censored, which seemed to anticipate Drakpa Gyaltsen's later humiliations in the year of the Water Horse. And then his throne, which was usually positioned at the same level as the Dalai Lama's during the general audiences and at the Monlam festival, was removed.

Drakpa Gyaltsen was torn between his feelings as a humble monk who should give no importance to negative worldly events, and those of the proud Dharma warrior within him, defender of a higher divine justice. As a monk, he was bound by respect for the sacred connection of the *samaya*, the devotee's bond with his brother and master. But in the latter role he was unable to contain either his indignation or his rage.

In the two long years when the Dalai Lama and his three thousand dignitaries and courtiers were absent, stationed at the Manchu Emperor's court, not a few came forward to remind the *tulku* from Gekhasa that he still held the highest rank after the Panchen Lama, and no human decree could revoke the power of his lineage from the celestial order. However,

Drakpa Gyaltsen knew that even the most beautiful fruit, if it falls off the branch before it has ripened, risks rotting on the ground untasted. For this reason, he wanted to maintain his firm resolve to serve the Dharma of the Yellow Hats, whatever course events might take. At an earlier, tragic juncture, he already had done this, once at the cost of the suffering of his elderly parents.

This had happened years before, when another band of ferocious Mongols, similar to the one that had kidnapped him as a child, again swooped down into the Gekhasa Valley. They slaughtered all his brothers without pity, leaving his mother, Agyal, with only one daughter who neither could neither inherit nor manage the immense family holdings on her own. According to a tradition of that era, women were excluded from owning property. And further suffering was added to Lady Agyal by the humiliation of having seen the *tulku* carried in her womb demoted. She tried to call Drakpa Gyaltsen home so that he could take care of the untended lands, and she wept at length, imploring him not to abandon her in that ocean of suffering.

But all she obtained was a poetic and heartbreaking ballad:

> Each one of us, oh Mother, must die in the end, there is no escaping this fact; it is particularly difficult to transform or change karmic causes and circumstances that we have created in the past. Therefore, do not be sad, because the situation in which we find ourselves is the fruit of our past actions. I protected the precepts as if they were the pupils of my eyes, and the opportunity I have had to practice the profound teachings has been a great fortune. To accept your proposal would be equal to refusing this good karma. I would not create anything positive in this life, only negative actions, and in the next one, we would all, children and parents, have an inferior rebirth. Even if I were to remain here, among you, as you request of me, the progeny of the family would not be assured, therefore, there is no reason for me to abandon a life dedicated to the teaching; I would rather die.

His words did not console Lady Agyal; rather, they threw her into an even deeper despair. The tulku's sister, her only other child to survive the Mongol massacre, had no choice but to marry the ambitious Nomsu

Norbu, a man proud of being a close relation of the Regent and Prime Minister of Tibet, Sonam Choepel. Nomsu had no personal property but was very practical and knew how to profit from circumstances. The marriage, besides making him a rich man, conferred upon him the noble title he needed to enter politics. Nomsu became notorious for the brutal—some said violent and unscrupulous—ways in which he later dealt on the regent's behalf with certain practical issues that were embarrassing for a high-ranking religious dignitary such as Choepel. It is impossible to say whether his evil deeds included the murder of Drakpa Gyaltsen, the *tulku* of the Upper Chamber, given the ambiguous and extraordinary events leading to the latter's death. There was a growing suspicion that Nomsu even had close ties to the tribes of Mongol raiders who were responsible for the assaults on Gekhasa. However, so many rumors flew between Lhasa and Drepung that they canceled one another out at lightning speed. Drakpa Gyaltsen may have been aware of his devious brother-in-law's diabolical plans, and this would leave open the hypothesis that Nomsu Norbu had decided to silence him. However, no judge except the supreme magistrate of karma can travel back so far in time and space.

A long time had passed since the return of the Great Fifth from China. His devoted Mongol patron, Gushri Khan, had departed this world, leaving an inheritance of immense, conquered territories to swarms of offspring who soon split up into different tribes and factions, contending with all the other clans that existed already. Among the new Mongol rulers there were murmurings, this time from the inside, of a danger threatening the Gelukpa school, which had been "contaminated" by the Nyingmapa tendencies of the Dalai Lama. The Princes of Oiro and Olkha invited Drakpa Gyaltsen to transmit the Dharma in their territories, but the ministers flatly refused, despite the offer of rich donations in silver coinage.

The tulku remained unperturbed, telling himself that perhaps those people had not accumulated sufficient merit to receive his precious teachings. Nonetheless, whispers that he desired to leave this world soon began to circulate insistently.

The old Panchen Lama of Tashi Lhunpo, who had been master to both the Drepung tulkus, had hoped, in the way that a patient father indulges his child, that time and experience would save the Gekhasa tulku from the cage he was building with meticulous perseverance around himself and his world. However, facts demonstrate that, at this crucial point of his existence, Drakpa Gyaltsen was no longer was able to read into the mirror of his clear mind.

In his autobiography, he wrote:[88]

> The Omniscient Panchen Lobsang Choegyen,
> With loving compassion and goodwill,
> Orally transmitted the divination and
> Identified me as the reincarnation of Gelek Pasang.[89]
> This divided my mind in two,
> And a blaze of perverted notions and jealousy,
> A display of incendiary words [(aimed at me)]
> Desperately stripped my naked karma to the raw bone.
> Considering the faith that I still maintain,
> I seek to find happiness
> In my present circumstances.

Night had coated the sky with luminous stars forming halos around the mountain peaks shrouded in a mellow, opaque light. Sleepless, the sage from the Upper Residence waited, deep in reflection, for the sun to rise. From his window open to infinity, he let in the sky and the dense vaporous mist of the new day. He absorbed the intense, perfumed smoke billowing forth from the resin of the burning branches of the juniper *sang* rite offered up to the gods from the monks' braziers. But, instead of finding relief in this ritual, he was assailed by a new, bitterly lacerating melancholy, the Tantric practitioner's worst enemy. This emotion not only impedes visions in dreams but, also, in the waking hours, throws a veil over the sense of past, present, and future, both near and distant.

Like a bonfire blazing in that mental and material fog, a single sublime thought continued to take shape and substance, not mingling with the others: the fate of the pure Gelukpa doctrine.

Suddenly a faint ray of oblique sunshine traversed the room like gold powder thrown onto the *thangka* of the mighty guardian deity. He had no doubt that this was another long-awaited sign.

---

[88] *Rangnam togjoe zamatok*, from the Tibetan government-in-exile's Scientific Study Committee on the Shugden affair.

[89] Sonam Drakpa's successor.

The Protector of Religion, Nechung's minister, Dorje Drakden, whose contours were outlined in gold embroidery and encircled by flames in relief on a black background, seemed to be reminding him yet again, "Remember the promise!" He had been waiting all too long for a development of the astonishing vision that had conditioned his recent life. This time he was not about to let slip another opportunity to discover it.

He instructed his assistants to go down and offer tea to the entire assembly of monks in Drepung. Then, his body trembling with excitement and fever, he went to call on the medium and awaited his trance. The Nechung Oracle rolled his head like a mad demon, hissed through his tongue and teeth, and finally placed a few grains of consecrated rice in the open palm of his hand, saying, "Take these and go into sealed strict retreat. That way you will remember."

Drakpa Gyaltsen returned to his residence in a strange euphoria. He asked his servants to prepare everything necessary for an indefinite period of meditation and prayer and closed himself in his room.

On the seventh day he had a vision of a peaceful spot near Ganden Monastery. The master Tsong Khapa was seated nearby, shrouded in azure light. He was resting together with some other disciples when a child dressed in white addressed him, repeating with petulant insistence, "You must help me."

One of the disciples took him aside and told him not to disturb the master's repose. "I shall give you what you are looking for. Tell me what you want."

The child smiled happily. "Remember, you have promised in front of the master and the other disciples to help me."

The vision dissolved as if by enchantment. Nevertheless, the monk for the first time had the distinct feeling that that disciple was himself, and that the child was the emanation of a deity, the celestial key to his enigma. If this were really so, he would surely manifest again soon and clarify his obsessive plea.

Some maintain that the pact with the ferocious guardian corresponds to the incubation period of Drakpa Gyaltsen's disease, and that the great design was on the verge of being accomplished. Yet, what mere humans, dedicated to mundane calculations, could not know or foresee was the vastness of the scheme that a man demoted in rank was weaving day after day.

During his long meditation, Drakpa Gyaltsen had overcome his doubts. There was no difference between him and Tsong Khapa's disciple; he had taken the commitment in a previous life to keep his promise to that mysterious, divine child. He now had to work out what to do concretely. He was not worried by the vision in itself, since he knew that everything is empty by nature and all is pure illusion. But he feared that a potent, invisible enemy could test his psychic perceptions, finding him weakened by fever and his own frame of mind.

Gathering his strength, he approached the window and looked at the reflection of rays of the sun in the river, abruptly remembering that this placid body of water was once turned into a fearsome and impetuous scourge during a thaw, connecting the monastery of Drepung and the Fifth Dalai Lama's government to the mystery of Nechung.

It was said that Nechung had arrived inside a chest borne by the river's flow and that, when opening it, someone had witnessed the miraculous manifestation of the spirit escaping the strong current by flying away and settling on top of a tree.

The *tulku* of the Upper Residence was struck by the symbolism of the freed *gyalpo* escaping out into the fresh air after having been locked for who knows how long in the chest. Was not the mind of an ordinary person comparable to that chest? Imprisoned, one is carried along by the course of events toward an undetermined destiny. And does did that turbulent water not represent the relentless passage of time?

Others said that, rather than Nechung, it actually was an ancient Bon mountain and tree spirit, subjugated by the Dalai Lama himself and his masters, the Nyingmapa magicians. Nevertheless, whichever version of these tales was more credible, the fact remained that a clairvoyant monk was possessed regularly by the god to serve as his medium, and that the Nechung Oracle became the main counselor and protector of the Tibetan government. Nechung's attention in this regard thus was doubly welcome, since it compensated for the lack of esteem shown by ordinary folk lacking wisdom.

On the mandala, its center occupied by the omniscient Buddha, stood the figures of Tsong Khapa, the *devas*, the *dakinis*,[90] and the bodhisattvas

---

[90] The *devas* and *dakinis* are various categories of divine male and female beings.

of the four directions, surrounded by the peaceful and wrathful deities of space. From the seed syllable in his heart, the *tulku* emanated a light that reached the mandala. From each figure, the glimmer spread all around, until its rays pervaded the entire dimension of the universe. In the end, he reabsorbed the vision into himself. This was the supreme guru yoga, the union with the primordial master. Finally, Drakpa Gyaltsen saw something arise from the state of bliss beyond concepts.

A sound, a light, rays, and at the end, the limpid projection in space; Nechung was addressing his predecessor, Sonam Drakpa, telling him, "The masters of your school have requested me repeatedly to become the principal guardian of the Virtuous Yellow Hats. However, in the past, at the feet of the Great Acharya Padmasambhava, I promised to protect the entire body of teachings, and I cannot only serve the Gelukpa school. You, Pandit, are the one who possesses the highest erudition. You have already promised to help me. Here is what I ask of you—you must manifest in your fierce wrathful form to defend the teachings of Tsong Khapa."

Now Drakpa Gyaltsen understood. He knew, or thought he knew, that all his predecessors were encompassed in his own mind, and from the void beyond space and time he felt all the weight of his old garment of flesh, bones, and blood. He would soon leave it to fly off, like the spirit from the chest, out of his trembling, feverish body; but this time not to take on another, similar one.

The presences in his room materialized in that state of concentration that lasts interminably.

His attendants, Lingto Chogye and Jangmo, entered and prostrated three times. "We went down to the Lower Residence ..." said Jangmo.

Drakpa Gyaltsen turned his gaze indifferently toward the window. Jangmo continued as if he had not noticed that gesture. "The regent and Governor Norbu have advised His Holiness against coming up, because of the infectious nature of your illness."

The learned monk was unable to hide a grimace. Lingto approached with a pitcher of hot water and a small box inlaid with turquoises containing four dark pills. He crushed them into powder in a stone bowl and handed it to the *tulku*, saying, "You must take this medicine, master," said the assistant as he poured the water into a cup.

Drakpa Gyaltsen remained silent as they administered to him tenderly, rubbing wet towels on his forehead and neck, and massaging his feet and ankles with oil. His fever had diminished and his mind also seemed pacified as positive thoughts started to move through it, like little boats pushed by a light breeze on a calm lake.

This sensation lasted long enough to allow Drakpa Gyaltsen to enjoy once again the imperturbable state that had sustained him throughout his reincarnations during the terrible visions of the *bardo*, which separates death from the next rebirth.

But the illusory game of mirrors reflecting one another, creating new lives and dimensions, left the cruel, fleeting, unresolved mystery of the emotions assaulting him as he emerged from a meditative contemplation. External figures, at times affable, at others adverse, crowded his thoughts. One of these was his spiritual brother and master, now the greatest and most revered lama in the history of Tibet. Drakpa Gyaltsen knew he should not judge him, yet he did. He knew that good and bad, right and wrong, are categories produced by a mind distracted from contemplation on equanimity, the enemy of the true and an obstacle to clear perception. These thoughts renewed the perennial challenge created by desire for revenge and regret for having surrendered to his impulses and instincts.

At that time, Drakpa Gyaltsen was thirty-eight years old, and his illness had started on the twenty-fifth day of the fourth month in the year of the Fire Monkey. His brother-in-law and Regent Sonam Choepel waited, biding their time, circling around him like birds of prey.

A Spirit for Posterity

Each one of us must die alone, whether to be reborn in a mother's womb or in another form. We, too, must leave Drakpa Gyaltsen to his last thoughts and relieve him of our indiscreet presence at the moment of extreme mystery that separates the mind from the body.

History and legend now replace his intimate, narrating voice. It is said that the enemies of the Gekhasa *tulku* had decided of common accord to eliminate him, even if he were to survive the fever. They had removed all his rank from him, but the danger remained. Gushri Khan was no longer there to defend the government of the Dalai Lama from external and internal enemies, and for some time now, newly rich and powerful Mongolian princes had been requesting an audience with Drakpa Gyaltsen, considered the only uncontaminated champion of the Gelukpa order left, like a single lotus growing in the mud. Thus, others joined those already demanding that he be given a role worthy of his lineage: the monks and the lamas in the faithful monasteries. His family, in particularly, his mother, would incessantly implore important members of the Lhasa aristocracy to intervene on his behalf.

Touched by the support and affection of so many, the *tulku* overcame the first critical phase of fever and seemed determined to recover. But at dawn on the third day, he died. One of the versions of the story claims that it was due to a relapse; another that it was suicide; and yet another that it was murder. The latter version was supported by Trijang Rinpoche. In any case, the date of his passing was the thirteenth day of the fifth month, July 1656.

From this point begin the conjectures. The most diverse hypotheses have been drawn from historical texts deemed improbable by some, while other theories have been born in the fervid fantasies of later generations.

Trijang Rinpoche, who was as devoted to Drakpa Gyaltsen's cause as he was to the Buddha Dharma, claims that they had first tried to kill him with weapons, but that because the swords could not pierce his body, they suffocated him with a ceremonial scarf.

"When those motivated by bad intentions strangled you with a silk scarf, you arose as a wrathful deity by the strength of your intention or your vow of bodhichitta," wrote Trijang in his prayer *The Cymbals Delighting an Ocean of Protectors*. His version appeared three centuries after those events and is very different from the Fifth Dalai Lama's account in his autobiography:

> As there was to be an eclipse on the fifteenth day of that month, I decided to stay in strictly sealed retreat after having consulted the astrological indications. When, on the morning of the eleventh day of the month I began to practice the recitation of the mantra of White Manjushri, I was overcome by sleepiness. I interrupted my meditation session and tried to wake myself up as best I could. Then I said: "If this feeling of heaviness takes over in my afternoon session too, my retreat will be in vain."

> When Drakpa Gyaltsen was struck by a highly infectious fever, Lingto Chogye and Jangmo cared for him and he made a full recovery. Saying that there was no danger to his life, the regent decided to send Nomsu Norbu to Mongolia to negotiate with certain tribal leaders. But the following morning his health deteriorated and donations were made to the monasteries on his behalf. The government functionaries then consulted the Oracle of Nechung and returned to Lhasa at noon, and warned me against visiting him [because of the nature of his illness]. Personally, though, the Oracle told me that I should confer the Mahakala empowerment on him so as to eliminate all interferences, and I felt embarrassed that I had not gone previously. I thought that what happened did not matter, and I decided to call on him anyway. I quickly ended my retreat and went to the Upper Residence. I granted him the initiation, but the *tulku* was as if possessed by a demon and his mind was not clear, therefore the practice had no effect, and on the thirteenth day of the month he died.

Trijang comments, "The Dalai Lama leads us to believe that Drakpa Gyaltsen died of disease, and as it is unthinkable that he would lie intentionally, he must have been deceived by the regent."

The strangling—if this is what happened—came after the Great Fifth Dalai Lama's attempt to save him from the demon, who had, he says, assailed the tulku. But who witnessed the crime? Drakpa's assistants and his servants probably would not have left him alone, especially in his debilitated physical condition. Thus, the assassins eventually also would have had to eliminate them in order to silence rumors. Who related these events? And why, after so many centuries, is the manner of his death and what took place in the Upper Residence still disputed?

The only fact unanimously agreed upon is that his body was burned on a pyre in the courtyard of the Tantric college of Drepung.

What happened during and after the cremation is also highly contested, one of the many enigmas surrounding the man who spent his life as a demoted tulku and then became a spirit. Or at least this is how he has been remembered.

Since the Fifth Dalai Lama was not present, let us refer once again to Trijang Rinpoche's account:

> Once the funeral pyre was set ablaze, the rite began. The white smoke rose straight up and divided into three distinct columns, which blew away. As Drakpa Gyaltsen's attendant watched those peaceful clouds ascend, he implored the master: "Motivated by jealousy and wicked intentions, they took your life, yet you still show kindness." Then he waved his monk's shawl in the air and the smoke separated. Two parts dissolved into the sky, and one darkened and assumed the shape of a closed fist as it spiraled down toward earth through the Dembag toward the direction of Tsangpu, the open space below the monastery, a sign that the wisdom mind of Drakpa Gyaltsen had asked for help from Sertrap.[91]
>
> The tulku's body was not consumed by the fire, and an octagonal silver stupa was constructed to contain it. The stupa was then transported temporarily to the Upper Residence. The wardens heard explosions, voices, lamentations, and terrifying sounds coming from inside. Nobody could approach it. After having called upon the Nechung Oracle, the regent had the silver stupa opened and the body removed and put into a wooden box, which was

---

[91] A famous guardian deity of the Kadampa order.

> thrown into the river Kyichu. The current dragged it to
> Dol in the land of Lhoka, to the place known as Dol
> Chumig Karmo.

No account of the cremation ceremony other than Trijang's is known. The
Fourteenth Dalai Lama, however, conducted research on these events
three and a half centuries later and recounted that it was Lak Agyal, the
Gekhasa tulku's mother, and not his assistant, who invoked his spirit as
the smoke arose and urged him explicitly to remember his promise and
seek revenge. The source from which the Tibetan leader drew this information is probably a passage in one of the autobiographical collections of
his predecessor, the Fifth Dalai Lama, who also states, "The false reincarnation of Tulku Sonam Gelek Palzang was successfully recognized because
of Lak Agyal's clever manipulations."

Let us now turn to the fate of Drakpa Gyaltsen's spirit, and the victims
of his first sweeping acts of revenge. The morning after the cremation
ceremony, the Fifth Dalai Lama wrote:

> In a deceptive vision I saw a monkey, black as a bear skin
> and with eyes with orange spiraling stripes, who was chas-
> ing a spirit benevolent to the teaching. At times the mon-
> key would be riding on the spirit's neck. Then when the
> body of Drakpa Gyaltsen was burned, Palden Lhamo said
> to me, "A man hiding nearby has set off for the Potala."

> On the deity's counsel I made offerings, reciting prayers
> and mantras in front of the statue of Avalokiteshvara for
> seven days. Positive signs started to manifest, indicating
> the purification of karma and of obstacles. One night I
> dreamed of a monk wearing a scarf six thumbs long
> whose ends resembled roots. When the monk pronounced
> a sentence, the scarf moved like a living creature. Another
> time I dreamed I was shoeless in the dark along a horse
> trail leading to a military fort. I had to escape when I saw
> a tiger leaping in through a door. This and other night-
> mares, together with serious physical disturbances, were
> certainly provoked by the spirit of Drakpa Gyaltsen.

Therefore I practiced a powerful form of Dorje Drolo,[92]
which also helped me keep an acute fever in check.

In his version of the story, Trijang Rinpoche again does his best not
to feed the hypothesis of an actual conflict between the spirit of Drakpa
Gyaltsen, now supposedly Shugden, and the Great Fifth Dalai Lama. He
writes:

> At the moment of death Drakpa Gyaltsen manifested
> miraculous signs to the Dalai Lama with the sole scope
> purpose of exalting him. In any case, after the Dalai Lama
> had unsuccessfully performed various rites to remove
> these magic manifestations, he ordered the construction
> of a temple to Shugden in Dol Chumig Karmo and made
> offerings of ritual implements to him. This action did not
> bring any concrete results either. Many people fell ill,
> two monks from Namgyal monastery died, and Shug-
> den's manifestations increased unrelentingly. It was at
> this point that the monks from Namgyal requested that
> His Holiness perform a fire offering ritual to destroy him.

As regards the fire offering ritual, the two versions by the Great Fifth and
by Trijang Rinpoche again contradict one each another.

But all the numerous sources of that epoch agree that grave turmoil
was signaled far and wide, all of it attributed "to Dolgyal," as the Fifth
Dalai Lama writes in his autobiography:[93]

> He is referred to as Dolgyal because he is a *gyalpo* [*king
> demon*] from Dol Chumig Karmo. *Gyalpo* is a class of
> interfering spirit. Since Shugden belongs to this group, he
> is also called Gyalchen [(the Great *Gyalpo*)], a very power-
> ful perfidious spirit (*dam sri*),[94] born due to distorted

---

[92] One of the numerous fierce divine manifestations created by Padmasambhava to subdue demons.

[93] Heavenly Silk Garment (Dukulai Gosang), vol. Kha, Lhasa edition.

[94] The spirit of one who has deliberately breached his oath or commitment to his lama out of resentment and dissension.

234 · *The Dalai Lama and the King Demon*

prayers, who has been harming the teaching of the Buddha
and sentient beings.

That he is indeed Dolgyal is no longer a mystery, at least not for the Fifth
Dalai Lama. However, he does not explain what kind of "distorted prayer"
was uttered by his contemporary. What we do know from the texts (possibly
rewritten more recently) that have reached us is that the Gekhasa tulku's
predecessors promised to defend the Gelukpa transmission in the form of a
fierce guardian. If we are to believe the later versions, they kept this promise through their last representative on earth, Drakpa Gyaltsen. We must
bear in mind that before the Gekhasa tulku's birth there was nothing to
defend. Yet the Gelukpas were attacked violently and at length by the
rulers of Tsang and their allies in the Kagyupa school. We can deduce,
then, that, for the Shugden supporters, the Fifth Dalai Lama was more
dangerous than the King of Tsang and his court. The intervention of an
authoritative new king or spirit was necessary and was launched, the day
after Drakpa Gyaltsen's death, against that singular "enemy of the faith."
An odd enemy it was, who, though practicing the Nyingmapa discipline,
had spread the school of the Yellow Hats all over the land.

Shugden's principal target was the Fifth Dalai Lama, whose own
court seemed disconcerted and paralyzed by fear. Quoting from the Great
Fifth's autobiography:

> The harmful activity of Gyalchen Shugden has intensified
> since the Fire Bird year (1657), and the spirit has been
> successful in many of his missions. But, as if this did not
> concern them, hardly anyone has taken any action.... At
> the end of the Earth Bird year, 1669, a new house was
> constructed at Dol Chumig Karmo and articles were placed
> there in the hope that it would become a place for the
> *gyalpo* to settle.

This did not, however, placate the spirit. The Fifth Dalai Lama continues:

> Toward evening on the first day of the month of the
> Earth Dog, I found myself in Drepung and was told by my
> attendant that Desi Sonam Choepel was ailing. I dispatched
> a mantra written on a slip of paper and some consecrated
> pills for him to swallow. But I learned that he had been
> struck by a serious paralysis, and in fact he died at noon .

on the third day. I practiced the transference of consciousness[95] for him.

The Dalai Lama also clearly ascribes Desi Sonam Choepel's death to
the spirit of Drakpa Gyaltsen. He writes:

> The potent Guardian Nechung had informed the regent
> that the stupas of the Upper Palace had been possessed by
> demons and had to be removed. Instead he only had the
> silver stupa dismantled—where Drakpa Gyaltsen's remains
> had been placed after the cremation—and left the other
> stupas standing. For this reason, Nechung told me, the
> regent fell ill and the problem became more serious,
> obliging us to demolish the other stupas too.

> I do not know if it is true that the spirits were really
> present, but before the eight stupas of the Upper Palace
> were dismantled, they were said to be emitting laments
> and voices.[96] On the base of these superstitions it was
> unanimously decided to send the various parts of the
> stupa to Tolung, the tulku's family home, and have the
> wooden structure thrown into the river. In their place by
> the Upper Palace a shrine to a wrathful spirit was built,
> where the monks of the three Drepung colleges would
> congregate to recite the scriptures.

The Fifth Dalai Lama does not censor the details of further misfortunes—
the earthquakes, the sudden deaths of his personal monks, the extinguished
butter lamps. He recounts, "In the Lhasa area many people starved to death
in a famine, and for five years[97] bad omens of the supernatural spirit of
Drakpa Gyaltsen were observed."

The Dalai Lama then decided to proceed with a powerful exorcism, a
fire offering ritual that he executed personally together with seven groups

---

[95] A special technique called "*powa*" that prevents the deceased's mind from regressing
into inferior realms.

[96] This was confirmed in Trijang Rinpoche's subsequent version.

[97] The years of the Fire Bird, Earth Dog, Earth Pig, Iron Rat, and Iron Ox.

of practitioners led by the greatest Tantric masters of the time. On that occasion, the Dalai Lama invoked all the guardian deities of Tibet, offering them a libation so that 'the so-called Drakpa Gyaltsen who pretends to be a sublime entity even if he is not, becomes "devoid of any help or refuge" and "reduced to dust." But in the eventuality that "human and animal diseases, hail, hunger, and drought were due to other harmful spirits," he invited the protectors of the Land of the Snows to reduce them to "tiny particles."

The rites started with this premise. They were conducted in different places, including the Upper Residence, where the first problems had arisen. According to the Dalai Lama, a great number of signs, among them a strong smell of burning flesh, demonstrated that the exorcisms were fully successful and that "many lives were saved," while these "infernal creatures" were being guided 'toward a peaceful state of being" and saved from the danger of "having to experience the intolerable suffering of bad states of rebirth due to their increasingly negative actions."

Here again, Trijang's version differs sharply. He writes:

> When they attempted to burn Shugden in the ritual, Sertrap manifested a magnificent monastery on the mountain called Bunpo near Drepung and shook the top of the Potala. The Dalai Lama's concentration vacillated and the ritual had no effect. After all, Drakpa Gyaltsen had practiced to reach the perfection stage of the yoga of *Guhyasamaja*.[98]

Trijang also lists further acts of sorcery that occurred while the other masters invited by the Fifth Dalai Lama to the fire sacrifice were trying to annihilate Shugden. The spirit always seemed to mock them by placing himself on the tip of the ritual instrument used to pitch him into the fire, a sort of long spoon. According to Trijang, the great Terdag Lingpa of the celebrated Mindroling lineage, who was the Fifth Dalai Lama's Nyingmapa master, was distracted in turn by a magic vision and the spirit of Shugden flew off in the form of a pigeon.

---

[98] One of the principal protector deities of the Gelukpa tradition.

Among these stories and legends, we may also consider the version from Terdak Lingpa's "inner biography."[99] The Nyingmapa lama recounts how, after having been summoned to the Potala by the Dalai Lama, he found him "slightly ill." (All the versions of the story are in accord regarding the Dalai Lama's ailment and the terrible occult phenomena following tulku Gyaltsen's death.) Terdak joined in the monks' prayers and the next day climbed up on the roof of the new palace dressed like Guru Padmasambhava and recited the "the oath to which demons and gods are subject." Terdak writes, "I clearly saw all the ferocious beings of the eight classes gathered together with their retinues. They listened to the pledge with respect and agreed to undertake what was asked of them. Then on the Dalai Lama's request I celebrated the fire rite, assuming the fiery form of Guru Dragpur's wrath."[100]

Terdak's account continues:

> I saw that at this point of the rite the untamable elemental spirit, wandering in the night, being seized, tied around the waist, killed, and eaten. All the participants heard screams and smelled a burnt odor. After these and other positive signs, the Dalai Lama completely recovered.

Terdak Lingpa then advances another hypothesis on Shugden's true nature.[101] "The one they call Dolgyal cannot be Drakpa Gyaltsen. He probably is the incarnation of a Karmapa monk born in Yarto who did not fulfill his commitment and had malevolent intentions rooted in his sectarian outlook."[102]

---

[99] *The Music that Reveals Infinite Qualities*, cited by the venerable contemporary Nyingmapa lama Chadral Rinpoche, author of a lengthy work on Shugden.

[100] Considered the most powerful of Padmasambhava's Tantric manifestations when he defeated the Bon demons.

[101] From the biography of another Tantric Nyingmapa master who was his disciple, quoted by Chadral Rinpoche in his book, *An Adamantine Rain of Fire*.

[102] The Karmapa is the head of the Kagyu school, the Tsangpa patron of which was at odds with the Fifth Dalai Lama's order during the war between U and Tsang. The hypothesis that one of his disciples could be the real spirit of Dorje Shugden has been referred to by many other sources, including the current Karmapa, who resides in India.

All that now remains is to conclude the last chapter of the sad adventures of Drakpa Gyaltsen, his ferocious, restless spirit, whoever he may be, and the Fifth Dalai Lama. With no refutation, the Great Fifth writes:

> With the intention of seeking refuge with the Panchen,
> the spirit circumambulated the monastery of Tashi Lhunpo,
> where, however, Vaishravana, god of wealth and guardian
> of the north, and the eight horse deities barred him access
> and chased him away.

Having left Tashi Lhunpo behind, one night Gyaltsen's poor roving spirit arrived at the walls of Sakya Monastery where, just then, Dagchen Sonam Rinchen was teaching three hundred people. Shugden began to disturb many of the participants. One night, the master dreamt of a monk's face with many eyes appearing next to the temple and asked him, "Who are you?" "I am the evil spirit (*dam sri*) of a Gelukpa master, and I ask you to give me my share of food." So then Dagchen told him he could stay and gave him a place where his soul[103] could remain. Subsequently, the master's son built him a shrine, and from this small refuge Shugden's adventure in the new century began. This would prove to be even more turbulent than the previous one for the embattled Land of the Snows and its ancient doctrines. Indeed, the seeds of intolerance and sectarianism sown before, during, and after the stormy relationship between Drakpa Gyaltsen and the Dalai Lama were bearing bitter fruit. That the two were in conflict was now undoubted. Perhaps neither of them imagined that the struggle would continue for centuries.

---

[103] The subtle energy of the body and mind.

PART FIVE

The Crime Scene

After days spent fully immersed in Drakpa Gyaltsen's universe, I went out and walked by the small building where Geshe Lobsang Gyatso had lived. I intended to visit it to get a precise idea of where the killings had taken place. I went to the office of the Ministry for Religious Affairs, where the Department of Security also had its headquarters. A number of its staff had worked with the Indian police during the investigation of the three homicides. One of them, Ngodup P., had accompanied me to meet the slain geshe's former assistant, Kalsang Damdul. When I asked him if I could visit the crime scene, Damdul said that would be no problem, since it had been decided to transform the room into a museum in remembrance of what had happened there. I could go that very morning.

As we were waiting, Ngodup spoke at length about the research their office had done. He urged me not to underestimate Beijing's interest in the entire affair. "Numerous articles have been published in the official Chinese press, particularly in *China's Tibet*, which describes His Holiness's decision to limit the cult of Shugden as "antidemocratic," "ridiculous," and "hysterical." He showed me a magazine with a shiny cover in the unmistakably naïve style of older Chinese publications. "Read this," said Ngodup. "Aren't you surprised to see atheists who destroyed hundreds of monasteries and killed millions of Tibetans defending the cult's request for 'religious freedom'? They claim to be the 'counter-resistance' to the Dalai Lama and say that His Holiness has by now lost all 'political and religious control over Tibetans.'"

I told Ngodup I had read about cases of spying here in Dharamsala, too. "Two Tibetans in Peking's Beijing's service were hiding detailed maps of the surrounding area and His Holiness's residence in an apartment," he confirmed. "One of them was called Chompel and came from Chamdo in eastern Tibet, the other, Migmar, was from Lhasa. During the questioning, Chompel admitted to having been trained by the People's Liberation Army for over four years and said that he entered India in the guise of a refugee to pass information to his superiors. But according to the Indian secret services, Migmar was the actual ringleader of the group, which was never entirely identified. They had precise plans of His Holiness's residence with the details of our security service's protection. That was a lot more worrying than what emerged from the cross-examination of the

241

arrested men, and we strengthened our security system against possible attacks.

"After the arrests, a spokesperson for China's Foreign Ministry swiftly denied any involvement of his nation in the spying, offering to reopen the dialogue with the exile authorities in Dharamsala to avoid 'separatist activities' on the part of the Tibetans. But the truth is that a plan to provoke divisions within our community had been established in various secret meetings, including one in May 1993 in Chengdu, in southwestern China, and one in Beijing in July 1994. Even a cook had managed to infiltrate His Holiness's kitchens before we succeeded in unmasking him. The Chinese government published a *Guide to Religious Instruction* for the political re-education of monks and nuns in Tibet in March, 1997. One of the chapters was dedicated to Shugden, with prayers and a series of declarations originally printed by the devotee press here in India and abroad. Did you know that they have numerous centers in the West?"

When I answered that I did, the security official showed me some press material issued by the "International Coalition" dedicated to the cult; most of it was the same as what I had been given at Ganchen Tulku's center in Milan.

I mentioned the name of "His Holiness" Kundeling. Ngodup, after thinking it over for a moment, said, "Ah, you mean "Nga lama." I asked him if that was his real name, and both Ngodup and the geshe burst out laughing. "No, '*Nga*' means 'me;' we use this Tibetan expression for someone who proclaims himself a lama—'Me lama,'" said Ngodup. "You must know he was not recognized as his predecessor's reincarnation by the Labrang, the true Kundeling Rinpoche's private institution...."[104]

"Actually, one of his disciples was calling him "His Holiness," I said.

"Really? Well, then he is rapidly going up in rank. Where did you meet him, in his center in Bangalore?"

"No, I had an interview with him in Milan in Ganchen Tulku's headquarters."

"As you see, they are very close," said Ngodup. "Ganchen and Nga lama are most active in the campaign against His Holiness, and their aim

---

[104] In Dharamsala and in his southern monastery, a young Kundeling tulku lives and studies, considered by the government-in-exile and his fellow lamas to be the genuine Kundeling reincarnation.

is to involve as many Westerners as possible. But there's something else I forgot to mention about China. The government has established a Shugden Foundation in Lhasa with financing to renovate the temple affiliated with the spirit in Panglung."

"What do the Indian police think of the links between Tibetan exiles and the authorities in Beijing?" I asked.

"The Indian police also are convinced that the geshe's assassins are under Chinese protection.... Did you speak to the investigators?" Ngodup asked me.

"I would like to meet Superintendent Singh."

"Mr. Singh has left his post and now lives in Delhi. If you see him, ask him for as many details as possible regarding the inquiry. You'll see for yourself what happened."

Ngodup returned to his office. Shortly afterwards, a young monk arrived with a bunch of keys in hand to take me to the building where Lobsang Gyatso and his two assistants had been stabbed. The entrance to the apartment was not visible from the street. The monk removed the lock, and as soon as he opened the door I saw the bloodcurdling photographs of the bodies displayed on the wall in front of me. *"What difference is there between a demon and a man possessed by hatred?"* I thought. Next to the pictures of the slaughter was a row of images of the exiled geshe in different situations: performing ordinations, inaugurating schools and monasteries, conducting private interview, and accompanying the Dalai Lama on ceremonial occasions.

The young monk explained that His Holiness the Dalai Lama was well aware of the dedication the geshe had put into his work to educate the young. For many years, he had taught children and youths in a school in Mussoorie, helping them in every way he could. "Sometimes he would wash their clothes and buy them food with his own money," he said.

I looked around and asked if any object there before the crime had been left. I learned that the bed where his sprawled body had been found was still in its place, but the rest of the room had been emptied to make room for display cases all around. The geshe's various publications in Tibetan were exhibited under glass, and the monk explained that these consisted mainly of philosophical treatises and critiques of the Shugden cult. There was also his speech at the inauguration of the School of Dialectics, founded in 1973 by the Dalai Lama and entrusted to his directorship. Since then, Lobsang Gyatso's activities had greatly expanded and led him all over the world. He also had been the first lama to give teachings in Israel, and he had students from Mongolia, Japan, the United States, Europe, and Australia.

I read his introduction to a small book written after the director had received quite a few letters from the so-called Shugden committee. "I would have preferred to respond directly," he explained, "but it was impossible because they did not give any address.[105] The fact that they have not provided a return address denotes their reluctance to show their true face, and on my part I have no burning desire to see them," he wrote. Then, from the shelf I picked up a book in a shiny jacket with a picture of a smiling Lobsang Gyatso. It was a biography written by his English disciple, Gareth Sparham. I opened it to a page at random. "Before I left the village my uncle told me, 'Your only duty is to study. I did not teach you any rites because once in town I don't want you to get distracted by rich families inviting you to perform paid ceremonies.'"

I noticed that the monk had left. Oddly, I felt perfectly at ease reading the victim's writings on my own, alone in the very room where he had met such an atrocious death. It was an opportunity to get to know him better. Several passages revealed his character. "I remember that my master did not want me to participate in the philosophical debates," he wrote, "and did not assign a teacher to prepare me. I insisted on going anyway. I listened to all the debates and studied like mad until finally one of the instructors presented me as an example to the monks, who had always treated me like an idiot."

In the pages of the book Lobsang Gyatso emerges as a man of religion, totally dedicated to his mission. One can guess that he would not have wanted to end his self-imposed isolation without having found an answer to the problem that had made him don monastic robes.

> One day, while I was thinking about going home to visit my family, I bought a text in a Lhasa bookstore. It said that one's birth place is the demon Mara's prison and family members are the bait that he uses to drag us in there. I asked my master for an explanation, and he said

---

[105] At that time the Shugden Society had not yet opened an office in Delhi.

that if you don't follow your vocation, training in practice and study in the monastery, you end up being a slave to attachment to your family, who will always be sending you letters, begging you to return. Each time you go to visit you discover that there is something that urgently needs doing in the house and outside it, and in this way you slowly build your own prison.

The history of the remarkably swift expansion of Buddhism at the time of the preaching of the former Prince Gautama came to mind. The Indian families in the villages surrounding his hermitage were distressed by the sudden calling of hundreds of young people who abandoned everything, the fields and their relatives, to follow the ascetic into the forests, sleeping on the ground and feeding themselves by begging. The same thing had also happened in Tibet, but the great monasteries of first the Sakyapas, then the Kadampas, the Kagyupas, and especially the Gelukpas, rapidly became self-sufficient. Thanks to their respective patrons, they owned vast cultivable lands, and the monks were by no means itinerant beggars like the Buddha's first disciples.

I skipped some pages and came to the more political sections of the book. They recounted anecdotes from the period of the Thirteenth Dalai Lama, who had passed on when the geshe was a child.

All his reforms to modernize Tibet were hindered by the more conservative members of the clergy and aristocracy. One day, during a ceremony, the medium of the Nechung Oracle offered consecrated water to the assembled government nobles, inviting them to favor the Dalai Lama's policies. When I was a monk in Drepung I heard that some of them drank the water, but many others poured it into their sleeves.... It was at this time that the problems related to Shugden began. The Thirteenth Dalai Lama wanted to cut short the cult's propitiation of the spirit, but since it was venerated by so many Tibetans a formal ban would have caused serious disorders. It would have been like requesting disciples to break their commitment to certain lamas.

In another text, Lobsang Gyatso maintained, "If the Thirteenth Dalai Lama's wishes had been respected, Tibet could have started on a new path of reform and progress and avoided subjugation by the Chinese Communists." He also explicitly blamed the "rivalries between the principal monastic colleges," which "made it easy for China to invade Tibet."

The geshe was particularly critical of Phabongka, who had not abided by the Thirteenth Dalai Lama's advice to put an end to the practice of the *gyalpo*. Instead, he introduced the practice in Drepung Monastery and among the government bureaucrats and the people of Lhasa.

One particularly critical chapter was dedicated to Tagdrak Rinpoche, the former regent who had taken over from Reting when the Thirteenth Dalai Lama was a child. The geshe at that time was a young monk, and the continual feuding between the two lamas' groups had caused revolts and deaths. He wrote:

> The situation was so dramatic that someone even recommended I go home. The government sectarians stoked the tension and enjoyed the continuing chaos while other problems arose in Kham, in Amdo, in central Tibet, and usually wherever the Shugden cult was more developed. In Drepung, it was said that the practice of this *gyalpo* brought problems and disturbances. I didn't pay much attention then, but I did later.

The monk came back into the room and asked if I wanted to stay much longer, but I felt it was not necessary to read his entire collection of writings to understand the lama's pugnacious personality. He believed wholeheartedly in proclaiming his ideas openly, even at the cost of his own life. In a note dated June 5, 1996, eight months before the assassination, he wrote:

> Their ingratitude toward the Dalai Lama and their irresponsible declarations are unacceptable and blasphemous to my ears. I suggest they use their acumen and make the right choice, even if I do not nourish much hope for their souls, already consumed by ignorance.... However, I would be more than happy to participate in a serious and appropriate debate, in an exchange of opinions based on logical reasoning and incontrovertible truths.

I left the room with a heavy heart. His tone was certainly harsh and not very conciliatory, despite his offer to discuss ideas peacefully. But the motive for choosing Geshe Lobsang as victim was incomprehensible to me. What is more, that bloodbath had also ended the lives of two young monks.

The Old Togden

It is certainly truer to say: the devil
created the world than to say that
God created it.

—A. Schopenhauer

Togden[106] Chawang lived a good distance from Dharamsala, in a
small Tantric monastery among forests and valleys opening onto high
mountain ranges, snow-clad for part of the year. The isolated hermitage
was the abode of yogis of different traditions who, in their approach to
the teachings, shared the nonsectarian Rimey[107] perspective. They had
overcome the divides of school and lineage and transmitted one to another
the teachings they had received. Thanks to the support of the monastery,
they were able to spend long periods in retreat in some nearby caves.

My friend Elio, the translator, knew the abbot of that monastery and
had run into him by chance in Dharamsala. Elio told the abbot about our
research and learned from him that Togden Chawang was an extremely
learned man who had studied the history of the conflict at length. He
could not guarantee that the yogi would receive us, but he said he would
use his influence and invited us to the monastery. This was a unique
opportunity to visit a hermitage about which we often had heard. When
we presented ourselves in his office a few days later, the abbot confirmed
that the yogis in the caves had truly special powers and wanted to
demonstrate this. One of them had recently left his body, and, after the
cremation, his relics were stored in a precious silver box inlaid with
precious stones. These relics looked like tiny phosphorescent balls. As
we peered at them through a microscope we discovered, to our wonder,
their shapes and colors. Some were perfect mother-of-pearl spheres while
others looked exactly like minuscule seashells.

---

[106] *Togden* (literally "realization holder") is a term of respect, by custom only accorded to
highly accomplished yogis.

[107] A movement that arose in Kham in the nineteenth century, inspired by Jamyang Khyentse
Wangpo and Jamgon Kongtrul.

We were astonished, and our admiration for those yogis and for Lama Chawang increased considerably. For two days in the village guesthouse we anxiously awaited his attendant's reply.

Finally Kunga, a young disciple, came to say that Togden Chawang had performed several *mo*, which had been positive. The next morning we walked to his retreat place hidden deep in the woods, where total silence reigned. With a sense of excitement, we stepped into a small cell built of simple bricks, permeated by the scent of incense and butter lamps. We had to bend over to avoid touching the ceiling with our heads while Kunga continuously sent us signals to make no noise and to be careful of any object lying around in the soft semi-darkness of that narrow space.

The old man had very long hair gathered in a coil on the top of his head, in the manner of the Indian *sadhus*. His face was completely lined with wrinkles, like a carved mask. Once our eyes got used to the darkness, however, we noticed, however, that the lama's skin was almost luminous. We offered him a *kata* with a small amount of money and were invited to make ourselves comfortable on the frayed carpet on the floor. Kunga sat down in the corner under a *thangka* of Jamgon Kongtrul, one of the founders of the Rimey tradition.

Togden Chawang understood our reasons for wanting to meet him, and while Elio was filling him in on the details, the old lama nodded his head, saying, "*La so, la so.*"[108] In his lap he held a text that seemed to be a prayer book, from which he began chanting recitations:

> This present era is rampant with the five forms of degeneration, in particular the red ideology.... In the future, this system will certainly be forced either from within or without on this land that cherishes the joint spiritual and temporal system. If, in such an event, we fail to defend our land, the holy lamas, including the "triumphant father and son" (the Dalai Lama and the Panchen Lama), will be eliminated without a trace of their names remaining; the properties of the incarnate lamas and of the monasteries, along with the endowments for the religious services, will all be seized.

---

[108] Yes indeed, that is so.

We all recognized the quotation from the prophecy written by the Thirteenth Dalai Lama a year before he died, in 1932. The Togden barely could hold back his tears as he read it. Then we felt the master gazing at us with a strange intensity, as if he were trying to discern our real motivation.

"Listen to what else His Holiness had to say in that prophecy." He continued:

> Moreover, our political system, originated by the three ancient [Dharma] kings, will be reduced to an empty name; my officials, deprived of their patrimony and property, will be subjugated like slaves by the enemy; and my people, subjected to fears and miseries, will be unable to endure day or night. Such an era will certainly come.

Lama Chawang put away the text and looked at the Buddha in the *thangka* hanging on the wall. Then he focused on me while Elio translated his words, whispering into my ear, "A prophecy, my dear stranger, is not a street magician's vision in a crystal ball. We Tibetans call it 'clarity.' It is the fruit of a mind trained to read the future from signs in the present, even when they seem obscure and indecipherable to others."

He paused as he looked intently at each of us. "You know that for the most part, these predictions already have come to pass. The Thirteenth was not the only one to know that our country has a history of wars, invasions, intrigue, betrayals, and lack of reciprocal love and respect. He tried to avoid the further degeneration of our people's karma but foresaw the selfishness of the men in government and the increase of the most deplorable result of their splits: sectarianism."

Are you referring to the cult of Shugden?

"Do not underestimate sectarianism abroad," said the old Togden, "because our suffering is born principally from the lack of unity and respect. I hope that the lesson of Tibet's history at least will be useful to the rest of the world. Do you understand what I mean? Important lamas with high-sounding names may tour Asia and the West, preaching the secrets of esoteric Tantric practices and reciting the scriptures by heart. Nonetheless, if they have not developed within themselves true equanimity, pure altruism, and sincere compassion, they risk creating irreparable damage in the minds of many, leading them toward abysses of intolerance, just like the fanatical terrorists. Look at how many hundreds of thousands, maybe even millions, of people in the modern world, are interested today in Tibetan Buddhism, among them intellectuals with strong followings and influence. But how many have knowledge of the essence of the spirituality originally developed in our land?"

The Shugden supporters say that they, too, are struggling against the corruption of the teachings.

"Je Tsong Khapa did not reestablish Vajrayana Buddhism in Tibet to separate Buddhists and venerate vindictive spirits. He wished to proffer the chance of a gradual access to the knowledge of the sutras and the higher Tantras, even to those who did not possess the innate qualities necessary for yoga. He presented them with sites to which they could retreat and practice a monastic lifestyle, following a strict discipline of meditation and study. But he warned them not to get ensnared in the many pitfalls on the path. One of these he called "the pitfall of partiality." In a famous dialogue[109] he wrote, "All persons who have the temporary view take refuge erroneously in scriptures by fastening upon the view given in the treatises of their own schools exclusively, and divide things into self and other, higher and lower factions...." Everybody knows that Tsong Khapa was not speaking empty words, he never sought worldly power, he even refused repeated invitations from the Chinese emperor, and he never enforced his model, either with swords and guns or by invoking ferocious spirits."

He took a sip of the tea the young man had poured and with a sad smile said, "Surely Tsong Khapa never could have imagined that partiality would, like a tumor, infect many of his heirs, who at times would become allies, at times mute spectators, of continual Mongol, Chinese, and Tibetan repression and intolerance of other traditions."

Do you mean to say that he did not have clarity?

---

[109] A dialogue between the esoteric divinities Vajrapani and Karmavajra (the Nyingma-Kadam master Lhodrak Khenchen in dialogue with Lama Tsong Khapa); translated in *The Life and Teachings of Tsongkapa* by Robert Thurman (Library of Tibetan Works and Archives).

"You know that karma has its own indecipherable ways. Like a subterranean river, once in a while it reemerges on the surface. But I don't want to philosophize too much, history speaks for itself."

Speaking of history: it seems that the most serious problems linked to the sectarian cult of Shugden started in the twentieth century, at the time of the Thirteenth Dalai Lama. Thinking back to your discourse on karma being like a subterranean river, I wonder, how can we trace its source?

Togden Chawang shook his head, sighing. "More than ever, in this last part of my life, so many past coincidences have me reflecting on the mysterious dark force that has tried and is still trying to obstruct not only the Dalai Lamas, but all activities that might benefit the Tibetan people."

Do you mean a kind of curse?

The lama crossed his legs in the lotus position and drank some more tea. "No malediction can affect the minds of beings capable of overcoming the barrier between life and death. But we cannot deny that the power of the bodhisattvas can be challenged by powerful beings able to recreate the same obstacles in the course of time. Only by studying history can we human beings with our limited perception follow the struggle between good and evil."

To what history are you alluding?

"Does it seem normal to you that five Dalai Lamas, one after the other, from the eighth to the twelfth, did not succeed in ruling their country as they should have? That some died in childhood and none reached old age?"

We moved closer to hear the lama better.

"I don't think I am revealing anything new. The current Dalai Lama's elder brother[110] said that some of them, if not all of them, had probably been poisoned, either by Tibetans, who considered them impostors nominated by the Chinese, or by the Chinese, who did not deem them trustworthy. Listen to what a certain Gunthang Rinpoche, a disciple of the

---

[110] Thubten Jigme Norbu, *An Account of the History, the Religion and the People of Tibet*.

great nonsectarian Gelukpa lamas, contemporaries of the Seventh Dalai Lama, wrote in the eighteenth century.[111]

> Though the traditions of the father remain excellent,
> Now they are besmirched with the dark dust of pollution,
> And many false spiritual guides
> Lead beings to the abyss of disaster and grief.

"'The traditions of the father' clearly refers to the teachings of Lama Tsong Khapa. Why did Gunthang write these words? Try to start, as I did, from a simple statement. Upon the death of the Fifth Dalai Lama, and especially around the beginning of the eighteenth century, incomprehensible historical events were taking place. Who is to say whether these events were caused by demonic interferences or not?"

To which events in particular are you referring?

"The regent had kept the Fifth Dalai Lama's death a secret for fifteen years, for fear that the kingdom would break up under the pressure from the numerous Mongol tribes and the Manchu empire. From his point of view, it was a brilliant move. But the Sixth Dalai Lama, Tsangyang Gyatso, had already reached adolescence when he was enthroned. Like the Great Fifth, he had been instructed by Nyingmapa masters and, without the constraints of the monkhood and the role of Dalai Lama, the Sixth Dalai Lama had already developed the great powers of a Tantric yogi. Do you understand what I am saying? I mean the capacity to use every contact of the senses, beginning with one of the greatest earthly pleasures, sex, to develop a specific type of energy generated in the subtle channels while preventing the loss of seed. At night he would carouse with his lovers quite openly, and already had decided to renounce his celibacy vows; he even was willing to sacrifice his investiture as Dalai Lama."

Had there ever been any doubts that he was not the true reincarnation of the Fifth Dalai Lama?

"Few disputed it, but among those who did was a prominent Gelukpa abbot named Kunkhyen Jamshey Lama,[112] who was not alone in considering

---

[111] The text is called *Töpa Dön Denma, Meaningful Praise*.

the Sixth Dalai Lama's behavior scandalous. That Dalai Lama, noted for his seeming transgressions, was eventually exiled and perhaps killed[113] by a Mongol, Prince Lhazang Khan. The Khan, unlike his ancestors, was intent on governing Tibet himself, after removing the regent, too. The legitimate reincarnation's libertine manner served as a pretext to impose another Dalai Lama whose manner was in line with the more orthodox Kunkhyen and Panchen Lamas and who was also endorsed by the Manchu Emperor of China."

It is said that Shugden created many difficulties for the Fifth Dalai Lama. Is it possible that this spirit continued to manifest during the period of his successive reincarnations?

The Togden looked into space and shook his head, saying, "Who can tell? It is certain that, at that time, the lineage of the Dalai Lamas had been distanced from the tenets of its school and that the *gyalpo* spirit had not disappeared at all. In the eighteenth century in the region of Dol, the principal area of Shugden worship, a Gelukpa lama by the name of Morchen Kunga had many visions of a terrifying being whom he regarded as a Dharma-guardian who protected Tsong Khapa's school."

Was it Shugden?

"Yes, even though he was then known as Dolgyal, the *gyalpo* of Dol. According to Morchen Kunga, the spirit was able to manifest more rapidly than any other worldly deity, including the State Oracle, Nechung, and also Palden Lhamo, the personal protector of the Dalai Lama. He even was said to be an emanation of the mighty Mahakala…. The rites for the new guardian transmitted by Morchen Kunga principally were practiced in Riwo Choling, a monastery in Lhoka, and in the Todre Kang of Lhasa. In that period, a student of Morchen[114] wrote a text dedicated to the *gyalpo*

---

[112] Comment by the Fourteenth Dalai Lama in a speech given in Dharamsala in October 1997: "The generally accepted fact that Tsangyang Gyatso was the Fifth Dalai Lama's reincarnation was not contested, except by Kunkyen Lama Jamshe Ngawang Tsondrue (1648–1721) of Tashi Kyil Labrang."

[113] There exists a secret biography according to which he survived and led the life of a wandering hermit.

[114] The lama Sakya Dagchen Sonam Rinchen.

with a significant title, *Destroy the One Who Does Not Believe*. In that text, the spirit was called Shugdenzel, and the name changed later from Dolgyal to Shugden. It was evident that it was the same spirit. As you know, while the cult proliferated, the problems of Tibet increased. Or perhaps without mechanically assuming a connection between the two, one could say the reverse: the problems of Tibet intensified as the cult spread. For me, however, the result was the same."

Is there other proof of devotion to Shugden in those years?

"The great Trichen Dorje Chang,[115] the Abbot of Ganden and tutor to the Seventh Dalai Lama, discovered that several of his predecessors who had been enthroned in Tsong Khapa's monastery had assiduously venerated the spirit and that other lamas and abbots even had erected an altar to him. The Trichen had it demolished, and in the great assembly hall of Ganden he invoked the Dharmaraja Kalarupa, who, along with Mahakala, was the chief deity of the monastery. Dharmaraja does not possess the sectarian characteristics of Shugden even though he traditionally is associated with the Gelukpa school. He is the guardian of respect for the "karmic law of cause and effect" and witness to both positive and negative actions. The biography of Trichen[116] recounts how, after that ritual, Dharmaraja manifested his fearsome power against the worshippers of the new spirit, and several abbots and lamas who had been practicing Shugden suddenly all died at the same time."

It really seems that the deities and spirits of Tibet are more vindictive than its people.

"Stranger, listen and reflect before you make judgments," said the lama, giving me a piercing look. "Peace and compassion need the right circumstances to appear, and if you want to eat bread you must separate the wheat from the weeds. Do you know what had happened while those so-called lamas paid homage to their spirit?"

I dared not reply.

---

[115] Trichen Ngawang Chokden (1677–1751); for his biography, see *A Brief History of Opposition to Shugden*, published by the Tibetan government-in-exile.

[116] Written by Changkya Rolpai Dorje (1717–1786).

The yogi continued; "When the Sixth Dalai Lama was banished and perhaps also murdered, there was a rumor that his reincarnation had been found in the eastern province of Lithang. News of the discovery of the new Dalai Lama put the Mongol prince, Lhazang Khan, in a serious quandary since he already had installed his choice. The clergy, supported by the majority of the Lhasa population, asked the other Mongol tribes, the nomad Dzungar warriors, for help in placing the Lithang tulku on the throne immediately. The Manchu emperor heard about this and had the child and his parents put under strict surveillance.

"The Dzungar Mongols did not succeed in freeing him from the Manchus, but lied to the Tibetans and pretended that the little Dalai Lama was safely under their protection and that soon they would transfer him to Lhasa. Misled by this promise, the members of the faction opposing Lhazang Khan helped the Dzungars penetrate the boundaries of the city by night. Once they were in, the Mongol soldiers put the capital to the sword, plundered the houses, raped the women, and in their savage fury killed anyone in their path. Upon reaching the Potala, where Lhazang had sought refuge, they sacked it and even profaned the remains of the Fifth Dalai Lama.

"After having hunted down and killed the fleeing prince, the Dzungars enforced their dominion, persecuting Nyingmapa practitioners and all the Gelukpas accused by orthodox lamas of having infringed the rules of the order. The memory of the religious wars in previous centuries paled in comparison to their barbarism. Nyingmapa, Kagyupa, and Bon practitioners, together with the followers of the Jonang sect, which had by now almost disappeared, were the prey of a ruthless manhunt. Over five hundred monasteries, statues, and sacred texts of Padmasambhava were destroyed, and the tongues of many Bon and Nyingmapa monks were cut out to prevent them from reciting their secret mantras.

"It was one of the darkest chapters in our history. Many lamas and most of the monks of the three huge monasteries near Lhasa were appalled by the brutality of the repression. Nobody could lift a hand to stop them. By the time the Emperor of China sent his army to Lhasa, the pillaging Dzungars had departed. Accompanying the soldiers from Beijing for the first time were two Manchu governors, called 'amban.' This episode still is used today by Beijing as a pretext to claim sovereignty over Tibet...."

During another brief pause in his tale, I told the Togden that it was difficult to distinguish the historical events from the religious interests linked to cults, traditions, power struggles, and cliques in monasteries and Buddhist schools.

Chawang nodded his head and smiled. Then he started to declaim:

> Prevailing demonic influences will thwart
> the monks who safeguard the teachings.
> The virtuous and well intentioned
> will be weak and suffer many torments.
> The advent of these signs will signify
> That the teaching of the Buddha is disappearing.

"I recited these verses by a renowned yogini[117] because we Buddhists believe strongly in the power of action. When religious and political figures in a country such as Tibet depart from the spirit of the Dharma, it indicates that the collective merit of a people incapable of defeating the ghosts of the past is being depleted."

What happened after the departure of the Dzungar Mongols and the arrival of the Chinese?

"The Manchu Emperor in Beijing had the young Seventh Dalai Lama brought back to Lhasa in triumph, and many members of the religious community together with the laypeople thought it preferable to rely directly on China rather than on the unstable and unpredictable Mongol hordes. And so, the Tibetans lost control of their land yet again. When the old Emperor Kangxi died, his son Yongzheng decided to unleash another campaign against the opponents of the Gelukpa school. The planned massacre was avoided only thanks to the intelligence and courage of Beijing's trusted man in Lhasa. His name was Pholhanay, and though he was a Gelukpa, he had been raised by a tolerant and open-minded Nyingmapa family. However, even under his guidance, intrigue and power struggles still were rife, and even the Seventh Dalai Lama's father was involved in them. All government posts were reserved for the lay and religious members of the community who observed strictly the practices of the Yellow Hats. The Dalai Lama's court also reflected this sectarian approach. The monks in the Great Fifth's personal monastery, Namgyal, were replaced

---

[117] Machig Labdronma.

by the Gelukpa Tantric college's monks, who eliminated all the Nying-mapa rituals.[118] History shows that this sectarianism did not bring about anything positive in the end. After the Seventh Dalai Lama's demise, there began a long and unfortunate series of events for his lineage."

Are you referring to the premature deaths?

"Four or five casualties, one after another, logically should have something in common."

What was the recurring feature of these deaths, apart from the young age of the Dalai Lamas?

"When the Eighth Dalai Lama turned nineteen, the former regent already was dead, and the young man should have taken the reins of the nation in hand. But he either decided, or was forced, to complete his schooling. An important Yellow Hat lama who had acted as spiritual mentor to the Emperor Qianlong for fifteen years was called back from Beijing to act as regent in Lhasa. When he had finished studying, the Dalai Lama accepted the government's invitation to assume his temporal duties; but four years later a new regent was again at his side. Then, unexpectedly, at the age of forty-five, he left his body. It cannot be said that the Eighth Dalai Lama ever really wished to become a sovereign, since he preferred to meditate and study. However, he never was given an opportunity to rule his country in any real way. The Emperor Qianlong was intent on keeping firm control over Tibet. He introduced the use of a golden urn to contain the names of the candidates for the reincarnations of the most important tulkus, including the Dalai Lama. It is a bit like what they did a few years ago with the latest Panchen Lama; indeed, they used the same urn...."

I have heard that the Chinese are thinking of doing the same thing with His Holiness when he dies.

---

[118] The monks in Namgyal started to perform ceremonies belonging to the other schools again only after the current Dalai Lama banned the practice of Shugden.

"We shall have to see what the Tibetans think of that. In any case, when the Emperor Qianlong discovered that the urn had not been used for choosing the name of the Ninth Dalai Lama, the young candidate did not have a long life. Officially, he was the victim of pneumonia, but others say he was poisoned. He was less than ten years old."

Did the emperor have him killed?

"Nobody can confirm the truth now. However, regarding Qianlong, there is another story that may interest you.... It seems that he presented a *thangka* of Shugden to a nonsectarian lama of the Gelukpa tradition.[119] Perhaps the emperor thought he would appreciate it, or else he had no idea who the painted figure was. Nevertheless, this is a sign that in the first half of the eighteenth century, the image of the demonic spirit was circulating in Peking."

And what happened to the Tenth Dalai Lama?

"Nor was he to have a long or leisurely life. His regent was a monk from Amdo who was in turn manipulated by China. The young tulku, obviously closely monitored, secretly would seek out the people of Lhasa, evading the Potala courtiers. When he was barely fifteen years old, he wrote a plan for a series of reforms based on his impressions. But he was not able to put his resolutions into practice. He also died suddenly, at the age of twenty-two, without ever having ruled.

"The Chinese-loving regent was under suspicion, but nonetheless was given the task of searching for the eleventh reincarnation. It took him five years. Not long afterwards, he also died. With him gone, the new Dalai Lama finally had the opportunity denied his predecessors. This was also because the Chinese were busy with other emergencies—the opium war, the peasant uprisings, and the Anglo-French military threat. Someone exclusively faithful to the Tibetan cause was nominated to act as regent until the Dalai Lama reached adulthood. On his eighteenth birthday, this regent stepped aside to let him govern. But on the eve of his enthronement, the Eleventh Dalai Lama also died."

---

[119] Changkya Rolpai Dorje (1717–1786).

The Togden paused to give us time to reflect on this incredible chain of events. He told us that the Eleventh Dalai Lama's death was attributed to a long illness caused by his weak constitution. But there was an additional twist to the story, and once more it concerned the cult of Shugden. "The ambassador from Beijing," recounted Togden Chawang, "one day took a series of heartfelt questions to the Trode Khangsar in Lhasa, where you still will find an altar dedicated to the demonic spirit. He had written these questions in Chinese characters on a piece of paper, and once inside the temple he burned the list in the flame of a butter lamp. The next day, Shugden was called upon to manifest through the oracle and gave answers, which, it is said, left the man speechless. The ambassador referred all of this to the Emperor Dhakong, requesting permission to offer verses of thanks and praise to the spirit in the temple. Once the authorization was obtained, numerous ceremonies were held in which Shugden was officially called—for the first time—'Guardian of the Doctrine of the Yellow Hats.'"[120]

So two Manchu emperors, even if only marginally, had something to do with Shugden in the past. This tale is really full of surprises....

"Indeed. In any case, the sequence of deaths of the Dalai Lamas did not end with the passing of the eleventh in line. His successor's story is just as sad, though not as mysterious. Since his childhood, the thirst for power displayed by the heads of Drepung Monastery and several unscrupulous laymen had created bloody feuds within the city of Lhasa. Barely two years after his investiture, the Dalai Lama died at the end of a journey. He was not yet twenty years old, and this time the perpetrators of the crime were identified, two dignitaries who were tortured and exiled."

The lama stopped and opened his arms. "There, I have finished this account of the list of strange events that preceded the arrival in this world of the man who finally has put an end to the misfortunes afflicting his lineage, a man truly different from his seven precursors, a figure we only can compare to the Great Fifth Dalai Lama."

---

[120] The episode is cited in the *Collected Works of Thu-bkwan Blo-bzang-chos-kyi-nyi-ma, 1.5–831, 221* (Delhi: Ngawang Gelek Demo. 1969–1971), also mentioned by the Dalai Lama in a speech, May 8, 1996, and in a text by Trijang Rinpoche.

What do the Fifth and Thirteenth Dalai Lamas have in common, besides the fact that they lived much longer than all the others?

"They were both elevated Tantric practitioners of all traditions, particularly the Nyingma.[121] I am not saying their life was longer because of this. Certainly not, especially since the Thirteenth Dalai Lama departed this world at the age of fifty-eight. But they clearly displayed strengths of intellect and character that the others did not possess or were not able to demonstrate because of the circumstances. To give you an idea, when the Thirteenth Dalai Lama was ten years old, he wrote a furious letter to the British and the Chinese who had 'arrogated to themselves the right' to carve up the Tibetan territory without consulting the Potala. His counselors told him that it was inappropriate for a child his age to express such opinions. But he already had a strong wish for the autonomy of his nation.

"Unfortunately, the vicissitudes of his reign after his investiture were clouded by dubious and ambitious protagonists who betrayed his trust. Although these are well-known facts, books hold no in-depth explanations of why the Thirteenth Dalai Lama wrote that shocking prophecy that I read to you earlier.

"The consolidation of his authority within a few years and Tibet's declaration of independence were not achieved without paying a price. Apart from the struggles between among different factions, the boycott of his attempts at modernization, and so forth, the usual problem of sectarianism raised its ugly head. Never before had the cult of Shugden spread at such a pace as during his reign; as you may know, one lama in particular dedicated himself to worshipping the spirit and succeeded in conditioning government officials and hundreds of monks."

Are you talking about Phabongka?

The Togden's expression was enigmatic.

---

[121] The annals of Dzogchen Monastery include the Thirteenth Dalai Lama among the most important discoverer of "treasures" hidden in the time of Padmasambhava. Vested with the mystical name Drakden Lingpa, the Thirteenth Dalai Lama composed complex Tantric commentaries and rediscovered the secret text of a practice of the deity Vajra Kilaya. This Tantric divinity is renowned for his power to defeat the *gyalpo* demons, the class of beings to which Shugden is said to belong.

"In his case, too, you can find many written explanations," were his only words.

The young Kunga motioned to us that perhaps it was time to let the elderly yogi rest. So I asked him a final question.

I still don't understand why so much attention has been lavished on Shugden and not on one of the other thousands of gods or spirits of your religion.

"Shugden's followers claim that he has set himself a sort of divine task, and that men never will be able to judge the essentially compassionate motivation behind his ferocious nature. But I think that what has convinced many to place themselves under his protection is the extreme ease with which he can be invoked, a quality that may have proved as fascinating to the faithful of the eighteenth century as it does to his adepts today. Aren't rapidity and efficiency distinctive of modern civilization? It is a great pity that not everyone is aware of the consequences we are facing."

What are you implying?

"Several things. To acquire power and wealth at all costs, one always has to establish a pact with the demon of the ego, and as in any pact with a demon, the price is very high. Stranger, don't you agree?"

Kunga gave us another meaningful glance. It was clear that we had taken up too much of the Togden's time. We said farewell, thanking him respectfully. The old man just smiled at us with a light wave of the hand. We had stayed hours in his cell and our limbs were stiff, but we gladly would have spent more time talking with him had it been appropriate.

Phabongka in the Time of the Thirteenth Dalai Lama

The day after our long interview with the Togden, Elio and I returned to Dharamsala to work further on the texts in the Library of Tibetan Works and Archives. By evening, we had found many new translations, mainly of the biographies and autobiography of Phabongka. I went back to reading and writing in my quiet room at the Tara Guest House.

In 1878, when the Thirteenth Dalai Lama was three years old, Kyabje Phabongka Dechen Nyingpo was born in Shan to a family of merchants and governors of Chapli. His father, considered a very generous man, would share his food with poor people and passersby, and his mother, Choedron, was thought to be a *dakini*. Miraculous dreams accompanied her pregnancy until a son was born, a breech baby. Even as an infant he was fat, with a round, white face. On the top of his head there was a protuberance the size of a thumb, which disappeared in time, and on his back were white spots like bone fragments.

Ever since she had carried him in her womb, his mother had prayed and made offerings to the tutelary deities that a great master be born to her. An episode in Phabongka's early childhood convinced her that her prayers might have been answered. During a visit to a temple, the little boy grasped at a great lama's tunic in a display case. "Give me my robe!" he shouted.

After a while, a delegation of monks arrived at the family home in search of the new human form of a tulku who had died in that area. "I had a yellow palanquin, did your lama have one?" the little Phabongka asked rather irreverently. "And my monastery has a gilded Chinese canopy, does your monastery have one?" The monks answered that there was neither palanquin nor canopy. "Well then, I cannot be the reincarnation of your teacher," said the child.

A long time went by, and his mother could not understand why nobody seemed able to discover which great master had been reincarnated in her chubby son. So she entrusted him to a monastery to make a simple monk out of him, saying to encourage him, "You are the new essence of a great lama,[122] but you haven't been recognized yet." And before leaving him to the tough monastic routine, she entreated him to manifest himself for the greater good of mankind.

One day, a niece of Phabongka's mother suddenly was possessed by a deity. They all gathered around trying to help her. In the confusion, Phabongka's mother asked, "Who is inside your body?"

"Don't you recognize me?" answered a strange voice. Phabongka was to uncover the mystery. He said it was Dorje Shugden, and from then on the guardian returned many times. While in trance states, he possessed family members and acquaintances in trance states, dispensing advice and various prophecies.

After becoming a novice at the age of seven, Phabongka was taken by his mother to visit a reputed lama, who was struck by that obese child who spoke in wise phrases and even in Chinese. "*Maybe he is my guru,*" thought the lama. But after a careful *mo* he deduced that this was not the case, though he was convinced that the boy possessed the signs of a reincarnate. Perhaps they could attempt to have him recognized as the abbot of Phabongka Monastery, even if he were not.

His mother was so delighted that her son finally was going to obtain a tulku title that she paid no attention to the precarious state of the monastery. Back home she put up with her husband's fury. "You got him accepted as tulku of that wretched place," said the man, "and now our son is no better off than a beggar." "Whether our son gains wealth or does not depends on his karma," was her answer.

In the monastery he was treated like a simple monk, though his mother saw to it that he was accorded the appropriate rank when he was ten years old. Nonetheless, because of his indigence, he could not find a teacher disposed to tutor him. His attendant turned to the college but could find no one for a month, until one of the elderly monks, feeling sorry for him, took him on as a student.

Luckily for Phabongka, this teacher was above worldly concerns and dedicated himself to the little boy's instruction each day, helping him develop visions and special dreams. Phabongka often would recount these to the servants, who dismissed them as jokes played by the devil. Thereafter, the visions gradually disappeared. Nevertheless, the tulku trained himself

---

[122] Changkya Rolpai Dorje (1717–1786).

with such commitment that one day the signs of practice manifested: ability in debate; faith in his masters; and, although this sounds odd now, faith in Padmasambhava.

When Phabongka met Dakpo, his root guru, the lama described to him events of his past lives and the dangers of his present one. Dakpo suggested that he start a long-life retreat, and together they found a suitable place, a cave indicated by a magic bird where Dakpo himself had experienced some extraordinary visions. Dakpo also had to perform many rites to save his disciple from a sudden illness. Imagining the dakinis of the four directions, he ritually offered them an effigy of Phabongka to bring with them to the Pure Land instead of taking his student. But he had the impression that the dakinis of the West did not want to leave and were waiting to take the real Phabongka along. The master therefore transformed himself into a gigantic wrathful deity, Hayagriva, as large as the entire universe, causing the dakas and the dakinis to flee in terror. However, some of the worldly beings present, such as the flesh-eating she-demons with animal heads, refused to budge, insisting they wanted Phabongka's life. Then Dakpo's wrathful manifestation beat the spirits with an enormous stick, chopped some of them up into pieces, and chased the rest away. Not long afterwards, his disciple, who was thirty-one years old, recovered from his disease.

Around that time, a frail five-year-old boy arrived from Gungtang. After various controversies, he had been recognized as the reincarnation of Trijang Rinpoche. The little tulku, destined to become Phabongka's main disciple, was a frequent guest of the master. His cheerful presence lit up the hermitage, where a regular flow of faithful devotees was continually requesting blessings and advice. Phabongka immediately intuited that they had a special connection and prayed to the guardian spirit Shugden to take him under his protection. Trijang stayed with him for two years before going to Chatreng Monastery in Kham, where the populace had risen against Trijang.

When Phabongka was thirty-two years old, the retired former abbot of Tashi Lhunpo Monastery told him that he had to work to preserve the pure teachings and practices of the Gelukpa school. He notified him that a disciple of Tsong Khapa's had warned the Yellow Hat lamas against haphazard practices, cautioning them against the rage of the Dharmaraja Dorje Shugden.

This former abbot was not the first to remind him of his commitment
to the spirit, and Phabongka anxiously recalled the illness from which his
master had saved him.

One day he went to Reting to meet the Thirteenth Dalai Lama, who had
just come back from China. Tibet's sovereign had heard of Phabongka
and of his ability to transmit the gradual path of the *Lam Rim*.[123] He
welcomed his offerings and invited him to teach in the Meru Chichö,
where the head of the Gelukpa monastery of Ganden would often sit on
the throne. He also asked him to perform the rain rituals against the hail
that was then destroying the crops.

When the Chinese invaded Tibet in 1910 and the Dalai Lama was
forced into exile again, Phabongka and other great masters were invited to
practice for two years in Sera Monastery to pacify the Land of the Snows.
Less than three years later, the Dalai Lama returned to Lhasa.

At the age of thirty-seven, Phabongka completed the reading transmission of the Buddhist canon as the Thirteenth Dalai Lama had ordered
him, to remove the obstacles to the doctrine and the nation. A short while
later, he fell ill again and received a letter from the Dalai Lama requesting
him to prolong his life.

At that time Phabongka was still practicing the Nyingmapa Tantras.
However, his biographers state that Shugden manifested by possessing
people close to him, to remind him that he had to maintain the uncontaminated Gelukpa teaching. Shugden also promised Phabongka that if he up-
held the purity of the school, he would help him realize all his activities
and wishes. Phabongka accepted.

Within a few years, Phabongka became the master of numerous lamas
and prominent lay government officials. Aristocrats with their families
would crowd his residence, and the master would give out advice and
teachings, and especially the prayer to Shugden.

The young Trijang often was present and transcribed Phabongka's
lessons on several occasions, including the time when Phabongka transmitted the practice of the protector in Drepung Monastery, a traditional site
of veneration for other deities such as Palden Lhamo and Pehar of Nechung.

---

[123] *The Stages of the Enlightenment Path*, a fundamental text of the Gelukpa school,
arranging the main themes of exoteric practices in a graded sequence of meditative practice.

Phabongka also said: "Nowadays, even among those who consider themselves Buddhists, there are presumptuous people who, instead of relying on the great classic texts, seek visions in Mahamudra or Dzogchen teachings based on short, simplified texts. To regard as deep the meditations practiced following those instructions is like believing that a piece of brass is gold, and you will wander astray on mistaken paths. You might confuse your torpor for meditation, but you will not succeed even in being reborn in the higher realms of form and formlessness. You will have to be satisfied with becoming animals. At best, your meditations will have the same effect as the practices of the non-Buddhists. Therefore, do not consider these inferior paths viable; learn to distinguish between the superior path and the paths that simply seem right."

Phabongka explained that he himself had been a victim of such errors and had fallen ill after having practiced Nyingmapa teachings without respecting the will of his mighty protector. He said that Shugden had appeared to him several times to warn him of the danger, and that finally he had understood and ended his deviant practices.

For this reason, he wished to share his experience with other religious and lay figures from all over Tibet. He also promised himself to extend his activities soon to the regions where the most serious violations were reported, especially in Kham, which had become a stronghold of the nonsectarian Rimey movement. For Phabongka, the Rimey was the most devious instrument at the disposal of the devil contaminating the purity of the Buddha's teaching. Only one remedy existed, he said, and that was to introduce the initiation of Shugden more widely.

Many already knew his name, since for quite some time a number of prominent disciples of the lama had been talking about the Gelukpa protector who was to replace Nechung sooner or later as State Oracle and defender of the Dharma. Before the ceremony, Phabongka spoke at length of the indications his teacher Dakpo had sent him in dreams, telling him the time had come for Shugden to assume his destined role.

He recounted Shugden's origins and his appearance as an emanation of the master Drakpa Gyaltsen, shielding the Fifth Dalai Lama's contemporary from the accusations of those who considered his rebirth demonic.

"Those people," Phabongka said, "scorn the law of karma and have no knowledge of the words spoken by the Bodhisattva Manjushri, Lord of Discriminating Wisdom, to the Buddha. These words are:

> For the sake of sentient beings, the [bodhisattvas even]
>   disguise themselves as demons—
> The worldly cannot realize this."

Trijang Rinpoche, transcribing word for word, was aware that in the near future it would be up to him to complete the master's mission and his teachings.

Before bestowing the formal initiation, Phabongka read the invocation that his guru Dagpo had taught, supposedly after having received it in a clear vision:

> I pay homage to Dorje Shugden, who is everywhere,
> I pay homage to you, Drakpa, second hero,
> Dorje Drakden,[124] fierce deity who urged you time and
>   time again
> To take the form of the sole guardian of the Gelukpa
>   teaching.
>
> I bow down to you, you who have developed a ferociously
>   courageous heart!
> When those in bad faith who had nurtured flawed inten-
>   tions tightened a silken scarf around your throat, by the
>   strength of your purpose, your vow of *bodhichitta*, you
>   rose in the aspect of a wrathful deity.
> Night and day you manifested mighty and awesome
>   miracles;
> I bow down to you, you who have also terrified men with
>   great minds.
>
> When four powerful knowledge holders
> Practiced the destroying activity to eliminate you,
> With the power acquired from perfecting the two stages
>   of Guhyasamaja,
> Their rites did not defeat you.
> I bow down to you, you who have heroic pride.

---

[124] The minister of Pehar who possesses the oracle medium of Nechung.

I bow down to you, who punish lamas and disciples
Who are not qualified because of lack of training on the
path, and who introduce corruption to the doctrine of
the Yellow Hats.
In this era, the teaching and learning of the Lam Rim have
degenerated, and the majority of monks are abandoning
the perfect refuge.

Many have lost their way. When with calumny some
cause useless damage to the monastic community,
your power, O divine being,
Strikes them down with life-threatening diseases....

Manifesting in the form of excellent abbots,
You create favorable circumstances and in empty space
make precious material objects rain down.
Through your oracle, which manifests in a ferocious mode,
you proffer adamantine words....

You eliminated and reduced to dust great beings, ordinary masters and authorities, who had corrupted the
teaching of Ganden [monastery].
I pay homage to you, you who defeat the enemies of the
teaching of the Yellow Hats, leader of beings towards
liberation.

In brief, your manifestation and your activities are an
infinitely transcendent and inconceivable magical
dance.
They are a wish-fulfilling jewel and auspicious vase.
I pay homage to Dorje Shugden, who is everywhere.

Phabongka's assistants began to prepare the necessary implements
for the ceremony, and when everything was ready, hundreds bent their
heads down to welcome the empowerment of the body, speech, and mind
of Shugden.

But not everyone agreed with the decision to hold that ritual in the
monastery dedicated to the guardian deity of the Dalai Lamas and the
Tibetan government. Among these was the Abbot of Drepung Monastery,
who immediately consulted Nechung, the State Oracle. The Oracle's silence

was more explicit than a thousand words. There could not be two protectors under the same roof, wrote the abbot to His Holiness, the Thirteenth Dalai Lama.

A month had gone by since Phabongka Rinpoche had conferred the initiation at Drepung. From that day the practice of the *gyalpo* spread like oil on water among the young students in the colleges.

The Dalai Lama, aware of the risk of open conflict, decided to have Phabongka formally rebuked by a government functionary. Then he wrote to him personally, revealing how disconcerted he was by his behavior.

A few days went by, and a messenger brought Phabongka's response to the Potala, with a gold coin and a white *kata*. Phabongka apologized, saying it was his fault alone and that he had nothing to add in his defense. "What I have done is unjustifiable and in the future, as you have asked of me, I shall take your instructions to heart. I ask your forgiveness for what I have done and written."

The Dalai Lama responded to Phabongka's apology with a second letter, which did not entirely mask his displeasure.

> There is much to be said about your words and deeds, in both in logistical and doctrinal terms, but I do not want to continue on this subject. Concerning your references to the practice of the refuge, first of all you are propitiating Shugden as a protector. And since these students now have a connection with you, the practice has notably spread at Drepung. Since the monastery was first founded by Jamyang Choejey, Nechung has been designated as guardian and protector of Drepung, and his oracle has expressed his great dissatisfaction to the abbot on several occasions, saying that appeasing Shugden has accelerated the degeneration of the Buddha's teaching. This is the root of the problem. In particular, your search for the support of a worldly guardian to ensure benefits in this life is contrary to the principle of the taking of refuge.
>
> Therefore, it is contradictory to affirm, as you do "from the bottom of your heart," that what happened is only the fruit of your "confusion and ignorance," and that you were not aware of having "followed a wrongful path and led others onto it.

Phabongka replied with apparent humility.

> You have asked me why I am interested in this protector. I must explain that, according to my old mother, Shugden was a guardian for my family from the start, and that is why I have honored him. But now I want to say that I have repented and I have understood my mistake. I shall perform purification and promise with all my heart that in the future I will avoid propitiating, praying to, and making daily offerings [to Shugden]. I admit to all the errors I have made, disturbing Nechung and contradicting the principle of the refuge, and I beg you, in your great heartfelt compassion, to forgive me and purify my actions.

Phabongka sent a white silk *kata* scarf and five silver coins along with the letter. However, Phabongka's statements to his biographer, Lobsang Dorje Jampa Tenzin Trinley Gyatso, cast doubt on the sincerity of his remorse. He told him:

> After the first letter from the government official I did not grasp the extent of the Dalai Lama's anger. So I offered an honest explanation of what had happened in Drepung. Many people had suggested that His Holiness was disturbed. In this case, as the biographies of the Kagyupa lamas maintain, if the guru says that the sun sets in the east, then I am obliged to think that whoever states the contrary is living in illusion, because the master cannot be mistaken. This is the reason I apologized and chose not to enter into an argument.

The irony in his words concealed an apparently serious difference with the Tibetan leader, who had openly criticized him. Phabongka had not forgotten that on another occasion, the Dalai Lama had punished him for having changed the ranking of the deities during a ceremony, and had prohibited him from teaching for three years. He also pleaded for forgiveness from Nechung, who, however, put him on his guard: "You have disobeyed my Omniscient Guru [the Thirteenth Dalai Lama], and tried to incriminate two eminent scholars. Your conduct has wounded me deeply.... If you do not exert some self-control and persist in performing nonvirtuous deeds, you will suffer my punishment."

Then, something happened that seemed to announce a radical change in the dynamics of power in their relationship. According to Phabongka's account to his biographer:

> During the seventh month of Hor, in the retreat of Reting Monastery, I heard someone who sounded like a monk in a trance possessed by Shugden declare twice in a loud and triumphant tone, "It is the thirtieth, after the completion of the ninth!" On the thirtieth day of the tenth month of Hor, corresponding to December 17, 1933, the Thirteenth Dalai Lama was to die.

For Phabongka, there was no doubt that this had been a prophecy of his guardian spirit. From then on, he no longer felt bound by the letters of apology and the promises addressed to the soon-to-be deceased Tibetan leader.

If previously there was little to be done against the power of the man who obstructed and punished him, Phabongka now felt free to act as he pleased. Almost all of the ministers were his disciples, and the situation at court was quite different than in the epoch of the historical figure he felt closest to, Drakpa Gyaltsen. That tulku had been isolated, humiliated, and killed during the reign of the Fifth Dalai Lama. From 1933 onwards, Phabongka took to diffusing widely the cult of Shugden, personally or by means of his disciples' actions. This he did wherever he was, in monasteries and in great celebrations with thousands of devotees, in central Tibet and in Kham. Numerous centers of the Nyingmapa and the other traditions were converted to the Gelukpa school, and the name of Phabongka became widely known, as Shugden had predicted.

Reting Rinpoche, the Regent of Tibet after the death of the Thirteenth Dalai Lama, was also dedicated to the cult of Shugden. He was a disciple of Phabongka's, as was his successor, Tagdrak, and Phabongka's pupil Trijang, who was destined to have a brilliant career. It was no coincidence that in the first month of the new year of the Iron Snake (1941), when Tagdrak was installed as regent, it was Trijang who officiated over the auspicious rituals in his honor in the private ceremony in the Potala. It was only a few days since Trijang Rinpoche had received the instructions and complete ritual practices connected to Gyalpo Shugden, and from that moment began a crescendo of glory and success. In that same month,

Phabongka "prophesied" that Trijang soon would be called upon to serve the young Dalai Lama "to the best of his ability."

Shortly afterwards, Trijang was granted a further Shugden initiation in Phabongka's residence, together with the new Minister of Finance, Lhalu, and his wife. On that occasion, Phabongka asked him to compile the texts of all the rituals related to the protector and instructed him on how to complete the work on his own, with the precise intent of transferring the responsibility for the transmission to him. This was just as Dakpo had done with Phabongka.

Evidently, he knew that the end of his life was approaching. The next day, Trijang was summoned to the Summer Palace, where the chamberlain communicated to him that Tagdrak had named him junior tutor to the new Dalai Lama in place of Ling Rinpoche, who was another disciple of Phabongka's. In turn, Ling Rinpoche had become senior tutor, replacing the new regent. How then could the fourteenth sovereign of Tibet have possibly escaped the fate of a reign so marked by the influence of the demonic spirit?

After having accomplished his mission to leave a host of heirs to continue the cult's propaganda, the time had come for Phabongka to depart this world. This took place in the Dakpo Podrang on the way to Yarlung, where the lama was headed to teach *The Stages of the Path* to the thousands of monks and laypeople who would converge for his teachings wherever he went.

The food for the honored guest was indeed particular in the family house of Depo Chaksur. For some time, Phabongka had experienced difficulties moving his heavy body and had received negative signs regarding his life. During a rite for the dakinis, he forgot to present offerings to the divinities of the eastern direction, which led to prophetic dreams. Then one day, he discovered a much more serious cause for alarm in his urine. To examine it, he had heated a white stone on which he deposited a few drops of the liquid. These divided into parts the size of grains of wheat, black as coal. He said this was a sign that he had ingested an artificially prepared poison.

At lunch, he ate some *tsampa* with butter tea, roots of the *droma* tuber, the yogurt of a *dzomo* (female yak), and vegetable soup. But he did not finish his meal. His words stuck in his throat as he was conversing with his hosts and his heart stopped beating. Everybody gathered around him and started to pray, imploring him to not leave his earthly body, but Phabongka could no longer hear them. Had he been poisoned? Had he been killed by a Nyingmapa spell? Were Bon shamans responsible? Had he wanted suddenly to abandon this world?

He certainly had many enemies. From his biography, it is difficult to understand what really happened in those last hours, and what the signs of his poor health were. Descriptions of the setting, in popular tradition and in his biography match, with only a slight discrepancy as to whether he died during the meal or not.

The official biography furnishes a less embarrassing epilogue:

> When on the 28th day of the fifth month his illness became apparent in Depo Chaksur's house, Phabongka took medicines to ease his pain, but they had no effect whatsoever. In the late afternoon he felt very heavy. Nonetheless, he dedicated himself as usual to his meditation. On the next day, the 29th of the month, his ailment gave no signs of remission. So one of his entourage asked which practices should be performed to remove the obstruction to his health and his life. Phabongka answered, "apart from the rite of propitiation to the guardian of the *labrang* [(the tulku's estate)], I need nothing."

After giving this response, he remained in deep meditation. That day, he experienced no specific disturbance, but his body felt very heavy. He did not disrupt his practice schedule. From time to time he would vomit a frothy liquid. Nevertheless, he would receive the people who wished to meet him. In the evening he went to bed and slept until the last few hours of the night. He rose before dawn, practicing the yoga of the moment of awakening, washed himself, and told his attendant, "The moment to dedicate myself to the *tugdam*[125] has arrived," and asked the servant for a ritual vase. The man thought that the lama was not feeling well and that the fever had made him delirious. "This is not the moment to give initiation and there is no need for the vase," he told him. "Oh, poor man," Phabongka answered, "you are not to blame." He then stood up suddenly, as

---

[125] *Tug dam*, "mind-focus," refers to the period of clear light after the death of a high lamas, when the body does not decompose for two or three days.

in one phase of the great empowerments of the Mahanuttarayoga Tantra,[126] reciting incomprehensible words.

Then the master sat down again. From that moment his eyes were closed and he no longer spoke. After a little while, he extended his legs in "the noble position." His biographer writes:

> At dawn on the first day of the sixth month in the year of the Iron Snake of the sixteenth sixty-year cycle, he dissolved his physical manifestation into the sphere of the Dharmadhatu.

The only point in common between the official biography and the account passed on by other non-Gelukpa sources is the heaviness of his body, probably due to undigested food. The froth issuing from his mouth, like the urine on the heated stone, seems to point to a form of poisoning.

Is it possible that the great Phabongka truly was poisoned? Here is another mystery, following the Thirteenth Dalai Lama's sudden death and Reting Rinpoche's similarly baffling end. But who could have had the capacity and the temerity to kill such a powerful lama? His biographer, Jampa Tenzin Trinley Gyatso, mentions a speech given by Phabongka in Chamdo shortly before he died. He said; "Even if a thousand Bonpos, famous for their powers, were to cast harmful spells against me, they would not be able to move a single hair of mine." He added: "I possess the secret instructions of Ra Lotsawa and Nyen Lotsawa,[127] and I apply them to protect and guard other beings. If the Bonpos were to perform the killing rites against me, they would be the ones to suffer the consequences."

However, despite Phabongka's repeated boasts of possessing greater powers than the ancient shamans, a considerable number of people were convinced that the Bonpo priests had practiced black magic to eliminate the man who so despised their doctrine. It was in this very area of Tashi Choeling, one of the Bonpo strongholds, that the high lama was struck by illness for the first time. And it was here again that his sickness resurfaced later, even more virulently.

---

[126] When the lama rises from the throne.

[127] Renowned Tantric practitioners.

The current Dalai Lama frequently has said that Phabongka's incarnations up to the present day have not been very fortunate. The first tulku died at the age of twenty-five from tuberculosis. The present one lives in Nepal. He was not able to complete his studies and lives in tranquil anonymity. One of his assistants, Gekula, considered an expert in the liturgy of Shugden, died under a passing train. This is all we managed to learn about the recent lives of Kyabje Phabongka Dechen Nyingpo.

The Demon and the Dalai Lama's Tutor

Phabongka's favorite disciple was born in 1900 in Lhasa, to a family descended from the Seventh Dalai Lama. Trijang Rinpoche was initiated by his master into the secret powers both of the protector and of his own previous incarnations. In several of these, he had occupied the Gelukpa throne of Ganden, and also a devotee of the spirit.

In his autobiography, *The Magic Play of Illusion*, Trijang recounts different episodes of his life linked to Shugden, including the sad fate reserved for anyone who, for whatever reason, was in discord or conflict with him.

Though born in Lhasa, Trijang had been recognized as the tulku of the distant, isolated town of Chatreng, in the wild region of Kham near the Chinese borderlands. The people there would have preferred to install a local child on the throne, since the people of Kham usually only received demands for tax payments from the holy city, making few of them fond of the government, with all its impositions and its declared reincarnates. The local candidate died after falling off a horse, however, and Trijang was installed despite the persistent hostility of an influential group of Khampas guided by Samphel Tenzin and Troti Tulku.

One night, Trijang Rinpoche dreamed that a man slaughtered a huge yak; immediately thereafter, Samphel fell ill and died. This was not the first such incident. As he makes clear in his autobiography, each time Trijang saw a sentient being slain in a dream, this swiftly would be followed "directly or indirectly" by the death of someone harboring "hostile intentions" towards him. It was Phabongka who had established a connection between the misfortunes of his enemies and the special protection granted him by Gyalchen Shugden, whom Phabongka believed capable of destroying any "external interference." Trijang explained: "During the Great Prayer Festival of the Water Monkey year in Lhasa, another geshe from Chatreng, aligned with Troti Tulku, fell ill and died. Seven days later the same fate befell Troti Tulku."

But the misfortunes did not end there. Trijang comments; "Many of the people from Kham who opposed me died in various unpleasant circumstances."

To get a better idea of the personality of the Fourteenth Dalai Lama's famed tutor, Elio and I went to McLeod to interview Ganji, the man who had served him as personal secretary and factotum for over thirty years.

Ganji[128] sat to receive us, his round, fleshy bulk spread on an armchair covered with white, hand-embroidered lace. I looked at him attentively in the shadows of the room, where only the dark red light of the sunset filtered through the heavy cotton curtains. The more I observed the man, the more puzzled I was by how such an acute and penetrating gaze could be reconciled with so good-natured a countenance. I was fully aware of the fact that he had been a *gyalpo* practitioner for many years, but it also could have been an expression of his psychological state.

The secretary, slowly fingering his *mala* rosary, began to speak. At times he focused on me and at times he looked at Elio, who was translating every word. An ineffable Trijang Rinpoche smiled enigmatically in an enormously enlarged photograph. Two oil lamps hanging on either side of the picture sent out flickering rays of light, which seemed to render that face alive and present. He began:

"It is not easy to become the assistant of a great lama such as Trijang Rinpoche. I think that if I have had this privilege it means I must have gained some merit in my past lives. I inherited the position from my uncle, who was Trijang's old helper, and I was only eight years old when I started to serve him. The lama and my uncle taught me the alphabet, how to read and write, fed and clothed me, and gave me everything I needed. When I was nine, they sent me to school and paid all my fees and expenses. In exchange for their kindness, I replied to the bulk of Rinpoche's mail; the number of his correspondents had been growing along with his fame because of his role at the Dalai Lama's court. Thanks to him I became a monk in Ganden Monastery, and after my studies I worked at copying Rinpoche's daily diary, in which he noted down absolutely everything he did and said.

"Trijang Rinpoche was forty-one when the Dalai Lama's senior tutor, the recently appointed Regent of Tibet, Tagdrak Rinpoche, offered him the position of *tsenshap*, or spiritual mentor, to the Dalai Lama, who at the time was six years old.

"I asked him if he knew why Tagdrak had recommended Trijang for the post. The man shook his big head and answered; "I don't know." One

---

[128] I have adhered to his request to be kept anonymous.

reason is that after the death of the Thirteenth Dalai Lama, he had overseen all the postfunerary rites, preparing the stupa and other necessities, all tasks he had performed to perfection. Rinpoche then had worked diligently on an edition of the Kangyur, the Buddhist canon, in the printing house under the Potala. He organized the index of the volumes, a job with great responsibilities. One day Tagdrak told him he had to teach the Dalai Lama to read, write, and memorize the sacred scriptures, and also see to it that the child recited his prayers morning and evening."

Elio and I had the same thought regarding those prayers, but we avoided exchanging glances. The secretary continued: "The Dalai Lama had seven spiritual assistants, and at that time Trijang was among them. The principal one was called the *dahren*, and the others were distinguished in order of importance according to the number of ribbons on their horses and the number of their servants. Trijang was *dahren* for ten years, until 1951, when the Dalai Lama returned from exile in Yatung. Two years later, in 1953, he was named *yongzin*, junior tutor, while the senior tutor was Ling Rinpoche. At this point I entered his service.

"It is not easy to be appointed tutor to the Dalai Lama. The tutor is examined by the government and also must receive the approval of his pupil. I remember that His Holiness was very pleased with the choice. As you can imagine, at this point Trijang became even better known, and everyone admired his great erudition. After his nomination, thousands of people would flock to his teachings."

"Did Trijang Rinpoche often go to Kham?" I asked.

"Not very often. Two or three times he went on his own and stayed at length, for months at a time."

"Did Phabongka ever go to visit him?"

"He never went, even though he had been invited on several occasions."

"And what can you tell me about the disputes that took place with the other Chatreng incarnation?"

"The local tulku went to study in Sera, and as soon as he arrived at the monastery, he fell off his horse. He was only nineteen years old. After the incident, his servant was so upset that he also became ill and died shortly thereafter. When Trijang first arrived in Chatreng from Lhasa, he was received with indifference. However, after several years passed, his fame as a great scholar reached the outpost and he was accepted by the majority of the population. Especially after listening to his teachings, they understood that he was a very special lama. Then something happened that struck their imagination. Trijang had painted frightened birds flying and images of flames destroying everything. Later on, Chatreng Monastery was bombed twice by the Chinese. And so, members of the village began to venerate Trijang Rinpoche, and when these folks are convinced by something and have faith in someone, they are ready to lay down their lives.

"In their character they are undisciplined, something they have in common with all other Khampas. Specifically, in Chatreng, if you are fifteen and do not know how to use a gun, you are considered effeminate. They are so renowned for their bravery that two of the Dalai Lama's personal bodyguards came from Chatreng. One of them later fled to India with us, and the other was killed by the Chinese.

"Trijang was so popular that even the Chinese were impressed by his fame. Before the 1959 escape, when a puppet government was formed in Lhasa, they conferred a certain authority on him as Vice-Director of the Autonomous Region. In short, the Chinese tried to involve him.

"He always dedicated special attention to the people of Chatreng, even if his reputation preceded him everywhere and his disciples were multiplying like stars in the sky. Ever since Trijang became the Dalai Lama's tutor, he has known no peace. A huge influx of people wanted to meet him, especially from the village in Kham. There also were long lines of Lhasa aristocrats, monastics, and laypeople, who turned to him for advice, and when the people from Chatreng came to see him they would have to wait their turn patiently for at least two months.

"Trijang was constantly sending scholars and geshes to Chatreng to teach, but the actual running of the monastery was decided on the spot. In 1954, when my master went to the village as His Holiness's envoy, all the inhabitants swore that they and their children would always venerate him.

"In Lhasa, there was a solid community of merchants from Chatreng that organized many festivities, to which Trijang Rinpoche always was invited. They would plant their tents in a pleasant spot, cook, and relax. Trijang would attend happily, enjoying the wrestling matches between the young monks, the games of tug-of-war, or stone-throwing competitions. Sometimes there was a gramophone for dances, and sometimes they would play their instruments. Trijang loved music and even wrote the Tibetan national anthem and other musical works.

"Eventually he became as well known as his master, Phabongka, and, like him, would attract great crowds at his teachings. In exile, he bravely put up with harsh new living conditions. During the first few years in

Mussoorie, he was obliged to wear a *chuba* and boots because none of us were certain how the local people would welcome monks. Then, when Nehru came to visit that town, the Dalai Lama put on his monk's robes, and since then all the Gelukpa lamas have followed suit.

"Trijang continued to study and practice, and he sometimes went on pilgrimage to sacred places or traveled abroad to give teachings. There were many Chatrengpas among his bodyguards, but he lived alone and had only one servant, his *tsopon*. All the Tibetan exiles considered him the most scholarly and realized of the lamas, and he was the first to meet the Pope, Paul VI."

I would have liked to ask his opinion on the suspicions of the police regarding the geshe's assassins from Chatreng, but Elio signaled that it was better not to. Indeed, the secretary urged us at length not to involve him in any discussion of the crimes. He insisted that he loved and respected the Dalai Lama.

So I asked him if he remembered the days of the escape from Lhasa in March 1959. He answered: "On March 8, Trijang Rinpoche had informed me that they could be leaving. He asked me to prepare everything necessary for our getaway: horses, mules, and food. Then he said, 'You and your uncle will come with us.' We had decided to flee by way of the river Kyichu, and luckily the telephone office on our route out of Lhasa had been destroyed so we were able to pass through without being intercepted. I had already made many trips between the Summer Palace and the house in Lhasa to gather everything necessary for our escape [on March 17]. The Khampas procured a boat for us to traverse the river. Once across, we looked for a spot to spend the night. The Dalai Lama, Trijang Rinpoche, and all their entourage reached us there under the cover of darkness to find the horses and mules ready."

This time I was unable to restrain my curiosity: "As far as you know, was the Shugden Oracle consulted to decide when and how to leave Tibet?"

The secretary was expecting this question. He responded with a gesture of annoyance; or perhaps more of fear than annoyance. "There is someone who knows all this," he said, "who is still alive in Sera Mey, in South India. His name is Chansog Lobsang Yeshe. He is the administrator of the monastery and at that time was the abbot's principal attendant. Ask him. I don't know what happened in Panglung."[129]

---

[129] The seat of the Oracle.

I inquired if he had ever met Zemey Rinpoche.

"Zemey studied grammar, literature, history, and many other subjects with Trijang. But even though they were very close, Trijang did not tell Zemey to write certain things,[130] if that is what you want to know. I give you my word on that. In my opinion, Trijang never told him if this or that person had been killed by Shugden. In fact, Zemey even says so in *The Yellow Book*: that he collected many of the stories on his own and that even if Trijang had recounted some incidents, he certainly had not told him to write them down. I recollect, too, that when Zemey published that book, Trijang asked him to go and apologize to the Dalai Lama, who was irate.

"I know that Zemey did what Trijang suggested and that when the Dalai Lama left for south India, Zemey was told that the Dalai Lama was no longer angry with him. 'You are an important lama, you are educated, and you must continue to teach, to transmit the knowledge of our literature,' the Dalai Lama had indicated. Had he still been angry, he certainly would not have made contact with him. As far as I know, it seemed that the issue had been resolved in the Dalai Lama's mind and there was no rancor. I also remember that when Zemey was on the way to Dehradun, he received word of Trijang's illness and came here to perform the funerary rites."

Elio then asked a question that completely surprised me. He wanted to know what the secretary thought of the rumor in Dharamsala about Trijang's transformation after his death.

Though I did not understand what they were talking about, the secretary again made a gesture of annoyance with his hand.

"He did not become a zombie, if that's what you mean. But when a lama dies, luck then deserts the place. Shortly afterwards, the Dalai Lama's mother and other important people died. But whoever says absurd things like that doesn't know what he is talking about. In Tibet, zombies are called '*rolang*,' people who weep over their own fate, because someone who dies with attachment becomes a '*rolang*.' Nothing like that could have happened to a lama of his stature.

"I remember that when his body was cremated near the Children's Village, a strong wind suddenly began to blow and everybody looked in that direction. They noticed that the smoke was propelled towards Dalhousie. In Tibet we say that when a great man dies, a falcon soars in flight, and

---

[130] The Yellow Book.

one of these birds was seen circling the funeral pyre more than once. Had he turned into a zombie, his physical body would have risen and walked; instead it burned, and in the ashes the imprint of a small child's foot was found, pointed in the same direction as the wind. At the end of the cremation, Zemey gathered the ashes with the relics and practiced the ritual of offering to the Buddha.

"I was driving the jeep, which was covered in decorations, while all along the road long trumpets were blowing and a special ritual was being performed. We had placed the ashes in a vase, and within it a sphere formed. Around eight or nine o'clock that evening, Zemey carefully washed his hands. Then he put on a clean tunic and started to look through the ashes. He discovered that Trijang Rinpoche was the size of a newborn baby and that on the top of his head was a tiny hole, as if someone had inserted a stalk in it. It was the first time in my life that I had seen anything like this. Then, all together, we performed a ritual. There were also bones that had remained intact, and His Holiness wanted those relics for himself. That is the story of how he died."

We were silent in the dark room for a while. Then we asked him if he knew why Trijang's reincarnation had preferred to go and live in Switzerland rather than at his previous residence in Dharamsala.

"Perhaps because there have been fanciful debates about the protector Shugden and all the rest. His parents lived in America, but Gonsar Rinpoche invited him to stay with him in Switzerland, and he's been there for years. Nowadays among Tibetans, the situation generally is much more difficult. Everyone is scattered, some here, some there; there is no more unity. I urge you to please write something positive, in the hope that harmony and reconciliation will return."

"I would be happy if my book helped bring about reconciliation among your people," I answered, "but it's not so easy."

The secretary replied, "Each Tibetan religious school has its own deity, cults, and rituals that we Tibetans always have performed. If, in the future, we were to become independent in our own land, we could say that from now on by law, we must practice this or that. But today, Gelukpas or not, we are all in a country that is not our own...."

The criticism of the Dalai Lama had surfaced, veiled, only at the end.

The Monk's Secrets

Night had fallen by the time I left the house of Trijang's former secretary, and I took a long walk through the streets of McLeod, teeming with Tibetans, Indians, and Westerners. I wondered how many of them knew about or were interested in the case. I thought that perhaps I was attaching too much importance to it, as one of the outstanding intellectuals of the local Tibetan community, Tashi Tsering, had said. He is the Director of the Amnye Machen Institute and co-founder of a respected journal, *Lung Ta*. "You Westerners like these tales of ghosts and mysticism," he joked.

Tsering was not the only person to want us to believe that the triple murder somehow had already been forgotten. Indeed, it was life as usual for the exiles with their customary problems: the small family issues; their prayers in the temples; nostalgia for their homeland; and, the hope of obtaining a visa to go and live in the United States or some other Western country. The judicial inquiry also had come to a halt after the discovery that the assassins had sought refuge in Tibet. The Shugden Society in Delhi still was appealing unsuccessfully to the Commission on Human Rights, with the expectation of obtaining the legal "right" to perform the practices of their protector—something that actually had never been denied to a single individual.

I was also feeling a certain weariness after so much time spent poring over books and discussing the same topic, day in day out. Then, practically all together, the awaited replies from Delhi arrived, one from the former superintendent, Rajeev Singh, and one from Chimi Tsering, the main suspect as being the instigator of the killings. They had both agreed to meet me in the next few days.

The first appointment was with Chimi Tsering, in the small building that housed the Dorje Shugden Devotees Religious and Charitable Society, the same one I already had visited in the Tibetan neighborhood in Delhi. Chimi Tsering had a bad cold. He was worried about having to start an intense practice retreat in that state. He was a man who knew what he was doing; you could guess this from his self-confident gestures and from the obsequious manner of the people who showed me into his room on the second floor. Dressed in the traditional Gelukpa style, his head shaved like every other Buddhist monk's, he was weakened and worn out by the unbearable summer heat. He obviously was suspicious of us at first and checked our identity papers carefully; he then invited us to sit on two chairs facing his bed.

He started by asking us if we were familiar with some of the literature concerning the subject in which we were so interested, and he rose wearily and walked over to his bookshelves. Glancing at the titles, he began to quote a great number of texts by Japanese researchers, "the best ones," he said. He then transcribed from the Tibetan some other names of suggested volumes.

He advised us to rely essentially on two sources, Dagpo Dorje Chang and Trijang Rinpoche; this we had done already. We asked Chimi why, apart from a few texts by lamas, practically no valid historical documentation of the cult exists. "After the death of the monk Drakpa Gyaltsen, the Fifth Dalai Lama's contemporary, the regent, Sonam Choepel, had all the documentation on this topic destroyed," he answered. He stared at us for a few seconds, and then added, "Anyway, where is the historical proof that the Dalai Lama's nature is the same as Avalokiteshvara's?"

We replied that in effect one could not be sure of anything in a country like Tibet, where every event seems to assume a mythical and supernatural dimension.

"The figure of the Fifth Dalai Lama," he continued, "was actually very different from the idea most Tibetans have of him. He encouraged a strong cult of his personality and, despite being of Nyingmapa extraction, he had 120 monasteries of that school taken over by the Gelukpas. I am not passing judgment on whether he was good or bad, I am just saying that he was imaginative, but also politically tough and determined. He was the one to maintain that the Dalai Lama lineage descends from Avalokiteshvara, and the first problem, as you say yourselves, is the lack of tangible information. The same is true for the real story of the relations between Gelukpas and the guardian deities."

I said that among the most controversial texts on Shugden, and perhaps the trigger of the harsh conflicts of recent years, was *The Yellow Book*, by his teacher, Zemey Rinpoche.

"Whoever rejects Shugden," he answered, "uses Zemey's book as a pretext. But Zemey never wrote that those who do Nyingmapa practices will have problems. He himself had a statue of Padmasambhava in his house."

"Actually he stated it very clearly. There are two types of Nyingma-pas, and one of them is very bad: this type maintains that Phabongka destroyed the statues of Padmasambhava. This type of Nyingmapa also thinks of the great master as a demonic being upon whose death the ground under his feet opened and swallowed him up. Yet if you read Phabongka's biographies, you will find nothing of this. The real problem always has lain between the Nyingmapas who follow Padmasambhava's teaching and those who invent it. In the eleventh century in Tibet, there were many who declared themselves Nyingmapas who tried to attribute practices, invented or of uncertain origin, to the celebrated exorcist by saying they were his hidden and rediscovered treasures. Zemey stated that the Panchen Lama and other religious figures had adopted erroneous practices, since, if you are a monk, you should behave like a monk. And if you have a title, it doesn't necessarily mean that you are spiritually elevated. 'Lama,' 'cardinal,' 'pope'—these are just titles.

"Zemey was my lama. I spent seventeen years with him, and in the last fourteen his credibility was utterly destroyed. If you look at those six large volumes up there, you will see how much has been written about him, thanks to the Fourteenth Dalai Lama. Yet so far, His Holiness has not uttered a single word in his defense. Usually if a lama falls ill in Tibet, many long-life practices are performed for him; but when Zemey was sick, the Dalai Lama did nothing, despite the fact that for forty years he had been a prominent literary and religious figure, also a great practi-tioner. After forty years he wanted to retire, but because at that time the library had no director, the Dalai Lama asked him to take charge, even though *The Yellow Book* already had been published. Shunning this new job, Zemey moved to the south of India, and His Holiness was very offended."

An attendant came in holding a pot full of steaming liquid that gave off scented balsamic vapors. After breathing these in, Chimi started speaking again.

"Spiritual practice is a very different matter from politics. Politics are black, white, or grey. Spiritual practice is used to attain buddhahood, and you will not become realized if your practice is not pure, if you combine it with politics. What we are discussing is not a controversy over Dorje Shugden, but an invention by the Dalai Lama's office. They say that the practice of Dorje Shugden is sectarian, simply because ecumenism is fashionable. However, we distinguish a practice by its degree of purity, either it is pure or it is impure. Each Buddhist tradition brings benefits, but if you try to blend them you will destroy them; by merging their diverse qualities, you take risks."

I told him that the Dalai Lama argued that there was a certain degree of danger in the practices linked to spirit cults such as Shugden.

"Dangerous? No. He certainly has tremendous power, is very direct, and is from an ancient society. However, if you read history attentively, you will not underestimate the strife it entails. Thanks to his devotion to Shugden, my master Zemey remained in meditation position, his body displaying no signs of decay, for three whole days after his death.

"It is true that many devotees of Shugden sometimes think they must practice constantly so as not to incur problems. But Dorje Shugden does not harm other beings. In reality, when you stop practicing, you no longer have any power, and as a consequence you are more exposed. It's like in politics, when you have a forceful protector, things go better."

I asked him why there was so much attention given to Shugden, since the Buddhist pantheon is practically infinite and includes guardians of every type. This is universally acknowledged in Tibet, by everyone from the Dalai Lama down to the simplest nomad youth.

"Take Palden Lhamo, one of the principal figures considered a 'guardian deity' by the Dalai Lama himself. She is very different from Shugden, because Palden Lhamo offers protection beyond this material world, while Shugden is a protector who lives in this dimension. Since he is of the world, he can communicate directly with you. Let us also take the example of Nechung, who is the State Oracle of Tibet. Among my people there is a belief that Nechung will progress and transcend samsara, our condition of suffering, and go to abide in the Pure Lands, while down here his place will be taken by Shugden."

"Taking your premise into account," I said, "one could think that this new oracle residing in the worldly dimension may not be impartial and so is just like the rest of us."

"People think that the oracles are always honest. But often the oracle says what the lama wants. Nechung actually plays the role of minister in the Tibetan government, and the Dalai Lama has used him politically, affirming that Nechung's answer was this or that according to whatever was convenient at the moment."

I asked Chimi Tsering what he thought of the constant danger posed by the *gyalpo* class of beings, to whom Shugden is said to belong.

"If Shugden is a *gyalpo*, then Nechung is too, and so is the divinity of which he is an emanation, Pehar, who was turned into a guardian deity of Buddhism by Padmasambhava. The *gyalpo*, the *tsen*, and the other classes of beings designated by Tibetan Buddhism cannot be defined as either good or bad; each one has its own characteristics, just as human beings do."

"Hence, in your opinion, what was the real motivation for the Dalai Lama's request to stop the practice of Shugden?"

"From a spiritual point of view it makes no sense. However, politically it does. Since 1959, he uninterruptedly had been proclaiming the need for Tibetan independence from China. At a certain point, though, he realized that if he wanted a role in history, he would have to allow Tibetan exiles to return home freely. The motive is clear: although the generations who have been raised in India consider him a great political and spiritual leader, the next ones may begin to reflect on the fact that, under his reign, the country has been completely lost for the first time. This is why he modified his position, asking only for autonomy rather than independence, in the hope that China would change its attitude and accept a compromise. But this position is not well regarded by many Tibetans. So he created a distraction by brandishing the threat of Shugden before the generations still devoted to him in the months of March and July of 1996, and by saying that the worship of Shugden divided Tibetans and damaged his own health. By August, he was able to relaunch the proposal of autonomy. The two matters are closely linked."

We reminded him that a ban on the practice of Shugden was in force during the reign of the Thirteenth Dalai Lama, and that Phabongka Rinpoche had written a letter admitting his mistakes. Chimi replied that at that time, it was impossible to go against the wishes of the Dalai Lama, on pain of death, but that in the Thirteenth Dalai Lama's biography there is no mention of that ban. "The problem," he insisted, "is that Phabongka was a brilliant orator, beloved by the people. During his teachings he would joke and recount tragic tales. He had great charisma, but not as far as the envious lamas were concerned."

We then asked why the Thirteenth Dalai Lama had requested him to cease bestowing the initiation of Gyalchen Shugden but did not do the same for those of the other deities whose initiation Phabongka also gave, such as Sertrap.

"Because he was a controversial deity."

"So the controversy was also of a political nature?"

"No, it was caused by jealousy, the jealousy of the other lamas, who saw Phabongka as a threat. Indeed, Phabongka was held in such high esteem that he was asked to become regent on the death of the Thirteenth Dalai Lama, but he refused because he would have had to change the entire government."

Before leaving him to his inhalations, we asked Chimi Tsering the mandatory question regarding the inquiry into the triple crime in Dharamsala, in which he was being investigated along with the other leaders of his association. According to the police, the killers had dialed his phone number while they were following the murdered geshe after he had just returned from Hong Kong.

The monk simply repeated that neither he nor the Dorje Shugden Devotees Religious and Charitable Society had anything to do with the death of the monks in Dharamsala. He pointed out that his room had no telephone and said that he had never had one. All the rest was invented to make them look guilty. I figured it was useless to ask more questions, since he already had been interrogated by the police and the judges had acquitted him.

Once the interview was finished, we entered the office of one of his young assistants. He was waiting for us, seated on a camp bed with his wife. Lobsang said that he had been born in exile, but that his family originally was from Chatreng. We wanted to know why there was such devotion to Shugden in his village and if it were was connected to the fact that Trijang Rinpoche had been the principal lama. Young Lobsang admitted that this could be the main reason, but he explained another reason for his choice to consider Shugden a true buddha. He said that before the public ban on the cult by the Dalai Lama, Shugden was just one of the many guardian deities to whom he and his family paid homage during their daily prayers. But after the clamor following what he considered an act of religious persecution, he decided that the spirit must be far mightier than he had imagined. Since then he had thought of him as his main deity, as did the rest of his family and his acquaintances.

Dinner with a Former Superintendent

The former superintendent Rajeev Kumar Singh was courteous on the phone and explained that after leaving his post as the Chief Superintendent of Police of the district of Kangra, he had become Director of Security for the Indian state airline. "Now that some time has gone by since my first investigation of the crimes," he said, "I can speak quite freely, if I can be of any use to you." He promised to bring along a copy of the last report he had written at the end of the first stage of the inquiry into the triple murder in Dharamsala.

We met in the office of a journalist friend of mine. I was waiting for him in the street, and as soon as he got out of the company car I recognized him from the photographs printed in the newspapers at the time of the investigation. He was wearing an elegant, cream-colored suit with a dark tie, a green raincoat under his arm. A round face and oiled hair, brushed back with from a receding hairline, framed his intense eyes. From our first exchange, a mutual feeling of friendliness was evident, accentuated by our common interest in a case that we both had taken to heart. We soon realized that we had much to talk about, and we decided to carry on with our conversation in an Italian restaurant. The superintendent enjoyed good food and a good book, spoke impeccable English, and evidently had studied the case in great depth. Fascinated, I listened as he described the precise details of his investigation and his rapport with his collaborators, particularly with his deputy. When I explained that I intended to recount the entire story in a book, he immediately approved of the idea with just one condition: I could use his real name only if I kept scrupulously to the facts. It would be better, however, to use an alias for his deputy.

First of all, I asked him if he was disappointed by the final outcome of the inquiry, which had brought no concrete judicial result.

"Believe me, we did our best to have the truth come out. But, as you may know, India has no extradition treaty stipulated either with Nepal, to where the assassins first fled, or with China, where they finally disappeared. As to the hand behind the killings, I suggest you read my report carefully. I don't believe there is any doubt about the responsibility of the directors of the Shugden followers' society here in Delhi. However, in this country, having good lawyers and some strong backing often counts for more than any judicial proof...."

He opened his arms with a resigned air.

"Do you have absolutely no doubt that it really was the followers of this cult who carried out the assassination?"

"Read my report. Not even the judges could contest the upshot of our findings after a long investigation in practically all the Tibetan settlements in India. We have names, surnames, and photographs of the killers identified by more than one witness, and all the evidence shows followers of the cult and disciples of lamas and geshes in conflict with the Dalai Lama. As you probably know, they left a series of clues that not even a blind man could have missed, starting with the rucksack left at the crime scene."

"On that point, how could they have been so careless as to leave behind in the room a bag with the "signature" of the Delhi society on it?"

"The dynamic of every crime always has a strong emotional component, especially if it stems from some kind of passion, be it sentimental or ideological, or, as in this case, religious. They did not execute their victims with a pistol in cold blood like professional assassins; they stabbed them, dozens of times. They were motivated by profound hatred, and perhaps they chose this tactic of an exemplary strike to prove something further. If, as seems to be the case, they were killing in the name of a demonic spirit, then they had to act accordingly, by reinforcing the diabolical element in their act. Anyway, these are all inferences. What is sure is that the geshe grabbed that bag away from his assassin, probably just before being stabbed to death, holding and held it in the crook of his arm. Maybe the killers had not foreseen this reaction, or perhaps they took too long and were interrupted."

"Since there were no eyewitnesses, your identification was based on the pursuit of the geshe by a taxi from Delhi and the photographic evidence of those six young passengers by the cab driver and the owner of the hotel where they stayed. But how can you be sure that those were the assassins?"

"To start with, they all vanished into thin air right after the event, and we have proof of their escape abroad. According to a confidential report, the six assailants fled to Kathmandu and then crossed the border into Tibet at Solu Khumbu at the end of March 1997. This same report reveals that once in Lhasa, they took lodgings in a guesthouse around the Barkhor. I don't know if you want to divulge its name, it may be better just to use the owner's initials, C.T., a relative of the wife of one of the leaders of the Shugden Charitable Society in Delhi. In case you need it, here is the list of all the names," he said, handing me another typewritten sheet of paper. "Bear in mind that these six men were arrested by the Chinese Public Security Bureau, I'm not sure why, maybe based on our alert. But on July 30, 1997, they were transferred under guard to their home villages in Kham."

"Chatreng?"

"Mostly."

"Tell me more about the rucksack. Could it not have belonged to one of the three victims?"

"The rucksack was recognized by the hotel staff. Don't forget that inside it we found a pamphlet produced by the Shugden Devotees Religious and Charitable Society in Delhi. It would be odd to imagine the dying geshe putting it there, don't you think? Or somebody who wanted to divert the inquiry before our arrival?... No, we sounded out many other leads, but no alternative emerged, not even many months after the murders."

"No one but the cult devotees could have had reasons strong enough to create the resentment needed to carry out such an act. Don't forget that some of the young men we indicated as the assassins had already been marked out for their acts of violence in the religious communities of the south. In addition to this, during our raids on the offices and apartments of the cult members, we found copies of the same threatening letters that were discovered at the crime scene.

"Regrettably, I must admit to a certain frustration in not having been able to get my hands on either the killers or the men who sent them out. But this is just one example of the highly sensitive nature of this episode, in which other countries also are involved, not just ours."

I asked him what he thought of the Tibetan government-in-exile's security experts, whose opinion it was that the Chinese authorities were behind this group.

"I confirm that some reports by our intelligence do point in that direction."

"What kind of reports?"

"Above all, analyses by the RAW, who have been worried by China's growing interest in the activities of the groups supporting the Tibetan cause here in India, first and foremost the Dalai Lama's office. Between 1995 and 1996, five spies were arrested in Dharamsala, and almost all of them admitted to having come here with a brief to gather intelligence for the Chinese. As you can imagine, the prospect of having hundreds of Tibetan monastics and laypeople as allies in India is a huge opportunity for the authorities in Beijing. If my intuition is right, over time they will build up their undercover network extensively with the Shugden devotee groups."

"Yet you exclude any direct involvement by the Chinese in the triple murder?"

"I certainly can rule out any hypothesis of the kind right away. Furthermore, there was no need to create a divide between among Tibetans. Practically speaking, it already existed, both in the exile communities and within their own country. Some of the characters in this anti-Dalai Lama coalition, such as Chimi Tsering, have had ties with the Chinese authorities for a long time, at least as far back as the classified RAW reports show. However, we have had to stick to the facts because of the sensitive nature of our diplomatic relations with Beijing. Long before the killings, the slain monk, together with various leading functionaries in the Tibetan government-in-exile, repeatedly received threats from members of the cult."

He opened a page of his report. "Look here, Minister Tashi Wangdi, Minister Sonam Topgyal, the President of the Parliament Samdhong Rinpoche,[131] the Secretary of the Dalai Lama Tenzin Chonyid, the Government Spokesperson Kalsang Yeshi, a reincarnate lama called Khamtrul Rinpoche."

"I read that during your investigation you also found explicit letters signed by the Delhi Shugden society and addressed to different Dharamsala offices."

Singh leafed through the pages of his report: "Read this, dated June 5, 1996: 'Some poison-affected persons are working towards turning Tibet into a sea of blood...' and, 'If the matter is not resolved, we will have to take some other step. In such an eventuality, the Indian government, the people, and the Tibetan community will suffer shame and regret before the world.' Look at this other undated letter sent to the Tibetan Women's Association: 'If there comes a division among prominent persons within the Gelukpa sect, there will be bloodshed in the monasteries and the settlements. It will not be possible to escape or run from this eventuality.'

---

[131] At present, prime minister.

"We transcribed several letters written in the same vein, and one of the recurring phrases is 'bloodbath,' as in this letter of August 8, 1996, addressed to 'the Dalai Lama and his asinine officials.' In some of the missives they threatened to turn their mission into a war, similar to those seen between Hindus and Muslims in India. Believe me, our government is not optimistic about the future. But what can we do?"

"In your first requests for collaboration with Interpol, you mentioned the groups of practitioners of the spirit cult abroad, in Britain and in Italy. Have you ever found clues of any operations in common?"

"The activities of the centers abroad, as you may know, orbited around two central characters, Kelsang Gyatso and Ganchen Tulku. The latter particularly was working with the Chinese, but this was an open secret. To understand what happened on the undercover and operational level, a police investigation is never sufficient."

For a while we spoke of other matters. I asked the superintendent about his deputy, Amitabha. I learned that they both had left the Kangra police district together and that his deputy had then experienced 'some problems.' He didn't want to specify, but he led me to think that perhaps he had been demoted or punished for his behavior. "Unfortunately, I wasn't able to help Amitabha. Although he truly was an excellent policeman, not everyone shared my point of view, and his behavior, both within and outside the service, did not help. But we all create our own destiny, don't you agree?"

"Tell me something, Superintendent. I know that some of your men were quite superstitious. Did you ever have any misgivings, fears; or, let's say, were you wary of treating this case as a simple crime? You know what I mean...."

"The truth is that this affair didn't rear up like some hybrid monster. I received a rational education and I don't believe, or at least I'm not interested, in spirits. I only know that in our *Shrimad Bhagavata Purana* there is the description of eight categories of superior beings with powers over places...."

"Like the eight classes catalogued by the Tibetans?"

"I don't know much about it," answered the superintendent, "only what the Dalai Lama's staff told me. But in the *Puranas* it also is written that after death, the souls of wicked human beings are transformed into evil spirits who try to harm us and only can be placated with gifts and rituals. They tell me that that is exactly what Shugden is, a spirit who must be offered devotion and ceremonies in exchange for small, worldly favors...."

"I realize that at any rate your Hindu upbringing has been useful in this case."

"Well, if I had to investigate the motive of a religious crime in Rome, within the walls of Saint Peter's, I would have a lot more problems... Franciscans, Dominicans, Cathars.... I read *The Name of the Rose*, but I can't say I understood much about the differences. For sure, I had a hard time with the Tibetans, too, with all their religious schools and Tantras, a first wave of translations, a second wave of translations...an arduous enterprise, don't you think?"

"That's for sure!" I replied. "It is a complex world. Even though I don't keep up much with the codes of the schools, I am interested in the essence of their teachings, to relax, to find a calm state of mind.... Undoubtedly it's not easy...."

"I agree with you. There's no point worrying too much. I've adopted this method since I was put in charge of dozens and then hundreds of people. And sometimes, believe me, it's difficult to keep your nerve. This is why I can't help wondering how certain monks, used to sitting in meditation for hours and days at a time, could get so worked up over a spirit.... From that point of view, I don't miss that investigation."

I asked him if there were any hope of reviving the search for the killers and those who had given gave them their orders. Superintendent Singh furnished a vague answer, the gist of which seemed to me strongly critical of the judicial system and the lack of coordination with the Nepalese and Chinese authorities. But I preferred not to insist on details that could have proved embarrassing for the former superintendent of Kangra, even years later. We said farewell with the hope that the situation would quiet down sooner or later. The former investigator, Mr. Singh, gave me the telephone numbers of the office in his old precinct where, theoretically, the investigation had never been dropped. Though I tried to contact his successors, I did not find them as easy to approach.

PART SIX

The Return to Italy

After leaving India, I slipped back into my professional routine. From the window of my office, which looked onto one of the busiest streets in the city, I saw how, as in my earlier dream, cars and pedestrians went backward and forward, their movement reminding me of the comings and goings of my life along its prescribed routes. These seemed my choice alone, although they actually were imposed by automatic mechanisms, work, sleep, waking time, work, rest, work again, rest, sleep. The green, red, and yellow rays of the traffic light reflected intermittently on the windowpane, symbolizing our conditioned rhythms. To be sure, I did not choose my own working hours, although I regarded myself as a lot more fortunate than those workers who had to clock in and out, but the pattern of repetition nevertheless was oppressing me. My research in Dharamsala had broken my routine, but it had not been enough to free me from the cycle. I could not devote myself full time to the matter I had spent so many months researching, although an indefinable sense of urgency drove me to keep on until I had completed what I had begun.

There had been no further dramatic episodes since the triple homicide, but the official Internet site of the Tibetan government dedicated ever more space to the Shugden case. There were declarations from the Dalai Lama and other masters, the government itself, and the parliament-in-exile. Evidently, there was great concern that the striking growth of centers in the Western world linked to the cult could have a slow but inexorable effect on the image of Tibetan Buddhism. I thought back to my conversation with Ganchen Tulku. "If Shugden is an insignificant spirit, why is there such fear of him?" he had asked. And now I had the impression that the Dalai Lama perhaps had personal experience of Shugden's powers. Certainly his devotees, as the former monk P. had said, believed the spirit capable of bestowing success in business and in life in general. Other organizations groups describing themselves as Buddhist, such as the Japanese Soka Gakkai sect, also spread the belief that the power of particular mantras[132] can resolve daily problems, whether great or small, and it was is no accident

---

[132] *Namu-myoho-renge-kyo*, Japanese for "I bow to the Holy White Lotus Dharma Sutra!" repeated as a mantra by followers of the Soka Gakkai school.

that it had has become a large and powerful organization with branches all over the world.

The Dalai Lama, instead, along with masters from other traditions, not only Tibetan, continued to warn practitioners against paying too much attention to gaining material benefits. There was a real danger of contradicting the essence of the original teachings and annulling the progress of spiritual evolution towards freedom from attachment to the world. Even if the principles of Buddhism are founded on the illusory nature of phenomena—as the Tibetan leader has repeated ever more frequently—few actually try to understand its their meaning. Many seek help in religions, not just Buddhism, to become wealthy, to support their families and groups—aims far from the ideal of the bodhisattva, which is difficult to achieve in this world.

In one of his most popular books, Geshe Kelsang Gyatso—who now ranks along with Ganchen Tulku as one of the leading opponents of the Dalai Lama—specifically explained his reasons for seeking support from the spirit. "Dorje Shugden," he writes in *The Melodious Drum Victorious in All Directions*, "always helps, guides, and protects pure and faithful practitioners by granting blessings, increasing their wisdom, fulfilling their wishes, and bestowing success on all their virtuous activities." It is difficult to criticize such aspirations.

The remarkable growth of Kelsang Gyatso's Manjushri Kadampa Meditation Centre seems to demonstrate that Shugden very satisfactorily has completed the task assigned by the geshe. In the evidence gathered at Dharamsala were included a number of texts, and, in particular, an article published in the *Guardian*,[133] after the first anti-Dalai Lama demonstration organized in London by the geshe's followers.

The activities of his center in Cumbria, and the first twenty other centers of the New Kadampa Tradition (NKT), were described in detail. Within the space of a few years, these had sprung up like mushrooms in the United Kingdom, with others in Australia, Malaysia, Europe, and the United States. According to the propaganda on their Websites, the number of centers or groups connected to the NKT already ran into several hundred, located all over the world, especially in the United States.

---

[133] Madeleine Bunting, July 6, 1996.

Kelsang Gyatso's organization possesses a castle in Derbyshire, which had cost over a million pounds, with thirty-eight acres of land, two tennis courts, a football field, and a covered swimming pool. It also owns the headquarters of the Manjushri Centre at Ulverston in Cumbria, another enormous Victorian gothic manor house surrounded by seventy acres of land and completely restored with vaulted arches, immense drawing rooms, stained-glass windows, and large, gilded statues of the Buddha.

The NKT's school for aspiring Buddhist masters turns out teachers as if by means of an assembly line, using precise, unbreakable, didactic rules. Foremost among them is the requirement to learn by heart the teachings of Kelsang Gyatso, described as "the Third Buddha." The library, as the *Guardian* explained, contains only the works of the geshe, or those he himself recommends. When the reporter visited, the Dalai Lama did not appear either as an author or in the hundreds of Buddhist images liberally distributed in the temple and around the rest of the center, which was crowded with worshippers and even tourists. The name of Lama Yeshe, the actual founder of the organization in England, had, completely disappeared, and the merit for its success was attributed entirely to Kelsang Gyatso.

The operation undertaken to separate his center from all other Gelukpa associations connected to the Dalai Lama had considerable financial implications. The *Guardian* article listed the many ways the Manjushri Centre financed itself, at least in the beginning, including selling objects and special prayers for those desiring to accumulate "merit," and demanding nonrepayable "loans" from disciples.

The severing of all links with Tibetan Buddhism's traditional organizations, the *Guardian* continued, began slowly and continued relentlessly with the marginalization of all the old members of Lama Yeshe's original association. Letters were sent to one family who had followed the teachings of another lama, forbidding them to frequent the NKT centers. The same ban applied to one of the trainee teachers who refused to repeat, parrot fashion, the lessons of Kelsang Gyatso. One of the most delicate issues raised in the article was that of "proselytizing," an activity, considered "off limits" in traditional Buddhism. The NKT advised its teachers in a form of handbook:

> Be very careful not to give the impression it is a recruit-
> ment drive.... We need to come over as really quite ordi-
> nary and quite matter-of-fact at the beginning.... We

should not worry about converting people at the beginning.... To start with we need to agree with people, to
show that we understand where they are at, not to resist
them or argue with them. If we have a wild horse, the
best way to tame it is to mount it, to go with it.

The article contained a lot of information, starting with economic
points. Certainly, the many thousands of pounds earned by the Manjushri
Centre since its change of direction were not even partly destined for the
Tibetan exile community and the Dalai Lama's projects in India. According
to Yvonne, the English disciple of Lama Kundeling, the NKT financed
projects of its own accord for Tibetans in the settlements in the south,
particularly the practitioners of cults "marginalized" by the official organizations in Dharamsala. But this was not made evident in any way on the
Websites.

Doubtless, the spread of Buddhism in the West has changed certain
of its characteristics. A more dynamic and less contemplative spirituality,
immersed in the contradictions of the age, has emerged. The speed of
change and the fast transmission of information have taken away the
magic and sacredness of long, slow pilgrimages that for centuries had
imposed great sacrifices on the disciples intent on reaching the ancient
caves of the Himalayas or the remote villages where the masters lived.
With distances shortened and with so many types of spirituality offered
today, everyone has a chance of encountering the right teaching for his or
her particular aptitude. What this means for the future is not clear. Risks
of a transformation or degeneration of the doctrine have existed for 2,500
years. The selection of a true master was as difficult in India in the time of
the Buddha as it was in the old, small, closed world of Tibetan monastic
communities, which often were victims of feudal customs or the ambitions
of unenlightened lamas and monks. Without doubt, outside Tibet, religion
has become a sort of tool of propaganda, with ever more attractive
"commercials" offered by various gurus who do their best to recreate the
"myth of Shambhala." But it is difficult to change the mindset of most of
the potential "customer-disciples" who await miracles and expect special
"vibrations," rather than the simple spiritual message of a deep teaching,
free of aesthetic ornaments.

I had to admit that, as a journalist and a sympathizer with the Tibetan
cause, I had to make an enormous effort to overcome my prejudices and

stereotypes regarding many aspects of the "Dharma business" all around us. But in the specific case of the Shugden dispute, without understanding its origins, there clearly was a risk of presenting only the superficial elements of the argument, pro-Dalai Lama on one side and anti-Dalai Lama on the other.

I wondered why it was that the Italian Gelukpas, and perhaps the Gelukpas elsewhere in Europe, continued to behave as if nothing unusual was happening. Not even the Tibetologists or the lamas I had contacted had wanted to enter into the rights and wrongs of the quarrel, perhaps from fear of a newspaper article appearing, or of arousing the anger of the parties involved. They said, "Best let sleeping dogs lie." I thought their attitude typical of those who follow the path of renunciation. But for how long would the dogs sleep?

In an online chat session held among experts on Buddhism, a certain participant named Mary wrote, "My friend Donald Lopez, an eminent Tibetologist from the University of Michigan, intended to write a book on the Shugden controversy in the mid 1970s. But he abandoned the project after he heard the opinion of Ling Rinpoche, the senior tutor to the Dalai Lama. Ling Rinpoche had said, 'Why waste your ink on this?'"

Many years later, Lopez dedicated a short chapter to Shugden in his work *Prisoners of Shangri-La*, in which he pointedly criticized the myth of Tibet and its religion, despite having studied and practiced it himself for many years. Apart from this, with the exception of a few short academic articles,[134] the silence of the media was absolute. It was suggested that this reticence stemmed from fear of a Buddhist version of a fundamentalist Muslim "*fatwa*," something similar to the decree against Salman Rushdie.

Only on the Internet, often under the guarantee of anonymity, was the debate continued, sometimes in heated terms. Many warned of a "witch hunt" against the spirit's practitioners. My own feeling was that the responsibility for the three murders inevitably fell on a small number of fanatics intent on raising tensions, and not on the devotees who were unaware of the more disturbing aspects of the cult. Moral responsibility was a more complex matter. Sharing ideas with a group of murderers is not equal to murdering, but without some attempt to reach an understanding,

---

[134] By George Dreyfus and Michael Von Bruck.

the conflict easily could have degenerated. That was plain from reading the emails on the Web, often full of factual errors and confused reasoning.

A bit of information no one could have found on the Internet was the 1998 letter that Geshe Kelsang Gyatso and his two disciples, James Belither and Rupert Brookes, wrote to all the lamas and geshes directing centers devoted to the cult in India and Nepal.[135] The NKT's leader recalled that since 1996, their organization had received

> many requests from Shugden practitioners in India and other lamas for help in their battle to gain religious liberty and to save the pure Gelukpa tradition. Thanks to our communal activities, it seems we have had some temporary success, but we are still far from our objective. Although we are still working towards our shared aim of religious liberty, our approaches are different. We know that the source of the problem is the Dalai Lama himself, and that if he does not change his views, there is no chance of further progress.... At any rate, it seems to us that you are reluctant to oppose the Dalai Lama completely, and that you believe there is a chance of maintaining a good relationship with him. Your direction is not clear. This difference in approach is a serious obstacle to our achieving our shared purpose. The solution is for us to unite in the International Dorje Shugden Coalition. We should meet and discuss together a plan on how to proceed. If you do not wish to work with the New Kadampa Tradition, then we have no choice but to end all our shared activities connected to the Dorje Shugden case.... Please discuss this among yourselves and let us have your answer by October 10th. [1998].

I found no trace of any answer to the letter. Nevertheless, a few months later Chimi Tsering, in the name of the Dorje Shugden Devotees Religious and Charitable Society of Delhi, responded by declaring officially at a

---

[135] The letter, dated September 22, 1998, is addressed to "Venerable Lamas Dragom Rinpoche, Tomo Geshe Rinpoche, Gonsar Rinpoche, Serkong Tritul Rinpoche, Gangchen Rinpoche, Geshe Chime Tsering."

press conference, "Until the Dalai Lama revokes his ban on our faith, we will not accept him as our leader."

But there were other indications showing that the international activities of groups of worshippers opposed to the Dalai Lama were intensifying, propelled by a great expenditure of money and resources. Kelsang Gyatso in the same letter listed clearly his "ultimate aims":

> 1. The Dalai Lama removed Dorje Shugden as the Dharma protector of the Geluk tradition. We want him to be reinstated.

> 2. The Dalai Lama removed Je Phabongka and Trijang Dorjechang from the lineage of gurus of the Geluk tradition. We want them to be reinstated.

> 3. The Dalai Lama is not giving freedom to those Tibetan people who wish to worship Dorje Shugden. We want them to have complete freedom to worship as they choose.

Besides the ultimatum of the English NKT, and more striking than the political propaganda, was the tone of the declarations that continued to be aimed at the poor geshe from Dharamsala, even after the tragedy of February 4, 1997. Amongst the post-mortem accusations was that he aroused the anger of many potential assassins, as mentioned by the Austrian monk, Helmut Gassner, one of the leading Western intellectuals of the "Shugden generation." After having translated the teachings of the Dalai Lama for many years, Gassner had become one of his most severe critics and, in a lengthy speech at Hamburg's Friedrich Naumann Foundation in 1999, he proposed alternative theories to those of the Indian police who had pursued the six Shugden-inspired killers.

"The Director of the School of Dialectics," he said, "was well known for the calumnies he wrote, dragging everything in the mud that was not absolutely in line with the course prescribed by the government-in-exile; famous masters, the great monastic universities, even the Tibetan resistance...."

The Austrian's attack on a man who could no longer defend himself revived the dispute that had preceded the crimes. His words proclaiming the Delhi group's innocence were cited repeatedly on the numerous Internet sites dedicated to the cult, and also, curiously, in the Chinese press.

The Chinese Octopus

Several years passed during which, between the demands of work and everyday routine, I merely kept an eye on the Shugden affair. There had been no significant new developments, other than the steady continual rise in tension, evident above all in the monastic communities of Southern India. But one morning, amongst my emails, I found an item from "*World Tibetan News.*" It was an extract from a newspaper article reporting the first conference of pro-Shugden associations in Asia. With two hundred participants, it was held in the conference room of a large hotel in Delhi and hosted by the Chinese embassy.

I could not be sure the report was true, but it showed that the large numbers of practitioners of the cult in the East did not depend solely on the initiatives of Kelsang Gyatso's NKT. I took the opportunity to write to Ngodup, the Director of Security for the government-in-exile in Dharamsala. He wrote back a few days later, attaching some confidential information on Ganchen Tulku and "Nga lama" Kundeling. In March 1998, shortly after we met, these two men were in Kathmandu, Nepal, with other Shugden followers and a member of the Communist Party of the Autonomous Region of Tibet, Gungthang Ngodup, who had come especially from Lhasa. A few days afterwards, wrote Director Ngodup, an adviser from the Chinese embassy in Nepal, one "Mr. Wang,"[136] visited Ganchen's house. As far as he could determine, the discussion revolved around the type of collaboration to be established between the Shugden followers and the Chinese authorities, including possible financial support.

In December of the same year, as reported by the *Indian Express* and the *Tribune*, the under-secretary of the Chinese embassy in Delhi, Zhao Hongang, went to the Ganden Monastery in India, accompanied by a devotee from Bylakuppe, Thupten Kunsang, and a monk who had arrived from Sera Mey. In July 1999, also in Kathmandu, other meetings were held between pro-Shugden activists and Chinese representatives. This time, "Mr. Wang" met with Chimi Tsering and other directors of the Delhi "Shugden Society," Lobsang Gyaltsen, Konchok Gyaltsen, Gelek Gyatso, and Soepa Tokhmey, the society's treasurer. After the final meeting, a

---

[136] Now deceased.

306

letter was drafted to be presented to the United Front Department of the Communist Party to ask for help in countering those discriminating against Shugden practitioners in India.

These reports were new breaches made by Tibetan counterespionage in an apparently insurmountable wall of secrecy. They tried to show, by means of information obtained who knows how, that by order of the highest echelons of the Communist Party, a new Chinese strategy for Tibet was being planned in Beijing, Lhasa, Kathmandu, and Delhi, with the particular aim of establishing a future alternative to the Dalai Lama. But while although there were legitimate doubts regarding the accuracy of the sources, the evidence of direct links between Chinese Communists and pro-Shugden associations soon appeared.

The main organ delegated to maintain that contact was the United Front Department (UFD). Created as a special agency of the Central Committee of the Politburo, the UFD, since the Mao era, has been one of the most power-ful instruments of the Chinese Communist Party, its "front" being an institutional wing established to monitor relationships with every sector of society. A more clandestine element of the organization, with branches throughout China and abroad, concerned itself with intelligence gathering. The Great Helmsman called the United Front, along with the Communist Party and the People's Liberation Army, "one of the three weapons with which we defeated the enemy." The United Front Department and its territorial subsections conducted operations in varying degrees of secrecy against the Nationalists in Taiwan, Hong Kong, and Macao in addition to, obviously, those against the "Dalai Lama clique" and independence groups suspected by Beijing of being in the government-in-exile's service.

In January 2000, after the meeting in Kathmandu between representa-tives of the cult and the Chinese emissaries, the Nepal National Dorje Shugden Society was born, with an office and a full-time staff of three, paid—according to the Dharamsala Security Services—with Communist Party funds funneled through the Chinese embassy. Ganchen Tulku was on the Committee of Consultants.

For all its powers, the United Front was unable to prevent the escape of the Karmapa, the young head of the Kagyu tradition, over the New Year of 2000, across the snowy passes of the Himalayas. In the barely disguised warfare between Beijing and Tibetans hostile to its rule, this defection, reported by the mass media all over the world, was a very serious blow. In response a few months later, the Communist authorities officially named their own candidate as reincarnation of Reting, the former Regent of Tibet, overriding the opinion of the monks of his monastery. Eight monks even were arrested and accused of trying to harm the child. Nothing was ever learned about their trial.

That news had little impact compared to the 1995 abduction of Gendun Choekyi Nyima, the Panchen Lama named by Dharamsala, and his replacement by the Chinese candidate, Gyaincain Norbu, to whom Ganchen Tulku paid homage in 1997. But this showed that the new Party strategy was increasingly aimed at controlling the effective leaders of Tibetan Buddhism, the tulku bodhisattva reincarnations. Among the Tibetan religious figures prepared to support their policy, along with Ganchen, were some of longstanding faith, such as Sengchan Lobsang Gyaltsen, head of Tashi Lhunpo Monastery, who had termed "illegal" the naming of the tulku chosen by the Dalai Lama. Sengchen also had asked for and obtained the arrest of the monk responsible for finding the child excluded by Beijing. After his arrest, this child and his family disappeared completely. For the official recognition ceremony it was Sengchen, once more, who had brought from Beijing the Party's candidate, along with two other children who had no chance of selection from the outset. The chosen one in fact was already waiting behind a curtain in his ceremonial robes for the investiture before the selection procedure was even over.

The story of Sengchen Gyaltsen shows how the Party guarantees to further the careers of Tibetans of proven Communist loyalty. He had been one of the fiercest accusers of the previous Panchen Lama, who was tortured during the famous "show trials" of the Cultural Revolution and held in prison for many years as an "enemy of the people and the Party." I wondered how Ganchen Tulku could back up the tyrants who had jailed and tortured his master. But it was clear that "the war of the lamas" over Shugden was being waged with no holds barred, and with long-term political aims ever more openly asserted.

Trijang Rinpoche's Tulku

In 2000, the year of the Karmapa's arrival in India after his dramatic New Year's Eve escape from Tibet, the Dalai Lama returned to Italy, where he was invited to a concert given by Luciano Pavarotti. He asked all the Gelukpa lamas resident in Europe, with the exception of the directors of the Italian "Unione Buddhista," to meet him in his hotel in Bologna. The reason for convening them was not difficult to guess. I learned that the Dalai Lama's sister, Jetsun Pema, had asked the director of the largest Italian Gelukpa monastery, the Lama Tsong Khapa Institute of Pomaia, why Ganchen Tulku's presence was tolerated in the Buddhist Union. The director, an Italian monk, answered that one should show compassion towards certain brothers who had "erred." The Dalai Lama's sister's reaction was probably unforeseen; she burst into tears as she told the monk that he had no idea of the suffering caused to so many people by the criticisms of the Dalai Lama and the government-in-exile, especially her brother, who bore the brunt of the attacks. Although years had passed since the murders, it was clear that memories of the case had not faded in Dharamsala. Indeed, the opposite may have been true.

I decided to go to Bologna to try to meet some of the Gelukpas summoned by the Dalai Lama to his hotel. I saw them slip into the elevator, in their maroon and yellow ochre robes, observed with great curiosity by the staff and guests. I waited for the end of the meeting to try to pick up some snippets of information or a chance indiscretion. One of those present, who had come from France, told me that the main subject was the reincarnation of Trijang. That young rinpoche had in fact left India for Switzerland, after the Dalai Lama asked him to stop performing the practices of Shugden, if he wished to receive his Tantric initiations.

"His Holiness was rather worried," the French Gelukpa said, "His former tutor had been very kind to him, and he wanted his reincarnation to study in our monastic universities under the greatest masters. But as it turned out, the boy had practically been held hostage by the lamas and monks of his entourage, leading the Dalai Lama to suspect that he might be pressured into becoming the leader of the Shugden worshippers, with serious consequences for himself and for relationships among Tibetans. The Dalai Lama also heard that the young rinpoche had been invited by Ganchen here in Italy."

For the tulku of His Holiness's former tutor, events during the next few years were to take a dramatic turn. In a radio talk broadcast in 2002 by a Tibetan station, the young Trijang offered a number of disturbing revelations. He recounted how, while still in Dharamsala, he was told of a plan by the Tibetan Youth Congress and the Tibetan Women's Association to attack his labrang.

> Consequently, the Chatreng community appealed to me to come immediately to Delhi and thereafter to leave for the Densa [Ganden Monastery in south India]. I did so, leaving my attendant, Tharchin, in Dharamsala to request an interview with His Holiness. Anonymous letters and telephone calls were received at the labrang, where masked men were seen trying to enter my residence at night. As a result, the Chatreng community deployed around twenty guards for my security. In 1996, Gonsar Rinpoche and others decided to move me to Switzerland. The situation in India deteriorated and tensions rose between the followers and non-followers of the protector, consequently delaying my return. Later that year, with my aide Tharchin, I had an audience with His Holiness during his visit to Switzerland. Tharchin apprised him of the threats to my life and we agreed I should continue my studies abroad. Six years have passed since then.

Trijang recounted how subsequently he had other audiences with the Dalai Lama in Europe, during which the Tibetan leader had asked him to choose between his spiritual guide and the protector.

> I could not decide against him, but nor could I stop propitiating Shugden, with whom my relationship dates back to previous incarnations. I find myself in an immensely difficult situation. The followers of the protector would not have listened to me, and no one seems to care about the difficulties I am facing.... I also don't want the people of Chatreng, who have great expectations of me, to be disheartened. But if I continue to propitiate the protector publicly, I could be compelled to become a sort of head of his worshippers, and this would be an offense to the

Dalai Lama, from whom I received my bhikshu monk's ordination and who always has treated me with extraordinary benevolence. I cannot even hope to keep a low profile since they [the Shugden devotees] would not let me.

The broadcast contained another series of remarkable revelations:

I have reason to believe that my return to India may possibly result in internal chaos, attempts on lives, and other immoral acts bringing disgrace to His Holiness.... I cannot sleep and I have had health problems. I am worried about what will happen next. It is quite terrifying to think that I might be a cause of disgrace instead of serving the Tibetan people and His Holiness.... Some have told me, "If you abandon the protector [Shugden], there is no knowing what will happen. We will not consider you a lama." The people of Chatreng are strange, very wild and unruly. We do not know what they may do.

It is very clear my life might be in danger. So I have decided to leave my labrang and disrobe, so that none of the Shugden worshippers can ask me to be their leader. I hope that this way I can respect the wishes of the Dalai Lama and still revere the protector, practicing in private and far from everyone. I intend to follow a middle way, neither for nor against Shugden. I appeal to both parties not to contact me.

His account ended with another dramatic twist:

In my own labrang, I have recently witnessed a kind of factionalism, and I have discovered that one person in particular was planning an evil conspiracy. This plan was to murder my assistant, Tharchin, and to implicate His Holiness's government-in-exile with this odious crime. The conspirator aimed to become *changzoe* [manager] of my estate. Tharchin has been very kind to me, more so than my own parents, and has taken care of me since I was three years old, as well as managing the affairs of my labrang. With my own ears I heard this person discussing

> on the telephone a plan to assassinate Tharchin. It is
> really a matter of great sadness and surprise, especially
> since the person involved in this ploy has been very close
> to me as well. If he had succeeded in his plan, it would
> have been a cause of great trouble for the labrang, as well
> as a cause of disgrace to the Tibetan government and His
> Holiness the Dalai Lama. These are not lies, but true facts
> which that I want everyone to know. That is why I made
> this statement.

Trijang concluded his message by urging the followers of the protector to
stop seeking him. "I do not wish to be in touch with you," he said.

The young Trijang Rinpoche's radio message created no little embarrassment among the *gyalpo* king demon's worshippers. The image of a
community "living peacefully and devoted to the Buddhadharma," promoted in their propaganda material was damaged seriously, and for a
long time, the polemics against the Dalai Lama seemed to be diminish-
ing. But hopes that they would fade away completely have not been
fulfilled—far from it. After this declaration, Trijang moved to the United
States with a small number of his most faithful followers.

The Secret Strategy

Dharamsala's security forces continued to receive information regarding the continual "pilgrimages" made by the cult's leaders to Chinese-occupied Tibet. The list of them included, from 1998 onwards: a lama based in Taiwan and Singapore, Serkong Tritul, who was the guru of one of the alleged Dharamsala murderers; Yongya Tulku, the Secretary of the Delhi Shugden Society; Phari Phuntsok, a lama resident in Kathmandu; Dagom Rinpoche, Vice-President of the Nepalese Shugden society; Basundara Lhakpa; Chatreng Thinley; and Chatreng Topgyal. The latter three were received in Lhasa as an official delegation from the authorities of the Tibet Autonomous Region (TAR).

The ever-closer links between the cult members and the Chinese authorities were not "invented" by Dharamsala's counterespionage team. In his long activist history, Kundeling Lama, the leader of the International Coalition who had met Ganchen in Milan, wrote,

> In the winter [of 2001] I took the bold step of visiting Beijing in the hope of reaching out to the Eleventh Panchen Lama and other prominent Buddhist leaders.[137] In April 2002, once again, I visited Beijing to apprise the Buddhist leaders and the authorities of the threats being faced by Shugden devotees within Tibet.

This odd request from a Tibetan for China to support the cult seems to have been granted, at least by the national media, which published several articles on the subject. On February 27, 2003, with money offered by the Chinese embassy in Kathmandu, a bimonthly review was started, called *Times of Democracy*, to which a reporter from the *Wen Hui Daily* of Shanghai contributed. Even the building that housed the offices of the journal and the headquarters of the Nepalese branch of the Shugden Society was paid for by the embassy, which contributed 700,000 rupees, then around 6,500 euros.

---

[137] The directors of the Chinese Buddhist Association are members of the Party directly linked to the United Front Department.

Despite the formal denials of the cult's practitioners, the common strategy of the Chinese authorities by now was obvious. In 2001 the Chinese ambassador was guest of honor at "The Millennium Conference on Human Rights" organized by the Shugden Devotees Religious and Charitable Society of Delhi and held March 20–22 at the most prestigious venue in the Indian capital, the India International Centre. If the reports of the pro-Shugden convention financed by the embassy were only "rumor" spread by *World Tibetan News*, the ambassador's presence at the Millennium Conference was hard to reconcile with his routine duties as a diplomat. For that reason, I began to regard the information I continued to receive from my good source in Dharamsala as very reliable. According to one item, Thubten Chodhen, suspected of being one of the killers of Geshe Lobsang, was stabbed to death in 2001 in his birthplace, the city of Lithang, near Chatreng. The motive appears to have been a disagreement over the cult of Shugden that arose between local Tibetans, famed for settling their arguments with fists and knives.

Chodhen had been recognized along with the others by several witnesses, but he managed to cover his tracks until the day of his death, news of which reached Dharamsala from Khampa informers who knew his previous record.

Meanwhile, the judicial whitewash for Chodhen and the other killers allowed those who ordered the triple homicide to present themselves shamelessly as victims of religious persecution.

In April 2005, the Shugden Charitable Society organized another conference to celebrate the ninth anniversary of its founding, detailing instances of supposed discrimination against the cult's practitioners — charges earlier judged as unfounded by the Human Rights Commission of India. Among them were supposed bans on Shugden followers becoming teachers, studying in exile government schools such as the Tibetan Children's Village, receiving assistance as newly arrived refugees, entering monasteries, marrying, or even eating at the same table as other Tibetans. Not surprisingly, they claimed to be "the new outcasts."

After my first trip, I returned to India several times, and from what I managed to understand, there was deliberate exaggeration employed in dramatizing a situation that was much more complex than the society's descriptions in letters, documents, press conferences, and even legal depositions.

The split over Shugden had occurred long before and was by that time decidedly a political rather than a spiritual question. There were a great number of Tibetans who, even after many years, had not managed to choose between their devotion to the Dalai Lama and the masters who had initiated them into the cult. But whoever decided not to abandon Shugden could already rely for support from various Indian and international organizations arrayed against the Tibetan leader. Substantial financial assistance continued to arrive for them from both East and West.

The Dalai Lama's position on the dangers of the cult by now certainly had been accepted by the heads of all the schools and by most Tibetans in exile, starting with the monastic community. Both laypeople and monastics increasingly seemed less and less willing to mix with Shugden worshippers, perceived as potential enemies of their bodhisattva leader. There was more than one reason for this.

In fact, the dissidents' request to be given responsible roles in the institutions of the exile community conflicted with the need to defend the community and the offices of the Dalai Lama and his government from the dangers of infiltration by Chinese-trained spies. The cult representatives continued to compare the Dalai Lama to Hitler, labeling him a dictator, as the minutes of the Shugden Society's ninth-anniversary conference show.

But the government-in-exile's mistrust was justified further by the news that kept arriving from China. On June 22, 2004, after several appearances at ceremonies and conferences transmitted on Chinese television, Ganchen Tulku took part as an actual member in the work of the "China-Tibet Committee for the Development and Preservation of Culture," presided over by Ja Qing-Lin, president of the powerful "People's Conference on Political Consultation." A few months earlier, on February 1 in Mysore, Kundeling "Nga-lama" had met two Chinese officials from the consulate in Mumbai, together with a leader of the Delhi Shugden Society, Lobsang Yeshi.

At the same time, on the other side of the world, the head of the Manjushri Centre, Kelsang Gyatso, gave the order to all the affiliated centers of the "New Kadampa" Tradition not to admit any student who refused to do the practices of Shugden. The NKT by then had acquired over five hundred such centers, and most of the new ones were in the United States. It seemed probable that many of the new adepts were Westerners who knew very little about the other Buddhist traditions before they discovered the teachings of Kelsang Gyatso and his "protector" spirit.

I had no wish to judge them, since, before becoming interested in the three murders, I personally had known little about the Gelukpa tradition, which, for better or worse, is at the religious, judicial, and political heart of the affair.

What increased my concern at the unfolding of events was a more general consideration: the lack of awareness in the international community regarding the implications of this case. What might be the consequences for an ancient civilization crushed by an unprecedented alliance between political atheists and enterprising mystics, gathered around a spirit whose origins and powers are so nebulous?

The only "glue" that seemed to hold these two hybrid components together was the power of money and "modernity." In exchange for relative prosperity (destined mostly for the exclusive benefit of the overwhelmingly Chinese community), Tibet progressively has been stripped of its values in the name of a socialist-capitalist model that carries the seeds of degeneration for both ideologies, leading to the dictatorial, collectivist control of the individual and the selfish exploitation of resources.

In many ways, the fate of Tibet resembles that of the lands once inhabited by the Native Americans, before an alien industry imposed by rifle and cannon polluted their environment and materialism eroded their culture. Tibet possesses nothing other than its mountains, its religion, and the great rivers that the Chinese slowly have devastated after conquering their sources.

The Himalayas were for centuries the last frontier, a buffer protecting the valleys where Chinese civilization evolved. Inaccessible peaks separated the Han from the other major Asian ethnic groups on the Indian continent, but, in the battle of the earth's giants, several million human beings who lived in almost complete isolation have been overwhelmed and now stand in danger of extermination. Given the numerical superiority of the Chinese, this fate lies not far ahead. In a few generations, the Mongols' presence in part of their own land, split off into "Inner Mongolia" as part of China, was heavily "diluted," and they now represent only twenty percent of those who live in their territory. Similarly, the Manchu barely exist as an autonomous ethnic group, Manchuria now containing approximately 2 million Manchus and 75 million Chinese.

The greatness of Tibet, despite the human errors described in these pages, is not only physical but moral and spiritual, in sharp contrast to the brutal force of a regime that tolerates no dissent whatsoever and allows no meaningful religious freedom. In China, tens of thousands of people have been arrested, most of whom are still incarcerated, for having practiced the yogic techniques of the Falun Gong sect; hundreds of practicing Catholics and priests obedient to the Vatican have been spied on, arrested, and discriminated against; and trade union members and political critics of the Party have experienced similar infringements of their freedom.

As the collaboration between Shugden followers and the authorities of Beijing and Lhasa gradually becomes evident, a common strategy absolutely unprecedented in the history of the Celestial Empire appears ever more paradoxical. Never before has the Party trusted entities that are "external" and not under the direct control of its apparatus. Buddhists, Muslims, Daoists, Catholics, and Protestants, members of the only religions tolerated in China, must be registered with one of the five related patriotic associations under the supervision of the Administration for Religious Affairs.

The Communist defense of the Shugden practitioners' cult against "the abuses of the Dalai Lama clique" has been the subject of continual analysis and exchanges of opinion, often reported in the official Beijing Chinese press. I also learned personally from the Dalai Lama that the negotiations between the Dharamsala delegation and the Chinese officials in 2002 foundered on the thorny question of the controversial spirit.

But what happened early in 2006 defies the imagination. On February 14, at Ganden Monastery, the original seat of the Gelukpa sect outside of Lhasa, a group of seventeen monks decided to destroy the statue of Shugden that the Chinese authorities had allowed devotees of the spirit to install.

First Xinhua, the official press agency, then the Under-Secretary of the Communist Party of Tibet, Zhang Qingli, and finally the Mayor of Lhasa, Norbu Dunzhub, attributed the statue's destruction to "the Dalai Lama clique," accusing it of "violating the religious liberty of believers," and "creating a conflict between different sects of Tibetan Buddhism in order to sabotage the unity of Tibet." The Communist leaders, for once, were not mistaken in attributing the act to the concern for the Dalai Lama felt by the monks in Tibet.

Traditionally Ganden had not permitted images of such mundane wrathful deities, as was recounted in the historical episodes cited earlier. As part of the campaign to diminish the cult, images of Shugden already had been removed years before from the reconstructed Ganden Monastery in India, after a divination by the Dalai Lama and meetings with the abbots. But it was definitely not the Tibetan leader who asked for that statue in Tibet to be destroyed.

The episode brought jail sentences and heavy fines imposed to pay for the reconstruction of the destroyed object, and it marked the beginning of a series of highly significant events.

Concerned about potential confrontations among the people over Shugden, the Party leaders held a series of meetings at the highest level to examine possible strategies. On September 12, the first Tibetan in history was elected to the post of Vice Minister of the Central United Front, with responsibility for the Seventh Office delegated to focus on Tibet. Mr. Sertar had distinguished himself for many years by his fervent opposition to the Dalai Lama, and, barely a week after his appointment, the government of the Autonomous Region of Tibet passed a new law regarding the "Regulation of Religious Affairs." Article 13 obliged all religious organizations to submit any plans for the construction of open-air statues, stupas, or Mani Lhakang[138] to the appropriate department of the TAR, Tibetan Autonomous Prefectures, or local administrations.

The law became effective on January 1, 2007, and three weeks later, the new statue of Shugden was unveiled in Ganden Monastery in the presence of numerous officials of the TAR government, the Party, and the Lhasa municipal administration, together with cult followers from the Ngaba and Chatreng areas and from Nepal. The statue was made by Nepalese artists and brought to Ganden by Ganchen Tulku, who offered to pay other monasteries at Qinghai and Gansu if they were willing to install similar images of Shugden in their prayer halls.

Four months later, a different fate awaited a great sculpture of Padmasambhava standing at Samye, a monastery founded in the eighth century by the guru himself when he brought Buddhism to Tibet. Over 10 meters tall, it was covered in gold and copper and had cost 800,000 yuan (75,000 euros), money donated by two Chinese devotees from Guangdong. In

---

[138] Small pagodas containing large prayer wheels or cylinders.

mid-May, in accord with the new laws on statues, a platoon of People's Armed Police agents arrived with trucks and bulldozers and smashed it into small pieces, which then were taken to a distant dump. For weeks, tourists were forbidden access to the monastery, until in June the Democratic Management Committee of Samye officially admitted the "removal" of the "illegal statue of the Buddha," which "failed to obey the laws of the People's Republic on cultural patrimony." Could there have been a more absurd choice of language for the destruction of a statue of a renowned figure venerated by all Tibetans, apart from Shugden worshippers, for over twelve centuries?

In July, the Administration for Religious Affairs passed a law on an issue more delicate than that of statues. It concerned the naming of tulkus, or "living buddhas," as the Chinese authorities called them. From September 1, 2007, every new reincarnation selected by the monasteries had to be examined and approved by the Department Administration of Religious Affairs or the governments above the municipal level. The political authorities already had decided "officially," as we saw earlier, on a number of important reincarnations, such as those of the Panchen Lama and Reting Rinpoche. However, this new ruling was the first formal step taken with regard to the future choice of the most important "living buddha" of all, the Dalai Lama.

These various moves made by the Party followed a precise, long-term strategy aimed at an even tighter control of Tibetan Buddhism and of Tibet itself. As events soon showed, this strategy would embitter the souls of the majority of Tibetans, while the particular minority of the Shugden worshippers continued to receive recognition and funding for the promotion of their own cult. At the start of 2007, an influential Tibetan Communist cadre, Phuntsog Wangyal, wrote a well-publicized letter to the Party President, Hu Jintao, in which he defined the lamas and worshippers of the spirit as people who "earn their living, promote wealth, and indeed prosper by opposing separatism."[139]

On September 28 of the same year, a group of Western tourists on a trip to the sacred Mount Kailash witnessed a curious event. At the starting point of the traditional route for the circumambulation of the mountain, the village of Darchen, they saw about twenty Tibetans surrounding a

---

[139] Tibetan Review, May 2007.

statue of Padmasambhava that stood about two meters tall. Dozens of police were trying to disperse them. A woman, in tears, drew one of the Western women aside and explained to her that the police wanted to destroy the statue. She begged the tourist to take photographs and deliver them to the Dalai Lama. Shortly afterwards, she and the other demonstrators were removed violently and the sculpture was smashed to pieces.

The police also tried to seize the tourists' cameras, but one of them nevertheless managed to take pictures of the statue before and after its destruction. "It seems absurd to see something like that happen," was his anonymous comment. He certainly could not have known the background, which is increasingly clear to those of us who have been following the issue. The choice of singling out statues of Padmasambhava for destruction was obviously not a casual one. Since the Cultural Revolution, no other image has received this treatment, especially since the Communist authorities realize that Tibet's religious sculptures are a tourist attraction and a source of revenue.

The explanation for this relentless attack against Padmasambhava was given by the Dalai Lama in his interview in Bolzano, which there is no need to repeat. But on a trip I made to China, sources there confirmed that, being highly superstitious, the authorities were influenced by hearing that Padmasambhava symbolized the independent soul of Tibet, and learning that he founded the Nyingmapa tradition so vehemently opposed by the extremist Gelukpas who venerate Shugden.

The Referendum in the Monasteries

This struggle between China and the "Shugdenites" on the one side, and the Dalai Lama's government-in-exile on the other, entered a new, decisive phase later in 2007, starting in Karnataka in south India, where over 15,000 monks live in the great Gelukpa monasteries of Drepung, Ganden, and Sera. The coexistence of pro- and anti-Shugden groups within them was becoming ever more strained. The Dalai Lama's followers, after numerous episodes of hostility and violence, had asked Dharamsala to intervene to separate them from the *gyalpo* practitioners.

The situation came to a head on the eve of the winter session of debates, during which the Gelukpa monks must demonstrate their intellectual ability in contests, displaying their knowledge of Buddhist scriptures, and in particular, the theories regarding dependent origination and emptiness. The monk making the challenge stands and asks a question, clapping his hands to invite his seated opponent to reply immediately. By tradition, the community watches with great interest. The excitement grows with the increasing difficulty of the theoretical subjects, studied for years by the participants, but in normal times the competitive tension of the monks is tempered by the brotherly feeling that usually bonds them. But in November 2007, feelings over Shugden were running high, and apprehension that the debates could degenerate into violence became terror.

Hundreds of monks had told the abbots and college heads that they did not wish to take part in the dialectical challenges while Shugden practitioners were present, nor did they even want to share the kitchens and dining rooms with them. For the first time, there was a critical problem in accommodating the two groups under one roof.

The monasteries of Sera Mey in Bylakuppe and Ganden Shartse in Mundgod, predictably, were at the heart of the conflict, since the highest percentage of monks devoted to the cult lived there. Their temples had been closed for a long time for fear of incidents, and the monks remained in their separate colleges, where, for the last two years, the two sides had divided into separate dormitories according to allegiance. At Sera Mey, on the second day of the debates, the *gyalpo* practitioners came to take part with the others, but a large number of the monks left the hall when they arrived.

The Dalai Lama, who had planned to go to the south to inaugurate the debate session, decided to take the bull by the horns. At the beginning of January 2008, he reached Mundgod, together with Samdhong Rinpoche, a high official who had been threatened repeatedly when he was head of the parliament-in-exile and had since become prime minister of the Dharamsala government.

Samdhong spoke first, revealing that many people had warned him not to continue to expose himself, as his life would be at risk. "Sooner or later I'll have to die anyway," he said, "whether it is Shugden practitioners who kill me or not. But my duty is to warn of the dangers of developing the cult of this demon.... I hope that one day everyone will understand this and His Holiness will be able to teach in every Tibetan settlement without having to check whether the place is safe from people connected to the practice of Dolgyal."

Samdhong explained that monks disagreeing over doctrines was nothing new, and he cited the stories of the *bhikshu* monks of Koshambi, and of Ananda, the Buddha's main disciple, not speaking to those of Nyenyoed. He was indicating that even in the time of the Buddha, according to the rules of the Vinaya, monks were free to refuse to live alongside other religious practitioners who did not follow their same doctrine.

"In the past," he said, 'the practice of Dolgyal was a matter of individual faith, but it now has a political element. Shugden worshippers are receiving special attention from the Chinese government and are invited to ceremonies and meetings. This is now spoken of publicly, and so the cult's practitioners unashamedly seek the patronage of China, which is using them for its own ends.... We have never taken away their political rights," continued the Prime Minister in Exile, "We have only insisted on their not taking part in religious rituals conducted by His Holiness. They, instead, continue to lie, and have appealed several times to the Indian government, to Amnesty International, and to the National Commission on Human Rights. Even though their lies have been seen as such by everyone, their behavior has created many political problems for us."

That day and for several days thereafter at Mundgod, the Dalai Lama spoke in a harsher tone than he had used before. In his first talk on January 5, in unequivocal terms, he accused the "Dorje Shugden Charitable Trust" of being responsible for "crimes, assaults, arson, falsehoods, exaggerated declarations, and unethical practices." His Holiness described the criticism that had been showered on him after repudiating Shugden, as if he had done so only "to please the Nyingmapa and other Buddhist schools." He stated, "They even went so far as to say that "the Dalai Lama was born with the express aim of abolishing the Buddhadharma in general and the teachings of Tsong Khapa in particular." They called me "the false Dalai Lama;" but such accusations do not bother me. During the Cultural Revolution, the Chinese called me "a wolf in monk's clothes"; but I don't have to kill lambs and crawl on all fours because of these accusations. As for my being born to abolish the Buddhadharma, each of you can judge for yourself whether I have contributed to the teachings of the Buddha or not."

One particularly sensitive issue touched on by the Tibetan leader was the case of Phabongka, who, through Trijang and his lineage, indirectly was the guru of a large number of the monks present at the meeting. After having expressed his esteem for the lama's erudition, he recalled that the Thirteenth Dalai Lama was "displeased with him and reprimanded him for his conduct." "There was no other reason for this," he explained, "than his propitiation of Shugden. And in the end, the practice harmed rather than favored Phabongka, while his spiritual heirs derived no benefit whatsoever. I, in turn, was mistaken in not following the path of my predecessors. At that time, I did not know and I was not aware. Trijang Rinpoche cannot be held responsible because he followed his lama, Phabongka, who had in turn become associated with this spirit as a result of a number of factors.... Can we blame Phabongka, then? His mistake lay in his attachment to Dolgyal."

The Dalai Lama's tone hardened when he spoke of the links between Shugden followers and the Beijing authorities. "The Chinese openly favor the Dolgyal practitioners, some of whom are helped financially, while the monasteries are encouraged to worship the spirit." Then he referred to the two episodes in which Padmasambhava statues had been destroyed, at Samye and near Kailash. Without saying so explicitly, he seemed to connect these incidents directly to the increasingly close links between the Communist authorities and the spirit's worshippers. "Those who do the practices of Shugden," he said, "have no real reason to be in India. We came here because we disapprove of the Chinese policies in Tibet. But the Dolgyal practitioners receive attention and favors, so it would be better for them to go where they are supported. They have no reason to stay here."

With this remark, the Tibetan leader introduced the idea of a referendum in the monasteries to decide once and for all if and how the followers of the cult could remain in the monastic universities. "In the Supreme Vinaya tradition, there are seven ways of resolving differences," he continued, "One of these is to vote with colored sticks. In modern democracies, the word 'referendum' means establishing the choice of the majority to resolve an issue. Now the time has come for us to discover which side the majority is on. When you return to your monasteries, you will be asked whether you are for or against the practice of Dolgyal. The other question will be whether you wish to continue to live beside the practitioners of the cult. If there is a majority of sixty percent in favor of the practice, then I will not say another word on this matter. In the opposite case, we shall see what measures to take."

News of the Dalai Lama's speech spread rapidly among the Tibetan exiles, south and north. The prospect of splitting the monastic community could have yet more dramatic consequences, but by now it was clear that the battle over Shugden had entered a new stage and the Dalai Lama was specifically asking all Tibetan society to be wary of collusion between the Shugdenites and the Chinese authorities.

The Revolt in Tibet

In the heated days of the referendum, Yvonne, the disciple of Kundeling "Nga lama," wrote a letter to the editor of my newspaper:

> A witch-hunt is taking place, with all the features of persecution, falsehoods, and excommunications. I am working with my lama Kundeling on a chronological account of events during these years of the ban. We present concrete evidence in the form of articles, video, and audio recordings of the Dalai Lama's speeches in his ferocious campaign of persecution. We are also working with the Indian authorities to show the injustices perpetrated on the territory of the world's largest democracy. We ask for an impartial and objective investigation of the facts. But it is URGENT. There is a movement to ELIMINATE the practitioners of Dorje Shugden, making it impossible for them to live in monasteries or in refugee communities or with their families. Every day we receive news from the monasteries of more injustice and suffering. And all this is done in the name of religion! It is difficult for a Westerner to comprehend all this. We can produce PROOF of his words and actions. We hope you will take an immediate interest in this, since the situation is truly grave.
>
> Sincerely,
>
> Yvonne K.

This letter to my newspaper provided confirmation that after several years of keeping a relatively low profile in the public controversy with the Dalai Lama, the devotees of the spirit had begun an international press campaign and other new initiatives. A few days later, the *China Daily*, Peking's Beijing's most widely sold English-language newspaper, published an article comparing the "persecution" of the Shugden followers to the days of the Inquisition in Europe. I was none too surprised by the turn that events were taking. For some time, I had been expecting the issue to flare up again, and now I decided that I would complete and publish my research on the subject.

I reached Dharamsala early in March 2008 and immediately requested an interview with the Dalai Lama. I hoped not to wait long to be received, despite his numerous commitments on the eve of the forty-ninth anniversary of the Lhasa Revolt against the Chinese occupation.

On March 10, the day of the anniversary, I went to the main temple to hear his speech, which the press agencies had been awaiting. Before thousands of exiles and a good number of foreigners who had come to receive spiritual teachings, the Tibetan leader, in a new, even firmer tone, described the "cultural genocide" taking place in his homeland. His speech was interpreted as an attempt to pacify internal dissent, since the Dalai Lama still was being criticized continually for his "Middle Way" of seeking autonomy rather than independence for Tibet. But few foresaw what would happen within a few days.

On March 14, the monks of Drepung and Ramoche in Lhasa took to the streets and soon were joined by lay Tibetans. This time, they did not stop at chanting "Free Tibet" or reciting mantras as they marched. In a series of attacks on shops and businesses, several Han Chinese were killed, victims of a long-repressed rage against political discrimination and the Chinese invasion that had made Tibetans a minority in their own land. Protests against the government exploded immediately, all over Tibet, and after initial surprise, the authorities reacted with mass arrests and massacres of demonstrators in Lhasa, Amdo, Kham, Gansu, and Sichuan. No journalist was allowed into the areas where the revolt was under way, and even Beijing correspondents had to rely on agency bulletins. But a lot of news reached Dharamsala through exile organizations and the exile government there.

During those critical days, while daily demonstrations were held on McLeod Ganj's main street in support of the Tibetan cause, news of the Shugden affair continued to arrive. I learned that between January and February, in fourteen monasteries in Karnataka, over twelve thousand monks had voted against the presence of *gyalpo* practitioners. Another three thousand were absent on the day of the referendum but already had announced they would accede to the Dalai Lama's request. One hundred and fifty monks from Sera Mey's Pomra House and six hundred from Dhokang House in Ganden Shartse monastery, a very small percentage of the total, had chosen to abstain, as a sign of protest against the referendum. These were the hostel residences with the most dedicated *gyalpo* worshippers, from which the killers of the geshe and his assistants had come.

A video shown posted on the Internet by the pro-Shugden organizations showed images of monks trying to overturn the boxes with colored sticks used in the voting, yellow for those supporting the Dalai Lama's request, red for those in favor of Shugden.

The Final Interviews with His Holiness

During the revolt in Tibet, dozens of journalists from all over the world came to Dharamsala seeking to interview the Dalai Lama, whose private office organized a series of press conferences. At one of these, the Tibetan leader recognized me and asked me to come back the following day.

"I know that Your Holiness is very busy, I wouldn't wish to disturb you," I answered.

"That's true, but I am responsible for everything that's happening, and seeing that your research has been going on for years, I'd like to do what I can to clear up any doubts you still have."

And so, for three days in a row, while Tibet rebelled and the world watched the Chinese army's dramatic response in alarm, I had the great fortune to be able to speak to the Dalai Lama at length on the diverse aspects of the Shugden problem. I had previously had two such opportunities since our first meeting in Bolzano, but for me to be received at this time of crisis showed that the topic was a burning issue, by no means marginal to the way events were unfolding.

Sometimes the meetings took place in his private office and at other times in a part of the grand reception room, with its large *thangkas* and an imposing gilded statue of Avalokiteshvara. Present at all the meetings were the translator, Dorji Damdul, and my friend, Jeremy Russell, an English scholar of Tibetan culture and philosophy who has followed the development of the Shugden case over the many years since the Dalai Lama made his first public statements about it.

Dalai Lama: My mental state has been troubled over the last few days, rather like my experience after March 10, 1959. Things are really becoming very tense: the Chinese side has decided to crush and the Tibetan side appears equally determined to go ahead. Bloodshed seems inevitable. However, fortunately, there is no disturbance of my sleep. Until I go to sleep I feel some kind of anxiety, but once I am asleep, I can get complete rest.

Had you expected something of this sort?

DL: Expected it? I don't know. It's like feeding a small deer into the lion's claws. Nothing can be done. But let's talk about our business. As you are writing a book on Shugden, I thought it had better be as thorough as possible. I think, essentially, there are three main points to consider: first, we must establish whether the worship of this spirit is a religious matter or not. No, it is not. So the question of religious freedom then is irrelevant.

Second, this organization's way of operating: at the beginning they killed Geshe-la. Subsequently there were cases of people being beaten up and an attempt to kill my representative in the south. The case is currently pending in the Indian courts, thus we consider this group as a kind of criminal organization.

Third, there is the political aspect: since the Chinese government wants to exploit and utilize anything that is potentially damaging to the Dalai Lama, it has come to believe that the pro-Shugden movement lends itself ideally to such purposes. It seems that now, because of Shugden, the Chinese have become more religious-minded. Now they are spirit worshippers.

Could I ask you to restate the basic reasons for Your Holiness's restrictions on this practice?

DL: Our Buddhism belongs to the pure tradition of Nalanda, and because of the conduct of some followers who consider this spirit to be more helpful than the Buddha, we are witnessing a degeneration of the standard of the teachings. As the Thirteenth Dalai Lama pointed out, this viewpoint contradicts the advice to take refuge[140] in the Buddha, the Dharma, and the Sangha. My commitment to promoting religious harmony implies a sense of nonsectarianism among Tibetan Buddhist traditions. The followers of Shugden, instead, are opposed to this. Since this problem began in the era of my fifth predecessor and led to a conflict, it is very bad for the Dalai Lama's government.

Are you also referring to the historical periods afterwards?

DL: A very old former monk from Pomra House at Sera Mey, who abandoned the practices of the spirit at my request, told me that when he was young he often visited Trode Khangsar, the main abode of Shugden in Lhasa. He told me that a medium from Pomra House performed daily rituals for the spirit, and whenever the Shugden Oracle went into trance,

[140] "Refuge" here has a literal meaning, i.e., to turn to for one's protection.

he would grip a spear and fling it, saying, "I aim at the head of the Ganden Phodrang government." That was not the medium alone speaking; it was the spirit's oracle in trance.

I have heard that during the era of the Fifth Dalai Lama there was a fire offering ritual, and that many other such rituals have been performed over the years to control the spirit. I am sure that His Holiness must have taken practical measures to diminish its power. I read of a dream in which you swallowed the spirit in the form of a child who was trying to claw his long fingernails into your flesh. My question is: if he is still alive, what is the source of his power? Does it come from those who worship him, perhaps? It seems that Phabongka, for example, in some way revitalized the spirit.

DL: That is right.

Then could you explain the difference between a being, a real entity, and a power that grows according to the veneration offered by human devotees?

DL: That is really mysterious. The writings of the Fifth Dalai Lama mention that this spirit appeared after the death of Drakpa Gyaltsen. For some time, the Dalai Lama attempted to rehabilitate this spirit. I think he created a shrine or cairn for it. In Tibet, almost every local deity is offered something like this and a place to burn incense: This being a common practice, it did not indicate that it was for a high spirit, but just an ordinary local one. Then, however, the Dalai Lama noticed that its negativity seemed to increase, and so he concluded that the only alternative left might be to destroy it. And so under his guidance, some lamas met to carry out the special rites necessary.

According to the writings of the Fifth Dalai Lama, the negative manifestations nevertheless increased.

DL: Both in the past and today, a number of people believe this spirit has the power to create trouble, but for some other lamas it doesn't seem to have much power. Likewise, since I imposed restrictions on the cult, of the many Sakya and Geluk lamas who used to place faith in the spirit, perhaps ninety percent then abandoned its practices; in most cases, they experienced no negative consequences. But a few lamas noticed some disturbances in their dreams: it is something that cannot be fully explained. It may also have as much to do with the individual's conceptualization as with the spirit itself. In my own case, nothing happened.

Is the spirit a real entity?

DL: Oh yes, it is real, but when we speak of its power, we must make a distinction. That entity also has another aspect. Terdak Lingpa of Mindroling was both a student of and tutor to the Fifth Dalai Lama. He had received some mysterious teachings that the Fifth Dalai Lama considered authentic, and so he gave the transmission requested of him. Thus, Terdak Lingpa became the Fifth Dalai Lama's guru. One of the followers of this Nyingma master explained that the true being of Drakpa Gyaltsen or Shugden was in reality burned in the fire offering ritual carried out in the Potala: subsequently, though, a spirit appeared proclaiming itself as Shugden. Actually, it was a monk faithful to the Karmapa faction who was a tenacious opponent of the government. You know that the King of Tsang ruled in central Tibet and was defeated when the Fifth Dalai Lama rose to power. So the story is truly mysterious.

Given all the conflicts surrounding this spirit, we can deduce that it still has a certain power. But is it a power that grows thanks to the veneration it receives? Is that why we should avoid having any relationship with it?

DL: Khenpo Jigme Phuntsok once explained that the real spirit of Shugden no longer exists, or at least is much weakened. A number of other indications suggest that this is true. Therefore, even if the spirit of Shugden were alive, or still existed, it certainly would be a lot weaker.

How would you describe this spirit? Some say it is a "gyalpo," others that it is a "dam-sri," a perfidious spirit.

DL: A *dam-sri*, a malicious spirit, is how the Fifth Dalai Lama described Shugden. Nechung also can be classified as a *gyalpo*, but *gyalpos* can be both positive and negative. Nechung is not a malicious spirit: indeed, he is the opposite because he made a pledge to Padmasambhava to serve the Buddhist cause. When Padmasambhava came to Tibet, Nechung tried to interfere with his activities, and so Padmasambhava subdued him. Nechung surrendered and Padmasambhava gave him a commitment. In

Shugden's case, however, no one subdued him or gave him any responsibility.

Was there no one of Padmasambhava's stature capable of taming him?

DL: That's right, so he was a sort of wild... wild spirit. During the fire sacrifice performed to destroy him, the Fifth Dalai Lama referred to him, saying, "The one who is without any pledge or commitments and pretends to bear the name of Drakpa Gyaltsen," and, "Tulku Drakpa Gyaltsen, who is the wrongly recognized incarnation of such noble beings as Tulku Sonam Gelek Palsang, appeared in this form by means of misdirected prayers." That is the cause.

What is meant by "misdirected prayers?" I have heard that often, but...

DL: These two lines written by the Dalai Lama explain the origin of Shugden clearly. The expression "by means of misdirected prayers" reveals the cause of Shugden.

Jeremy Russell: Is it that he broke his pledges or that he never was offered the chance to make any, so that he remained a wild, untamed spirit? Is this a spirit who did something wrong, who displeased or defied his lama, or is it simply that he is wild and uncontrolled? It seems important to clarify this. Does it mean he broke trust? In what way?

DL: In the sense that he supported harmful deeds and engaged in harmful deeds. Obviously, he broke his pledge to the Fifth Dalai Lama. Then, after becoming a spirit, he tried to visit the monastery of Tashi Lhunpo, but Vaishravana stopped him from entering. There is some significance to this. Trijang Rinpoche also mentions it. So then, somewhat disappointed, he visited Sakya Monastery. When the Sakya Tripa lama met him and asked him who he was, he replied, "The Gelukpa *dam-sri*." Later in Kham, when Phabongka promoted the cult of Shugden, the spirit reappeared by entering mediums in trance states; as a result, some monasteries discarded their statues of Guru Rinpoche [Padmasambhava]. He then was clearly a *dam-sri*, born from misdirected prayers and the perpetrator of harmful actions.

Forgive me if I am belaboring the point, but I think it is important to clarify as much as possible the "malevolent" nature of this spirit, since we continue to talk about him so much.

DL: From a Buddhist viewpoint, the manifestation of such a spirit is a mystery. Only those who have clairvoyant power can understand its nature. As we have seen, this evil spirit appeared for the first time during the lifetime of the Fifth Dalai Lama, who witnessed everything to do with him. The Fifth Dalai Lama had the ability to receive information through visions of his guru, meditational deities, and Dharma protectors. He often had visions of Palden Lhamo, and there are three volumes of teachings that he received in that way. For more than three hundred years, no one has argued that these teachings are controversial. All lamas, including the Gelukpas, consider them to be authentic. I myself have done several retreats based upon these teachings, and on each occasion I have had significant dreams, so they must have some authenticity. Furthermore, the Fifth Dalai Lama, as a Buddhist monk, would not have lied. Although he was involved in politics, I do not think he deliberately would have told lies. Therefore, his word should be reliable. If someone had wanted to question the Fifth Dalai Lama's statements, or his attitude towards the spirit, he or she would have had to have been a person of equal spiritual realization. However, in over three hundred years, no one has challenged the Fifth Dalai Lama's statements on this matter; on the contrary, everyone has followed his advice. There actually have been many people in the past who have criticized the spirit, as in the eras of the Seventh and Eighth Dalai Lamas. However, it only has been in the last seventy years, since the death of the Thirteenth Dalai Lama, that the issue has suddenly come alive once more.

Are you referring to Phabongka Rinpoche?

DL: I think it is very hard to establish whether Phabongka Rinpoche had a status or realization equal to that of the Dalai Lama, and, unfortunately, he maintained complete silence regarding what the Fifth had said. The proper way would have been to spell out clearly where he rejected the Dalai Lama's point of view and explain his new interpretation. Then everything would have been clear. But Phabongka and Trijang Rinpoche must have heard and read his words, yet they kept quiet. They did not have the courage to challenge him or to explain their new interpretation.

Therefore, the Fifth Dalai Lama's statements still stand and continue to retain their validity.

As for myself, bearing his same title, I really feel that I made an error earlier on, but eventually I felt it my duty to adhere to the Fifth and Thirteenth Dalai Lamas' positions over this question.

A position that conflicted with that of Trijang and Phabongka Rinpoche?

DL: I believe that they themselves were superior to the spirit, and so the spirit should have served them. I'd like to cite an example. Trijang Rinpoche often told me that the beings that can appear before us through trance states are not supramundane or transcendental deities. That applies to Shugden, Nechung, and also to Dulzin, one of the five forms of Shugden; they go into trance-mediums, so they are worldly spirits. Its followers consider Dulzin to be the peaceful form.

It would be interesting to know what really happened in the time of the Fifth Dalai Lama and Drakpa Gyaltsen.

DL: Trijang Rinpoche mentions in his writings that after Drakpa Gyaltsen's death, as his body was being cremated, white smoke rose at first; then his mother, who was still alive, shouted out, "Remember! Take revenge!" and in that moment the white smoke turned to black.

We must not forget that, according to the Fifth Dalai Lama, it was "thanks to the cunning of his mother" that Drakpa Gyaltsen was successful in being recognized as the reincarnation of Sonam Gelek Palzang. Another story I have heard, which I am not certain is authentic, is that at the time of the Fifth Dalai Lama's selection, Tulku Drakpa Gyaltsen was one of the candidates. His mother, a most astute and well-connected woman, showed great manipulating skill in the course of what was a sort of competition created to recognize the next Dalai Lama. But in the end, before a special statue of Guhyasamaja in Reting Monastery, the divination rite indicated the boy from south Tibet, who became the Fifth Dalai Lama.

According to one school of Western thought, it can be said that a demonic identity is latent in every human being to some degree. Your Holiness once told me that a demon is an obstructive force.

DL: My basic stand is that whether you worship this spirit or not is entirely up to the individual. Whether you observe religion or not is also a personal choice. But if you are a genuine Buddhist, in particular a follower of the school of the Yellow Hats, then you must follow the authentic, traditional way strictly. Similarly, a Catholic who enters a monastery must respect the basic guidelines. If you are a Christian and you start to worship a malevolent angel... Doesn't Satan belong to the tradition of demonic angels?

Satan (Lucifer) was an angel who fell because of his arrogance.

DL: Thus, he was a negative force. For someone to remain in the Catholic or Protestant church, but meanwhile worship a demonic being, makes no sense. If he or she worships something of the sort, they should leave the church: in that case they can do what they want, believe in God or not. If you are really a Buddhist and a true follower of Tsong Khapa, you have to follow the traditional guiding principles of the Yellow Hats.

JR: How is it that this spirit changes, or is presented as a worldly spirit, while one story has it that he is even considered a sort of protector of the Geluk tradition?

DL: I don't know. We need further research. My knowledge also is limited. It seems that Kyabje Phabongka Rinpoche personally was fond of the spirit, and that was fine as far as it went. Then he gave it a special sort of recognition, such as that accorded to local spirits, a type of rank or position. And so I think that since Phabongka worshipped him, while deep inside having a somewhat rebellious attitude towards the Thirteenth Dalai Lama, he took the chance to follow his own inclinations after the death of my predecessor. I believe Phabongka behaved in such a way, precisely because of his link to the spirit. Many of his disciples followed him in this, out of ignorance.

So he was mainly responsible for the spread of the cult?

DL: Phabongka Rinpoche, in my view, was a highly qualified, very good lama, and even the Thirteenth Dalai Lama at first regarded him as such. He was quite fond of him and showed him great respect. However, later the Dalai Lama's stance toward this lama changed, becoming negative, and there was no other reason for this than Shugden. In the early part of his life, Phabongka had followed a nonsectarian course, receiving all the teachings of *The Secret Visions of the Fifth Dalai Lama* and also Terdak Lingpa's *Doncho Bumsung* teachings, typical of the Nyingma tradition.

Suddenly, though, Shugden began to display a very negative attitude. It was at that point that Phabongka changed direction. It is clear that his nonsectarian approach changed because of the spirit, as did the Thirteenth Dalai Lama's estimation of him. My feeling is, and I have often said this, that had Phabongka Rinpoche not treated Shugden as a sort of high deity but employed him as a sort of lieutenant, all the subsequent problems might not have arisen.

Do you think that Phabongka was very angry with the Thirteenth Dalai Lama?

DL: That is very clear from his biography.

JR: But when the Thirteenth Dalai Lama challenged him, Phabongka did not say, "This is a special spirit or a special protector," he said the connection came through his mother.

DL: At that time Phabongka said exactly what he thought, but at the death of the Dalai Lama the spirit exulted. So naturally, after the Thirteenth had passed, Phabongka did as he wished.

JR: The Thirteenth Dalai Lama was very firm about this issue, but everyone seems to have forgotten that.

DL: Not only that. I also think something has to be said about the attitude of Tibetans at that time, which paved the way for this disastrous situation.

That's a very interesting point. Could you explain it more fully?

DL: After his return from India and China in 1912–1913, the Thirteenth Dalai Lama paid greater attention to modern education and in the 1920s he sent four students to England, led by Lungshar.[141] From personal experience, he realized the importance of foreign relations, and he recognized the value of technology and knowledge of the English language and the significance of a Western education. However, his efforts were hindered by the opposition of certain obtuse monks. These were orthodox and highly conservative in mentality and maintained that if Western culture came to Tibet, it would be an enemy of the Buddhadharma. This attitude prevailed, and people paid little attention to what the Dalai Lama had to say.

In his final testament he indicated clearly what was going to happen, but our regents, including Reting Rinpoche, who was then a boy, completely ignored all this. And so we missed the moment, our best chance in history.

Regarding Reting Rinpoche, in The Yellow Book, *Zemey argues that despite worshipping Shugden, his problems actually arose from having followed the Nyingma practices.*

DL: Reting Rinpoche, too, turned to Shugden because of Phabongka. According to what Trijang Rinpoche writes, Shugden annihilated Reting just as he previously destroyed Kundeling, who also was a Nyingmapa practitioner. But all this, once again, shows how heavily sectarian rifts weighed at the time, especially in their widening after the death of the Thirteenth Dalai Lama.

I'll tell you a story. The attendant whose duty it was to cook for me was old and very ignorant, but he was a very nice person and a good monk. He was unable to tell stories, he had no education, either traditional or modern, and he wasn't even capable of playing with me. But because he fed me, I was attached to him, almost as if he were my mother. When I was just a silly schoolboy, I always had to have him near me; even if he were outside the door, I had to be able to see the hem of his robe to reassure myself he was there, otherwise I cried. We were very, very close. He had

---

[141] A powerful minister during the time of the Thirteenth Dalai Lama, mentioned in Zemey's *Yellow Book* for having aroused the anger of Shugden because of his Nyingma practices. Lungshar's wife, who did practices for the spirit, became pregnant in England and urged her husband to return to Tibet, fearing superstitiously that if she bore the child in England, it could have blue eyes. See M. Goldstein, *The Demise of the Lamaist State*.

begun serving the Thirteenth Dalai Lama from the age of nineteen, because his teacher had held the same post for a long time, and when he retired, his cousin or nephew—this attendant named Lobsang Jinpa—began to work in the kitchen. I was so fond of this man that when I sat in his lap I used to suck a mole on his face for comfort until it became red. My mother came to see me occasionally, but the monk never let me out of his sight. He died, at about eighty-one years old, and when his body was taken away, I wept as I saw his face. I had never shed tears, even when my mother passed, and so I realized that we are animals, for whom food is the most important thing. At any rate, the main point of this story is that this old, illiterate monk once said to me, "All those people, officials and lamas who were kept under control by the Thirteenth, rose up once he died, and Phabongka Rinpoche was one of them." This attendant was uneducated and unsophisticated, yet he was astute in his observation of that period of transition.

Was it always the cult of Shugden that was the root of sectarian problems in Tibet at that time? It is well known that many monks and laypeople in the government were disciples of Phabongka and followers of the spirit. Did no one challenge them?

DL: In the era when Phabongka held influence, one lama who was highly respected and not inferior in rank and stature to Phabongka, expressed clear reservations about the prevalence of the worship of Shugden. He was a famous master from the monastery of Drepung Loseling, and he was called Khangsar Dorje Chang. The lineage of teachings of the Kalachakra that Ling Rinpoche transmitted to me came through him.

It seems that Phabongka's influence also extended to eastern Tibet.

DL: The Director of the School of Dialectics, Lobsang Gyatso, the murdered geshe, once told me that after visits from Phabongka, and in particular from his disciple, Dragyap Thongden, some Gelukpa monasteries in the Kham region became extremely critical of the Nyingmapa tradition. As I said earlier, several monks welcomed the spirit of Shugden when in trance and threw statues of Guru Rinpoche into the river. Khyentse

Chokyi Lodroe wrote a letter to Alak,[142] quoting Phabongka regarding the fact that some of his followers considered this spirit a sort of supreme protector. This started a tendency towards sectarianism. The late director of the School of Dialectics explained to me that, following the introduction of Shugden into those monasteries by Dragyab Thongden, struggles, clashes, and internal conflicts began.

The arrival of the Chinese in the mid-50s seriously harmed Buddhism in that region, since many monasteries were destroyed. But, as Lobsang Gyatso pointed out, many religious centers had begun to disintegrate as a result of internal warring before they were flattened by the steamroller of the People's Liberation Army.

JR: You have said in the past that instructions sent out from Lhasa to recite certain prayers never were followed.

DL: That's a long story. But around 1948–49, the Governor of Chamdo was Mister Lhalu,[143] a staunch follower of the Gelukpa school, like the renowned master Geshe Jhampa Thaye.[144] A monk who served under the governor as an official and later became one of my assistants told me that when Lhalu received instructions from the Tibetan government to perform certain rituals, he consulted Geshe Thaye, who answered, "It is awful that they are asking for these Nyingmapa rites; they are not necessary. Forget about them!" This was something my assistant witnessed. The fact is that those rituals had the precise aim of promoting a nonsectarian bond among the various monasteries in the name of Tibetan unity. Therefore, the political implications of that interference are something very serious.

Chogyal Namkhai Norbu told another story about Dragyap Thongden. He said that this disciple of Phabongka, wishing to convert two small Sakyapa and Nyingmapa monasteries, challenged a scholar named Lodroe to debate. But Dragyap was defeated. At the end of the debate, Lodroe said that since he had lost, Dragyap should convert his own Gelukpa monastery

---

[142] Two famed masters.

[143] As mentioned previously, he was the son of the official sent to England by the Thirteenth Dalai Lama.

[144] *Gyalpo* practitioner, disciple of Phabongka and Trijang.

to the Sakyapa tradition. But Governor Lhalu, who was present, ordered instead that Lodroe should receive three hundred lashes for his "arrogance," and that he was to be imprisoned. Lama Lodroe is said to have lost his sanity later in prison. The other monks attributed his madness to Shugden.

DL: It must also be remembered that in Golok and Kham, there were quite a number of Gelukpa masters who were genuinely *rimey*, nonsectarian.[145] Therefore, such traditions, healthy traditions, do exist, and in Kham for centuries there was an atmosphere of openness, even if in some parts of the country, such as Lhasa, there have been periods of strong sectarianism.

During our meeting in Bolzano, you said that, before the invasion, Khyentse Choekyi Lodro, the master of Sogyal Rinpoche, advised the Tibetan government to put a large statue of Padmasambhava in the Jokhang and to place beneath it an image of Shugden. But this advice was never followed. The idea, if I'm not mistaken, was that it would have helped to keep the Chinese at bay.

DL: The recommended form of the statue of Guru Rinpoche was Nangsi Silnon, "Overcomer of Obstacles," like the one in the temple here. Another form depicts Padmasambhava as an ordinary Indian pandit.

Khyentse Choekyl Lodro, I remember clearly, advised the Kashag [Cabinet] to construct an image in the form of Nangsi Silnon.[146] But among the Gelukpas opinions differ: the Overcomer of Obstacles is a true image of Guru Rinpoche, but some argue that he visited Tibet only once, while others say twice. His appearance on the second occasion is supposed to have been in the form of Nangsi Silnon. Some Gelukpas maintain that was not the real Padmasambhava but a false apparition, and so they prefer an image in the form of an Indian pandit. So a decision was made and reported to Choekyl Lodro. The master replied sadly, "Oh, what a pity! Now perhaps the Dalai Lama and only a small entourage may be able to escape to India." That I know. I had great regrets. And, as

---

[145] His Holiness refers to Lama Jamru in Golok, to his disciple Tulku Songrab, and, in Kham, to Draggar Rinpoche.

[146] The same form destroyed by the Chinese authorities in 2007 at Samye and at Kailash.

I told you, when we settled here, I had a statue of Guru Rinpoche constructed according to his instructions.

JR: Is the episode that you cited connected to the Shugden issue?

DL: I don't know. It was a sectarian decision and a source of sectarian disagreement. I shall tell you another story. I don't know if I should name names, but another of my teachers, T. Rinpoche, told me that once, when in Lhasa on pilgrimage, he met an old lady on the street in the capital. She asked him, "Who are you and where do you come from?" Rinpoche replied that he was from western Tibet. She then asked him to what tradition he belonged. He did not dare say he was a Nyingmapa and gave a vague response that excluded that possibility. Hearing this, the old lady said, "Oh, very good! Otherwise, if you followed the Nyingmapa practices, you would be defiled and suffer all sorts of obscurations." That is an example of the dangerous sectarian feelings that used to prevail, and they clearly had to do with Shugden.

This very lama I mentioned also received teachings from a Gelukpa master, though before receiving the teaching he took the precaution of asking the master if he was a *gyalpo* Shugden practitioner. T. Rinpoche also told me about an episode many years ago in northeast India, when the arrival of the Dalai Lama created embarrassment in some monasteries belonging to other schools. Since, on the one hand, he was the head of the Tibetan government and the leader of Tibet, they thought they should invite him, but at the same time he was a practitioner of Shugden. Therefore, by welcoming him to their monastery, they risked contamination. And so it seems that after my visit, some of them began to carry out purification rituals. Such a pity and so unnecessary! *(Laughs)* But can you imagine it! In Bhutan too, some officials were very negative towards the Gelukpa tradition. "The Gelukpas are fine," they said, "no danger there, but wherever one sees a Gelukpa, there goes Shugden behind him."

T. Rinpoche continued to explain to me how after my decision to restrict the cult, all the other schools in the Himalayan regions, Nyingmas, Kagyus, and so on, became followers of the Dalai Lama. Lately, I have noticed how all the lamas from the Nyingma, Kagyu, and other monasteries are eager to come here and meet me. This is the result of my serious commitment to nonsectarianism. What better outcome can there be than a genuine harmony among the different Tibetan traditions?

You had a number of dreams, did a great deal of research, and had many divinations performed before abandoning the practice. What was the final factor determining your decision?

DL: The decision to end the worship of Shugden came with the help of the divination before Palden Lhamo. That same day, when I told my senior tutor Ling Rinpoche, he confessed he was very happy, since he always had harbored doubts regarding the practice. He told me it certainly was the right decision. Until that moment, Yongzin Ling Rinpoche, by means of his silence, always had assumed a defensive stand. He said nothing until I had abandoned the practice, but the moment that I told him of my choice, he also confessed something he never had told me. Rinpoche was a disciple of Phabongka. He came from Sera but belonged to Drepung Monastery, so he was connected to the deity Nechung. Every time he went to his master to ask him a question, he came back happy and satisfied with the answer.

Once, however, Ling Rinpoche raised a doubt with Phabongka that was shared by many others. "If we at Drepung start to worship Shugden, isn't there a risk of a conflict between the two that could bring us harm? Nechung will not be happy," he said. Phabongka replied that there was no basis for thinking this, since the deity used to invoke Shugden was actually Nechung. But for the first time, Ling Rinpoche felt uneasy with his master's reply, as he told me personally. This was how I learned that my principal teacher, who gave me full ordination, had taken a defensive position, never having dared to tell me the truth. Perhaps this was because Trijang Rinpoche, my other tutor, was a great devotee of Shugden, and this obliged Ling Rinpoche to show prudence.

And what did Trijang Rinpoche say to you after Palden Lhamo's divination?

DL: He appeared a bit puzzled, saying, "It's quite strange that Palden Lhamo would be displeased because someone worshipped Shugden." However, he did believe one hundred percent in the result of my oracle rite. He said that this divination is very accurate and reliable when performed in front of the *thangka* of Palden Lhamo. The *thangka* dates from the time of the Second Dalai Lama, and this was an absolute guarantee. When the Great Fifth left his earthly body, the regent [Desi Sangye Gyatso] was thrown into panic because the red building of the Potala was still under construction and there were many other problems to be faced. "How can I solve them?" he cried out in desperation. Then the body of the Dalai Lama came back to life and said, "Don't worry, the small matters you can decide on by yourself, and for the more important questions, perform the divination rite in front of the *thangka* of Palden Lhamo." I took special care to carry this painting personally when I escaped in 1959.

You know that one of the reasons why the Shugden followers have criticized you is over what they regard as a lack on your part of the respect due from a disciple to Trijang and the lineage of Phabongka.

DL: I have great respect for them and admire them as practitioners of Chakrasamvara,[147] but where their worship of Shugden is concerned, I completely disagree with them.

JR: Some say that if one accepts this viewpoint, according to which Phabongka made a mistake, the entire tradition is shattered.

DL: That is an error. Arya Vimuktisena, a pupil of Vasubhandu, corrected his master's interpretation of the teachings on the *Perfection of Wisdom*, and reinterpreted them according to the Madhyamika perspective. The great logician Dharmakirti rejected some of the positions taken by his celebrated teacher, Ishvarasena. These examples show that the Buddhist approach is genuinely open.

So when can one consider the sacred samaya *vow-bond between master and disciple to be broken?*

DL: When there is no longer respect. If one turns away from one's master in one's mind, then the *samaya* is broken.

Could you say something about the results of the referendum on Shugden in the south?

DL: Yes, as to this story, I never expected something like that would happen, even though there had been tension over the years between Shugden

---

[147] Tantric deity.

worshippers and others at Ganden Shartse and Sera Mey. Over time, very disagreeable feelings had been stirred up to the point that, just before my visit to Drepung for the annual debate competition between monks of different monasteries, some students from Sera Jey independently organized a boycott of the students who still were Shugden practitioners. During the ceremony, some monks in authority, worrying about my imminent visit and that of Sakya Trizin, were afraid that this movement started at Sera Jey could be the source of further problems. Some of the directors of Loseling, wanting to guarantee a regular, orderly debate, acted a little too zealously and not only used monks of a certain rank but also called in the Indian police. The monks at Sera Jey were so upset by all of this that, ever since then, they have resolved not to participate in debates with Shugden worshippers, not to share the teachings with them, nor to eat alongside them. I had noticed previously that in the monasteries, especially among the abbots, there had been a way of handling this problem of coexistence, with many fine intentions being expressed to me but with never any follow-up action. At least that had been my impression. The monks at Sera Jey had created a dilemma within the entire monastic order, and since the discontent had emerged from below, I decided I would not leave these monks, who had exposed themselves in order to support the Dalai Lama, isolated. Of course, I could not sanction the separation: this would have been a real malfeasance, so I suggested that the matter be resolved by a referendum among the monks themselves, to let them decide by majority, democratically.

The cult's followers claim the referendum was unjust and a source of division.

DL: In the Vinaya, the monastic code, Buddha himself fixed the rules to be followed when conflict arises within a monastic community, indicating seven ways to resolve them. One of these is to vote in the traditional manner by choosing different colored sticks or colored cards. I let it be known that if sixty percent of the monks declared their intention to continue the practices of Shugden, I would acknowledge this and drop the subject. Instead, the results showed over ninety percent in favor of abandoning the cult of Shugden. So that's the story.

A couple of monastic houses, though, did not adhere to the process.

DL: Yes, Pomra House in Sera Mey and Dokhang House in Shartse opted out. But even in their cases we must make a distinction: I think that at Pomra around 300 monks formed the majority while 270 continued the practices of the spirit. At Dokhang I am not exactly sure of the situation, but it appears that those who voted to continue the cult practices were under some degree of internal pressure.

The Dokhang leaders are very resolute practitioners and effectively control the whole body of monks. At Pomra, for example, there was a monk who secretly had compiled a list of those who wished to receive the teachings of the Dalai Lama. The head of the college, upon learning this, confronted that him; when the monk claimed his right of religious freedom, he was beaten. "If you want to kill me," the monk said to the head, "you can, but I will never abandon my wish to receive His Holiness's teachings."

I have heard that many of the monks devoted to Shugden come from Nepal.

DL: In Dokhang House, over two hundred monks are actually Nepali Tamangs sent there by Serkhong Tritul, who lives in Singapore and is openly critical of me. He opened or sponsored a monastery in Nepal where the practice of the spirit is kept up. It is a fact that over the last fifty years, the number of Tibetan lamas and of Buddhist activities in Nepal has increased greatly. This may be positive in that there are more opportunities to obtain general instruction, and in that sense, Serkong Tritul then may be helpful and well accepted. However, at the same time, he is seeking to add to the number of Shugden worshippers.

Your Security Service has indicated that contacts between lamas dedicated to the cult and the Chinese authorities have increased.

DL: That brings me to the third point, the political implications. Just three days ago, we received information that Chinese officials held a meeting in which they decided that around fifty of their agents in India should become more active in creating friction and clashes between the Tibetans themselves and between Tibetans and Indians.

As happened in 1995?

DL: Yes, and in 1975, or 1980, if I remember rightly, we received definite information that a Shugden worshipper in Simla planned to set fire to an Indian shop to create trouble in the area. I remember it being mentioned in a local newspaper, too.

Were they trying to create trouble among the Tibetans or between Tibetans and Indians?

DL: Both. A short while ago, in Tibet, Chinese officials approached some monks at the Sera Monastery in Lhasa who were Shugden worshippers to tell them that the Dalai Lama's restrictions on Shugden practices were a violation of religious freedom. They were exhorted to continue their worship and told that they could turn to the Party if they needed anything. Among other things, the Chinese officials offered to have teachers brought in from India.

What kind of teachers?

DL: I don't know, perhaps geshes or lamas. The Chinese are offering them open support.

Are you referring to Ganchen or the so-called Kundeling, Nga lama?

DL: Nga Lama, yes. *(Chuckles)*

Regarding this leader of the cult in the West, what can you tell us about Kelsang Gyatso of the Manjushri Centre in England? He originally worked for Lama Yeshe's organization.

DL: Oh, yes. There were endless quarrels.

Kelsang Gyatso took over the Manjushri Institute. But Lama Yeshe was also a worshipper.

DL: Yes, that's right....

What's the difference between them? I never met either of them.

DL: Yes, both of them worshipped Shugden, so there was no reason to quarrel on that point; their differences arose over money, power, and things of that sort. And when Lama Zopa turned to me, asking for my support and intervention, I sent Kalsang Yeshi-la, who was Secretary of the Religious Office, and he had dreams with negative signs concerning a black hat or something of that sort.

A student of Kelsang Gyatso, wishing to follow the instructions of His Holiness, once asked Lama Zopa for advice regarding conduct. The lama answered him, "Until you go to Kelsang Gyatso and ask him to release you from your commitments, he is still your guru. You must still obey him." Is that possible?

DL: I don't know about that. But anyway, once one has received instructions from someone, a link is created between master and disciple for the rest of this lifetime, until the next. But I'll repeat the Buddha's words: the follower or disciple does not necessarily have to accept the words of the teacher just as they are. A disciple has the choice of which parts of the teachings he or she wishes to apply. The Buddha made it very clear. The same applies to the disciples of Kelsang Gyatso and the worship of Shugden; they can stop that worship and still remain followers of their master, the master-disciple relationship remains the same.

I would like to dedicate my last question to the news coming from Tibet. You have often mentioned in the past and also more recently the links between the Chinese and the cult worshippers. In Your Holiness's view, is the spirit of Shugden hanging over Tibet in these days of tension and uprising?

DL: No, not in the sense that the spirit is linked to the protests. I think that the monks of Drepung, Sera, and Ganden who rose up in Tibet are generally against the spirit. The monks who worship Shugden, like those in Chamdo, kept quiet. They are perfectly satisfied, since the Chinese are their bosses. In India it is the same: the cult followers in the south are paying little attention to the struggle in Tibet.

Before leaving his residence, I asked the Dalai Lama another question about another critical period, 1950, when at the Dromo Monastery at Yatung the Tibetan leader came into contact with the Shugden Oracle for the first time.

On that occasion, did you consult the spirit on political matters?

DL: Oh yes! I even let it be known that it could become something like a minor State Oracle, which was a mistake.

Do you remember some of the political questions that you asked?

DL: Yes, I asked whether I should return to Lhasa, and it said I should.

Essentially that was a positive answer, good for Your Holiness… do you remember mistaken answers?

DL: No, but a wrong answer was given to Trijang Rinpoche in 1959. I think around the month of February, just as the crisis began to develop. Shugden told Trijang Rinpoche, "Now the Dalai Lama should leave, escape. Or, otherwise, Trijang Rinpoche should leave." He even gave a date. At the latest, according to the prophecy, Trijang Rinpoche must leave by the end of March. However, the crisis peaked between March 10 and 17. If my tutor had relied on this advice and waited till the end of the month, then he would have been lost.

PART SEVEN

The Western Shugden Society

In those days spent in Dharamsala I acquired a considerable amount of new information, but the core of it already had been widely disseminated on hundreds of Internet sites. The Chinese press had made much of the results of the referendums in the southern monasteries, and the International Shugden Coalition meanwhile had changed its name, probably because of internal struggles over its leadership. In its place, the Western Shugden Society had emerged, its activities publicized on its Website in eleven languages. No legal headquarters existed, but two telephone numbers were given, in the United States and in England, strongholds of Kelsang Gyatso's Manjushri Centre, which already boasted over a thousand branches under the control of the main one. In published articles it insistently was denied that the New Kadampas were the leaders of the new "Shugden Society," which was presented as "an ad hoc coalition of practitioners from many countries."

In India, the leadership of the "Shugden Devotees Religious and Charitable Society" was, or certainly appeared to be, taken decisively by Kundeling Rinpoche. In January 2008, one of the leaders of the society visited Ganchen Tulku in Milan (the latter was banned from entering India), and in February, Kundeling denounced the Dalai Lama at the High Court in Delhi, claiming that his restrictions on the cult were "illicit and unconstitutional." Kundeling then presented an urgent petition on March 17; three days after this, the Lhasa revolt began. Forcing a possible appearance of the Dalai Lama before the magistrates was a dramatic move, and the legal action was publicized during a series of press conferences, which were attended in force by numerous representatives of the Chinese media in Delhi.

Concerned about this lawsuit, the disorder, and the demonstrations against the referendums in the south, the Indian government sent a representative to meet with the Dalai Lama. This was just when I happened to be in Dharamsala. The private office authorized me to read what the Tibetan leader had told the high official. The text contained important new details, and I asked for permission to publish it. Here is an extract of the most significant passages.

> In 1950, the Chinese army started to invade.... At that
> time, many lamas and monasteries of the non-Gelukpa

schools that were influential in that area [of the invasion, i.e., eastern Tibet] were not fully co-operative, because the governor of that part of Kham, [Lhalu,] had a sectarian attitude and very little contact with them. Therefore, the other sects were distant from him and from the Dalai Lama's government, because they had the impression it was a government for the Yellow Hats.

In the last few centuries, particularly the twentieth, the entry of Chinese forces into Tibet was actually made easier by this somewhat sectarian attitude. Even here in exile in the early 1960s, a lama who represented the Nyingmapa sect said that in Dharamsala there is a "yellow umbrella," on the top of which is the Dalai Lama's government. Among important individuals in other schools there remained some doubt. In those very years I intended to receive teachings from a certain Khunu Lama, a lama in the Nyingmapa school, but my senior tutor, Ling Rinpoche, suggested it would be better to wait. He was very cautious about it, because of this spirit, because I was still worshipping this spirit. So this is how my personal religious freedom was restricted, because of fear of this spirit. The State Oracle and later my own investigations made it very clear that this demonic force was hostile to the Dalai Lama's government.

After reminding the Indian official of the attacks on him by the Delhi "Shugden Society," the Tibetan leader described in detail the triple homicide and the results of the police inquiry. The Dalai Lama explained that he met Geshe Lobsang, with whom he had an excellent relationship, for the last time on the very day of his murder. He underlined the fact that one of the young monks killed was his best translator into and from Mandarin, "and since interest in my teachings was growing among Chinese students, his death was truly a great loss." After the crime, he revealed further, came an anonymous message, that said: "We have already offered you three corpses, you will find others if you continue with your approach."

As regards the investigation, the Dalai Lama made a serious accusation. "It seems that the Delhi police, either under pressure of some sort, or because money changed hands somewhere along the line, managed to discourage a detailed investigation. They did not search the building [in Delhi Majnuka Tilla] in an appropriate manner."

The Dalai Lama cited the testimony of a bodyguard of one of the resistance leaders, Lithang Athar from Chushi Gangdruk, in which he said that on the night of the raid on Majnu Ka Tilla, clothes with bloodstains from the crime were still on the roof of the Shugden Society's building, which never was properly searched.

The Dalai Lama referred to a report from "the relevant Indian government department assigned to ensure the safety of the government-in-exile." This said that his very life had been threatened by the worshippers of the cult. It accused them explicitly of "behaving like extremists and acting as terrorists," and it concluded that the geshe's assassins "were immediately sent to Tibet through Nepal." When they reached Lhasa, it said, "the Chinese security services certainly knew what they had been connected to" and "opened up their network." In recent years, it went on to explain, "the Chinese officials have shown particular favoritism to these people, not only here but also abroad." His Holiness mentioned the case of the center in Switzerland opened by Geshe Rabten, which he said now had become "a seat of Shugden practitioners. Previously, some Tibetans had gone there, but after my restrictions, almost everyone in the community avoids it. Now the accommodation once occupied by Tibetans is used by Chinese officials, who sometimes come in delegations, and particularly by those who work in the embassy and consulates in Switzerland."

The Dalai Lama then revealed that he had been informed by a Tibetan Party leader of a secret plan for a demonstration against him in Beijing during the Olympics. "Chinese officials," he said, "have been recruiting Tibetans to join some group in Beijing, for which they receive a 10,000 yuan reward." The demonstration, however, never took place, for reasons unknown.

The last of these new elements of interest to emerge from the conversation contained a prophecy of sorts.

> If the Indian government would like the Tibetan community here to be more united under the leadership of the Dalai Lama, which I believe is in its interest, it should know that it is now Chinese policy to use this issue to destabilize the Tibetan community and weaken the Dalai Lama's authority, not only here but also within Tibet. In

our country, those monasteries that carry on with this practice are generally boycotted by the public. This also happened in south India.... But now that these people have found a strong backer[148] and a good source of money, their activities will increase.

It is difficult to say whether the numerous demonstrations that coincided with all the Dalai Lama's subsequent foreign trips were organized with Chinese financial support. The fledgling Western Shugden Society claimed exclusive responsibility. The following is a timeline of some of the activities of the society.

April 2008: The Dalai Lama received an ultimatum in a letter that circulated on the Internet. Its four points demanded that he withdraw all restrictions and end all discrimination against worshippers of the cult. If by April 22, there was no reply by letter to the Delhi headquarters of the society in Majnu Ka Tilla, a worldwide protest campaign would begin. That is exactly what happened.

April 22: At Colgate University in Hamilton, New York, during the Dalai Lama's conference, several hundred people gathered; some were Tibetans, but the majority were Westerners, mostly from the 389 (at that time, according to the NKT) North American centers of Kelsang Gyatso's New Kadampa Tradition. Several Chinese students also were interviewed by journalists. They stated that they had come to express their rage against the negative image of their country that the Western media had projected during the boycott of the Olympic torch in Paris and London. Many of the journalists present there were Chinese, and their articles provided extensive coverage of both demonstrations.

April 28: During a Delhi Shugden Society press conference, Kundeling "Nga lama" went so far as to accuse the United States and the West in general of feeding the flames of the controversy over the spirit in order to attack China. The Gold Medal of Honor given to the Dalai Lama by the U.S. Congress and President

---

[148] i.e., from the Chinese government.

George W. Bush and the visit to Dharamsala by the Speaker of the House, Nancy Pelosi, during the revolt, were cited as proof of the connection between the Tibetan leader and the American intelligence services. Kundeling also stated explicitly, as did the Chinese Communist authorities, that it was the Dalai Lama personally who had incited the March revolt in Lhasa.

May 8: During another meeting held by the Dalai Lama, the Western Shugden Society protest shifted to Oxford, outside the Sheldonian Theatre. The press reported that supporters of the society gathered in Oxford from centers as far away as Brazil, New Zealand, and Hong Kong. The same happened on June 11 at Olympic Park in Sydney. Even if the number of protesters was lower, many had come from abroad, paying their own way. Here, too, a large body of Chinese journalists was present.

Shugden and the Young Panchen Lama

At this point, my research could have been considered complete. It was impossible to synthesize the mound of historical and religious material, the thousands of articles and commentaries abounding on the Internet, in favor of, against, or neutral regarding this controversy.

But a couple of these, taken from the site of the "Dorje Shugden Administration," clearly deserved attention. Under the title, "Why not kill him?" a brief article explained, "Recently there was a new attempt to eliminate him and as a result Dorje Shugden was declared 'dead.' But the day after, he [an oracle] went into trance and said, 'They may bury me underground, drown me in water, burn me in fire, but they can never destroy what is immune to destruction.'"

While the oracle's trance suggested the mystical aspect of Shugden's latest "message," the political aspect was condensed in a single photograph published by the above-mentioned site and others linked to it. The image was of the young Panchen Gyaincain Norbu, appointed by the Chinese, sitting on his throne with the long yellow hat of the school; behind him hung a *thangka* of Shugden. Not only did the photo confirm the prior influence that the lamas of the cult, particularly Ganchen, had exerted over his education, but it also functioned as a very specific warning, as the text bearing the signature of the "Dorje Shugden Administration" confirms:

> The Panchen Lama named by China, today is nineteen years old, and is increasingly fulfilling his role as "Supreme Lama of Tibet" in the Communist-administered country. The Chinese government declares that it is socialist and believes in no religion, nonetheless it supports the highest-ranking lama in Tibet. The Panchen Lama has the support of the Beijing central government, which also meets all of his expenses and gives him an institutional rank…. China supports the practice and the diffusion of the worship of Shugden, and no one can stop it doing so; neither the Dalai Lama, nor his government-in-exile, nor the various Dharma centers of the four schools of Buddhism spread all over the world. In the end, their protests against the worship of Shugden will

be confused with all the others raised against the policies of China. They will have little effect.

Ironically, the more the Dalai Lama and his Tibetan government-in-exile attempt to suppress Shugden, the more Chinese support for this practice increases. The Dalai Lama and his Tibetan government will never be able to overwhelm the Beijing government; nor will they ever be able to shout more loudly or have more influence in the world. If that were possible, Tibet would already be free. The Dalai Lama is already over seventy years old, and China is growing stronger all the time. If he continues his arguments, Dorje Shugden, with Chinese support, will expand among a billion, two hundred million Han who will believe in its benefits one hundred percent. In the end, who should they believe? In their government, which is opening the doors to free trade to create free citizens, or the Dalai Lama?

Even today, many states are doing everything possible not to offend Beijing in the hope of ensuring lucrative business deals for themselves. When all is said and done, isn't bringing prosperity to one's people one of the main duties of any government, be it socialist or democratic?

The Dalai Lama is doing everything possible to make Shugden greater and more famous and important. Does he not know, does he not realize that is exactly what he is doing? In China, he is indirectly making Shugden the best-known and most popular Buddhist deity of our time.

I was stunned as I read the commentary, and a strong sense of unease gripped me. Was all this just exaggeration? Perhaps. But it contained that basis of reality Ganchen Tulku had spoken of in our interview ten years earlier. I couldn't be sure if he himself had written or inspired the article, but the ideas were his, and the style resembled that of his friends, Kundeling the "Nga lama" and Chimi Tsering. The logic corresponded to that of the Chinese authorities.

The text continues:

> The Dalai Lama himself has condensed into three points the essential reasons that spur the Chinese government to promote the practice.
>
> Shugden damages the movement for Tibetan independence. Shugden damages the Dalai Lama's welfare. Shugden confers easy material gains and is an earthly spirit that foregoes spiritual goals.
>
> Aren't these points listed above the very political reasons why China should promote Shugden? Basically, the Chinese have not said or carried out any policy to make Shugden an anti-Dalai Lama force. That has been achieved by the Dalai Lama himself. China knew nothing about Shugden until the Dalai Lama made it famous. Now, with substantial help from Beijing, the rise of Shugden seems inevitable. After the ill-omened death of the Dalai Lama, it can only grow stronger and will become a torrent because the rush has already begun.

The article then went beyond even those enthusiastic predictions:

> In future, denigrating the practice of Shugden, his lamas, his centers, or anything to do with him will be tantamount to an indirect attack or a protest against the policies of the Chinese government. Therefore, it will be politically unsound to oppose the practice of Shugden.... After all, who will the world listen to: the Dalai Lama and his moralisms or China's promises of economic wealth? The image of the Beijing-backed Panchen Lama with the *thangkas* of Dorje Shugden hanging behind him speaks volumes. Every photograph of the Panchen Lama, what he wears, who is with him, what is behind and around him, needs to be approved by the Chinese government. Since the Shugdenites support this false Panchen Lama, their backing provides the definite proof: the cult followers are on the payroll of the government of China, and therefore what the Dalai Lama says is true.... But if we

> look more closely, we see that not only have the Shug-
> denites promoted Shugden on behalf of the Chinese gov-
> ernment, but the Dalai Lama and his government have
> too. The more they speak out, the more China supports
> Shugden. Simple logic.

After reading these comments released on the internet by the "Dorje Shugden Administration," I could not help noting the author's evident attempt to appear neutral, (clearly unsuccessful), by referring explicitly to the "Shugdenites" in the third person. The hierarchy of the former "International Coalition," alternately led by Kelsang Gyatso and Ganchen, must indeed be feeling some embarrassment when justifying their pro-Chinese position to their Western followers, given the blatant violations of human rights in the Land of the Snows and the ever more frequent expressions of discontent and dissent among both monastics and laypeople. The latest example has been the numerous acts of self-immolation by Tibetan monks and nuns since 2011.

The course of events has shown that the collaboration of the *gyalpo* devotees is essential to the political strategy of the Communist authorities. The current policy of the pro-Shugden coalition leaders, who de facto have decided to align themselves with the Chinese powers, is to share control with them of the entire process of identification and enthronement of the future Dalai Lama, exploiting as much as possible this unprecedented opportunity of a profitable relationship with the current political powers. The Chinese need a Dalai Lama who will be faithful to the Party so as to avoid the danger of deeper social rifts. The education of their chosen Dalai Lama will be entrusted to *gyalpo* practitioners, as was the case with the Panchen Lama. A Dalai Lama chosen by Shugden oracles and mediums could even be enthroned in the sacred Potala, a seat that has been empty for half a century, in a form of posthumous "rehabilitation" of Drakpa Gyaltsen, over whom another child tulku reincarnation was preferred 390 years ago.

Like the Chinese, who continue to adjust the history of Tibet to suit their own interests, not only do the followers of the cult dispute the recognition of the Fifth Dalai Lama, (they considering that Drakpa Gyaltsen was the rightful claimant), they even question the legitimacy of the current Fourteenth. A recently distributed Western Shugden Society pamphlet goes so far as to argue that the Fourteenth Dalai Lama, Tenzin Gyatso, is from a Muslim family, and that mistaken criteria were applied in his selection. If everything goes according to this plan, the task of "recognizing" a Dalai Lama pleasing to both Chinese and Shugdenites can only be entrusted to the Panchen Lama. It is certainly not difficult to surmise which deity will be invoked to receive the signs of that rebirth.

It has happened often that the emanations of these two principal bodhisattvas identify one each another's reincarnations after one has died. The difference is that, in the past, the choices were made principally by following rituals based on the omens of the traditional divinities, usually recognized by all schools of the Vajrayana teachings of Tibet.

Shugden was born as an extremely controversial figure and has always created strife, from the disturbances provoked at the death of Drakpa Gyaltsen, to the successive attempts to establish this spirit as the main protector of the most influential school of Tibetan Buddhism. For this reason, the present Dalai Lama's concern is that the cult could shake the very foundations of Tibetan culture, which has been inspired for many centuries by Padmasambhava and the guardians of the Dharma, some of whom were wild spirits tamed by the great exorcist.

From what the lamas devoted to Shugden have written, and said, their form of religion, expressed through their practice, leads to the same spiritual goal as that of the schools inspired directly or indirectly by Guru Rinpoche. This theory is openly contested by the Dalai Lama, who maintains that an inexpert practitioner may succumb to the worldly powers of a spirit who has never been "tamed," i.e. turned away from egoism to altruism.

As in the past, when numerous inauspicious omens followed the first appearances of Shugden, the present phase of affirmation of the "new protector" of Tibet in place of the "old" Oracle of Nechung has been accompanied by dark signs. The Party's announcement that it intends to choose the next spiritual leader of Tibet, and the erecting of statues of the *gyalpo* king demon in monasteries, have created a deep crisis for the majority of Tibetan faithful.

It is in this context that the escalation of the number of self-immolations among monks and nuns in Amdo and Sichuan took began in 2011 and continued in 2012. Their desperate acts reveal the weight of the defeats suffered by the Tibetan people in these years, and an awareness that they soon risk being subjected to Chinese power for a long time without the guidance and inspiration of their leader in cultural and religious matters.

For this reason, the Dalai Lama recently released a long statement dedicated entirely to the issue of his reincarnation. He wrote: "While I remain physically and mentally fit, it seems important to me that we draw up clear guidelines to recognize the next Dalai Lama, so that there is no room for doubt or deception."

After explaining the general criteria used in the past and the powers of the numerous figures of the buddhas and bodhisattvas who have inspired Tibetan spirituality, he added:

> Since the Manchu era, Chinese political authorities repeatedly engaged in various deceitful means using Buddhism, Buddhist masters, and tulkus as tools to fulfill their political ends as they involved themselves in Tibetan and Mongolian affairs. Today, the authoritarian rulers of the People's Republic of China, who as Communists reject religion but still concern themselves in religious matters, have imposed the so-called re-education campaign and declared "Order No. Five" on the control and recognition of reincarnations, which came into force on September 1, 2007. This is outrageous and disgraceful. The enforcement of various inappropriate methods for recognizing reincarnations to eradicate our unique Tibetan cultural traditions is doing damage that will be difficult to repair. Moreover, they say they are waiting for my death and will recognize a Fifteenth Dalai Lama of their choice. It is clear from their recent rules and regulations and subsequent declarations that they have a detailed strategy to deceive Tibetans, followers of the Tibetan Buddhist tradition, and the world community. Therefore, I have a responsibility to protect the Dharma and sentient beings and counter such detrimental schemes.

This statement, which is available on official Websites such as http://www.dalailama.com/, traces the history and the significance of the tradition of the buddhas and bohisattvas of Tibet and concludes with this solemn announcement:

> When I am about ninety, I will consult the high lamas of the Tibetan Buddhist traditions, the Tibetan public, and

other concerned people who follow Tibetan Buddhism, and re-evaluate whether the institution of the Dalai Lama should continue or not. On that basis we will take a decision. If it is decided that the reincarnation of the Dalai Lama should continue and there is a need for the Fifteenth Dalai Lama to be recognized, responsibility for doing so will primarily rest on the concerned officers of the Dalai Lama's Ganden Podrang Trust. They should consult the various heads of the Tibetan Buddhist traditions and the reliable oath-bound Dharma protectors who are linked inseparably to the lineage of the Dalai Lamas. They should seek advice and direction from these concerned beings and carry out the procedures of search and recognition in accordance with past tradition. I shall leave clear written instructions about this.

Aside from his reiteration that he would never be reborn in a country deprived of religious freedom, such as China, His Holiness lets it be known that, even while he is still alive, one of his "emanations" might lead his followers (literally in Tibetan, a *ma 'das sprul sku*, a "tulku emanation without passing away"). He left open the possibility that it could be either a monastic or a layperson, an ordinary man or perhaps—and why not?—a woman, capable of receiving or already in possession of his spiritual powers (he has already relinquished his temporal powers, having announced his "retirement" from politics).

None of us can know if this "transfer" will be possible. If we examine the achievements of the Fourteenth Dalai Lama, there is no doubt that the "monk" Tenzin Gyatso, as we have said before, already has manifested extraordinary powers, becoming a unique spiritual reference point for men and women all over the world, and the most celebrated teacher and exemplar of the message of the Buddha in his time.

Some fear that the death of the Fourteenth Dalai Lama will compromise the future of one of our world's most ancient and profound cultural heritages. But it is by no means inevitable that the future will take shape in the ways desired by the devotees of Shugden.

The teachings of the Dharma, as the Dalai Lama has often said, have survived thousands of years of history and its conflicts. This time they will survive once again. This is his message.

EPILOGUE

Epilogue

The Dalai Lama, guided as ever by the compassion that governs his bodhisattva nature, has demonstrated that he needs no defenders. This does not mean that those who share his principles and ethics should not lend their support to his cause. As His Holiness admits himself, Tibet has never been so threatened as at present, under the shadow of "cultural genocide."

The appeal to "freedom of worship," launched during the Western Shugden Society's demonstrations, is part of a precise strategy aimed at capturing the imagination of Western readers who know next to nothing regarding the historical and religious implications surrounding the cult. Signs with messages such as, "Dalai Lama, give us religious freedom!" would have little impact in Tibet, where most Buddhists, by tradition, trust in the guidance of their spiritual leader.

The triggers of any phenomenon, whether social, religious, or political, are created by an infinite number of circumstances, by men and women who, through their individual actions, shape the course of history. It is impossible to tell if spirits or ancestral divinities played a part in the unfolding of events. One only can examine the basic facts in the issue of the dispute now surrounding the name of Shugden to understand that any alliance in his name is as dangerous as worshipping him.

From this perspective, it is easier to understand why the present Dalai Lama defines his invisible enemy as "mysterious," evidently aware that the spirit is a part of a subtle mechanism of karmic links often hidden from history, like those underground rivers mentioned by Togden Chawang, which emerge and disappear again, before they then reappear in places distant from their origin.

In samsara, where human beings and animals are born and die in pain numberless times, each of us knows that we can have influence in one way or another by means of our actions, our example, and sometimes simply our presence. Like an untamed fire, every conflict, even those generated very far away, sooner or later may reach our house of straw. Everything that we consider "mine" or "ours," and what we regard as real, concrete, or palpable, can be swept away suddenly by means of atomic warfare, climatic natural disaster, human damage to the environment, or any other reason that science neither can explain nor prevent.

In past centuries, no one could have imagined the enormous reciprocal influences generated today by commercial, cultural, and spiritual contact between the two hemispheres, East and West. Perhaps not even today, in the context of globalization, can we fully appreciate the innovative yet also deadly potential of this encounter between worlds that apparently are so diverse.

The implications of the Shugden case deserve deeper examination because they show the directions that relations among China, Tibet, and the rest of the world may be taking. Perhaps Beijing's leaders themselves, not to mention the cult's members, should realize that dividing the Tibetan people in fact could lead to the repetition of some of the most serious mistakes in history.

The master Chogyal Namkhai Norbu has taught me that, where individual experience of the Dharma path is concerned, the more the power of good grows, the more evil will adopt underhanded tactics of ever greater sophistication in order to prevail. For this reason we need the strength nurtured by practice. This means developing undistracted presence in our daily life, so as not to fall subject to the caprices of the mind, which is the source of all dualistic conceptions.

Buddha urged his disciples to understand the power of the mind. He defeated the devil Mara, driving him away from his mind, into which the demon had attempted to intrude by inflating the former prince's pride and ego. The Buddha did not manage this by eliminating his thoughts, because one can neither add nor take away anything from the nature of phenomena, of which the passions, the spirit, and the fear of death are all part. He succeeded by neutralizing the weight of egoistic thought, the real demon, the true enemy of human beings, certain of its power to exploit beings considered "inferior" and to change at will our very environment.

APPENDIXES

WANTED BY DISTT. KANGRA POLICE (H.P.)
AWARD OF TWO LAKH RUPEES

Name : Tenzin
Father's name : Dhondup
Age : 28 years
Height : 5'11" (Approx)
Complexion : Wheatish Brown

Name : Lobsang Chodak @ Jharu
Father's name : Kelsang Dawa
Age : 25 Years
Height : 5'7" (Approx)
Complexion : Wheatish Brown

These two Tibetan youths are involved in triple murder of Principal Lobsang Gyatso and two other students namely Lobsang Ngawang and Ngawang Lodoe, which took place on 4-2-97 at Mcleod Ganj District Kangra (H.P.) on which case FIR No. 48/97 dated 5-2-97 u/s 302/452 IPC was registered in PS Dharamshala. Both these Tibetans are resident of B-97 Chatering Guest House Majnu-Ka-Tilla Delhi-54. Deptt. of Tibetan Security, Central Tibetan Administration (Govt. in Exile) Dharamshala has announced reward of Two Lac Rupees to informant supplying definite information leading to trace abovementioned Tibetans. Name of such informer will be kept secret. Information can be given on following address/Telephone :

Superintendent of Police,
Distt. Kangra at Dharamshala (HP)
Tel-01892—22244, 24905 (Office)
24942 (Res.)

Secretary,
Deptt. of Security (CTA),
Gangchen Kyishong, Dharamshala,
Tel-01892—24954, 22254 (off.)

Buddhist School of Dialectics,
Mcleod Ganj, Dharamshala,
Tel-01892—21215

Tibetan Welfare Office,
Mcleod Ganj, Dharamshala,
Tel-01892—21059

1500.

Interpol on the Trail of Buddhist Killers

Jane Macartney from Beijing (*The Times*, June 22, 2007).

Interpol has issued wanted notices for two followers of a Tibetan sect accused of the ritualistic killing of one of the Dalai Lama's closest associates a decade ago.

The attack, in which two students were also killed, was apparently in revenge for the Nobel Peace Laureate's decision to ban the group after more than three centuries of mystic controversy.

The Interpol Red Notices for Lobsang Chodak, 36, and Tenzin Chozin, 40, issued at the request of the Indian police, are believed to be among the first demands by another country to arrest Chinese citizens living within their own country's borders. A Red Notice is not an arrest warrant but is a means by which Interpol notifies member nations that an individual is wanted in another country.

The notice leaves Beijing in a difficult position since China has been an active member of Interpol, frequently turning to the organization for help in trying to capture its citizens who have fled abroad.

The Fourteen Dalai Lamas

I—Gendun Drub (1391–1474)

Born of a family of pastoral nomads from Tsang, he later moved to Narthang Monastery in central Tibet, where he met Lama Tsong Khapa, head of the Gelukpa school, becoming one of his leading disciples. In 1447, he founded the great Tashi Lhunpo Monastery, which became the seat of the Panchen Lama. He wrote numerous texts based on the Kadampa teachings and suggested starting the system of reincarnations for the Gelukpas, which already existed among the Kagyupa and Sakyapa masters. He was recognized as the First Dalai Lama by the third of the line, Sonam Gyatso, who received the title of "Ocean of Wisdom" from the Mongol Emperor Altan Khan.

II—Gendun Gyatso (1475–1542)

Born of a noble family in Tsang, he entered Tashi Lhunpo at the age of eleven after having been instructed by his father, a lama of the Nyingmapa school. He studied at Drepung and in 1509 founded the Chokhorgyal Monastery in a high valley near the glacial Lake Lhamo Latso, sacred to the transmundane protector goddess, Palden Lhamo, and considered miraculous for inspiring the visions that enabled the discovery of subsequent Dalai Lamas. In 1518, at Drepung, he had the Ganden Podrang built. This became the residence of his successors and the future nucleus of the Tibetan government. He wrote over seven hundred texts and treatises on Tantra. He, too, was identified as a Dalai Lama, the second, after the recognition of Sonam Gyatso by the Mongol emperor.

III—Sonam Gyatso (1543–1588)

Born in the valley of Tolung, the domain of the Karmapa of the Kagyupa school, he was recognized as the reincarnation of Gendun Gyatso and taken to Drepung Monastery, where he later became abbot. In 1563 a civil war broke out, which marked the decline of the Phagmodrupa family, a Kagyupa family who were major patrons of the Gelukpa school. In 1565 the Tsang state was born, dominated by a royal family devoted to the Karma Kagyupa school. The danger of invasion led Sonam Gyatso to seek the help of the Tumed Mongols under Altan Khan. In 1578, he reached Mongolia and was honored with the title "Ocean of Wisdom" (Mongolian: *"dalai"* ("ocean") is the translation of the Tibetan word *gyatso*, and the title was extended retroactively to the first two well-known reincarnations). Sonam Gyatso persuaded the Mongols to abandon many barbarous practices, leading Altan Khan to declare, "The Ocean of Blood has now become an Ocean of Milk." The Emperor of Ming China also invited him to his court, but Sonam Gyatso died after his second journey to Mongolia, on his way back to Lhasa.

IV — Yonten Gyatso (1589–1616)

The successor to the Third Dalai Lama was a great-grandson of Altan Khan, the only non-Tibetan member in the history of the line. In 1602 he left for Tibet, where the struggle between Tsang and U soon resumed. The young Mongol Dalai Lama was in the thrall of regents and high officials of the great monasteries and died at only twenty-seven years of age. The cause of death remains a mystery and has been attributed either to a rheumatic illness or to poisoning.

V — Lobsang Gyatso (1617–1682)

Born in the valley of Yarlung into a family of Nyingmapa nobles descended from the first kings of Tibet, he was educated at Drepung by the Abbot of Tashi Lhunpo. In 1642, the leader of the Qoshot Mongols, Gushri Khan, defeated the King of Tsang and conferred on Lobsang Gyatso supreme authority over all of Tibet (U and Tsang). This was the start of the temporal power of the Dalai Lama. Known as the Great Fifth, Lobsang Gyatso, in his role as spiritual and political leader, visited the Manchu emperor in Beijing. He built the imposing Potala Palace in Lhasa and conferred the title of "Panchen Lama" on his master, Lobsang Choegyen, who was the Abbot of Tashi Lhunpo. He considered Lobsang Choegyen the Fourth Panchen Lama, acknowledging three previous well-known reincarnations.

At his own request, his death was kept secret for fifteen years by the Regent Sangye Gyatso. He wrote numerous Tantric treatises, often based on his own personal visions.

VI — *Tsangyang Gyatso (1683–1706)*

Born near the frontier with Bhutan into a family of the Nyingmapa tradition, his recognition was kept secret for fifteen years by the Regent Sangye Gyatso. In 1697, the Fifth Panchen Lama proceeded with his investiture, but Tsangyang Gyatso did not take religious vows, and without renouncing sexual relations, instead lived the life of a layman. In 1705, Lhazang Khan, leader of the Qoshot Mongols supported by the Manchu emperor, killed the regent and exiled the Dalai Lama, whom he replaced with his own son. The last trace of Tsangyang Gyatso was in 1706. According to one theory, he was killed on his journey to China, while others believe he lived incognito as a prominent teacher of the Mongolians.

VII — *Kalzang Gyatso (1708–1757)*

Born in Lithang, he was enthroned in 1720 at the end of a merciless period of wars and disorder in Lhasa. He rarely participated directly in the management of political affairs, even although his father had an important but ambiguous role in the government. Temporal power was exercised by a lay official in the service of China. His successors down to the Twelfth similarly were unable to govern the country. All of them died young, and it is suspected that they all were killed, either by the Chinese or by the regents themselves, who in turn were controlled by the Manchu imperial power in Beijing.

VIII — *Jampel Gyatso (1758–1804)*

IX — *Lungtog Gyatso (1805–1815)*

X — *Tsultrim Gyatso (1816–1837)*

XI — *Khedrup Gyatso (1838–1855)*

XII — *Trinley Gyatso (1856–1875)*

XIII — *Thubten Gyatso (1876–1933)*

Born into a peasant family in southeast Tibet, he was recognized in 1878 and assumed full powers in 1895. From childhood, he was aware of the risks posed by the expansionist aims of other nations, namely Russia and Britain in addition to China. In 1904, a British military expedition reached Lhasa after a bloody massacre of poorly armed Tibetan soldiers, and the Dalai Lama took refuge in Mongolia. After the British had left the country, he stayed in Mongolia and taught widely. In 1908 he visited Beijing, where he tried in vain to enlist the support of the enfeebled Manchu empire. Escaping to Tibet two years later, the Manchus sent an army to Lhasa to kill him, and so he had to flee a second time, this time to the British in Darjeeling. In 1911, the republican revolution dissolved the Manchu empire, and in 1912, the Dalai Lama returned to Lhasa and proclaimed Tibet's independence from China. The Thirteenth tried to safeguard the country from foreign ambitions and wished to introduce modernization. He met fierce opposition from the clergy and aristocracy, however. After seeing the Russian and Mongolian Communist destruction of Buddhism in that country, he predicted the same fate for Tibet, coming from China, and decided to pass away before the natural time, in order to be old enough to help when it would happen. Before dying, he made an apocalyptic prophecy in which he foretold the full extent of the tragic suffering of the Tibetan people since the Chinese Communist invasion of 1951.

XIV — Tenzin Gyatso (b. 1935–present)

The present Dalai Lama was born into a family of peasants on July 6, 1935, in Takster in the Amdo region, near the Chinese border. On February 22, 1940, an investiture ceremony was held in Lhasa, and the young Lhamo Dhondrup was renamed Jetsun Jamphel Ngawang Lobsang Yeshe Tenzin Gyatso ("His Holiness, Gentle Splendor Lord of Speech, Good-hearted One, Oceanic Defender of the Wisdom Teaching"). On November 17, 1950, at only fifteen years of age, he assumed full political powers as head of state after the invasion of Tibet by the People's Liberation Army. After a brief retreat at Yatung on the Indian border, he returned to Lhasa in 1951 to try to work with the Chinese. In 1954, he went to Beijing, where he met Mao Zedong and the other Chinese leaders. In 1959, after a popular revolt in Lhasa, he was forced to flee to India. Ultimately, more than 100,000 Tibetans followed him, from whence they spread out gradually around the world during the last sixty years. Since 1960 he has resided in Dharamsala in Himachal Pradesh, where the Tibetan government-in-exile has its seat.

With his support, a modern education system that includes the teaching of Tibetan culture has been organized for the children of the refugees, while religious education has been provided for the monastic community.

Sera, Ganden, and Drepung monasteries have been reconstructed in the southern Indian state of Karnataka. In 1963, the Dalai Lama promulgated a democratic constitution as the model for the future free Tibet. Members of parliament and, beginning in the spring of 2001, the prime ministers (Kalon Tripa), have been elected directly by the exile community.

In Washington in October, 1987, on the occasion of the meeting of the U.S. Congressional Caucus on Human Rights, the Dalai Lama proposed a Five-Point Peace Plan regarding the future status of Tibet. He asked for Tibet to be transformed into a "Peace Zone," an end to the massive transfer of the ethnic Chinese population to Tibet, the restoration of fundamental human rights and democratic liberties, and the discontinuation of Chinese use of Tibetan territory for the production of nuclear arms and the dumping of radioactive waste. He also expressed his sincere wish for "serious negotiations" to begin on the future of Tibet.

On June 15, 1988 at the European parliament in Strasbourg, France, the Dalai Lama further elaborated his Five-Point Peace Plan for an autonomous and democratic Tibet, "within the Chinese People's" Republic." In 1989, he was awarded the Nobel Peace Prize.

In September 2002, and in June 2003, two delegations of the government-in-exile paid official visits to China and Tibet, but the negotiations came to a halt. The next informal meetings took place only after the revolts of March 2008.

Since 1967, the Dalai Lama has undertaken a series of journeys that have brought him to over fifty nations as a spiritual leader, a Buddhist teacher, and a Nobel Laureate, often provoking the anger of the Chinese leadership against the heads of state who have received him. From his first visit to the West at the start of 1973, numerous universities and Western institutions have conferred upon His Holiness awards and honorary degrees. The latest gesture of recognition came in October 2007, in the form of the U.S. Congressional Medal of Honor for Human Rights.

SELECT BIBLIOGRAPHY

Select Bibliography

History

The Water Horse and Other Years: A History of Seventeenth- and Eighteenth-Century Tibet
K. Dhondup
Dharamsala: Library of Tibetan Works and Archives, Dharamsala 2003

The Water Bird and Other Years: A History of the Thirteenth Dalai Lama and After
K. Dhondup
New Delhi: Rangwang Publishers, New Delhi 1986

A History of Modern Tibet, 1913–1951: Demise of the Lamaist State
Melvyn C. Goldstein
New Delhi: Munshiram Manoharlal Publishers, New Delhi 1991

Tibet: A Political History
Tsepon W.D. Shakabpa
New Haven: Yale University Press, New Haven 1967

The Dragon in the Land of Snows: A History of Modern Tibet Since 1947
Tsering Shakya
London: Pimlico, London 1999

Tibetan Civilization
Rolf A. Stein
Stanford: Stanford University Press, Palo Alto 1972

Lhasa, Lieu du divin
Françoise Pommaret
Geneva: Editions Olizane, Geneva 1996

*The Dalai Lamas of Tibet and Their Relations with the Manchu
Emperors of China; 1644–1908*
W. W. Rockhill
Dharamsala: Library of Tibetan Works and Archives, Dharamsala
1998

A Cultural History of Tibet
David Snellgrove and Hugh Richardson
New York: G. Weidenfeld & Nicholson, New York 1968

The Story of Tibet: Conversations with the Dalai Lama
Thomas Laird
London: Atlantic Books, London 2006

The Necklace of gZi
Namkhai Norbu
Dharamsala: Information Office of the Dalai Lama, Dharamsala 1981
Arcidosso: Shang Shung Edizioni, Arcidosso 1997

Buddhism and Tantra

The World of Tibetan Buddhism
The Fourteenth Dalai Lama
London: Wisdom Publications, London 1995

Essential Tibetan Buddhism
Robert Thurman
San Francisco: HarperSanFrancisco, San Francisco 1995

What the Buddha Taught
Walpola Rahula
New York: Grove Press, New York 1962

Buddha e il Buddhismo
Oscar Botto
Fossano: Editrice Esperienze, Fossano 1984

Life and Teachings of Tsong Khapa
Robert Thurman
5th ed.
Dharamsala: Library of Tibetan Works and Archives, Dharamsala
2001

*Sects in Tibetan Buddhism: Comparing Practices Between Gelukpa
and Nyingmapa Sects*
Vijay Kumar Singh
New Delhi: D.K. Printworld, New Delhi 2005

The Bodhicaryāvatāra
Śāntideva
Oxford: Oxford University Press, Oxford 1995

Buddhist Sects in India
Nalinaksha Dutt
New Delhi: Motilal Banarsidass, New Delhi 1978

The Sound of Two Hands Clapping
George Dreyfus
Berkeley: University of California Press, Berkeley 2003

*Guru Yoga: According to the Preliminary Practice of Longchen
Nyingtik*
Dilgo Khyentse Rinpoche
Ithaca, N.Y.: Snow Lion, Ithaca 1999

Introduction to Tibetan Buddhism
John Powers
Revised ed.,
Ithaca, N.Y.: Snow Lion, Ithaca 2007

The Tibetan Book of Living and Dying
Sogyal Rinpoche
Revised and updated ed.,
New York: HarperOne, New York 1994

The Tibetan Book of the Dead: Liberation Through Understanding in the Between
Padma Sambhava (trans. Robert Thurman)
New York: Bantam, New York, 1994

Mahayana Buddhism
Paul Williams
New York: Routledge, New York 1989

Civilized Shamans: Buddhism in Tibetan Societies
Geoffrey Samuel
Washington, D.C.: Smithsonian Institution Press, Washington, D.C. 1993

Padmasambhava. La Magie de l'"Eveil.
Philippe Cornu
Paris: Editions du Seuil, Paris 1997

Texts by the Fourteenth Dalai Lama

My Land and My People: The Original Autobiography of His Holiness the Dalai Lama
New York: McGraw Hill, New York 1962

Freedom in Exile
San Francisco: HarperOne, San Francisco 1991

How to See Yourself as You Really Are
New York: Atria Books, New York 2006

Kindness, Clarity, and Insight
Ithaca, N.Y.: Snow Lion, Ithaca 1984

Bon and Dzogchen

Dzogchen: The Self-Perfected State
Namkhai Norbu
Ithaca, N.Y.: Snow Lion, Ithaca 1996

The Crystal and the Way of Light
Namkhai Norbu
New York and London: Routledge and Kegan Paul, New York and
London 1986

Dream Yoga and the Practice of Natural Light
Namkhai Norbu
Ithaca, N.Y.: Snow Lion, Ithaca 1992

Dzogchen: The Heart Essence of the Great Perfection
The Fourteenth Dalai Lama
Ithaca, N.Y.: Snow Lion, Ithaca 2001

*Oral Tradition from Zhang Zhung: An Introduction to the Bonpo
Dzogchen Teaching of the Oral Tradition from Zhang Zhung*
John Myrdhin Reynolds
Kathmandu: Vajra Bookshop, Kathmandu 2007

The Golden Letters
John Myrdhin Reynolds
Ithaca, N.Y.: Snow Lion, Ithaca 1996

Shugden and Tibetan Divinities

The Shuk-den Affair: Origins of a Controversy
George Dreyfus
Williamstown, Mass.: Williams College, Williamstown 1999

A Brief History of Opposition to Shugden
Dolgyal Research Committee
Dharamsala: Department of Religion and Culture, Central Tibetan
Administration, Dharamsala 1998

The Guardian Deities of Tibet
Ladrang Kelsang
Dharamsala: Little Lhasa Publications, Dharamsala 2000

Oracles and Demons of Tibet
René de Nebesky-Wojkowitz
Oxford: Oxford University Press, Oxford 1956

Other

Prisoners of Shangri-La: Tibetan Buddhism and the West
Donald S. Lopez Jr.
Chicago: University of Chicago Press, Chicago 1998

Reincarnation: The Phoenix Fire Mystery: An East-West Dialogue on Death and Rebirth from the Worlds of Religion, Science, Psychology, Philosophy
Joseph Head and S. L. Cranston
New York: Crown Publishers, New York 1977

Hostage of Beijing: The Abduction of the Panchen Lama
Gilles Van Grasdorff
Boston: Element Books, Boston 1999

Songs of the Sixth Dalai Lama
K. Dhondup
New Delhi: Paljor Publications, New Delhi 2002

Fourteen Dalai Lamas: A Sacred Legacy of Reincarnation
Glenn H. Mullin
Santa Fe: Clear Light Books, Santa Fe 2001

Memoirs of a Tibetan Lama
Lobsang Gyatso
Ithaca, N.Y.: Snow Lion, Ithaca 1998

Dalai Lama, My Son: A Mother's Story
Diki Tsering
London: Virgin Books, London 2000

The Legend of the Great Stupa
Guru Padmasambhava (trans. K. Dowman)
Berkeley: Dharma Publishing, Berkeley 1973

Journey Among the Tibetan Nomads: An Account of a Remote Civilization
Namkhai Norbu
New Delhi: Paljor Publications, New Delhi 1997

Witness to Tibet's History
Baba Phuntsok Wangyal
New Delhi: Paljor Publications, New Delhi 2007

Why the Dalai Lama Matters: His Act of Truth as the Solution for China, Tibet, and the World
Robert Thurman
New York: Beyond Words & Atria Books, 2008